VOLUME ONE

MEDICAL TERMINOLOGY
with Human Anatomy

Jane Rice

CUSTOM EDITION

Taken from:
Medical Terminology with Human Anatomy, Fifth Edition
by Jane Rice

PEARSON
Custom
Publishing

PEARSON
Prentice
Hall

Printed in the United States of America

10 9 8 7 6 5 4

ISBN 0-536-91915-1

2005280002

AP

Please visit our web site at *www.pearsoncustom.com*

PEARSON CUSTOM PUBLISHING
75 Arlington Street, Suite 300, Boston, MA 02116
A Pearson Education Company

In special memory of my parents, Warren Galileo and Elizabeth Styles Justice.

CONTENTS IN BRIEF

DETAILED CONTENTS

CHAPTER 4   THE SKELETAL SYSTEM   89

CHAPTER 5   THE MUSCULAR SYSTEM   127

PREFACE

The fifth edition of *Medical Terminology with Human Anatomy* continues its tradition of excellence with a new and refreshed approach to covering all aspects of medical terminology.

Over the years, this book has helped thousands gain a firm grasp of the challenging, yet exciting, new language of medicine. This revised edition embraces the philosophy that has made the book so successful, and incorporates fresh new features that will be sure to engage readers of all learning styles.

There are two driving goals of this text:

1. To teach students how to build medical terms by using word parts, and
2. To teach the basics of anatomy and physiology.

NEW TO THIS EDITION

- *Medical Terminology with Human Anatomy*'s unique **word building** approach has been further strengthened, and **pathology** has been highlighted in new and exciting ways: The terminology and vocabulary sections that were present in the 4th edition have been updated and rearranged into one feature entitled **Building Your Medical Vocabulary**, so that students can learn about terms that are built from word parts concurrently with vocabulary words. This more logical approach groups each important term by relevance in a single study list. The list is alphabetical, which is important because words with common prefixes follow each other, thereby creating a repetition that aids learning. Words listed in black are shown with their component word parts, while words in pink represent vocabulary terms that are not build from word parts. Pronunciations are provided for all terms.

- This section is followed by **Pathology Spotlights** and **Pathology Checkpoints**—new features that embody our initiative to fortify the pathology content in this edition. Pathology Spotlights highlight 4–6 conditions related to the chapter content, with artwork and links to media as well as the CD-ROM. Pathology Checkpoints provide the student with a concise list of the pathology terms they have encountered in the chapter. Students may check off those terms that they understand, and go back and review any that are not clear.

- Nearly 75 **new** illustrations and photos have been added to highlight important areas of the text.

- The Spanish component of the text has been removed and will now be included, along with French and German, as part of a **Terminology Translator** feature on the **free** CD-ROM (found at the back of the text). This Terminology Translator provides an innovative tool to translate medical words into Spanish, French, and German.

• A **free** CD-ROM is included with every text, and provides a wide variety of interactive activities such as labeling, word building, spelling, multiple-choice, true/false, fill-in-the-blank, and a variety of quiz games. An audio pronunciation glossary is included, along with a custom flashcard generator on the CD-ROM, that allows students to select glossary terms and print out flashcards for any or all terms for study. Finally, pathology concepts come alive with the presentation of one feature video per chapter that correlates to selected content in the Pathology Spotlight sections of the text.

MEDICAL WORD BUILDING TECHNIQUE—A TIME-PROVEN APPROACH

The fifth edition of *Medical Terminology with Human Anatomy* is still organized by body systems and specialty areas, with the component parts of medical words presented as they relate to each system of the body and specialty area. Prefixes and suffixes are repeated throughout the text, while word roots and combining forms are presented according to the system or specialty area to which they relate. Once the material in Chapters 1 and 2 has been mastered, the student should know approximately 87 prefixes, 68 roots/combining forms, and 77 suffixes. To build a medical vocabulary, all the student has to do is recall the word parts that they have learned and link them with the new component parts presented in each chapter. This word-building technique, while not complicated, is different from other terminology texts that have students learn prefixes, roots, combining forms and suffixes as separate entities generally not related to the terminology of a body system. It is much easier to learn component parts directly associated with a body system or specialty area and this is the key to the time-proven approach of *Medical Terminology with Human Anatomy*.

KEY FEATURES

• **Chapter Outlines and Objectives**   These appear at the beginning of each chapter. The outlines identify the organizational content of the chapter. The objectives state the learning concepts that should be obtained by the learner.

• **A Full Color Art Presentation**   Art provides visual references of diseases, disorders, and/or conditions. Color photographs are strategically placed throughout the text.

• **Full Color Illustrations**   Beautiful anatomy and physiology illustrations give the student access to essential diagrams of the human body. This is a perfect complement to the discussion of the anatomy and physiology overview in Chapters 2–16.

• **Anatomy and Physiology Overview** (Chapters 2–16)   Comprehensive coverage of the structure and function of the body with full-color art and tables.

• **Life Span Considerations**   Presents interesting facts about the human body as it relates to the child and the older adult.

• **Building Your Medical Vocabulary—NEW!**   This section provides the foundation for learning medical terminology. By connecting various word parts in an organized sequence, thousands of words can be built and learned. In this text the word list is alphabetized so one can see the variety of meanings created when common prefixes and suffixes are repeatedly applied to certain word roots and/or combining forms. Words shown in pink are additional words related to the content of the chapter that are not built from word parts. These words are included to enhance the student's vocabulary. Each medical word has a pronunciation guide directly under it.

- **Terminology Translator—NEW!** This feature, found on the **free** CD-ROM, provides an innovative tool to translate medical words into Spanish, French, and German. In our multicultural society, it is becoming more and more important that students be able to communicate in a variety of languages.

- **Pathology Spotlights—NEW!** This feature provides an in-depth focus on diseases and conditions related to the topic of the chapter. Presented are current findings in medicine along with interesting facts about the various medical conditions that are spotlighted.

- **Pathology Checkpoint—NEW!** This feature provides a concise list of pathology-related terms that the student has seen in the chapter. The student should review this checklist to make sure they are familiar with the meaning of each term before moving on to the next section.

- **Drug Highlights** Presents essential drug information that relates to the subject of the chapter.

- **Diagnostic and Laboratory Tests** Provides a snapshot of current tests and procedures that are used in the physical assessment and diagnosis of certain conditions/diseases.

- **Abbreviations** Selected abbreviations with their meanings are included in each chapter. These abbreviations are in current use and directly associated with the subject of the chapter.

- **Study and Review** Provides the student with the opportunity to write in or identify correct answers for questions that relate to each section of the chapter.

- **Case Studies** Highlight a disease, disorder, and/or condition that relates to the subject of the chapter. A synopsis of a patient's visit to a physician is presented with present history, signs and symptoms, diagnosis, treatment, and prevention. Case study questions follow the synopsis, and answers are provided at the back of the text.

COMPREHENSIVE TEACHING–LEARNING PACKAGE

To enhance the teaching and learning process, an attractive media-focused supplements package for both students and faculty has been developed for *Medical Terminology with Human Anatomy*. The various components of the package is also described on the inside front cover of this text. The full complement of supplemental teaching materials is available to all qualified instructors from your Prentice Hall sales representative.

Student CD-ROM

The Student CD-ROM is packaged **free** with every copy of the textbook. It includes:

- Custom flashcard generator
- Audio glossary with pronunciations of the key terms presented in the text
- Terminology Translator

- Pathology Spotlights videos, with additional content and weblinks related to diseases and conditions

- Medical terminology exercises, games, and activities that quiz students on spelling, word-building concepts, anatomy, and more.

Instructor's Resource Manual

This manual contains a wealth of material to help faculty plan and manage the medical terminology course. It includes lecture suggestions and outlines, learning objectives, a complete test bank, and more for each chapter. Through MediaLink boxes, the IRM also guides faculty on how to assign and use the text-specific Companion Website, www.prenhall.com/rice, and the CD-ROM that accompany the textbook.

Instructor's Resource CD-ROM

Packaged with the Instructor's Resource Manual, the Instructor's Resource CD-ROM provides many resources in an electronic format. First, the CD-ROM includes the complete test bank that allows instructors to generate customized exams and quizzes. Second, it includes a comprehensive turn-key lecture package in PowerPoint format. The lectures contain discussion points along with embedded color images from the textbook as well as bonus animations and videos to help infuse an extra spark into the classroom experience. Instructors may use this presentation system as it is provided, or they may opt to customize it for their specific needs.

Companion Website and Syllabus Manager®

Students and faculty will both benefit from the **free** Companion Website at www.prenhall.com/rice. This website serves as a text-specific, interactive online workbook to *Medical Terminology with Human Anatomy*. The Companion Website includes:

- A variety of quizzes in multiple-choice, true/false, labeling, fill-in-the-blank, and essay formats. Instant feedback and rationales are provided.

- An audio glossary in which key terms, as well as their component word parts, are pronounced.

- Instructors adopting this textbook for their courses have **free** access to an online Syllabus Manager with a whole host of features that facilitate the students' use of this Companion Website and allow faculty to post their syllabi online for their students. For more information or a demonstration of Syllabus Manager®, please contact your Prentice Hall sales representative or visit www.prenhall.com/demo, click on Companion Websites, and select Syllabus Manager Tour.

Finally, those instructors wishing to facilitate on-line courses will be able to access our premium on-line course management option, which is available in WebCT, Blackboard, or CourseCompass formats. For more information or a demonstration of our on-line course systems, please contact your Prentice Hall sales representative or visit www.prenhall.com/demo.

ACKNOWLEDGMENTS

It does not seem possible, but *Medical Terminology with Human Anatomy*, my "dream" text, is 18 years old. During these 18 years many people have stood by my side, guided me, and helped me in so many ways. A special thank you to all the Medical Assisting, Radiologic Technology, Respiratory Therapy, Nursing, and Business and Office Technology students that I have had the privilege to teach.

To Elena Mauceri, because of your hard work, your diligent persistence, and your knowledgeable foresight, the fifth edition is the best of the best. Words cannot express my gratitude, but a very special thank you goes to you, Julie Levin Alexander, Mark Cohen, and Melissa Kerian for believing in my book.

There are many other special people who help me in all that I do and I extend to each of you my warmest appreciation and gratitude:

Patrick Walsh   Mary Ellen Ruitenberg
Cheryl Asherman   John Jordan
Christopher Weigand   Nicole Benson
Danielle Newhouse   Amy Peltier
Jessica Balch   Barbara Cousins

I would like to express my appreciation to the following people for their valuable contributions to the supplements:

CD-ROM

Pamela A. Eugene, B.A.S., L.R.T. (R)
Delgado Community College
New Orleans, Louisiana

Patricia McLane, RHIA, MA
Henry Ford Community College
Dearborn, Michigan

Mindy A. Goldberg, PA-C, MPH
Pellissippi State Technical Community
  College
Knoxville, Tennessee

Instructor's Resource Manual

Pamela A. Eugene, B.A.S., L.R.T. (R)
Delgado Community College
New Orleans, Louisiana

I would also like to express my appreciation to the following reviewers for their valuable input:

Judy Anderson, MEd
Coastal Carolina Community College
Jacksonville, North Carolina

Ann Barton, CMT
Riverside, California

Cheryl Bernhardt, MS
John A. Logan College
Carterville, Illinois

Jamie L. Flower, MS, RN
University of Arkansas—Fort Smith
Fort Smith, Arkansas

Rebecca L. Gibson, MSTE, CMA, ASPT
The University of Akron
Akron, Ohio

Laura C. Gilliam, BS, MS
Western Piedmont Community College
Morganton, North Carolina

Marta Lopez, LM, CPM
Miami-Dade Community College
Miami, Florida

Ford Matipa, MD
The New York School for Medical and Dental Assistants
Forest Hills, New York

Mildred Norris, BS, RHIT, CCS, CPC
Hillsborough Community College
Tampa, Florida

Martha L. Rew, MS, RD, LD
Texas Woman's University
Denton, Texas

Marie Rogers, RNC, MSN, MA
Kalamazoo Valley Community College
Kalamazoo, Michigan

Jonathan Allen Thorsen, BS, RRT
Long Beach City College
Long Beach, California

Linda G. Toomer, MSN, RN
J. Sargeant Reynolds Community College
Richmond, Virginia

Renee Twibell, DNS, RN
Ball State University
Muncie, Indiana

Portions of the Pathology Spotlights sections are from Discovery Communications (www.discovery.com) and Adam, Inc. We thank them for their contributions.

ABOUT THE AUTHOR

School Days
1946-47

I would like for you to close your eyes and go back in time with me. To a time before most of you were born. The year is 1947 and I am a little girl with brown hair that is braided into pigtails. I am very shy and afraid—for, you see, I am in the second grade and I cannot read. Not one little word. The teacher discovered this and made me sit on a tall metal stool in front of the classroom with a dunce cap on my head. Still to this day, I get very nervous when I have to get up in front of a crowd of people.

My mother taught me to read because back then, there were no special classes for children with learning disabilities. I did not learn "phonetics," but memorized everything. I still have trouble pronouncing words, but I can tell you all you want to know about a medical word.

After the death of two brothers, my father, and the impending death of my mother, I prayed for something else to do, something that would help take away the pain and the hurt. In 1982 my prayers were answered with a most precious gift: *Medical Terminology with Human Anatomy*, which was first published in September of 1985.

I owe so much to God and my best friend and husband, Charles Larry Rice. Larry helps me in all that I do. We have a lovely adopted daughter, Melissa, who came into our lives 34 years ago when she was 3 weeks old. She has blessed us with a son-in-law, Doug, and five precious grandchildren: Zachary, Benjamin, Jacob, Mary Katherine, and Elizabeth Ann.

Although I am now retired, I had a wonderful teaching career. Because of my childhood experiences I became a caring and devoted teacher. As Medical Assisting Program Director at Coosa Valley Technical Institute, I developed the original curriculum for the medical assisting program and taught my favorite subject, medical terminology, for 29 years. I am grateful to my many wonderful students who taught me so much and touched my life with their unique qualities.

Jane Rice, RN, CMA-C

Build student SUCCESS with these time-proven tools!

Start with a strong foundation of anatomy and physiology . . .

BODY SYSTEMS ORGANIZATION

The chapter organization clearly places medical terms in context with their related body system.

BRIEF CONTENTS

THE CARDIOVASCULAR SYSTEM 7

Anatomy and Physiology Overview

Through the cardiovascular system, blood is circulated to all part the action of the heart. This process provides the body's cells nutritive elements and removes waste materials and carbon dio a muscular pump, is the central organ of the system, which also include and **capillaries.** The various organs and components of the cardiovas described in this chapter, along with some of their functions.

ANATOMY AND PHYSIOLOGY

Found at the beginning of each chapter, this section provides a comprehensive yet concise overview of the body system to which the terminology relates.

FULL COLOR ARTWORK

Our high-quality art provides a visual reference drawn with a consistent style throughout the book–fostering a comfortable experience for visual learners. **Nearly 75 new photos and illustrations** have been added to this edition!

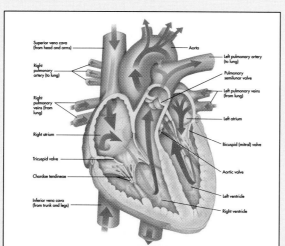

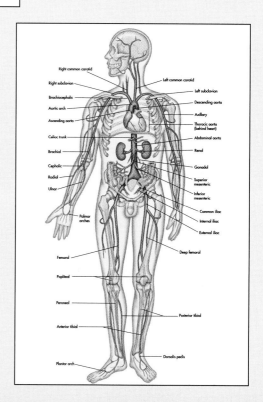

. . . and a unique word building approach

BUILDING YOUR MEDICAL VOCABULARY

This section provides the foundation for learning medical terminology. Medical words can be made up of four different types of word parts:

BUILDING YOUR MEDICAL VOCABULARY

This feature is at the core of the book's approach. Students can learn about terms that are built from word parts **concurrently** with vocabulary words. This logical approach groups each important term by relevance in a single study list.

Highlights of this feature are:

- Medical word and pronunciation are included in the left column.

- Components word parts in the center colum each clearly identify a prefix (P), root (R), combining form (CF), or suffix (S).

- The list is alphabetical, which places similar words together, thereby creating repetition that aids learning.

- Words shown in pink represent vocabulary words that are not built from word parts.

- Words related to diseases and conditions are integrated into this section. Those that are covered in the Pathology Spotlights section are highlighted with an asterisk icon ✱

- A CD icon indicates a corresponding media element such as an animation or video.

MEDICAL WORD	WORD PARTS (WHEN APPLICABLE)			DEFINITION
	Part	Type	Meaning	
coronary heart disease (CHD)				Coronary heart disease (CHD), also referred to as coronary artery disease (CAD), refers to the narrowing of the coronary arteries sufficient to prevent adequate blood supply to the myocardium. ✱ See Pathology Spotlight: Coronary Heart Disease.
cyanosis (sī-ă n-ō′ sĭs)	cyan -osis	R S	dark blue condition of	A dark blue condition of the skin and mucus membranes caused by oxygen deficiency
diastole (dī-ăs′ tō-lē)	diast -ole	R S	to expand small	The relaxation phase of the heart cycle during which the heart muscle relaxes and the heart chambers fill with blood
dysrhythmia (dĭs-rĭth′ mē-ă)	dys rhythm -ia	P R S	difficult rhythm condition	An abnormal, difficult, or bad rhythm. ✱ See Pathology Spotlight: Dysrythmias.
echocardiography (ĕk″ ō-kăr′ dē-ŏg′ rah-fē)	ech/o cardi/o -graphy	CF CF S	echo heart recording	A noninvasive ultrasound method for evaluating the heart for valvular or structural defects and coronary artery disease
electrocardiograph (ē-lĕk″ trō-kăr′ dĭ-ō-grăf)	electr/o cardi/o -graph	CF CF S	electricity heart to write, record	A device used for recording the electrical impulses of the heart muscle
electrocardio-phonograph (ē-lĕk″ trō-kăr″ dĭ-ō-fō′ nō-grăf)	electr/o cardi/o phon/o -graph	CF CF CF S	electricity heart sound to write, record	A device used to record heart sounds
embolism (ĕm′ bō-lĭzm)	embol -ism	R S	a throwing in condition of	A condition in which a blood clot obstructs a blood vessel; a moving blood clot
endarterectomy (ĕn″ dăr-tĕr-ĕk′ tō-mē)	end arter -ectomy	P R S	within artery excision	Surgical excision of the inner portion of an artery
endocarditis (ĕn″ dō-kăr-dī′ tĭs)	endo card -itis	P R S	within heart inflammation	Inflammation of the endocardium. See Figure 7-16.
endocardium (ĕn″ dō-kăr′ dē-ŭm)	endo card/i -um	P CF S	within heart tissue	The inner lining of the heart

Add focused pathology coverage . . .

Two new features embody our initiative to fortify the pathology content in this edition. With these features, readers can focus their learning on the most common diseases and disorders related to the body system.

PATHOLOGY SPOTLIGHTS

These features highlight 4-6 common conditions related to the chapter content, with illustrations and photos.

PATHOLOGY SPOTLIGHTS

Coronary Heart Disease (CHD)

Coronary heart disease (CHD) is the most common form of heart disease. It is also referred to as coronary artery disease (CAD) and refers to the narrowing of the coronary arteries that supply blood to the heart. It is a progressive disease that increases the risk of myocardial infarction (heart attack) and sudden death.

CHD usually results from the buildup of fatty material and plaque (**atherosclerosis**). See Figures 7–27, 7–28, and 7–29. As the coronary arteries narrow, the flow of blood to the heart can slow or stop. Blockage can occur in one or many coronary arteries.

Small blockages may not always affect the heart's performance. The person may not have symptoms until the heart needs more oxygen-rich blood than the arteries can supply. This commonly occurs during exercise or other activity. The pain that results is called stable angina.

If a blockage is large, angina pain can occur with little or no activity. This is known as unstable angina. In this case, the flow of blood to the heart is so limited that the person can-

✓ PATHOLOGY CHECKPOINT

Following is a concise list of the pathology-related terms that you've seen in the chapter. Review this checklist to make sure that you are familiar with the meaning of each term before moving on to the next section.

Conditions and Symptoms ✳

- ❑ aneurysm
- ❑ anginal
- ❑ angiocarditis
- ❑ angioma
- ❑ angiostenosis
- ❑ aortomalacia
- ❑ arrhythmia
- ❑ arteriosclerosis
- ❑ arteritis
- ❑ atheroma
- ❑ atherosclerosis
- ❑ bradycardia
- ❑ bruit
- ❑ cardiomegaly
- ❑ cardiomyopathy
- ❑ cardiopathy
- ❑ carditis
- ❑ claudication
- ❑ constriction
- ❑ coronary heart disease (CHD)
- ❑ cyanosis
- ❑ dysrhythmia
- ❑ embolism
- ❑ endocarditis

- ❑ heart failure (HF)
- ❑ hemangiectasis
- ❑ hemangioma
- ❑ hypertension
- ❑ hypotension
- ❑ infarction
- ❑ ischemia
- ❑ mitral stenosis
- ❑ murmur
- ❑ myocardial infarction (MI)
- ❑ myocarditis
- ❑ occlusion
- ❑ palpitation
- ❑ pericarditis
- ❑ phlebitis
- ❑ Raynaud's phenomenon
- ❑ rheumatic heart disease
- ❑ shock
- ❑ spider veins
- ❑ tachycardia
- ❑ telangiectasis
- ❑ thrombophlebitis
- ❑ thrombosis
- ❑ vasoconstrictive
- ❑ vasospasm

Diagnosis and Treatment ✳

- ❑ anastomosis
- ❑ angiocardiography
- ❑ artificial pacemaker
- ❑ auscultation
- ❑ cardiocentesis
- ❑ cardiometer
- ❑ cardiotonic
- ❑ catheterization
- ❑ coronary bypass
- ❑ echocardiography
- ❑ electrocardiograph
- ❑ electrocardiophonograph
- ❑ endarterectomy
- ❑ extracorporeal circulation
- ❑ heart-lung transplant
- ❑ heart transplant
- ❑ oximetry
- ❑ percutaneous transluminal coronary angioplasty
- ❑ phlebotomy
- ❑ sphygmomanometer
- ❑ stethoscope
- ❑ vasodilator
- ❑ venipuncture

PATHOLOGY CHECKPOINTS

Provide a concise list of the pathology terms covered in the chapter. Readers can "check off" those terms that they understand, and go back and review any that are not clear. Consistent headings are provided to separate Conditions/Symptoms from Diagnosis/Treatment.

. . . and practical applications

LIFESPAN
CONSIDERATIONS

■ THE CHILD

The development of the fetal heart is usually completed during the first 2 months of intrauterine life. It is completely formed and functioning by 10 weeks. At 16 weeks fetal heart tones can be heard with a **fetoscope**. Oxygenenated blood is trasported by the umbilical

mal aging heart is able to pro
output. But in some older ad
harder to pump blood beca
arteries (arteriosclerosis) and
in the arterial walls (ather
gradually become stiff and lo
aorta and arteries supplying

LIFESPAN CONSIDERATIONS

Presents interesting facts about the human body as it relates to the child and the older adult. Learning about these populations and their special needs prepares readers to work in a variety of settings.

DRUG HIGHLIGHTS

Presents essential drug information that relates to the subject of the chapter.

DRUG HIGHLIGHTS

Drugs that are generally used for cardiovascular diseases and disorders i
tions, antiarrhythmic agents, vasopressors, vasodilators, antihypertensi
demic, antiplatelet drugs, and thrombolgtic agents.

Digitalis Drugs — Strengthen the heart muscle, increase the force and velocity of contraction, slow the heart rate, and decrease conduction velo

DIAGNOSTIC & LAB TESTS

TEST	DESCRIPTION
angiogram (ăn′ jē-ō-grăm)	A test used to determine the size and shape of arteries and veins of organs and tiss A radiopaque substance is injected into the blood vessel, and x-rays are taken.
angiography (ăn′′ jē-ŏg′ ră-fē)	The x-ray recording of a blood vessel after the injection of a radiopaque substance Used to determine the condition of the blood vessels, organ, or tissue being studie

DIAGNOSTIC AND LAB TESTS

Provides a snapshot of current tests and procedures that are used in the physical assessment and diagnosis of certain diseases and conditions

ABBREVIATIONS

Selected abbreviations with their meanings are included in each chapter. These abbreviations are in current use and are directly associated with the subject of the chapter.

ABBREVIATIONS

ABBREVIATION	TERM	ABBREVIATION	
ACG	angiocardiography	Hgb	h
AI	aortic insufficiency	H&L	h
AMI	acute myocardial infarction	IHSS	i
AS	aortic stenosis		s
ASD	atrial septal defect	JNC	J
ASH	asymmetrical septal	A	t

And reinforce learning with integrated media . . .

MedMedia

Included at the beginning of each chapter, this feature prompts readers to use the various media components on the accompanying CD-ROM and Companion Website. MedMedia serves as a gateway to deeper understanding.

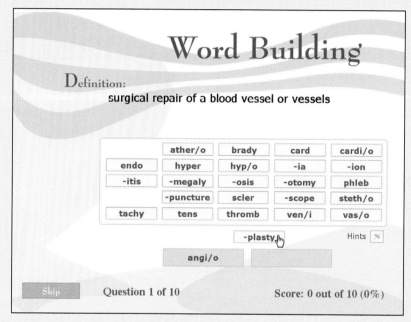

CD-ROM

A **free** CD-ROM is included with every text, and provides a wide variety of interactive games, animations, videos, an audio glossary, as well as exercises such as labeling, word building, spelling, and more. A custom flashcard generator is also available on the CD-ROM–allowing students to select glossary terms and printout flashcards for any or all terms for study.

TERMINOLOGY TRANSLATOR

This unique NEW feature, found on the FREE CD-ROM, provides an innovative tool to translate medical words into **Spanish, French,** and **German.** In our multicultural society, it is becoming more and more important that students be able to communicate in a variety of languages.

ON-LINE LEARNING

This text breaks new ground by offering on-line options in both a **free-access** Companion Website as well as **premium-level** distance learning courses. The Companion Website (www.prenhall.com/rice) serves as a text-specific, interactive online workbook and includes a variety of quizzes, links, and an audio glossary. Instructors adopting this textbook for their courses have **free** access to an online Syllabus Manager with a host of features that facilitate the students' use of this Companion Website and allow faculty to post their syllabi online for their students. Finally, those instructors wishing to facilitate on-line courses will be able to access our premium on-line course management option, which is available in **WebCT, Blackboard** or **CourseCompass** formats. For more information or a demonstration of our on-line course please visit www.prenhall.com/demo.

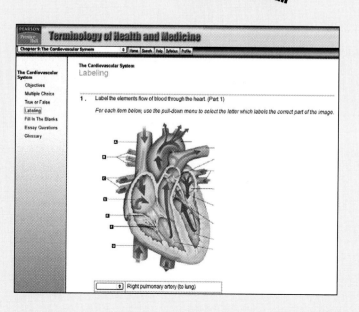

. . . and tools for student success

STUDY AND REVIEW

This section provides the student with the opportunity to review and reinforce their knowledge with activities that relate to each section of the chapter. Students can check their answers in the back of the book.

A variety of activities can be found in this section, including:

- Anatomy and physiology fill-in questions
- Word part definition fill-in exercises
- Identifying Medical Terms
- Spelling exercises
- Matching exercises
- Abbreviation exercises

STUDY AND REVIEW

Anatomy and Physiology

Write your answers to the following questions. Do not refer to the text.

1. The cardiovascular system includes:

   a. _____   b. _____

   c. _____   d. _____

2. Name the three layers of the heart.

   a. _____   b. _____

   c. _____

PREFIXES

Give the definitions of the following prefixes:

1. a- _____

3. brady- _____

5. end- _____

Identifying Medical Terms

In the spaces provided, write the medical terms for the following meanings:

1. _____ A tumor of a blood vessel

2. _____ The germ cell from which blood vessels develop

3. _____ Surgical repair of a blood vessel or vessels

Spelling

In the spaces provided, write the correct spelling of these misspelled terms:

1. astomosis _____   2. athrosclerosis _____

3. atriventrcular _____   4. endcarditis _____

5. extracoporal _____

Matching

Select the appropriate lettered meaning for each word listed below.

_____ 1. cholesterol

_____ 2. claudication

_____ 3. dysrhythmia

a. The two separate heart sounds that can be h with the use of a stethocope

b. Quivering of muscle fiber

c. Fat and protein molecules that are bound together

Abbreviations

Place the correct word, phrase, or abbreviation in the space provided.

1. acute myocardial infarction _____

2. atrioventricular _____

3. BP _____

CASE STUDIES

This feature highlights a disease, disorder, and/or condition that relates to the subject of the chapter. A patient scenario includes present history, signs and symptoms, diagnosis, treatment, and prevention. Case Study questions follow the synopsis, and answers are provided in the back of the text.

CASE STUDY — ANGINA PECTORIS

Read the following case study and then answer the questions that follow.

A 45-year-old male was seen by a cardiologist; the following is a synopsis of his visit.

Present History: The patient states that during a workout session he felt tightness in his chest, became short of breath, and felt very apprehensive. He states that this uncomfortable sensation went away after he stopped exercising.

Signs and Symptoms: Tightness in his chest, dyspnea, apprehension.

Diagnosis: Angina pectoris. Diagnosis was determined by a complete physical examination, an electro-cardiogram, and blood enzyme studies.

Treatment: Nitroglycerin sublingual tablets 0.4 mg as needed for chest pain. The patient is instructed to seek medical attention without delay if the pain is not relieved by three tablets, taken one every 5 minutes over a 15-minute period.

Prevention: Teach the patient to avoid situations that precipitate angina attacks. Proper rest and diet, stress management, lifestyle changes, avoidance of alcohol and tobacco are recommended.

CASE STUDY QUESTIONS

1. Signs and symptoms of angina pectoris include tightness in the chest, _____ (short-ness of breath), and apprehension.

2. The diagnosis of angina pectoris was determined by a complete physical examination, an _____ _____, and blood enzyme studies.

3. The medication regimen prescribed included _____ 0.4 mg as needed for chest pain.

4. If the patient follows the recommended medica-tion regimen and it does not relieve the pain, he should _____.

FUNDAMENTAL WORD STRUCTURE

1

OBJECTIVES

On completion of this chapter, you will be able to:

- Describe the fundamental elements that are used to build medical words.
- List three guidelines that will assist you with the identification and spelling of medical words.
- Analyze, build, spell, and pronounce medical words.
- Describe selected medical and surgical specialties, giving the scope of practice and the physician's title.
- Identify and define selected abbreviations.
- Successfully complete the study and review section.

MedMedia
www.prenhall.com/rice

Additional interactive resources and activities for this chapter can be found on the Companion Website. For Terminology Translator, animations, videos, audio glossary, and review, access the accompanying CD-ROM in this book.

Understanding Fundamental Word Structure

Medical terminology is the study of terms that are used in the art and science of medicine. It is a specialized language with its origin arising from the Greek influence on medicine. Hippocrates was a Greek physician who lived from 460 to 377 BC and whose vital role in medicine is still recognized today. He is called "The Father of Medicine" and is credited with establishing early ethical standards for physicians. Because of advances in scientific computerized technology, many new terms are coined daily; however, most of these terms are composed of word parts that have their origins in ancient Greek or Latin. Because of this foreign origin, it is necessary to learn the English translation of terms when learning the fundamentals of word structure.

FUNDAMENTALS OF WORD STRUCTURE

The fundamental elements in medical terminology are the component parts used to build medical words. The terms for component parts used in this text are P = **prefix**, R = **root**, CF = **combining form**, and S = **suffix**. Each of these component parts is described in detail below.

Prefix

The term **prefix** means to fix before or to fix to the beginning of a word. A prefix may be a syllable or a group of syllables united with or placed at the beginning of a word to alter or modify the meaning of the word or to create a new word.

For example: the word **abnormal** means pertaining to away from the normal. Note its component parts below:

ab	P or prefix meaning	away from
norm	R or root meaning	rule
-al	S or suffix meaning	pertaining to

Word Root

A **root** is a word or word element from which other words are formed. It is the foundation of the word. The root conveys the central meaning of the word and forms the base to which prefixes and suffixes are attached for word modification.

For example: the word **autonomy** means condition of being self-governed. Note its component parts below:

auto	P or prefix meaning	self
nom	R or root meaning	law
-y	S or suffix meaning	condition

Combining Form

A **combining form** is a word root to which a vowel has been added to join the root to a second root or to a suffix. The vowel "o" is used more often than any other to make combining forms. Combining forms may be found at the beginning of a word or within the word.

For example: the word **chemotherapy** means treatment of disease by using chemical agents. Note the relation of its component parts:

chem/o	CF or combining form meaning	chemical
-therapy	S or suffix meaning	treatment

Suffix

The term **suffix** means to fasten on, beneath, or under. A suffix may be a syllable or group of syllables united with or placed at the end of a word to alter or modify the meaning of the word or to create a new word.

For example: the word **centigrade** means having 100 steps or degrees and the word *centimeter* means one-hundredth of a meter:

centi	P or prefix meaning	a hundred
-grade	S or suffix meaning	a step
centi	P or prefix meaning	a hundred
-meter	S or suffix meaning	measure

In many medical terminology textbooks, all the prefixes and suffixes used throughout the text are grouped into one or two beginning chapters. Under this arrangement, you are forced to refer repeatedly to these chapters to identify or define these word elements. In this book, however, prefixes and suffixes, along with their definitions, are integrated into each chapter throughout the text and provide a ready reference. Naturally, many of these same prefixes and suffixes will be used in each chapter. This repetition serves to reinforce the learning of the terms and their definitions and makes this text an improved learning tool.

Word roots and combining forms, together with their definitions, are included in each chapter according to the cell, tissue, organ, system, or element they describe. This arrangement makes it possible for you to form associations between medical terms and the various body systems. To reinforce this relation, this text provides you with a general anatomy and physiology overview for each of the body systems that it includes.

PRINCIPLES OF COMPONENT PARTS

As you learn definitions for prefixes, roots, combining forms, and suffixes, you will discover that some component parts have the same meanings as others. This occurs most often with words that relate to the organs of the body and the diseases that affect them. The existence of more than one component part for a particular meaning can be traced to differences in the Greek or Latin words from which they originated. Most of the terms for the body's organs originated from Latin words, whereas terms describing diseases that affect these organs have their origins in Greek.

For example:

- **Uterus**—a Latin word for one of the organs of the female reproductive system
- **Hyster**—a Greek R (root) for womb
- **Hysterectomy**—surgical excision of the womb from hyster R (root) meaning womb + -ectomy S (suffix) meaning surgical excision
- **Metr/i**—a Greek CF (combining form) for uterus
- **Myometrium**—muscular tissue of the uterus from my/o CF meaning muscle + metr/i CF meaning uterus + -um S meaning tissue

Many prefixes and suffixes have more than a single definition. When learning medical terminology, you must learn to use the definition that best describes the term. The following are commonly used prefixes that have more than a single definition:

PREFIXES WITH MORE THAN ONE MEANING

Prefix	Meanings	Prefix	Meanings
a-, an-	no, not, without, lack of, apart	extra-	outside, beyond
ad-	toward, near, to	hyper-	above, beyond, excessive
bi-	two, double	hypo-	below, under, deficient
de-	down, away from		
di-	two, double	in-	in, into, not
dia-	through, between	mega-	large, great
dif-, dis-	apart, free from, separate	meta-	beyond, over, between, change
dys-	bad, difficult, painful	para-	beside, alongside, abnormal
ec-, ecto-	out, outside, outer	poly-	many, much, excessive
		post-	after, behind
end-, endo-	within, inner	pre-	before, in front of
ep-, epi-	upon, over, above	pro-	before, in front of
eu-	good, normal	super-	above, beyond
ex-, exo-	out, away from	supra-	above, beyond

The following prefixes and their meanings have been selected to aid you in building a medical vocabulary:

PREFIXES THAT PERTAIN TO POSITION OR PLACEMENT

Prefix	Meanings	Prefix	Meanings
ab-	away from	hyper-	above, excessive
ad-	toward	hypo-	below, deficient
ana-	up	infra-	below
ante-	before	inter-	between
cata-	down	intra-	within
circum-, peri-	around	meso-	middle
endo-	within	para-	beside, alongside
epi-	upon, above	retro-	backward
ex-	out, away from	sub-	below, under
extra-	outside, beyond	supra-	above, beyond

PREFIXES THAT PERTAIN TO NUMBERS AND AMOUNTS

Prefix	Meanings	Prefix	Meanings
ambi-	both	poly-	many
bi-	two, double	primi-	first
centi-	a hundred	quadri-	four
deca-	ten	quint-	five
dipl-	double	semi-, hemi-	half
di(s)-	two, apart	tetra-	four
milli-	one-thousandth	tri	three
multi-	many, much	uni-	one
nulli-	none		

PREFIXES THAT ARE DESCRIPTIVE AND ARE USED IN GENERAL

Prefix	Meanings	Prefix	Meanings
a, an-	without, lack of	hetero-	different
anti-, contra-	against	homeo-	similar, same
auto-	self	hydro-	water
brachy-	short	mega-	large, great
brady-	slow	micro-	small
cac-, mal-	bad	oligo-	scanty, little
dia-	through	pan-	all
dys-	bad, difficult	pseudo-	false
eu-	good, normal	sym-, syn-	together

The following are commonly used suffixes that have more than a single definition:

SUFFIXES WITH MORE THAN ONE DEFINITION

Suffix	Meanings	Suffix	Meanings
-ate	use, action	-plasm	a thing formed, plasma
-blast	immature cell, germ cell		
-ectasis	dilatation, dilation, distention	-plegia	stroke, paralysis
-gen	formation, produce	-ptosis	prolapse, drooping
-genesis	formation, produce	-rrhea	flow, discharge
-genic	formation, produce	-scopy	to view, examine
-gram	weight, mark, record	-spasm	tension, spasm
-ic	pertaining to, chemical	-stasis	control, stopping
-ive	nature of, quality of	-staxia	dripping, trickling
-lymph	serum, clear fluid	-trophy	nourishment, development
-lysis	destruction, to separate		
-megaly	enlargement, large	-y	process, condition, pertaining to
-penia	lack of, deficiency		

The following suffixes and their meanings have been selected to aid you in building a medical vocabulary:

SUFFIXES THAT PERTAIN TO PATHOLOGIC CONDITIONS

Suffix	Meanings	Suffix	Meanings
-algia, -dynia	pain	-pathy	disease
-cele	hernia, tumor, swelling	-penia	deficiency
-emesis	vomiting	-phobia	fear
-itis	inflammation	-plegia	paralysis, stroke
-lith	stone	-ptosis	drooping
-lysis	destruction, separation	-ptysis	spitting
-malacia	softening	-rrhage	bursting forth
-megaly	enlargement, large	-rrhagia	bursting forth
-oid	resemble	-rrhea	flow, discharge
-oma	tumor	-rrhexis	rupture
-osis	condition of		

SUFFIXES USED IN DIAGNOSTIC AND SURGICAL PROCEDURES

Suffix	Meanings	Suffix	Meanings
-centesis	surgical puncture	-pexy	surgical fixation
-desis	binding	-plasty	surgical repair
-ectomy	excision	-rrhaphy	suture
-gram	a weight, mark, record	-scope	instrument
-graph	to write, record	-scopy	to view
-graphy	recording	-stasis	control, stopping
-meter	instrument to measure, measure	-stomy	new opening
		-tome	instrument to cut
-opsy	to view	-tomy	incision

SUFFIXES THAT ARE USED IN GENERAL

Suffix	Meanings	Suffix	Meanings
-blast	immature cell, germ cell	-phraxis	to obstruct
-cyte	cell	-physis	growth
-ist	one who specializes, agent	-pnea	breathing
-logy	study of	-poiesis	formation
-phagia	to eat	-therapy	treatment
-plasia	formation, produce	-trophy	nourishment, development
-phasia	to speak		
-philia	attraction	-uria	urine

IDENTIFYING MEDICAL WORDS

When identifying medical words you will learn to distinguish between and select the appropriate component parts for the meaning of the word. It is most important that you learn the words as they are listed, for the slightest change in the arrangement of a medical word's component parts can change its meaning.

For example: the word **microscope** means an instrument used to view small objects. Compare the following:

micro + -scope   Proper placement of component parts (P + S) although the definitions translate micro = small and scope = instrument.

-scope + micro   Improper placement of component parts (S + P). Although incorrect, this arrangement of word parts seems to correspond to the term's definition.

SPELLING

Medical words of Greek origin are often difficult to spell because many of them begin with a silent letter or have a silent letter within the word. The following are examples of words that begin with silent letters:

Silent Beginning	Pronounced	Medical Term	Pronunciation Guide
cn	n	**c**nemial	(nē′mĭ-al)
gn	n	**g**nathic	(năth′ĭk)
kn	n	**k**nuckle	(nŭk′ĕl)
mn	n	**m**nemic	(nē′mĭk)
pn	n	**p**neumonia	(nū′-mō′nĭ-ă)
ps	s	**p**sychiatrist	(sī-kī′ă-trĭst)
pt	t	**p**tosis	(tō′sĭs)

The following are examples of medical terms that contain silent letters within the word:

Silent Letter	Medical Term	Pronunciation Guide
g	phle**g**m	(flĕm)
p	ble**p**har**opt**osis	(blĕf″ă-rō-tō′ sis)

Correct spelling is extremely important in medical terminology, as the addition or omission of a single letter may change the meaning of a word to something entirely different. The following examples illustrate this point:

Term/Letter Change	Meaning of Term	Term/Letter Change	Meaning of Term
a**b**duct	To lead **away** from the middle	arte**ri**tis	Inflammation of an **artery**
a**d**duct	To lead **toward** the middle	arth**ri**tis	Inflammation of a **joint**

Listed below are some of the prefixes and suffixes that often contribute to spelling errors:

PREFIXES AND SUFFIXES THAT ARE FREQUENTLY MISSPELLED

Prefix	Meaning	Suffix	Meaning
ante-	before	-poiesis	formation
anti-	against	-ptosis	prolapse, drooping
		-ptysis	spitting
ecto-	outside		
endo-	within	-rrhagia	bursting forth
		-rrhage	bursting forth
hyper-	above, beyond, excessive		
hypo-	below, under, deficient	-rrhaphy	suture
		-rrhea	flow
		-rrhexis	rupture
inter-	between	-scope	instrument
intra-	within	-scopy	to view
para-	beside, alongside, abnormal	-tome	instrument to cut
peri-	around	-tomy	incision
per-	through	-tripsy	crushing
pre-	before	-trophy	nourishment, development
pro-	before		
super-	above, beyond		
supra-	above, beyond		

The following guidelines are provided to help with the identification and spelling of medical words:

1. If the suffix begins with a vowel, drop the combining vowel from the combining form and add the suffix.

    For example: hemato + -oma becomes hematoma when we drop the "o" from hemato.

2. If the suffix begins with a consonant, keep the combining vowel and add the suffix to the combining form.

    For example, kilo + -gram becomes kilogram and we keep the "o" on the combining form kilo.

3. Keep the combining vowel between two or more roots in a term.

    For example: electro + cardio + -gram becomes electrocardiogram and we keep the combining vowels.

FORMING PLURAL ENDINGS

To change the following singular endings to plural endings, substitute the plural endings as illustrated:

Singular Ending	Plural Ending	Singular Ending	Plural Ending
a as in burs**a**	to **ae** as in burs**ae**	**ix** as in append**ix**	to **ices** as in append**ices**
ax as in thor**ax**	to **aces** as in thor**aces** or	**nx** as in phala**nx**	to **ges** as in phalan**ges**
	es as in thorax**es**	**on** as in spermatozo**on**	to **a** as in spermatozo**a**
en as in foram**en**	to **ina** as in foram**ina**	**um** as in ov**um**	to **a** as in ov**a**
is as in cris**is**	to **es** as in cris**es**	**us** as in nucle**us**	to **i** as in nucle**i**
is as in ir**is**	to **ides** as in ir**ides**	**y** as in arter**y**	to **i** and add **es** as in arter**ies**
is as in femor**is**	to **a** as in femor**a**		

PRONUNCIATION

Pronunciation of medical words may seem difficult; however, it is very important to pronounce medical words with the same or very similar sounds to convey their correct meanings. As in spelling, one mispronounced syllable can change the meaning of a medical word. This text uses a phonetically spelled pronunciation guide adapted from *Taber's Cyclopedic Medical Dictionary*, and you should practice speaking each term aloud when working with the various lists of medical terms or vocabulary words. Accent marks are used to indicate stress on certain syllables. A single accent mark (′) is called a primary accent and is used with the syllable that has the strongest stress. A double accent (″) is called a secondary accent and is given to syllables that are stressed less than primary syllables.

Diacritics are marks placed over or under vowels to indicate the long or short sound of the vowel. In this text, the macron (‾) shows the long sound of the vowel, the breve (˘) shows the short sound of the vowel, and the schwa (ə) indicates the uncolored, central vowel sound of most unstressed syllables [for example: antiseptic (an″ tĭ-sep′ tik) or diathermy (di′ ə-thĕr″ mē)].

BUILDING YOUR MEDICAL VOCABULARY

This section provides the foundation for learning medical terminology. Medical words can be made up of four different types of word parts:

- Prefixes (P)
- Roots (R)
- Combining forms (CF)
- Suffixes (S)

By connecting various word parts in an organized sequence, thousands of words can be built and learned. In this text the word list is alphabetized so one can see the variety of meanings created when common prefixes and suffixes are repeatedly applied to certain word roots and/or combining forms. Words shown in pink are additional words related to the content of this chapter that are not built from word parts. These words are included to enhance your vocabulary.

MEDICAL WORD	WORD PARTS (WHEN APPLICABLE)			DEFINITION
	Part	**Type**	**Meaning**	
abate (ă-bāt′)				To lessen, decrease, or cease
abnormal (ăb-nōr′ măl)	ab norm -al	P R S	away from rule pertaining to	Pertaining to away from the normal or rule
abscess (ăb′ sĕs)				A localized collection of pus, which may occur in any part of the body
acute (ă-cūt′)				Sudden, sharp, severe; a disease that has a sudden onset, severe symptoms, and a short course
adhesion (ăd′ hē-zhŭn)	adhes -ion	R S	stuck to process	The process of being stuck together
afferent (ăf′ ĕr ĕnt)				Carrying impulses toward a center
ambulatory (ăm′ bŭ-lăh-tŏr″ ē)				The condition of being able to walk, not confined to bed
antidote (ăn′ tĭ-dōt)				A substance given to counteract poisons and their effects
antipyretic (ăn″ tĭ-pī-rĕt′ĭk)	anti pyret -ic	P R S	against fever pertaining to	Pertaining to an agent that works against fever

MEDICAL WORD	WORD PARTS (WHEN APPLICABLE)			DEFINITION
	Part	Type	Meaning	
antiseptic (ăn″ tĭ-sĕp′ tĭk)	anti sept -ic	P R S	against putrefaction pertaining to	Pertaining to an agent that works against sepsis; *putrefaction*
antitussive (ăn″ tĭ-tŭs′ ĭv)	anti tuss -ive	P R S	against cough nature of, quality of	Pertaining to an agent that works against coughing
apathy (ăp′ ă-thē)				A condition in which one lacks feelings and emotions and is indifferent
asepsis (ā-sĕp′ sĭs)	a -sepsis	P S	without decay	Without decay; *sterile,* free from all living microorganisms
autoclave (ŏ′ tō-klāv)	auto -clave	P S	self a key	An apparatus used to sterilize articles by steam under pressure
autonomy (ăw-tŏ′ nōm-ē) (ŏ-tŏ′ nōmē)	auto nom -y	P R S	self law condition	The condition of being self-governed; to function independently
axillary (ăks′ ĭ-lār-ē)	axill -ary	R S	armpit pertaining to	Pertaining to the armpit
biopsy (bī′ ŏp-sē)	bi(o) -opsy	R S	life to view	Surgical removal of a small piece of tissue for microscopic examination; used to determine a diagnosis of cancer or other disease processes in the body
cachexia (kă-kĕks′ ĭ-ă)	cac -hexia	P S	bad condition	A condition of ill health, malnutrition, and wasting
centigrade (sĕn′ tĭ-grād)	centi -grade	P S	a hundred a step	Having 100 steps or degrees, like the Celsius temperature scale; boiling point = 100°C and freezing point = 0°C
centimeter (sĕn′ tĭ-mē-tĕr)	centi -meter	P S	a hundred measure	Unit of measurement in the metric system; one hundredth of a meter
centrifuge (sĕn′ trĭ-fūj)	centr/i -fuge	CF S	center to flee	A device used in a laboratory to separate solids from liquids
chemotherapy (kē″ mō-thĕr′ ă-pē)	chem/o -therapy	CF S	chemical treatment	Treatment using chemical agents
chronic (krŏn ik)				Pertaining to time; a disease that continues over a long time, showing little change in symptoms or course

MEDICAL WORD	WORD PARTS (WHEN APPLICABLE)			DEFINITION
	Part	**Type**	**Meaning**	
diagnosis (dī″ ăg-nō′ sĭs)	dia -gnosis	P S	through knowledge	Determination of the cause and nature of a disease
diaphoresis (dī″ ă-fō-rē′ sĭs)	dia -phoresis	P S	through to carry	To carry through sweat glands; *profuse sweating*
disease (dĭ-zēz′)				Lack of ease; an abnormal condition of the body that presents a series of symptoms that sets it apart from normal or other abnormal body states
disinfectant (dĭs″ ĭn-fĕk′ tănt)	dis infect -ant	P R S	apart infection forming	A chemical substance that destroys bacteria
efferent (ĕf′ ĕr ĕnt)				Carrying impulses away from a center
empathy (ĕm′ pă-thē)				A state of projecting one's own personality into the personality of another to understand the feelings, emotions, and behavior of the person
epidemic (ĕp″ i-dĕm′ ik)	epi dem -ic	P R S	upon people pertaining to	Pertaining to among the people; the rapid, widespread occurrence of an infectious disease
etiology (ē″ tē-ŏl′ ō-jē)	eti/o -logy	CF S	cause study of	The study of the cause(s) of disease
excision (ĕk-si′ zhŭn)	ex cis -ion	P R S	out to cut process	The process of cutting out, surgical removal
febrile (fē′ brĭl)				Pertaining to fever
gram (grăm)				A unit of weight in the metric system; a cubic centimeter or a milliliter of water is equal to the weight of a gram
heterogeneous (hĕt″ ĕr-ō-jē′ nĭ-ŭs)	hetero gene -ous	P R S	different formation, produce pertaining to	Pertaining to a different formation
illness (ĭl′ nĭs)				A state of being sick

MEDICAL WORD	WORD PARTS (WHEN APPLICABLE)			DEFINITION
	Part	**Type**	**Meaning**	
incision (ĭn-sĭzh′ ŭn)	in cis -ion	P R S	in, into to cut process	The process of cutting into
kilogram (kĭl′ ō-grăm)	kil/o -gram	CF S	a thousand a weight	Unit of weight in the metric system; *1000 g*
liter (lē′ tĕr)				A unit of volume in the metric system; equal to 33.8 fl oz or 1.0567 qt
macroscopic (măk″ rō-skŏp ĭk)	macr/o scop -ic	CF R S	large to examine pertaining to	Pertaining to objects large enough to be examined by the naked eye
malaise (mă-lāz′)				A bad feeling; a condition of discomfort, uneasiness; often felt by a patient with a chronic disease
malformation (măl″ fōr-mā′ shŭn)	mal format -ion	P R S	bad a shaping process	The process of being badly shaped, deformed
malignant (mă-lĭg′ nănt)	malign -ant	R S	bad kind forming	A bad wandering; pertaining to the spreading process of cancer from one area of the body to another area
maximal (măks′ ĭ-măl)	maxim -al	R S	greatest pertaining to	Pertaining to the greatest possible quantity, number, or degree
microgram (mī′ krō-grăm)	micro -gram	P S	small a weight	A unit of weight in the metric system; *0.001 mg*
microorganism (mī″ krō-ōr′ găn-ĭzm)	micro organ -ism	P R S	small organ condition	Small living organisms that are not visible to the naked eye
microscope (mī′ krō-skōp)	micro -scope	P S	small instrument	An instrument used to view small objects
milligram (mĭl′ ĭ-grăm)	milli -gram	P S	one-thousandth a weight	A unit of weight in the metric system; *0.001 g*
milliliter (mĭl′ ĭ-lē″ tĕr)	milli -liter	P S	one-thousandth liter	A unit of volume in the metric system; *0.001 L*
minimal (mĭn′ ĭ-măl)	minim -al	R S	least pertaining to	Pertaining to the least possible quantity, number, or degree
multiform (mŭl′ tĭ-form)	multi -form	P S	many, much shape	Occurring in or having many shapes

MEDICAL WORD	WORD PARTS (WHEN APPLICABLE)			DEFINITION
	Part	**Type**	**Meaning**	
necrosis (nĕ-krō′ sis)	necr -osis	R S	death condition of	A condition of death of tissue
neopathy (nē-ŏp′ ă-thē)	neo -pathy	P S	new disease	A new disease
oncology (ŏng-kŏl′ ō-jē)	onc/o -logy	CF S	tumor study of	The study of tumors
pallor (păl′ or)				Paleness, a lack of color
palmar (păl′ mar)	palm -ar	R S	palm pertaining to	Pertaining to the palm of the hand
paracentesis (păr″ ă-sĕn-tē′ sĭs)	para -centesis	P S	beside surgical puncture	Surgical puncture of a body cavity for fluid removal
prognosis (prŏg-nō′ sĭs)	pro -gnosis	P S	before knowledge	A condition of foreknowledge; the prediction of the course of a disease and the recovery rate
prophylactic (prō-fi-lăk′ tĭk)	prophylact -ic	R S	guarding pertaining to	Pertaining to preventing or protecting against disease
pyrogenic (pī″ rō-jĕn′ ĭk)	pyr/o -genic	CF S	heat, fire formation, produce	Pertaining to the production of heat; *a fever*
radiology (rā″ dē-ŏl′ ō-jē)	radi/o -logy	CF S	ray study of	The study of radioactive substances
rapport (ră-pōr′)				A relationship of understanding between two individuals, especially between the patient and the physician
syndrome (sĭn′ drōm)	syn -drome	P S	together, with a course	A combination of signs and symptoms occurring together that characterize a specific disease
thermometer (thĕr-mŏm′ ĕ-tĕr)	therm/o -meter	CF S	hot, heat instrument to measure	An instrument used to measure degree of heat. See Figure 1–1.
topography (tō-pŏg′ răh-fē)	top/o -graphy	CF S	place recording	A recording of a special place of the body
triage (trē-ahzh′)	tri -age	P S	three related to	The sorting and classifying of injuries to determine priority of need and treatment

FIGURE 1–1

Electronic thermometer.

Terminology Translator

Medicine **Medicina** **Médecine** **Medizin**

This feature, found on the accompanying CD-ROM, provides an innovative tool to translate medical words into Spanish, French, and German.

MEDICAL AND SURGICAL SPECIALTIES

Today, the practice of medicine involves many areas of specialization. The American Board of Medical Specialties (ABMS) was founded in 1933. This board established standards for and monitoring of specialty practice areas. A physician who has met standards beyond those of admission to licensure and has passed an examination in a specialty area becomes board certified. There are various medical professional organizations that establish their own standards and administer their own board certification examinations. Individuals successfully completing all requirements are called Fellows, such as Fellow of the American College of Surgeons (FACS) or Fellow of the American College of Physicians (FACP). Board certification may be required by a hospital for admission to the medical staff or for determination of a staff member's rank. See Table 1–1 for selected medical and surgical specialties and Table 1–2 for types of surgical specialties with description of practice.

TABLE 1–1 SELECTED MEDICAL AND SURGICAL SPECIALTIES

Specialty and Scope of Practice/Physician/Word Parts

Allergy and Immunology: The branch of medicine concerned with diseases of an allergic nature. The physician is an **allergist** or **immunologist** (*immun/o—immune; log—study of; -ist—one who specializes*).

Anesthesiology: The branch of medicine concerned with appropriate anesthesia for partial or complete loss of sensation. The physician is an **anesthesiologist** (*an—without; esthesi/o—feeling; log—study of; -ist—one who specializes*).

Cardiology: The branch of medicine concerned with diseases of the heart, arteries, veins, and capillaries. The physician is a **cardiologist** (*cardi/o—heart; log—study of; -ist—one who specializes*).

Dermatology: The branch of medicine concerned with diseases of the skin. The physician is a **dermatologist** (*dermat/o—skin; log—study of; -ist—one who specializes*).

Endocrinology: The branch of medicine concerned with diseases of the endocrine system. The physician is an **endocrinologist** (*endo—within; crin/o—to secrete; log—study of; -ist—one who specializes*).

Epidemiology: The branch of medicine concerned with epidemic diseases. The physician is an **epidemiologist** (*epi—upon; demi/o—people; log—study of; -ist—one who specializes*).

Family Practice: The branch of medicine concerned with the care of members of the family regardless of age and/or sex. The physician is a **Family Practitioner.**

Gastroenterology: The branch of medicine concerned with diseases of the stomach and intestines. The physician is a **gastroenterologist** (*gastr/o—stomach; enter/o—intestine; log—study of; -ist—one who specializes*).

Geriatrics: The branch of medicine concerned with aspects of aging. The physician is a **gerontologist** (*geront/o—old age; log—study of; -ist—one who specializes*).

Gynecology: The branch of medicine that studies diseases of the female reproductive system. The physician is a **gynecologist** (*gynec/o—female; log—study of; -ist—one who specializes*).

Hematology: The branch of medicine that studies diseases of the blood and blood-forming tissues. The physician is a **hematologist** (*hemat/o—blood; log—study of; -ist—one who specializes*).

Infectious Disease: The branch of medicine concerned with diseases caused by the growth of pathogenic microorganisms within the body.

Internal Medicine: The branch of medicine concerned with diseases of internal origin, those not usually treated surgically. The physician is an **internist** (*intern—within; -ist—one who specializes*).

Nephrology: The branch of medicine concerned with diseases of the kidney and urinary system. The physician is a **nephrologist** (*nephr/o—kidney; log—study of; -ist—one who specializes*).

Neurology: The branch of medicine concerned with diseases of the nervous system. The physician is a **neurologist** (*neur/o—nerve; log—study of; -ist—one who specializes*).

Obstetrics: The branch of medicine concerned with treating the female during pregnancy, childbirth, and the postpartum. The physician is an **obstetrician.** The Latin word element *obstetrix* means midwife.

Oncology: The branch of medicine that studies tumors. The physician is an **oncologist** (*onc/o—tumor; log—study of; -ist—one who specializes*).

Ophthalmology: The branch of medicine concerned with diseases of the eye. The physician is an **ophthalmologist** (*ophthalm/o—eye; log—study of; -ist—one who specializes*).

Orthopedic Surgery (*Orthopaedic*): The branch of medicine concerned with diseases and disorders involving locomotor structures of the body. The physician is an **orthopedist** (*orthopaedist*) (*orth/o—straight; ped—child; -ist—one who specializes*).

Otorhinolaryngology: The branch of medicine concerned with diseases of the ear, nose, and larynx. The physician is an **otorhinolaryngologist** (*ot/o—ear; rhin/o—nose; laryng/o—larynx; log—study of; -ist—one who specializes*).

TABLE 1–1 SELECTED MEDICAL AND SURGICAL SPECIALTIES (CONTINUED)

Specialty and Scope of Practice/Physician/Word Parts

Pathology: The branch of medicine that studies structural and functional changes in tissues and organs caused by disease. The physician is a **pathologist** (*path/o—disease; log—study of; -ist—one who specializes*).

Pediatrics: The branch of medicine concerned with diseases of children. The physician is a **pediatrician** (*ped—child; iatr—treatment; -ician—physician*).

Physical Medicine and Rehabilitation: The branch of medicine concerned with the treatment of disease by physical agents. The physician is a **physiatrist** (*phys—nature; iatr—treatment; -ist—one who specializes*).

Psychiatry: The branch of medicine concerned with diseases of the mind. The physician is a **psychiatrist** (*psych/o—mind; iatr—treatment; -ist—one who specializes*).

Pulmonary Disease: The branch of medicine concerned with diseases of the lungs. The physician is a **pulmonologist** (*pulmon/o—lung; log—study of; -ist—one who specializes*).

Radiology: The branch of medicine that studies radioactive substances and their relationship to prevention, diagnosis, and treatment of disease. The physician is a **radiologist** (*radi/o—ray; log—study of; -ist—one who specializes*).

Rheumatology: The branch of medicine concerned with rheumatic diseases. The physician is a **rheumatologist** (*rheumat/o—rheumatism; log—study of; -ist—one who specializes*).

Urology: The branch of medicine concerned with diseases of the urinary system. The physician is a **urologist** (*ur/o—urine; log—study of; -ist—one who specializes*).

TABLE 1–2 TYPES OF SURGICAL SPECIALTIES
WITH DESCRIPTION OF PRACTICE

Surgical Specialty	*Description of Practice*
Surgery is defined as the branch of medicine dealing with manual and operative procedures for correction of deformities and defects, repair of injuries, and diagnosis and cure of certain diseases.	
Cardiovascular	Surgical repair and correction of cardiovascular dysfunctions
Colon and Rectum	Surgical repair and correction of colon and rectal dysfunctions
Cosmetic, Reconstructive, Plastic	Surgical repair, reconstruction, revision, or change the texture, configuration, or relationship of contiguous structures of any part of the human body
General	Surgical repair and correction of various body parts and/or organs
Maxillofacial	Surgical treatment of diseases, injuries, and defects of the human mouth and dental structures
Neurologic	Surgical repair and correction of neurologic dysfunctions
Orthopedic (Orthopaedic)	Surgical prevention and repair of musculoskeletal dysfunctions
Thoracic	Surgical repair and correction of organs within the rib cage
Trauma	Surgical repair and correction of traumatic injuries
Vascular	Surgical repair and correction of vascular (vessels) dysfunctions

ABBREVIATIONS

ABBREVIATION	MEANING	ABBREVIATION	MEANING
AB	abnormal	FACP	Fellow of the American College of Physicians
ABMS	American Board of Medical Specialties	FACS	Fellow of the American College of Surgeons
ac	acute	FP	family practice
ax	axillary	g	gram
Bx	biopsy	GYN	gynecology
C	centigrade, Celsius	kg	kilogram
cm	centimeter	L	liter
CT	computerized tomography	mcg	microgram
CVD	cardiovascular disease	mg	milligram
D/C	discontinue	mL, ml	milliliter
derm	dermatology	OB	obstetrics
Dx	diagnosis	Peds	pediatrics
DRGs	diagnosis related groups	Psy	psychiatry, psychology
ENT	otorhinolaryngology		

STUDY AND REVIEW

Word Parts

1. In the spaces provided, write the definition of these prefixes, roots, combining forms, and suffixes. Do not refer to the listings of medical words. Leave blank those words you cannot define.

2. After completing as many as you can, refer back to the medical word listings to check your work. For each word missed or left blank, write the word and its definition several times on the margins of these pages or on a separate sheet of paper.

3. To maximize the learning process, it is to your advantage to do the following exercises as directed. To refer to the word building section before completing these exercises invalidates the learning process.

PREFIXES

Give the definitions of the following prefixes:

1. a- _____

2. ab- _____

3. anti- _____

4. auto- _____

5. cac- _____

6. centi- _____

7. dia- _____

8. hetero- _____

9. mal- _____

10. micro- _____

11. milli- _____

12. multi- _____

13. neo- _____

14. para- _____

15. pro- _____

16. syn- _____

17. tri- _____

18. dis- _____

19. epi- _____

20. ex- _____

21. in- _____

ROOTS AND COMBINING FORMS

Give the definitions of the following roots and combining forms:

1. adhes _____
2. axill _____
3. centr/i _____
4. chem/o _____
5. format _____
6. gene _____
7. kil/o _____
8. macr/o _____
9. necr _____
10. nom _____
11. norm _____
12. onc/o _____
13. organ _____
14. pyret _____
15. pyr/o _____
16. radi/o _____
17. scop _____
18. sept _____
19. therm/o _____
20. top/o _____
21. tuss _____
22. infect _____
23. dem _____
24. eti/o _____
25. cis _____
26. malign _____
27. maxim _____
28. minim _____
29. palm _____
30. prophylact _____

SUFFIXES

Give the definitions of the following suffixes:

1. -age _____
2. -al _____
3. -ary _____
4. -centesis _____
5. -clave _____
6. -drome _____
7. -form _____
8. -fuge _____
9. -genic _____
10. -gnosis _____
11. -grade _____
12. -gram _____
13. -graphy _____
14. -hexia _____
15. -ic _____
16. -ion _____
17. -ism _____
18. -ive _____

19. -liter _____

20. -logy _____

21. -meter _____

22. -osis _____

23. -ous _____

24. -pathy _____

25. -phoresis _____

26. -scope _____

27. -sepsis _____

28. -therapy _____

29. -ar _____

30. -y _____

Identifying Medical Terms

In the spaces provided, write the medical terms for the following meanings:

1. _____ Process of being stuck together

2. _____ Without decay

3. _____ Pertaining to the armpit

4. _____ Treatment using chemical agents

5. _____ Pertaining to a different formation

6. _____ Process of being badly shaped, deformed

7. _____ An instrument used to view small objects

8. _____ Occurring in or having many shapes

9. _____ A new disease

10. _____ The study of tumors

Spelling

In the spaces provided, write the correct spelling of these misspelled terms:

1. antseptic _____

2. autnomy _____

3. centmeter _____

4. diphoresis _____

5. miligram _____

6. necosis _____

7. parcentesis _____

8. radilogy _____

Matching

Select the appropriate lettered meaning for each word listed below.

_____ 1. abate

_____ 2. antipyretic

_____ 3. cachexia

_____ 4. diagnosis

_____ 5. disease

_____ 6. etiology

_____ 7. illness

_____ 8. prognosis

_____ 9. prophylactic

_____ 10. triage

a. Lack of ease
b. A state of being sick
c. Pertaining to protecting against disease
d. Pertaining to an agent that works against fever
e. The sorting and classifying of injuries to determine priority of need and treatment
f. To lessen, decrease, or cease
g. Determination of the cause and nature of a disease
h. A new disease
i. The prediction of the course of a disease and the recovery rate
j. A condition of ill health, malnutrition, and wasting
k. The study of the cause(s) of disease

Abbreviations

Place the correct word, phrase, or abbreviation in the space provided.

1. AB _____

2. ax _____

3. biopsy _____

4. CVD _____

5. DRGs _____

6. otorhinolaryngology _____

7. family practice _____

8. gram _____

9. GYN _____

10. Peds _____

MedMedia
Wrap-Up

www.prenhall.com/rice

Additional interactive resources and activities for this chapter can be found on the Companion Website. For animations, videos, audio glossary, and review, access the accompanying CD-ROM in this book.

Audio Glossary
Medical Terminology Exercises & Activities
Terminology Translator
Animations
Videos

Objectives
Medical Terminology Exercises & Activities
Audio Glossary
Drug Updates
Medical Terminology in the News

THE ORGANIZATION OF THE BODY

2

OBJECTIVES

On completion of this chapter, you will be able to:

- Define terms that describe the body and its structural units.
- List the systems of the body and give the organs in each system.
- Define terms that are used to describe direction, planes, and cavities of the body.
- Understand word analysis as it relates to Head-to-Toe Assessment.
- Analyze, build, spell, and pronounce medical words.
- Review Drug Highlights presented in this chapter.
- Identify and define selected abbreviations.
- Successfully complete the study and review section.

MedMedia
www.prenhall.com/rice

Additional interactive resources and activities for this chapter can be found on the Companion Website. For Terminology Translator, animations, videos, audio glossary, and review, access the accompanying CD-ROM in this book.

Anatomy and Physiology Overview

This chapter introduces you to terms describing the body and its structural units. To aid you, these terms have been grouped into two major sections: the first offers an overview of the units that make up the human body, and the second covers terms used to describe anatomical positions and locations. The human body is made up of atoms, molecules, organelles, cells, tissues, organs, and systems. See Figure 2–1. All of these parts normally function together in a unified and complex process. During **homeostasis** these processes allow the body to perform at its maximum potential.

THE HUMAN BODY: LEVELS OF ORGANIZATION

Atoms

An **atom** is the smallest chemical unit of matter. It consists of a nucleus that contains protons and neutrons and is surrounded by electrons. The **nucleus** is at the center of the atom and a **proton** is a positively charged particle, while a **neutron** is without an electrical charge. The **electron** is a negatively charged particle that revolves about the nucleus of an atom.

Chemical elements are made up of atoms. In chemistry, an **element** is a substance that cannot be separated into substances different from itself by ordinary chemical means. It is the basic component of which all matter is composed. There are at least 105 different chemical elements that have been identified.

Elements found in the human body include aluminum, carbon, calcium, chlorine, cobalt, copper, fluorine, hydrogen, iodine, iron, manganese, magnesium, nitrogen, oxygen, phosphorus, potassium, sodium, sulfur, and zinc. See Table 2–1.

TABLE 2–1 ELEMENTS FOUND IN THE HUMAN BODY

Symbol	Element	Atomic Weight
Al	aluminum	13
C	carbon	6
Ca	calcium	20
Cl	chlorine	17
Co	cobalt	27
Cu	copper	29
F	fluorine	9
H	hydrogen	1
I	iodine	53
Fe	iron	26
Mn	manganese	25
Mg	magnesium	12
N	nitrogen	7
O	oxygen	8
P	phosphorus	15
K	potassium	19
Na	sodium	11
S	sulfur	16
Zn	zinc	30

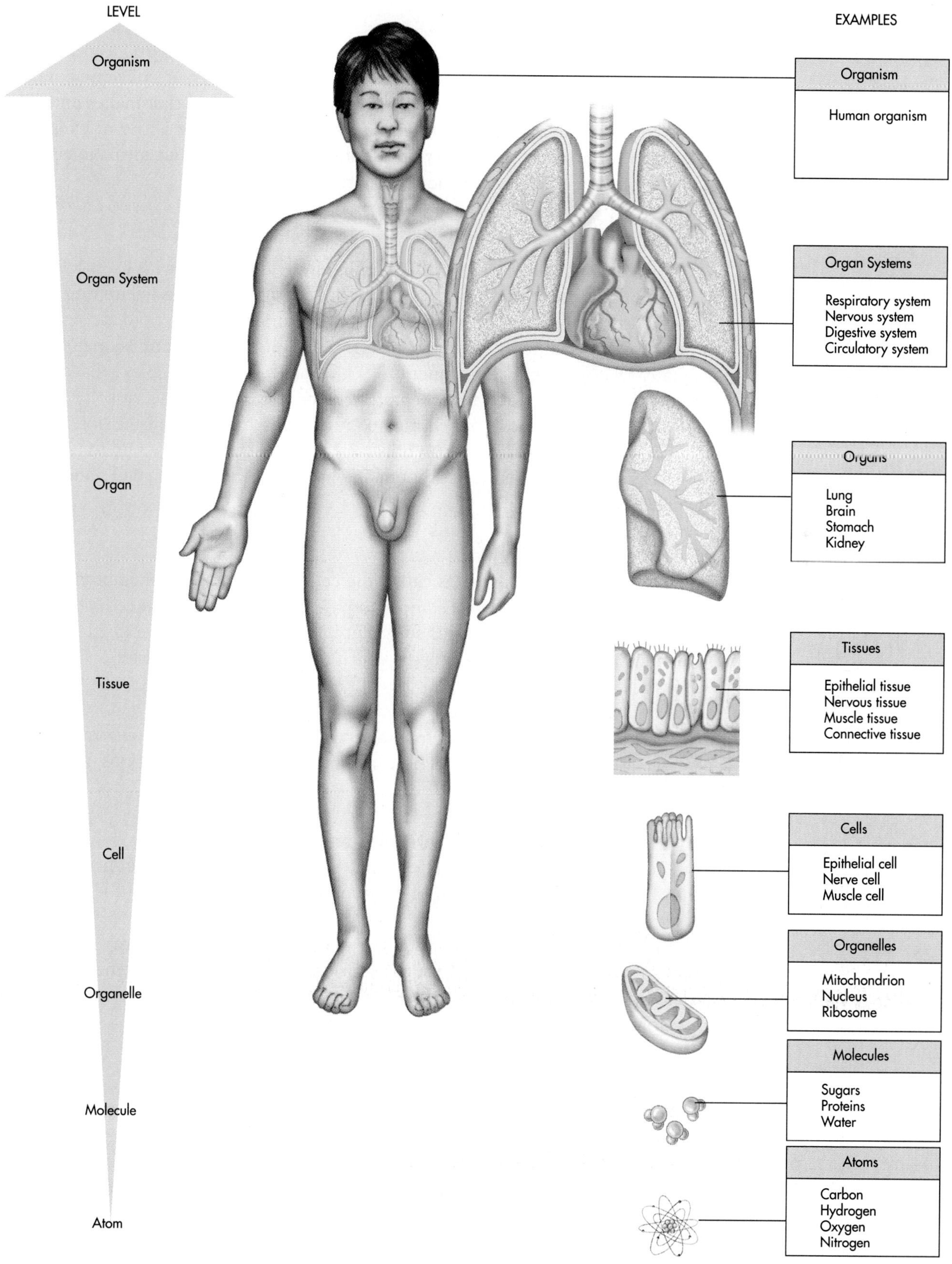

LEVEL

Organism

Organ System

Organ

Tissue

Cell

Organelle

Molecule

Atom

EXAMPLES

Organism
Human organism

Organ Systems
Respiratory system Nervous system Digestive system Circulatory system

Organs
Lung Brain Stomach Kidney

Tissues
Epithelial tissue Nervous tissue Muscle tissue Connective tissue

Cells
Epithelial cell Nerve cell Muscle cell

Organelles
Mitochondrion Nucleus Ribosome

Molecules
Sugars Proteins Water

Atoms
Carbon Hydrogen Oxygen Nitrogen

FIGURE 2–1

The human body: levels of organization.

Molecules

A **molecule** is a chemical combination of two or more atoms that form a specific chemical compound. In a water molecule (H_2O), oxygen forms polar covalent bonds with two hydrogen atoms. **Water** is a tasteless, clear, odorless liquid that makes up 65% of a male's body weight and 55% of a female's body weight. Water is the most important constituent of all body fluids, secretions, and excretions. It is an ideal transportation medium for inorganic and organic compounds.

Cells

The body consists of millions of cells working individually and with each other to sustain life. For the purposes of this book, **cells** are considered the basic building blocks for the various structures that together make up the human being. There are several types of cells, each specialized to perform specific functions. The size and shape of a cell are generally related directly to its function. See Figure 2–2. For example, cells forming the skin overlap each other to form a protective barrier, whereas nerve cells are usually elongated with branches connecting to other cells for the transmission of sensory impulses. Despite these differences, however, cells can generally be said to have a number of common components. The common parts of the cell are the **cell membrane** and the **protoplasm**.

THE CELL MEMBRANE

The outer covering of the cell is called the **cell membrane**. Cell membranes have the capability of allowing some substances to pass into and out of the cell while denying passage to other substances. This selectivity allows cells to receive nutrition and dispose of waste just as the human being eats food and disposes of waste.

PROTOPLASM

The substance within the cell membrane is called **protoplasm**. Protoplasm is composed of cytoplasm and karyoplasm. These substances and their functions are described below.

Karyoplasm.   Enclosed by its own membrane, **karyoplasm** is the substance of the cell's nucleus and contains the genetic matter necessary for cell reproduction as well as control over activity within the cell's cytoplasm.

Cytoplasm.   All protoplasm outside the nucleus is called **cytoplasm**. The cytoplasm provides storage and work areas for the cell. The work and storage elements of the cell, called organelles, are the endoplasmic reticulum, ribosomes, Golgi apparatus, mitochondria, lysosomes, and centrioles. See Figure 2–3 and Table 2–2.

Tissues

A **tissue** is a grouping of similar cells that together perform specialized functions. There are four basic types of tissue in the body: **epithelial**, **connective**, **muscle**, and **nerve**. Each of the four basic tissues has several subtypes named for their shape, appearance, arrangement, or function. The four basic types of tissue are described for you.

EPITHELIAL TISSUE

Epithelial tissue appears as sheet-like arrangements of cells, sometimes several layers thick, that form the outer layer of the skin, cover the surfaces of organs, line the walls of cavities, and form tubes, ducts, and portions of certain glands. The functions of epithelial tissues are protection, absorption, secretion, and excretion.

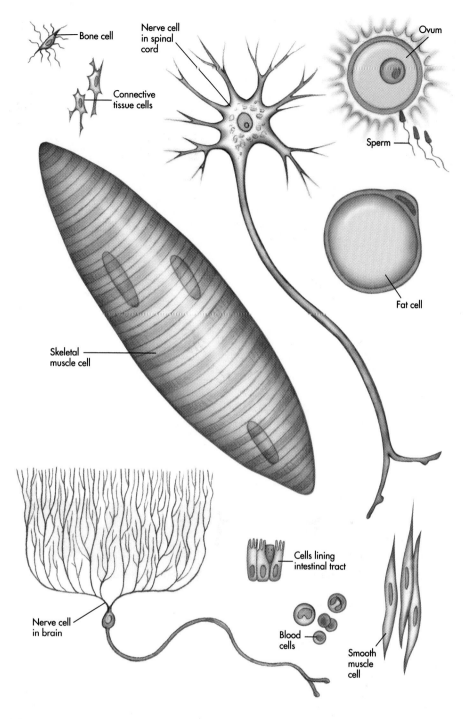

Bone cell

Nerve cell
in spinal
cord

Ovum

Connective
tissue cells

Sperm

Skeletal
muscle cell

Fat cell

Nerve cell
in brain

Cells lining
intestinal tract

Blood
cells

Smooth
muscle
cell

FIGURE 2–2

Cells may be described as the basic building blocks of the human body. They have many different shapes and vary in size and function. These examples show the range of forms and sizes with the dimensions they would have if magnified approximately 500 times.

CONNECTIVE TISSUE

The most widespread and abundant of the body tissues, **connective tissue** forms the supporting network for the organs of the body, sheaths the muscles, and connects muscles to bones and bones to joints. Bone is a dense form of connective tissue.

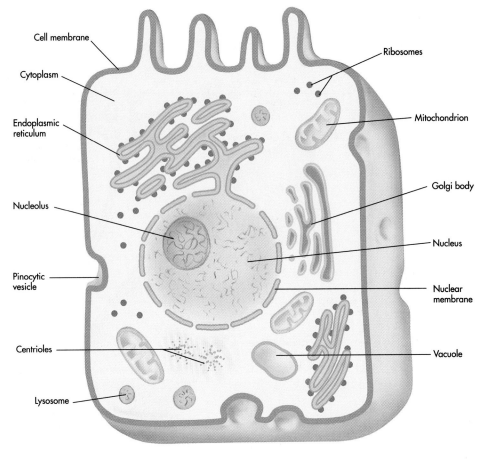

FIGURE 2–3

The major parts of a cell.

MUSCLE TISSUE

There are three types of **muscle tissue**: voluntary or striated, cardiac, and involuntary or smooth. Striated and smooth muscles are so described because of their appearance. Cardiac muscle is a specialized form of striated tissue under the control of the autonomic nervous system. Involuntary or smooth muscles are also controlled by this system. The striated or voluntary muscles are controlled by the person's will.

NERVE TISSUE

Nerve tissue consists of nerve cells (neurons) and interstitial tissue. It has the properties of excitability and conductivity, and functions to control and coordinate the activities of the body.

Organs

Tissues serving a common purpose or function make up structures called **organs**. Organs are specialized components of the body such as the brain, skin, or heart.

Systems

A group of organs functioning together for a common purpose is called a **system.** The various body systems function in support of the body as a whole. Listed in Figure 2–4 are the organ systems of the body.

TABLE 2–2 MAJOR CELL STRUCTURES AND PRIMARY FUNCTIONS

Cell Structures	Primary Functions
Cell membrane	Protects the cell; provides for communication via receptor proteins; surface proteins serve as positive identification tags; allow some substances to pass into and out of the cell while denying passage to other substances; this selectivity allows cells to receive nutrition and dispose of waste
Protoplasm	Composed of cytoplasm and karyoplasm
Karyoplasm	Substance of the cell's nucleus; contains the genetic matter necessary for cell reproduction as well as control over activity within the cell's cytoplasm
Cytoplasm	All protoplasm outside the nucleus. The cytoplasm provides storage and work areas for the cell:
Ribosomes	Make enzymes and other proteins; nicknamed "protein factories"
Endoplasmic reticulum (ER)	Carries proteins and other substances through the cytoplasm
Golgi apparatus	Chemically processes the molecules from the endoplasmic reticulum, then packages them into vesicles; nicknamed "chemical processing and packaging center"
Mitochondria	Complex, energy-releasing chemical reactions occur continuously; nicknamed "power plants"
Lysosomes	Contain enzymes that can digest food compounds; nicknamed "digestive bags"
Centrioles	Play an important role in cell reproduction
Cilia	Hair-like processes that project from epithelial cells; help propel mucus, dust particles, and other foreign substances from the respiratory tract
Flagellum	"Tail" of the sperm that makes it possible for the sperm to "swim" or move toward the ovum
Nucleus	Controls every organelle (little organ) in the cytoplasm; contains the genetic matter necessary for cell reproduction as well as control over activity within the cell's cytoplasm

ANATOMICAL LOCATIONS AND POSITIONS

Four primary reference systems have been adopted to provide uniformity to the anatomical description of the body. These reference systems are **direction, planes, cavities,** and **structural unit.** The standard anatomical position for the body is erect, head facing forward, arms by the sides with palms to the front. Left and right are from the subject's point of view, not the examiner's.

Direction

The following terms are used to describe direction:

- **Superior.** Above, in an upward direction
- **Anterior.** In front of or before
- **Posterior.** Toward the back
- **Cephalad.** Toward the head
- **Medial.** Nearest the midline
- **Lateral.** To the side

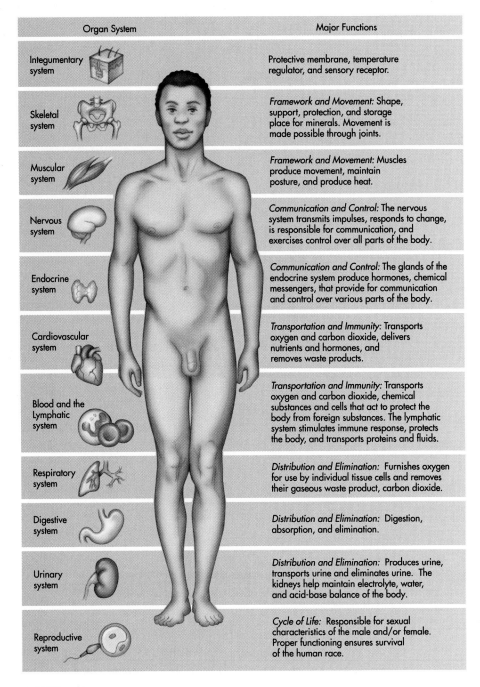

Organ System		Major Functions
Integumentary system		Protective membrane, temperature regulator, and sensory receptor.
Skeletal system		*Framework and Movement:* Shape, support, protection, and storage place for minerals. Movement is made possible through joints.
Muscular system		*Framework and Movement:* Muscles produce movement, maintain posture, and produce heat.
Nervous system		*Communication and Control:* The nervous system transmits impulses, responds to change, is responsible for communication, and exercises control over all parts of the body.
Endocrine system		*Communication and Control:* The glands of the endocrine system produce hormones, chemical messengers, that provide for communication and control over various parts of the body.
Cardiovascular system		*Transportation and Immunity:* Transports oxygen and carbon dioxide, delivers nutrients and hormones, and removes waste products.
Blood and the Lymphatic system		*Transportation and Immunity:* Transports oxygen and carbon dioxide, chemical substances and cells that act to protect the body from foreign substances. The lymphatic system stimulates immune response, protects the body, and transports proteins and fluids.
Respiratory system		*Distribution and Elimination:* Furnishes oxygen for use by individual tissue cells and removes their gaseous waste product, carbon dioxide.
Digestive system		*Distribution and Elimination:* Digestion, absorption, and elimination.
Urinary system		*Distribution and Elimination:* Produces urine, transports urine and eliminates urine. The kidneys help maintain electrolyte, water, and acid-base balance of the body.
Reproductive system		*Cycle of Life:* Responsible for sexual characteristics of the male and/or female. Proper functioning ensures survival of the human race.

FIGURE 2–4

Organ systems of the body with major functions.

- **Proximal.** Nearest the point of attachment
- **Distal.** Away from the point of attachment
- **Ventral.** The same as anterior, the front side
- **Dorsal.** The same as posterior, the back side

Planes

The terms defined below are used to describe the imaginary planes that are depicted in Figure 2–5 as passing through the body and dividing it into various sections.

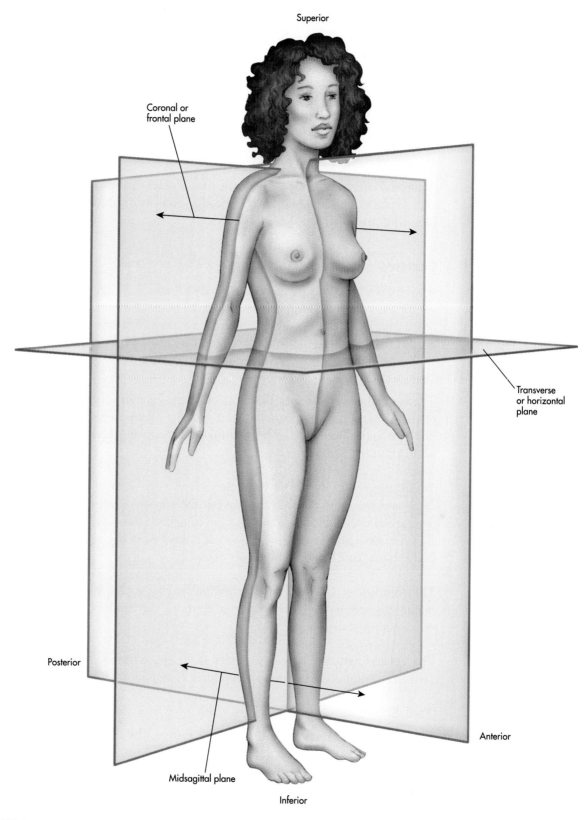

FIGURE 2–5

Planes of the body: coronal or frontal, transverse, and midsagittal.

MIDSAGITTAL PLANE

The **midsagittal plane** vertically divides the body as it passes through the midline to form a **right** and **left half**.

TRANSVERSE OR HORIZONTAL PLANE

A **transverse** or **horizontal plane** is any plane that divides the body into **superior** and **inferior** portions.

CORONAL OR FRONTAL PLANE

A **coronal** or **frontal plane** is any plane that divides the body at right angles to the midsagittal plane. The coronal plane divides the body into **anterior** (ventral) and **posterior** (dorsal) portions.

Cavities

A **cavity** is a hollow space containing body organs. Body cavities are classified into two groups according to their location. On the front are the **ventral** or **anterior cavities** and on the back are the **dorsal** or **posterior cavities**. The various cavities found in the human body are depicted in Figure 2–6.

THE VENTRAL CAVITY

The **ventral cavity** is the hollow portion of the human torso extending from the neck to the pelvis and containing the heart and the organs of respiration, digestion, reproduction, and elimination. The ventral cavity can be subdivided into three distinct areas: thoracic, abdominal, and pelvic.

The Thoracic Cavity.   The **thoracic cavity** is the area of the chest containing the heart and the lungs. Within this cavity, the space containing the **heart** is called the **pericardial** cavity and the spaces surrounding each **lung** are known as the **pleural** cavities. Other organs located in the thoracic cavity are the esophagus, trachea, thymus, and certain large blood and lymph vessels.

The Abdominal Cavity.   The **abdominal cavity** is the space below the diaphragm, commonly referred to as the belly. It contains the kidneys, stomach, intestines, and other organs of digestion.

The Pelvic Cavity.   The **pelvic cavity** is the space formed by the bones of the pelvic area and contains the organs of reproduction and elimination.

THE DORSAL CAVITY

Containing the structures of the nervous system, the **dorsal cavity** is subdivided into the cranial cavity and the spinal cavity.

The Cranial Cavity.   The **cranial cavity** is the space in the skull containing the brain.

The Spinal Cavity.   The **spinal cavity** is the space within the bony spinal column that contains the spinal cord and spinal fluid.

THE ABDOMINOPELVIC CAVITY

The **abdominopelvic cavity** is the combination of the abdominal and pelvic cavities. It is divided into nine regions.

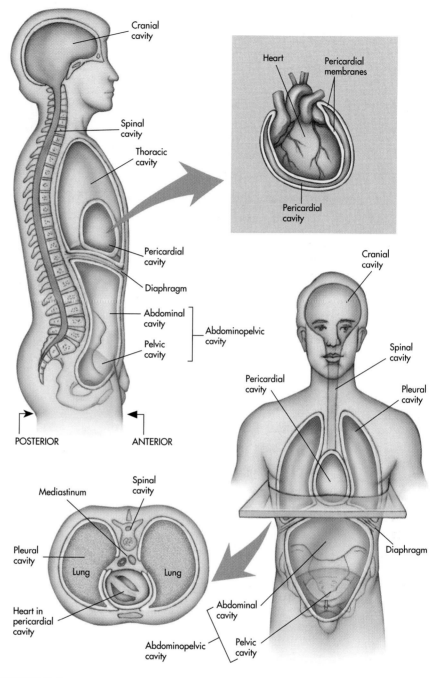

FIGURE 2–6

Body cavities.

Nine Regions of the Abdominopelvic Cavity

As a ready reference for locating visceral organs, anatomists divided the abdominopelvic cavity into nine regions. A tic-tac-toe pattern drawn across the abdominopelvic cavity (Fig. 2–7A) delineates these regions:

- **Right hypochondriac**—upper right region at the level of the ninth rib cartilage
- **Left hypochondriac**—upper left region at the level of the ninth rib cartilage
- **Epigastric**—region over the stomach
- **Right lumbar**—right middle lateral region

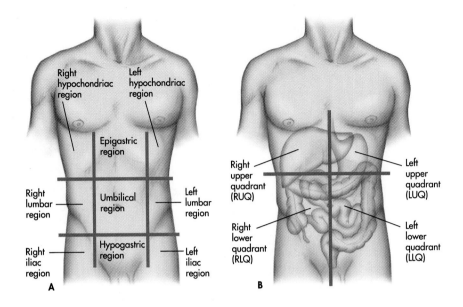

FIGURE 2–7

(A) The nine regions of the abdominopelvic cavity. (B) The four regions of the abdomen that are referred to as quadrants.

- **Left lumbar**—left middle lateral region
- **Umbilical**—in the center, between the right and left lumbar region; at the navel
- **Right iliac (inguinal)**—right lower lateral region
- **Left iliac (inguinal)**—left lower lateral region
- **Hypogastric**—lower middle region below the navel

Abdomen Divided into Quadrants

The **abdomen** is divided into four corresponding regions that are used for descriptive and diagnostic purposes. By using these regions one may describe the exact location of pain, a skin lesion, surgical incision, and/or abdominal tumor. The four **quadrants** are (Fig. 2–7B):

- **Right upper (RUQ)**
- **Left upper (LUQ)**
- **Right lower (RLQ)**
- **Left lower (LLQ)**

HEAD-TO-TOE ASSESSMENT

The terminology associated with head-to-toe assessment can be useful when studying the organization of the body. The following body areas, along with their word parts and/or related terminology, are provided for your study.

Body Area	Word Part/Terminology
abdomen (belly)	abdomin/o (ăb-dō′-mĭ-nō)
ankle	ankyl/o (ăn-kĭ′-lō)
arm	brach/i (bră′-chĭ)
back	poster/i; posterior (pŏs-tĕ-rĭ; pŏs-tĕ-rĭ-ōr)
bones	oste/o (ŏs-tē-ō)
breast	mast; mamm/o; mammary (măst; măm′-ō; măm′-ă-rē)
cheek	bucc/o; buccal (bŭk′-kō; bŭk′-ăl)
chest	thorac/o; thorax (thō-ră′-kō; thō′ raks)
ear	ot/o; otic (ō-tō; ō′ tĭk)
elbow	cubital (cū-bĭ-tăl′)
eye	ophthalm/o; ocul/o; opt/o (ōp-thăl′-mō; ō-kū-lō; ōp-tō)
finger	dactyl/o; digit; phalanx (dăk′-tĭ-lō; dĭj′-ĭt; făl′-ănks)
foot	illus (il-lus)
gums	gingiv; gingiva (gĭn-gĭv-; gĭn-gĭv-vă)
hand	manus (mă-nūs)
head	cephal/o; cephalad (sĕ-fă-lō; sĕf′ ă-lăd)
heart	cardi/o; cardiac (kăr-dĭ-ō; kăr′ dē-ăk)
hip	coxa (kŏk′-să)
leg	crural; femoral (crū-răl; fĕ-mō-răl)
liver	hepat/o; hepatic (hĕ-pă-tō; hĕ-păt ĭk)
lungs	pulm/o; pulmonary (pūl-mō; pŭl′ mō-nĕ-rē)
mouth	or/o; oral (ō-rō; or′ ăl)
muscles	muscul/o (mūs-cū-lō)
navel	umbilic; umbilicus (ŭm-bĭ-lĭ′-k; ŭm-bĭ-lĭ′-kŭs)
neck	cervic/o; cervical (sĕr′-vĭ-cō; sĕr′ vĭ-kă)
nerves	neur/o; neural (nū′-rō; nū′ răl)
nose	rhin/o; nas/o; nasal (rĭ′-nō; nă′-sō; nā′ zl)
ribs	cost/o; costal (cōs′-tō; cos′ tăl)
side	lateral (lă-tĕ-răl′)
skin	derm/a; dermad (dĕr′-mă; dĕr-măd)

Body Area	Word Part/Terminology
skull	crani/o; cranial (kră'-nĭ-ō; kră'-nē-ăl)
stomach	gastr/o; gastric (găs'-trō; găs' trĭk)
teeth	dent; dental (dĕnt'; dĕn-tăl)
temples	tempora; temporal (tĕm-pō'-ră; tĕm' pōr-ăl)
thigh	femoral; crural (fĕ-mō-răl; crŭ-răl)
throat	pharyng/o; pharyngeal (fă-rĭn'-hō; făr-ĭn' jē-ăl)
thumb	pollex (pōl'-lĕx)
tongue	lingu/o; gloss/o; lingual; glossal (lĭn-gū-ō; glōs-sō; ling' gwal; glŏs-săl)
wrist	carp/o; carpal (căr'-pō; căr-păl)

BUILDING YOUR MEDICAL VOCABULARY

This section provides the foundation for learning medical terminology. Medical words can be made up of four different types of word parts:

- Prefixes (P)
- Roots (R)
- Combining forms (CF)
- Suffixes (S)

By connecting various word parts in an organized sequence, thousands of words can be built and learned. In this text the word list is alphabetized so one can see the variety of meanings created when common prefixes and suffixes are repeatedly applied to certain word roots and/or combining forms. Words shown in pink are additional words related to the content of this chapter that are not built from word parts. These words are included to enhance your vocabulary.

MEDICAL WORD	WORD PARTS (WHEN APPLICABLE)			DEFINITION
	Part	**Type**	**Meaning**	
adipose (ăd" ĭ-pōs)	adip -ose	R S	fat like	Fatty tissue throughout the body
ambilateral (ăm" bĭ-lăt' ĕr-ăl)	ambi later -al	P R S	both side pertaining to	Pertaining to both sides

MEDICAL WORD	WORD PARTS (WHEN APPLICABLE)			DEFINITION
	Part	Type	Meaning	
anatomy (ăn-ăt′ ō-mē)	ana -tomy	P S	up incision	Literally means to cut up; the study of the structure of an organism such as humans
android (ăn′ droyd)	andr -oid	R S	man resemble	To resemble man
anterior (an-tĕr′ ē-ōr)	anter/i -or	CF S	toward the front a doer	In front of, before
apex (ā′ pĕks)				The pointed end of a cone-shaped structure
base (bās)				The lower part or foundation of a structure
bilateral (bī-lăt′ ĕr-ăl)	bi later -al	P R S	two side pertaining to	Pertaining to two sides
biology (bi-ŏl′ ō-jē)	bi/o -logy	CF S	life study of	The study of life
caudal (kŏd′ ăl)	caud -al	R S	tail pertaining to	Pertaining to the tail
center (sĕn′ tĕr)				The midpoint of a body or activity
cephalad (sĕf′ ă-lăd)	cephal -ad	R S	head pertaining to	Toward the head
chromosome (krō-mō-sōm)	chromo -some	P S	color body	Microscopic bodies that carry the genes that determine hereditary characteristics
cilia (sĭl′ ē-ă)				Hair-like processes that project from epithelial cells; they help propel mucus, dust particles, and other foreign substances from the respiratory tract
cytology (sī-tŏl′ ō-jē)	cyt/o -logy	CF S	cell study of	The study of cells
deep (dēp)				Far down from the surface
dehydrate (dē-hī′ drāt)	de hydr -ate	P R S	down, away from water use, action	To remove water away from the body

MEDICAL WORD	WORD PARTS (WHEN APPLICABLE)			DEFINITION
	Part	**Type**	**Meaning**	
diffusion (di-fū′ zhŭn)	dif fus -ion	P R S	apart to pour process	A process in which parts of a substance move from areas of high concentration to areas of lower concentration
distal (dĭs′ tăl)	dist -al	R S	away from the point of origin pertaining to	Farthest from the center or point of origin
dorsal (dōr′ săl)	dors -al	R S	backward pertaining to	Pertaining to the back side of the body
ectogenous (ĕk-tŏj′ ĕ-nŭs)	ecto gen -ous	P R S	outside formation, produce pertaining to	Pertaining to formation outside the organism or body
ectomorph (ĕk′ tō-morf)	ecto -morph	P S	outside form, shape	A slender physical body form
endomorph (ĕn″ dō-morf)	endo -morph	P S	within form, shape	A round physical body form
filtration (fĭl-trā′ shŭn)	filtrat -ion	R S	to strain through process	The process of filtering or straining particles from a solution
gene (jēn)				The hereditary unit that transmits and determines one's characteristics or hereditary traits
histology (hĭs-tŏl′ ō-jē)	hist/o -logy	CF S	tissue study of	The study of tissue
homeostasis (hō″ mē-ō-stā′ sĭs)	homeo -stasis	P S	similar, same control, stopping	The state of equilibrium maintained in the body's internal environment
horizontal (hŏr′ă-zŏn′ tăl)	horizont -al	R S	horizon pertaining to	Pertaining to the horizon, of or near the horizon, lying flat, even, level
human genome (hū′ măn jē′ nōm)				The complete set of genes and chromosomes tucked inside each of the body's trillions of cells
inferior (ĭn-fē′ rē-or)	infer/i -or	CF S	below a doer	Located below or in a downward direction
inguinal (ĭng′ gwĭ-năl)	inguin -al	R S	groin pertaining to	Pertaining to the groin, of or near the groin

MEDICAL WORD	WORD PARTS (WHEN APPLICABLE)			DEFINITION
	Part	**Type**	**Meaning**	
internal (ĭn-tĕr′ nal)	intern -al	R S	within pertaining to	Pertaining to within or the inside
karyogenesis (kăr″ i-ō-jĕn′ ĕ-sĭs)	kary/o -genesis	CF S	cell's nucleus formation, produce	Formation of a cell's nucleus
lateral (lăt′ ĕr-ăl)	later -al	R S	side pertaining to	Pertaining to the side
medial (mē′ dē al)	medi -al	R S	toward the middle pertaining to	Pertaining to the middle or midline
mesomorph (mĕs′ ō-morf)	meso -morph	P S	middle form, shape	A well-proportioned body form
organic (or-găn′ ĭk)	organ -ic	R S	organ pertaining to	Pertaining to an organ
pathology (pă-thŏl′ ō-jē)	path/o -logy	CF S	disease study of	The study of disease
perfusion (pur-fū′ zhŭn)	per fus -ion	P R S	through to pour process	The process of pouring through
phenotype (fē′ nō-tīp)	phen/o -type	CF S	to show type	The physical appearance or type of makeup of an individual
physiology (fiz″ i-ŏl′ ō-jē)	physi/o -logy	CF S	nature study of	The study of the nature of living organisms
posterior (pŏs-tē′ rĭ-ōr)	poster/i -or	CF S	behind, toward the back a doer	Toward the back
protoplasm (prō-tō-plăzm)	proto -plasm	P S	first a thing formed, plasma	The essential matter of a living cell
proximal (prŏk′ sĭm-ăl)	proxim -al	R S	near the point of origin pertaining to	Nearest the center or point of origin; nearest the point of attachment
somatotrophic (sō″ mă-tō-trŏf′ ĭk)	somat/o troph -ic	CF R S	body a turning pertaining to	Pertaining to stimulation of body growth
superficial (sū″ pĕr-fĭsh′ ăl)	superfic/i -al	CF S	near the surface pertaining to	Pertaining to the surface, on or near the surface

MEDICAL WORD	WORD PARTS (WHEN APPLICABLE)			DEFINITION
	Part	**Type**	**Meaning**	
superior (sū-pēr' rĭ-ōr)	super/i -or	CF S	upper a doer	Located above or in an upward direction
systemic (sis-tĕm' ĭk)	system -ic	R S	a composite whole pertaining to	Pertaining to the body as a whole
topical (tŏp' ĭ-kăl)	topic -al	R S	place pertaining to	Pertaining to a place, definite locale
unilateral (ū″ nĭ-lăt' ĕr-ăl)	uni later -al	P R S	one side pertaining to	Pertaining to one side
ventral (vĕn' trăl)	ventr -al	R S	near the belly side pertaining to	Pertaining to the front side of the body, abdomen, belly surface
vertex (vĕr' tĕks)				The top or highest point; the top or crown of the head
visceral (vĭs' ĕr-ăl)	viscer -al	R S	body organs pertaining to	Pertaining to body organs enclosed within a cavity, especially abdominal organs

Terminology Translator

This feature, found on the accompanying CD-ROM, provides an innovative tool to translate medical words into Spanish, French, and German.

DRUG HIGHLIGHTS

A drug is a medicinal substance that may alter or modify the functions of a living organism. There are thousands of drugs that are available as over-the-counter (OTC) medicines and do not require a prescription. A prescription is a written legal document that gives directions for compounding, dispensing, and administering a medication to a patient.

In general, there are five medical uses for drugs. These are: therapeutic, diagnostic, curative, replacement, and preventive or prophylactic.

- **Therapeutic Use.** Used in the treatment of a disease or condition, such as an allergy, to relieve the symptoms or to sustain the patient until other measures are instituted.
- **Diagnostic Use.** Certain drugs are used in conjunction with radiology to allow the physician to pinpoint the location of a disease process.

- **Curative Use.** Certain drugs, such as antibiotics, kill or remove the causative agent of a disease.
- **Replacement Use.** Certain drugs, such as hormones and vitamins, are used to replace substances normally found in the body.
- **Preventive or Prophylactic Use.** Certain drugs, such as immunizing agents, are used to ward off or lessen the severity of a disease.

Drug Names

Most drugs may be cited by their chemical, generic, and trade or brand (proprietary) name. The chemical name is usually the formula that denotes the composition of the drug. It is made up of letters and numbers that represent the drug's molecular structure. The generic name is the drug's official name and is descriptive of its chemical structure. The generic name is written in lowercase letters. A generic drug can be manufactured by more than one pharmaceutical company. When this is the case, each company markets the drug under its own unique trade or brand name. A trade or brand name is registered by the US Patent Office as well as approved by the US Food and Drug Administration (FDA). A trade or brand name is written with a capital.

Undesirable Actions of Drugs

Most drugs have the potential for causing an action other than their intended action. For example, antibiotics that are administered orally may disrupt the normal bacterial flora of the gastrointestinal tract and cause gastric discomfort. This type of reaction is known as a side effect. An adverse reaction is an unfavorable or harmful unintended action of a drug. For example, the adverse reaction of Demerol may be lightheadedness, dizziness, sedation, nausea, and sweating. A drug interaction may occur when one drug potentiates or diminishes the action of another drug. These actions may be desirable or undesirable. Drugs may also interact with foods, alcohol, tobacco, and other substances.

Medication Order and Dosage

The medication order is given for a specific patient and denotes the name of the drug, the dosage, the form of the drug, the time for or frequency of administration, and the route by which the drug is to be given.

The dosage is the amount of medicine that is prescribed for administration. The form of the drug may be liquid, solid, semisolid, tablet, capsule, transdermal therapeutic patch, etc. The route of administration may be by mouth, by injection, into the eye(s), ear(s), nostril(s), rectum, vagina, etc.

It is important for the patient to know when and how to take a medication. See Terminology Translator for some hows, whens, and directions for taking medications. To assist you in communicating this information to a patient, English, Spanish, French, and German are provided for you to use.

 ABBREVIATIONS

ABBREVIATION	MEANING	ABBREVIATION	MEANING
abd	abdomen, abdominal	LAT, lat	lateral
A&P	anatomy and physiology	LLQ	left lower quadrant
AP	anteroposterior	LUQ	left upper quadrant
CNS	central nervous system	PA	posteroanterior
CV	cardiovascular	resp	respiratory
ER	endoplasmic reticulum	RLQ	right lower quadrant
GI	gastrointestinal	RUQ	right upper quadrant

STUDY AND REVIEW

Anatomy and Physiology

Write your answers to the following questions. Do not refer to the text.

1. The _____ consist of millions of _____ working individually and with each other to _____ life.

2. The outer covering of the cell is known as the _____, which has the capability of allowing some substances to pass into and out of the cell.

3. The substance within the cell is known as _____ and is composed of _____ and _____.

4. The cell's nucleus is composed of _____, which contains its genetic material.

5. The two primary functions of the cell's nucleus are _____ and _____.

6. List the four functions of epithelial tissue.

   a. _____   b. _____

   c. _____   d. _____

7. _____ tissue is the most widespread and abundant of the four body tissues.

8. Name the three types of muscle tissue.

   a. _____   b. _____   c. _____

9. Two properties of nerve tissue are _____ and _____.

10. Define organ. _____.

11. Define body system. _____.

12. Name the organ systems listed in this text.

   a. _____   b. _____

   c. _____   d. _____

   e. _____   f. _____

   g. _____   h. _____

   i. _____   j. _____

   k. _____

13. Define the following directional terms:

    a. superior _____   b. anterior _____

    c. posterior _____   d. cephalad _____

    e. medial _____   f. lateral _____

    g. proximal _____   h. distal _____

    i. ventral _____   j. dorsal _____

14. The _____ _____ vertically divides the body. It passes through the midline to form a right and left half.

15. The _____ plane is any plane that divides the body into superior and inferior portions.

16. The _____ plane is any plane that divides the body at right angles to the plane described in question 14.

17. List the three distinct cavities that are located in the ventral cavity.

    a. _____   b. _____   c. _____

18. Name the two distinct cavities located in the dorsal cavity.

    a. _____   b. _____

Word Parts

1. In the spaces provided, write the definition of these prefixes, roots, combining forms, and suffixes. Do not refer to the listings of medical words. Leave blank those words you cannot define.

2. After completing as many as you can, refer back to the medical word listings to check your work. For each word missed or left blank, write the word and its definition several times on the margins of these pages or on a separate sheet of paper.

3. To maximize the learning process, it is to your advantage to do the following exercises as directed. To refer to the word building section before completing these exercises invalidates the learning process.

PREFIXES

Give the definitions of the following prefixes:

1. ambi- _____   2. ana- _____

3. bi- _____   4. chromo- _____

5. de- _____   6. dif- _____

7. ecto- _____   8. endo- _____

9. homeo- _____   10. meso- _____

11. per- _____   12. proto- _____

13. uni- _____

ROOTS AND COMBINING FORMS

Give the definitions of the following roots and combining forms:

1. adip _____   2. andr _____

3. bi/o _____   4. caud _____

5. cyt _____   6. cyt/o _____

7. fus _____   8. gen _____

9. hist/o _____   10. hydr _____

11. kary/o _____   12. later _____

13. path/o _____   14. physi/o _____

15. pin/o _____   16. somat/o _____

17. topic _____   18. troph _____

19. viscer _____   20. anter/i _____

21. cephal _____   22. dist _____

23. dors _____   24. filtrat _____

25. horizont _____   26. infer/i _____

27. inguin _____   28. intern _____

29. later _____   30. medi _____

31. organ _____   32. phen/o _____

33. poster/i _____   34. proxim _____

35. superfic/i _____   36. super/i _____

37. system _____   38. ventr _____

SUFFIXES

Give the definitions for the following suffixes:

1. -al _____
2. -ate _____
3. -genesis _____
4. -ic _____
5. -ion _____
6. -logy _____
7. -morph _____
8. -oid _____
9. -ose _____
10. -osis _____
11. -ous _____
12. -plasm _____
13. -some _____
14. -stasis _____
15. -tomy _____
16. -or _____
17. -ad _____
18. -type _____

Identifying Medical Terms

In the spaces provided, write the medical terms for the following meanings:

1. _____ To resemble man

2. _____ Pertaining to two sides

3. _____ The study of cells

4. _____ A slender physical body form

5. _____ Formation of a cell's nucleus

6. _____ Pertaining to the stimulation of body growth

7. _____ Pertaining to one side

Spelling

In the spaces provided, write the correct spelling of these misspelled terms:

1. adpose _____
2. caual _____
3. cytlogy _____
4. difusion _____
5. histlogy _____
6. mesmorph _____
7. prefusion _____
8. proxmal _____
9. somattrophic _____
10. unlateral _____

Matching

Select the appropriate lettered meaning for each word listed below.

_____ 1. ambilateral

_____ 2. anatomy

_____ 3. cephalad

_____ 4. chromosome

_____ 5. cilia

_____ 6. homeostasis

_____ 7. human genome

_____ 8. phenotype

_____ 9. physiology

_____ 10. vertex

a. Hair-like processes that project from epithelial cells
b. The top or highest point
c. Pertaining to both sides
d. The study of the structure of an organism such as humans
e. Toward the head
f. Microscopic bodies that carry the genes that determine hereditary characteristics
g. The complete set of genes and chromosomes
h. The physical appearance or type of makeup of an individual
i. The state of equilibrium maintained in the body's internal environment
j. The study of the nature of living organism
k. The study of disease

Abbreviations

Place the correct word, phrase, or abbreviation in the space provided.

1. abdomen _____

2. A&P _____

3. CNS _____

4. cardiovascular _____

5. gastrointestinal _____

6. LAT, lat _____

7. resp _____

8. ER _____

9. AP _____

10. PA _____

MedMedia Wrap-Up

www.prenhall.com/rice

Additional interactive resources and activities for this chapter can be found on the Companion Website. For animations, videos, audio glossary, and review, access the accompanying CD-ROM in this book.

Audio Glossary
Medical Terminology Exercises & Activities
Terminology Translator
Animations
Videos

Objectives
Medical Terminology Exercises & Activities
Audio Glossary
Drug Updates
Medical Terminology in the News

THE INTEGUMENTARY SYSTEM

3

OBJECTIVES

On completion of this chapter, you will be able to:

- Describe the integumentary system and its accessory structures.
- List the functions of the skin.
- Describe skin differences of the child and the older adult.
- Analyze, build, spell, and pronounce medical words.
- Describe each of the conditions presented in the Pathology Spotlights.
- Complete the Pathology Checkpoint.
- Review Drug Highlights presented in this chapter.
- Provide the description of diagnostic and laboratory tests related to the integumentary system.
- Identify and define selected abbreviations.
- Successfully complete the study and review section.

MedMedia
www.prenhall.com/rice

Additional interactive resources and activities for this chapter can be found on the Companion Website. For Terminology Translator, animations, videos, audio glossary, and review, access the accompanying CD-ROM in this book.

Anatomy and Physiology Overview

The integumentary system is composed of the **skin** and its accessory structures: **hair, nails, sebaceous glands,** and **sweat glands** (Table 3–1). This overview of the anatomy and physiology of the skin offers a general description of the integumentary system as an aid to those learning the terminology associated with its functions.

FUNCTIONS OF THE SKIN

The **skin** is the external covering of the body. In an average adult it covers more than 3000 square inches of surface area, weighs more than 6 pounds, and is the largest organ in the body. The skin is well supplied with blood vessels and nerves and has four main functions: **protection, regulation, sensation,** and **secretion.**

Protection

The skin serves as a **protective membrane** against invasion by bacteria and other potentially harmful agents that might try to penetrate to deeper tissues. It also protects against mechanical injury of delicate cells located beneath its epidermis or outer covering. The skin also serves to inhibit excessive loss of water and electrolytes and provides a reservoir for food and water storage. The skin guards the body against excessive exposure to the sun's ultraviolet rays by producing a protective pigmentation, and it helps to produce the body's supply of vitamin D.

TABLE 3–1 THE INTEGUMENTARY SYSTEM

Organ/Structure	*Primary Functions*
Skin	Protection, regulation, sensation, and secretion
Epidermis	The outer layer of the skin. It is divided into four strata:
Stratum corneum	Forms protective covering for the body
Stratum lucidum	Translucent layer that is frequently absent and not seen in thinner skin
Stratum granulosum	Active in the keratinization process, its cells become hard or horny
Stratum germinativum	Responsible for the regeneration of the epidermis
Dermis	Nourishes the epidermis, provides strength, and supports blood vessels
Papillae	Produce ridges that are one's fingerprints
Subcutaneous Tissue	Supports, nourishes, insulates, and cushions the skin
Hair	Provides sensation and some protection for the head. Hair around the eyes, in the nose, and in the ears serves to filter out foreign particles.
Nails	Protects ends of fingers and toes
Sebaceous Glands	Lubricates the hair and skin
Sweat (Sudoriferous) Glands	Secretes sweat or perspiration, which helps to cool the body by evaporation. Sweat also rids the body of waste.

Regulation

The skin serves to raise or lower body temperature as necessary. When the body needs to lose heat, the blood vessels in the skin dilate, bringing more blood to the surface for cooling by **radiation**. At the same time, the sweat glands are secreting more sweat for cooling by means of **evaporation**. Conversely, when the body needs to conserve heat, the reflex actions of the nervous system cause constriction of the skin's blood vessels, thereby allowing more heat-carrying blood to circulate to the muscles and vital organs.

Sensation

The skin contains millions of microscopic nerve endings that act as **sensory receptors** for pain, touch, heat, cold, and pressure. When stimulation occurs, nerve impulses are sent to the cerebral cortex of the brain. The nerve endings in the skin are specialized according to the type of sensory information transmitted and, once this information reaches the brain, any necessary response is triggered. For example, touching a hot surface with the hand causes the brain to recognize the senses of **touch**, **heat**, and **pain** and results in the immediate removal of the hand from the hot surface.

Secretion

The skin contains millions of sweat glands, which secrete **perspiration** or **sweat**, and sebaceous glands, which secrete **oil** for lubrication. Perspiration is largely water with a small amount of salt and other chemical compounds. This secretion, when left to accumulate, causes body odor, especially where it is trapped among hairs in the axillary region. Sebaceous glands produce **sebum**, which acts to protect the body from dehydration and possible absorption of harmful substances.

LAYERS OF THE SKIN

The skin is essentially composed of two layers, the **epidermis** and the **dermis**.

The Epidermis

The **epidermis** can be divided into four strata: the stratum corneum, the stratum lucidum, the stratum granulosum, and the stratum germinativum. See Figure 3–1 for the locations of these strata within the epidermis.

THE STRATUM CORNEUM

The **stratum corneum** is the outermost, horny layer, consisting of dead cells filled with a protein substance called **keratin**. It forms the protective covering for the body, and its thickness varies with the use made of the particular body part. Because of the pressure on their surfaces during use, the soles of the feet and palms of the hands have thicker layers of stratum corneum than do the eyelids or the forehead.

THE STRATUM LUCIDUM

The **stratum lucidum** is a translucent layer lying directly beneath the stratum corneum. It is frequently absent and is not seen in thinner skin. Cells in this layer are also dead or dying.

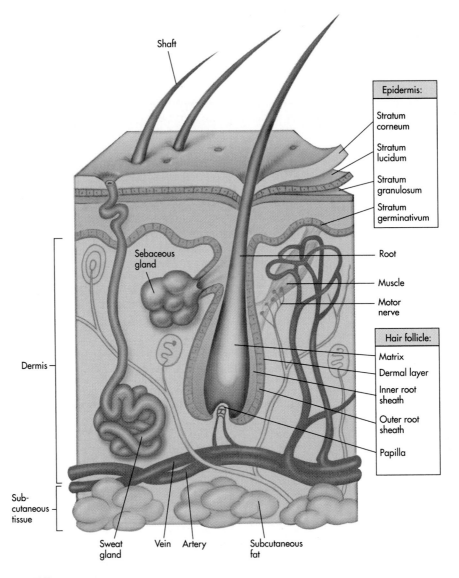

Shaft

Epidermis:

Stratum corneum

Stratum lucidum

Stratum granulosum

Stratum germinativum

Sebaceous gland

Root

Muscle

Motor nerve

Hair follicle:

Matrix

Dermal layer

Inner root sheath

Outer root sheath

Papilla

Dermis

Sub-cutaneous tissue

Sweat gland

Vein   Artery

Subcutaneous fat

FIGURE 3–1

The integument: the epidermis, dermis, subcutaneous tissue, and its appendages.

THE STRATUM GRANULOSUM

The **stratum granulosum** consists of several layers of living cells that are in the process of becoming a part of the previously mentioned strata. Its cells are active in the **keratinization** process, during which they lose their nuclei and become hard or horny.

THE STRATUM GERMINATIVUM

The **stratum germinativum** is composed of several layers of living cells capable of **mitosis** or cell division. Sometimes called the **mucosum** or **Malpighii**, the stratum germinativum is the innermost layer and is responsible for the regeneration of the epidermis. Damage to this layer, as in severe burns, necessitates the use of skin grafts. **Melanin**, the pigment that gives color to the skin, is formed in this layer. The more abundant the melanin, the darker the color of the skin.

The Dermis

Sometimes called the **corium** or **true skin**, the **dermis** is composed of connective tissue containing lymphatics, nerves and nerve endings, blood vessels, sebaceous and sweat glands, elastic fibers, and hair follicles. It is divided into two layers: the **upper** or **papillary layer** and the **lower** or **reticular layer**. The papillary layer is arranged into parallel rows of microscopic structures called **papillae**. The papillae produce the ridges of the skin that are one's fingerprints or footprints. The reticular layer is composed of white fibrous tissue that supports the blood vessels. The dermis is attached to underlying structures by the **subcutaneous tissue**. This tissue supports, nourishes, insulates, and cushions the skin.

ACCESSORY STRUCTURES OF THE SKIN

The hair, nails, sebaceous glands, and sweat glands are the accessory structures of the skin.

Hair

A **hair** is a thin, thread-like structure formed by a group of cells that develop within a hair **follicle** or **socket**. Each hair is composed of a **shaft**, which is the visible portion, and a **root**, which is embedded within the follicle. At the base of each follicle is a loop of capillaries enclosed within connective tissue called the **hair papilla**. The **pilomotor muscle** attaches to the side of each follicle. When the skin is cooled or the individual has an emotional reaction, the skin often forms "**goose pimples**" as a result of contraction by these muscles. Hair is distributed over the whole body with the exception of the palms of the hands and soles of the feet. It is thicker on the scalp and thinner on the other parts of the body. Hair around the eyes, in the nose, and in the ears serves to filter out foreign particles. The color of one's hair is a product of genetic background and is determined by the amount of pigmentation within the hair shaft. Hair grows at approximately 0.5 inch a month, and its growth is not affected by cutting.

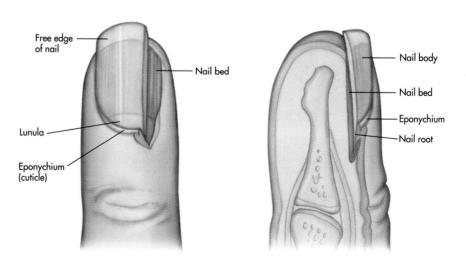

FIGURE 3–2

The fingernail, an appendage of the integument.

Nails

Finger- and **toenails** are horny cell structures of the epidermis and are composed of hard keratin. A nail consists of a **body**, a **root**, and a **matrix** or **nailbed** (Fig. 3–2). The crescent-shaped white area of the nail is the **lunula**. Nail growth may vary with age, disease, and hormone deficiency. Average growth is 1 mm per week, and a lost fingernail usually regenerates in 3½ to 5½ months. A lost toenail may require 6 to 8 months for regeneration.

Sebaceous Glands

The oil-secreting glands of the skin are called **sebaceous glands**. They have tiny ducts that open into the hair follicles, and their secretion, **sebum**, lubricates the hair as well as the skin. The amount of secretion is controlled by the endocrine system and varies with age, puberty, pregnancy, and senility.

Sweat (Sudoriferous) Glands

There are approximately 2 million **sweat glands**. These coiled, tubular glands are distributed over the entire surface of the body with the exception of the margin of the lips, glans penis, and the inner surface of the prepuce. They are more numerous on the palms of the hands, soles of the feet, forehead, and axillae. Sweat glands secrete **sweat** or **perspiration**, which helps to cool the body by evaporation. Sweat also rids the body of waste through the pores of the skin. Left to accumulate, sweat becomes odorous by the action of bacteria. The body loses about 0.5 L of fluid per day through sweat.

LIFE SPAN CONSIDERATIONS

■ THE CHILD

Vernix caseosa, a cheese-like substance, covers the fetus until birth. At first the fetal skin is transparent and blood vessels are clearly visible. In about 13 to 16 weeks downy lanugo hair begins to develop, especially on the head. At 21 to 24 weeks, the skin is reddish and wrinkled and has little subcutaneous fat. At birth, the subcutaneous glands are developed and the skin is smooth and pink. Preterm and term newborns have less subcutaneous fat than adults; therefore, they are more sensitive to heat and cold. Babies can blister easily.

Skin conditions may be acute or chronic, local or systemic, and some are congenital, such as strawberry nevi and Mongolian spots. Certain children's skin conditions may be associated with age, such as milia in babies and acne in adolescents. **Milia** are white pinhead-size papules occurring on the face, and sometimes the trunk, of a newborn. They usually disappear in several weeks. **Acne** is an inflammatory condition of the sebaceous glands and the hair follicles (**pimples**). See Figure 3–3.

Skin infections in children generally produce systemic symptoms, such as fever and malaise. Sebaceous glands do not produce sebum until about 8 to 10 years of age; therefore, a child's skin is more dry and chaps easily.

The hair of the child will vary according to race, texture, quality, and distribution. A newborn may have no hair on its head or a head covered with hair. Hair can become dry and brittle, due to improper nutrition. During a severe illness hair loss and color change may occur.

■ THE OLDER ADULT

With increasing years beyond reproductive maturity, the body begins the process of aging. By the year 2030 one in five people in the United States will be at least 65 years old. The process of aging varies with each individual. Aging is not a disease but rather a sequence of events regulated by complex processes.

The Integumentary System

As one ages, the skin becomes looser as the dermal papilla grows less dense. Collagen and elastic fibers of the upper dermis decrease and skin loses its elastic tone and wrinkles more easily. Skin conditions are common in the older adult. Dryness (**xerosis**) and itching (**pruritus**) are common. Premalignant and malignant skin lesions increase with aging. Carcinomas appear frequently on the nose, eyelid, or cheek. **Basal cell carcinomas** account for 80% of the skin cancers seen in the older adult. See Figure 3–4.

By age 50 approximately half of all people have some gray hair. Scalp hair thins in women and men. The hair becomes dry and often brittle. Older women may have an increase in facial hair. Men may have an increase in hair of the nares, eyebrows, or helix of the ear. In addition to the changes in the skin and hair, nails flatten and become discolored, dry, and brittle.

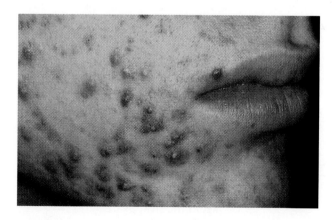

FIGURE 3–3

Acne. (Courtesy of Jason L. Smith, MD.)

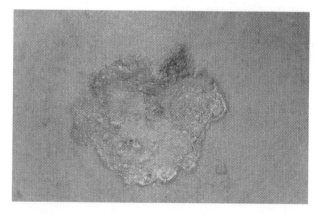

FIGURE 3–4

Basal cell carcinoma. (Courtesy of Jason L. Smith, MD.)

BUILDING YOUR MEDICAL VOCABULARY

This section provides the foundation for learning medical terminology. Medical words can be made up of four different types of word parts:

- Prefixes (P)
- Roots (R)
- Combining forms (CF)
- Suffixes (S)

By connecting various word parts in an organized sequence, thousands of words can be built and learned. In this text the word list is alphabetized so one can see the variety of meanings created when common prefixes and suffixes are repeatedly applied to certain word roots and/or combining forms. Words shown in pink are additional words related to the content of this chapter that are not built from word parts. These words are included to enhance your vocabulary. Note: an asterisk icon (✱) indicates terms that are covered in the Pathology Spotlights section in this chapter.

MEDICAL WORD	WORD PARTS (WHEN APPLICABLE)			DEFINITION
	Part	**Type**	**Meaning**	
acne (ăk′ nē)				An inflammatory condition of the sebaceous glands and the hair follicles; *pimples*. See Figure 3–3.
acrochordon (ăk″ rō-kor′ dŏn)	acr/o chord -on	CF R S	extremity cord pertaining to	A small outgrowth of epidermal and dermal tissue; *skin tags*. See Figure 3–5.
actinic dermatitis (ăk-tĭn′ ĭk dĕr″ mă-tī′ tĭs)	actin -ic dermat -itis	R S R S	ray pertaining to skin inflammation	Inflammation of the skin caused by exposure to radiant energy, such as x-rays, ultraviolet light, and sunlight. See Figure 3–6.
albinism (ăl′ bĭn-ĭsm)	albin -ism	R S	white condition of	Absence of pigment in the skin, hair, and eyes
alopecia (al″ ō-pē′ shĭ-ă)	a lopec -ia	P R S	without, lack of fox mange pertaining to	Loss of hair, baldness; *alopecia areata* is loss of hair in defined patches usually involving the scalp. See Figure 3–7. Male pattern alopecia begins in the frontal area and proceeds until only a horseshoe area of the hair remains in the back and temples. See Figure 3–8.

MEDICAL WORD	WORD PARTS (WHEN APPLICABLE)			DEFINITION
	Part	**Type**	**Meaning**	
anhidrosis (ăn″ hī-drō′ sĭs)	an hidr -osis	P R S	without, lack of sweat condition of	A condition in which there is a lack or complete absence of sweating
autograft (ŏ-tō-grăft)	auto -graft	P S	self pencil, grafting knife	A graft taken from one part of the patient's body and transferred to another part
avulsion (ă-vŭl′ shŭn)	a vuls -ion	P R S	away from to pull process	The process of forcibly tearing off a part or structure of the body, such as a finger or toe.
basal cell carcinoma (bā′ săl sel kăr″ sĭ-nō′ mă)				An epithelial malignant tumor of the skin that rarely metastasizes. It usually begins as a small, shiny papule and enlarges to form a whitish border around a central depression. See Figure 3–4.
bite (bīt)				An injury in which a part of the body surface is torn by an insect, animal, or human, resulting in an abrasion, puncture, or laceration. See Figures 3–9, 3–10, 3–11, and 3–12.
boil (boil)				An acute, painful nodule formed in the subcutaneous layers of the skin, gland, or hair follicle; most often caused by the invasion of staphylococci; *furuncle.* See Figure 3–13.
bulla (bŭl′ lă)				A larger blister; *a bleb.* See Figure 3–14.
burn (burn) (bərn)				An injury to tissue caused by heat, fire, chemical agents, electricity, lightning, or radiation; burns are classified according to degree or depth of skin damage. See Figure 3–15.
callus (kăl′ ŭs)				Hardened skin
candidiasis (kăn″ dĭ-dī′ ă-sĭs)				An infection of the skin or mucous membranes with any species of *Candida,* but chiefly *Candida albicans. Candida* is a genus of yeasts and was formerly called *Monilia.* See Figure 3–16.

MEDICAL WORD	WORD PARTS (WHEN APPLICABLE)			DEFINITION
	Part	**Type**	**Meaning**	
carbuncle (kăr′ bŭng″ kl)				An infection of the subcutaneous tissue, usually composed of a cluster of boils. See Figure 3–17.
causalgia (kŏ-săl′ jĭ-ă)	caus -algia	R S	heat pain	Intense burning pain associated with trophic skin changes in the hand or foot after trauma to the part
cellulitis (sĕl-ū-lī′ tĭs)	cellul -itis	R S	little cell inflammation	Inflammation of cellular or connective tissue. See Figure 3–18.
cicatrix (sĭk′ ă-trĭks)				The scar left after the healing of a wound
comedo (kŏm′ ē-dō)				Blackhead
corn (korn) (ko(ə)rn)				A horny induration and thickening of the skin on the toes caused by ill-fitting shoes.
cutaneous (kū-tā′ nē-ŭs)	cutane -ous	R S	skin pertaining to	Pertaining to the skin
cyst (sĭst)				A bladder or sac; a closed sac that contains fluid, semifluid, or solid material
decubitus (dē-kū′ bĭ-tŭs)	de cubit -us	P R S	down to lie pertaining to	Literally means a lying down; *a bedsore.* ✱ See Pathology Spotlight: Decubitus Ulcer.
dehiscence (dē-hĭs′ ĕns)				The separation or bursting open of a surgical wound. See Figure 3–19.
dermatitis (dĕr″ mă-ti′ tĭs)	dermat -itis	R S	skin inflammation	Inflammation of the skin. See Figures 3–20 and 3–21.
dermatologist (dĕr′ mah-tol′ŏ-jĭst)	dermat/o log -ist	CF R S	skin study of one who specializes	One who specializes in the study of the skin
dermatology (dĕr″ mah-tol′ ŏ-jē)	dermat/o -logy	CF S	skin study of	The study of the skin
dermatome (dĕr″ mah-tōm)	derm/a -tome	CF S	skin instrument to cut	An instrument used to cut the skin for grafting
dermomycosis (dĕr′ mō-mī-kō′ sĭs)	derm/o myc -osis	CF R S	skin fungus condition of	A skin condition caused by a fungus

MEDICAL WORD	WORD PARTS (WHEN APPLICABLE)			DEFINITION
	Part	**Type**	**Meaning**	
ecchymosis (ĕk-ĭ-mō′ sĭs)	ec chym -osis	P R S	out juice condition of	A condition in which the blood seeps into the skin causing discolorations ranging from blue-black to greenish-yellow
eczema (ĕk′ zĕ-mă)				An inflammatory skin disease of the epidermis. ✳ See Pathology Spotlight: Eczema.
erythema (ĕr″ ĭ-thē′ mă)				A redness of the skin; may be caused by capillary congestion, inflammation, heat, sunlight, or cold temperature. *Erythema infectiosum* is known as Fifth disease, a mild, moderately contagious disease caused by the human parvovirus B-19. It is most commonly seen in school-age children and is thought to be spread via respiratory secretions from infected persons. See Figure 3–22.
erythroderma (ĕ-rĭth″ rō-dĕr′-mă)	erythr/o -derma	CF S	red skin	Abnormal redness of the skin occurring over widespread areas of the body. See Figure 3–23.
eschar (ĕs′ kăr)				A slough, scab
excoriation (ĕks-kō″ rē-ā′ shŭn)	ex coriat -ion	P R S	out corium process	Abrasion of the epidermis by scratching, trauma, chemicals, burns, etc.
exudate (ĕks′ ū-dāt)				The production of pus or serum
folliculitis (fō-lĭk″ ū-lī′ tĭs)	follicul -itis	R S	little bag inflammation	Inflammation of a follicle or follicles. See Figure 3–24.
herpes simplex (hĕr′ pēz sĭm′ plĕks)				An inflammatory skin disease caused by a herpes virus (Type I); *cold sore or fever blister.* See Figures 3–25 and 3–26.
hidradenitis (hī-drăd-ĕ-nī′ tĭs)	hidr aden -itis	R R S	sweat gland inflammation	Inflammation of the sweat glands
hives (hīvz)				Eruption of itching and burning swellings on the skin; *urticaria.* See Figure 3–27.

MEDICAL WORD	WORD PARTS (WHEN APPLICABLE)			DEFINITION
	Part	**Type**	**Meaning**	
hyperhidrosis (hī″ pĕr-hī-drō′ sĭs)	hyper hidr -osis	P R S	excessive sweat condition of	A condition of excessive sweating. See Figure 3–28.
hypodermic (hī″ pō-dĕr′ mĭk)	hypo derm -ic	P R S	under skin pertaining to	Pertaining to under the skin or inserted under the skin, as a hypodermic injection
icteric (ik-tĕr′ ik)	icter -ic	R S	jaundice pertaining to	Pertaining to jaundice
impetigo (ĭm″ pĕ-tī′ gō)				A skin infection marked by vesicles or bullae; usually caused by streptococci or staphylococci. See Figure 3–29.
integumentary (ĭn-tĕg″ ū-mĕn′ tă-rē)	integument -ary	R S	a covering pertaining to	A covering; the skin, consisting of the dermis and the epidermis
intradermal (in″ trăh-dĕr′ măl)	intra derm -al	P R S	within skin pertaining to	Pertaining to within the skin, as an intradermal injection
jaundice (jawn′ dĭs)	jaund -ic(e)	R S	yellow pertaining to	Yellow; a symptom of a disease in which there is excessive bile in the blood; the skin, whites of the eyes, and mucous membranes are yellow; *icterus*
keloid (kē′ lŏyd)	kel -oid	R S	tumor resemble	Overgrowth of scar tissue caused by excessive collagen formation. See Figure 3–30.
lentigo (lĕn-tī′ gō)				A flat, brownish spot on the skin sometimes caused by exposure to the sun and weather; *freckle*. See Figure 3–31.
leukoderma (lū″ kō-dĕr′ mă)	leuk/o -derma	CF S	white skin	Localized loss of pigmentation of the skin
leukoplakia (lū″ kō-plā′ kē-ă)	leuk/o plak -ia	CF R S	white plate pertaining to	White spots or patches formed on the mucous membrane of the tongue or cheek; the spots are smooth, hard, and irregular in shape and may become malignant
lupus (lū′ pŭs)				Originally used to describe a destructive type of skin lesion; current usage of the word is usually in combination with the words *vulgaris* or *erythematosus*: *lupus vulgaris* or *lupus erythematosus*

MEDICAL WORD	WORD PARTS (WHEN APPLICABLE)			DEFINITION
	Part	**Type**	**Meaning**	
melanocarcinoma (měl″ ă-nō-kar″ sĭn-ō′ mă)	melan/o carcin -oma	CF R S	black cancer tumor	A cancerous tumor that has black pigmentation
melanoma (měl″ ă-nō′ mă)	melan -oma	R S	black tumor	A malignant black mole or tumor. ✱ See Figures 3–50 and 3–51 in Pathology Spotlight: Skin Cancer.
miliaria (mĭl-ē-ā′ rē-ă)	miliar -ia	R S	millet (tiny) pertaining to	Is called *prickly heat* and is commonly seen in newborns and/or infants. It is caused by excessive body warmth. There is retention of sweat in the sweat glands, which have become blocked or inflamed, and then rupture or leak into the skin. *Miliaria* appears as a rash with tiny pinhead-sized papules, vesicles, and/or pustules. See Figure 3–32.
mole (mōl)				A pigmented, elevated spot above the surface of the skin; a *nevus*. See Figure 3–33.
onychitis (ŏn″ ĭ-kī′ tĭs)	onych -itis	R S	nail inflammation	Inflammation of the nail
onychomycosis (ŏn″ ĭ-kō-mī-kō′ sĭs)	onych/o myc -osis	CF R S	nail fungus condition of	A condition of the nail caused by a fungus. See Figure 3–34.
pachyderma (păk-ē-der′ mă)	pachy -derma	R S	thick skin	Thick skin
paronychia (păr″ ō-nĭk′ ĭ-ă)	par onych -ia	P R S	around nail condition	An infectious condition of the marginal structures around the nail
pediculosis (pě-dĭk″ ū-lō′ sĭs)	pedicul -osis	R S	a louse condition of	A condition of infestation with lice. See Figure 3–35.
petechiae (pē-tē′ kĭ-ē)				Small, pinpoint, purplish hemorrhagic spots on the skin
pruritus (proo-rī′ tŭs)	prurit -us	R S	itching pertaining to	A severe itching
psoriasis (sō-rī′ ă-sĭs)				A chronic skin disease characterized by pink or dull-red lesions surmounted by silvery scaling. ✱ See Figure 3–49 in Pathology Spotlight: Psoriasis.

MEDICAL WORD	WORD PARTS (WHEN APPLICABLE)			DEFINITION
	Part	**Type**	**Meaning**	
purpura (pur′ pū-ră)				A purplish discoloration of the skin caused by extravasation of blood into the tissues. See Figures 3–36 and 3–37.
rhytidoplasty (rĭt′ ĭ-dō-plăs″ tē)	rhytid/o -plasty	CF S	wrinkle surgical repair	Plastic surgery for the removal of wrinkles
roseola (rō-zē′ ō-lă)				Any rose-colored rash marked by *maculae* or red spots on the skin. See Figure 3–38.
rubella (roo-bĕl′ lă)				A systemic disease caused by a virus and characterized by a rash and fever; also called *German measles* and *three-day measles*
rubeola (roo-bē′ ō-lă)				A contagious disease characterized by fever, inflammation of the mucous membranes, and rose-colored spots on the skin; also called *measles*
scabies (skā′ bēz) or (skā′ bĭ-ēz)				A contagious skin disease characterized by papules, vesicles, pustules, burrows, and intense itching; it is caused by the itch mite and is also called "*the itch*" or the "*seven-year itch*." See Figure 3–39.
scar (skahr)				The mark left by the healing process of a wound, sore, or injury
scleroderma (skli rō-dĕr′ mă)	scler/o -derma	CF S	hard skin	A chronic condition with hardening of the skin and other connective tissues of the body
seborrhea (sĕb″ or-ē′ ă)	seb/o -rrhea	CF S	oil flow	Excessive flow of oil from the sebaceous glands
sebum (sē′ bŭm)				The fatty or oil secretion of sebaceous glands of the skin
senile keratosis (sĕn′ ĭl kĕr″ ă-tō′ sĭs)	senile kerat -osis	R R S	old horn condition of	A condition occurring in older people wherein there is dry skin and localized scaling caused by excessive exposure to the sun. See Figure 3–40.
striae (plural) (strī′ ē)				Streaks or lines on the breasts, thighs, abdomen, or buttocks caused by weakening of elastic tissue. See Figure 3–41.

MEDICAL WORD	WORD PARTS (WHEN APPLICABLE)			DEFINITION
	Part	**Type**	**Meaning**	
subcutaneous (sŭb″ kū-tā′ nē-ŭs)	sub cutane -ous	P R S	below skin pertaining to	Pertaining to below the skin, as a subcutaneous injection
subungual (sŭb-ŭng′ gwăl)	sub ungu -al	P R S	below nail pertaining to	Pertaining to below the nail
taut (tŏt)				Tight, firm; to pull or draw tight a surface, such as the skin
telangiectasia (tĕl-ăn″ jē-ĕk-tā′ zē-ă)	tel ang/i -ectasia	R CF S	end, distant vessel dilatation	Dilatation of small blood vessels that may appear as a "*birthmark*"
thermanesthesia (thĕrm″ ăn-ĕs-thē′ zē-ă)	therm an -esthesia	R P S	hot, heat without, lack of sensation	Inability to distinguish between the sensations of heat and cold
tinea (tĭn′ ē-ă)				Contagious skin diseases affecting both man and domestic animals, caused by certain fungi, and marked by the localized appearance of discolored, scaly patches on the skin; also called *ringworm*. See Figures 3–42 and 3–43.
trichomycosis (trĭk″ ō-mi-kō′ sĭs)	trich/o myc -osis	CF R S	hair fungus condition of	A fungus condition of the hair
ulcer (ŭl′ sĕr)				An open lesion or sore of the epidermis or mucous membrane. See Figure 3–44.
varicella (văr″ i-sĕl′ ă)				A contagious viral disease characterized by fever, headache, and a crop of red spots that become macules, papules, vesicles, and crusts; also called *chickenpox*. See Figure 3–45.
vitiligo (vĭt″ ĭl-ĭ′ gō)				A skin condition characterized by milk-white patches surrounded by areas of normal pigmentation. See Figure 3–46.
wart (wōrt)				An elevation of viral origin on the epidermis; *verruca*. See Figure 3–47. A plantar wart is known as *verruca plantaris*. It occurs on a pressure-bearing area, especially the sole of the foot. See Figure 3–48.

MEDICAL WORD	WORD PARTS (WHEN APPLICABLE)			DEFINITION
	Part	Type	Meaning	
wound (woond)				An injury to soft tissue caused by trauma; generally classified as open or closed
xanthoderma (zăn″ thō-dĕr′ mă)	xanth/o -derma	CF S	yellow skin	Yellow skin
xanthoma (zăn-thō′ mă)	xanth -oma	R S	yellow tumor	Yellow tumor
xeroderma (zē″ rō-dĕr′ mă)	xer/o -derma	CF S	dry skin	Dry skin
xerosis (zē-rō′ sĭs)	xer -osis	R S	dry condition of	Abnormal dryness of skin, mucous membranes, or the conjunctiva.

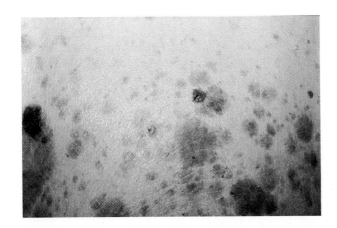

FIGURE 3–5

Acrochordon (skin tags). (Courtesy of Jason L. Smith, MD.)

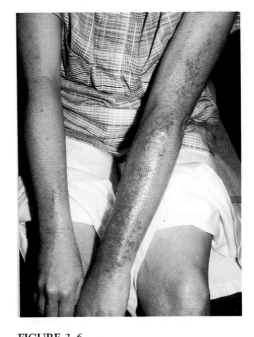

FIGURE 3–6

Photodermatitis. (Courtesy of Jason L. Smith, MD.)

FIGURE 3–7

Alopecia areata. (Courtesy of Jason L. Smith, MD.)

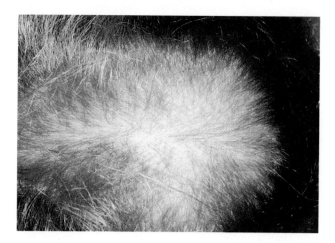

FIGURE 3–8

Male pattern alopecia. (Courtesy of Jason L. Smith, MD.)

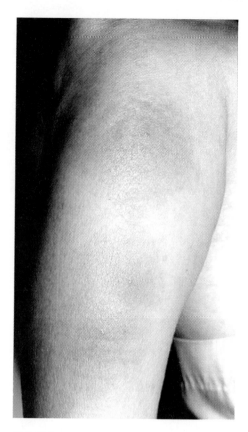

FIGURE 3–9

Fire ant bites. (Courtesy of Jason L. Smith, MD.)

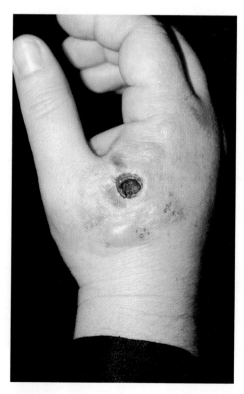

FIGURE 3–10

Brown recluse spider bites. (Courtesy of Jason L. Smith, MD.)

FIGURE 3–11

Tick bite. (Courtesy of Jason L. Smith, MD.)

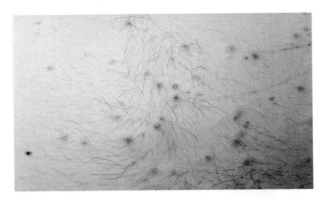

FIGURE 3–12

Flea bites. (Courtesy of Jason L. Smith, MD.)

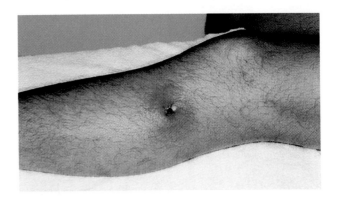

FIGURE 3–13

Furuncle. (Courtesy of Jason L. Smith, MD.)

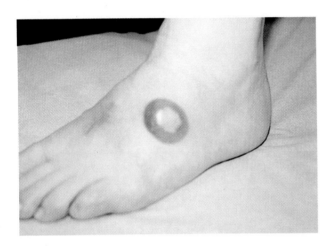

FIGURE 3–14

Bulla. (Courtesy of Jason L. Smith, MD.)

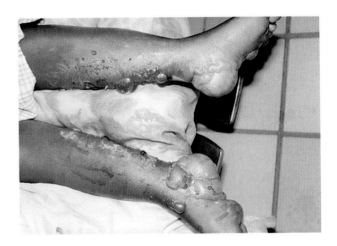

FIGURE 3–15

Burn, second degree. (Courtesy of Jason L. Smith, MD.)

FIGURE 3–16

Candidiasis. (Courtesy of Jason L. Smith, MD.)

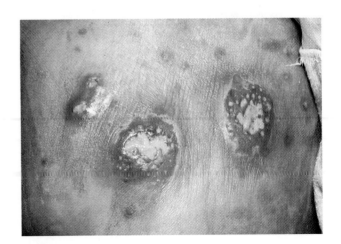

FIGURE 3–17

Carbuncles. (Courtesy of Jason L. Smith, MD.)

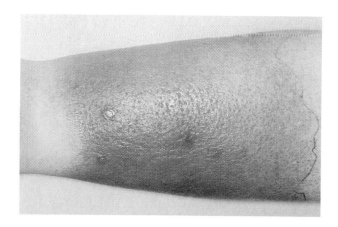

FIGURE 3–18

Cellulitis. (Courtesy of Jason L. Smith, MD.)

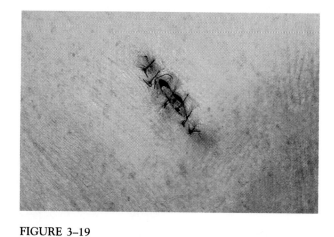

FIGURE 3–19

Wound dehiscence, back. (Courtesy of Jason L. Smith, MD.)

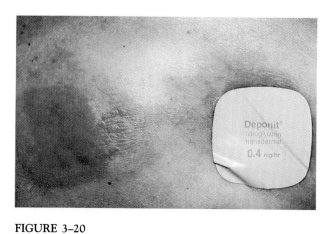

FIGURE 3–20

Contact dermatitis; adhesive reaction. (Courtesy of Jason L. Smith, MD.)

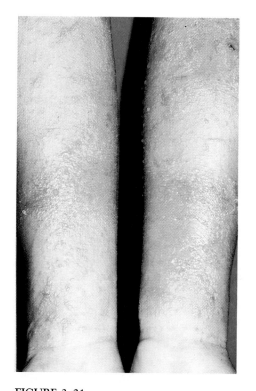

FIGURE 3–21

Dermatitis; poison ivy. (Courtesy of Jason L. Smith, MD.)

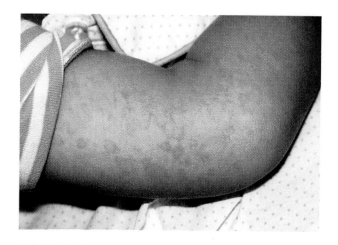

FIGURE 3–22

Erythema infectiosum (Fifth disease). (Courtesy of Jason L. Smith, MD.)

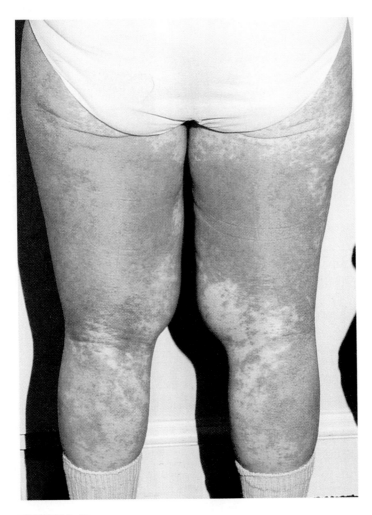

FIGURE 3–23

Erythroderma. (Courtesy of Jason L. Smith, MD.)

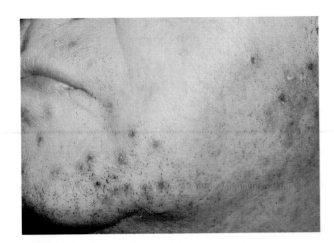

FIGURE 3–24

Staphylococcal folliculitis. (Courtesy of Jason L. Smith, MD.)

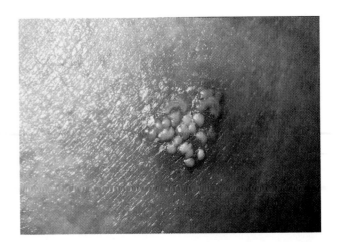

FIGURE 3–25

Herpes simplex. (Courtesy of Jason L. Smith, MD.)

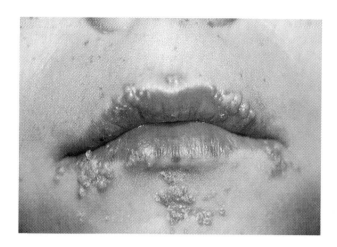

FIGURE 3–26

Herpes labialis. (Courtesy of Jason L. Smith, MD.)

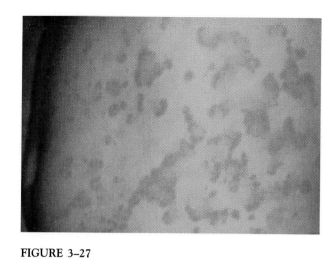

FIGURE 3–27

Urticaria (hives). (Courtesy of Jason L. Smith, MD.)

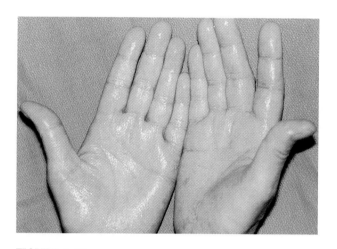

FIGURE 3–28

Hyperhidrosis. (Courtesy of Jason L. Smith, MD.)

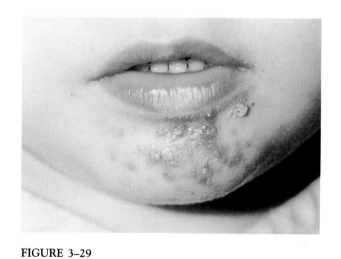

FIGURE 3–29

Impetigo. (Courtesy of Jason L. Smith, MD.)

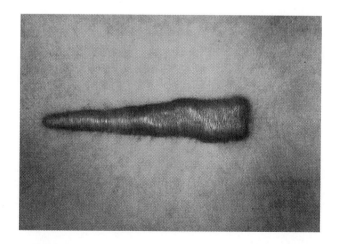

FIGURE 3–30

Keloid. (Courtesy of Jason L. Smith, MD.)

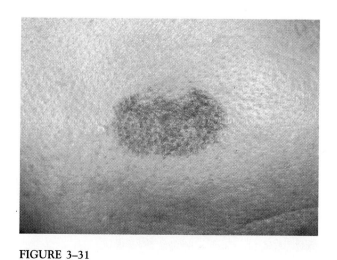

FIGURE 3–31

Lentigo. (Courtesy of Jason L. Smith, MD.)

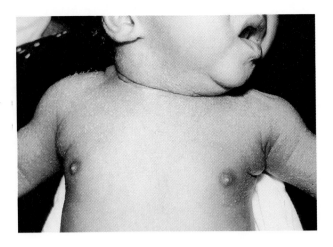

FIGURE 3–32

Miliaria. (Courtesy of Jason L. Smith, MD.)

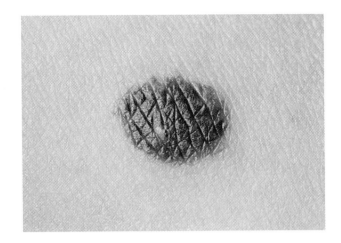

FIGURE 3–33

Nevus (mole). (Courtesy of Jason L. Smith, MD.)

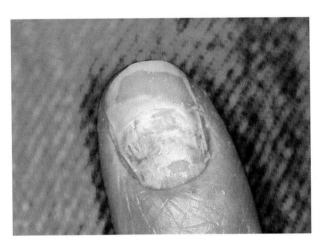

FIGURE 3–34

Onychomycosis. (Courtesy of Jason L. Smith, MD.)

FIGURE 3–35

Pediculosis capitis. (Courtesy of Jason L. Smith, MD.)

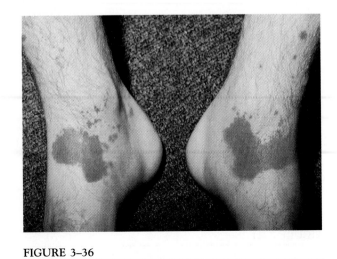

FIGURE 3–36

Purpura. (Courtesy of Jason L. Smith, MD.)

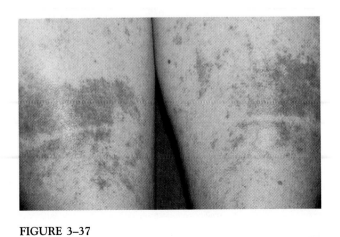

FIGURE 3–37

Benign pigmented purpura. (Courtesy of Jason L. Smith, MD.)

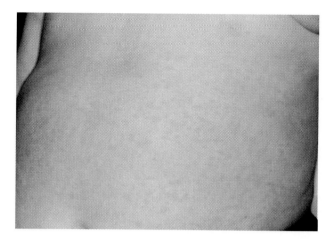

FIGURE 3–38

Roseola. (Courtesy of Jason L. Smith, MD.)

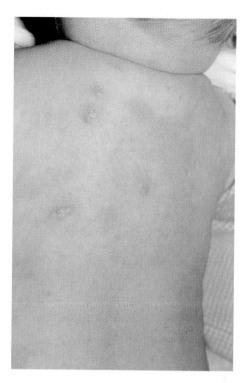

FIGURE 3–39

Scabies. (Courtesy of Jason L. Smith, MD.)

FIGURE 3–40

Photoaging solar elastosis; senile keratosis. (Courtesy of Jason L. Smith, MD.)

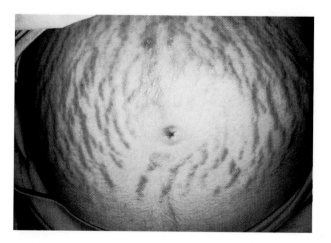

FIGURE 3–41

Striae. (Courtesy of Jason L. Smith, MD.)

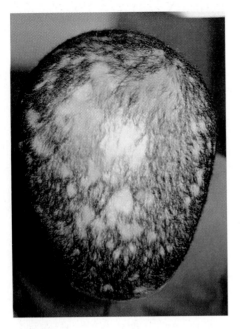

FIGURE 3-42

Tinea capitis. (Courtesy of Jason L. Smith, MD.)

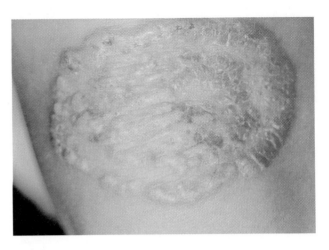

FIGURE 3-43

Tinea corporis. (Courtesy of Jason L. Smith, MD.)

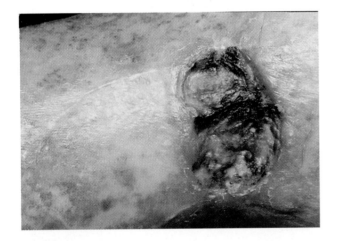

FIGURE 3-44

Leg ulcer radiation site. (Courtesy of Jason L. Smith, MD.)

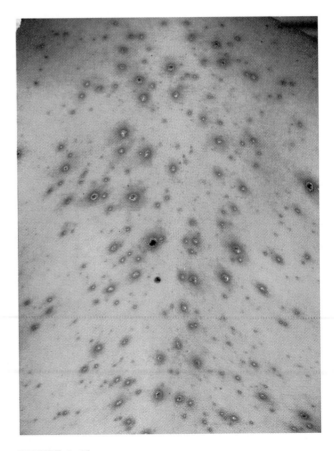

FIGURE 3-45

Varicella (chickenpox). (Courtesy of Jason L. Smith, MD.)

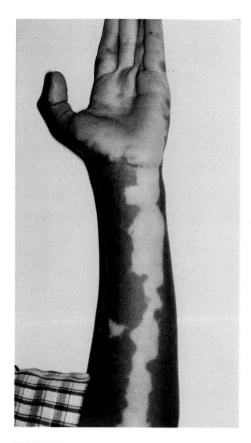

FIGURE 3–46

Vitiligo. (Courtesy of Jason L. Smith, MD.)

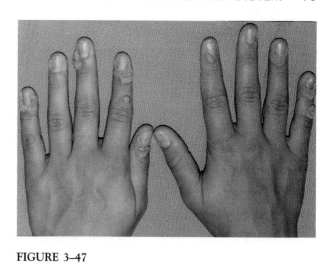

FIGURE 3–47

Verrucae (warts). (Courtesy of Jason L. Smith, MD.)

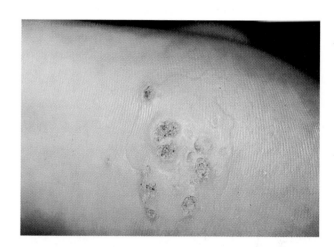

FIGURE 3–48

Plantar wart. (Courtesy of Jason L. Smith, MD.)

Terminology Translator

Medicine   Medicina   Médecine   Medizin

This feature, found on the accompanying CD-ROM, provides an innovative tool to translate medical words into Spanish, French, and German.

PATHOLOGY SPOTLIGHTS

PATHOLOGY SPOTLIGHTS

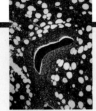

Decubitus Ulcer

Also known as a bedsore or pressure ulcer, a decubitus ulcer is an area of skin and tissue that becomes injured or broken down. See the "Skin Signs" section that follows, as well as Figure 3–52. The literal meaning of the word, decubitus, is a lying down. This meaning points to what causes a decubitus (pressure) ulcer: When a person is in a sitting or lying position for too long without shifting his or her weight, the constant pressure against the tissue causes a decreased blood supply to that area. Without a blood supply, the affected tissue dies. The most common places for pressure ulcers are over bony prominences such as the elbow, heels, hips, ankles, shoulders, back, and the back of the head.

Although it is more common for people to get pressure ulcers if they spend most of their time in bed or use a wheelchair, those who can walk can also get pressure ulcers when they are bedridden as a result of an illness or injury.

The National Pressure Ulcer Advisory Panel (NPUAP) created a system for evaluating pressure sores, which is based on a staging system from Stage I (earliest signs) to Stage IV (worst):

Stage I: A reddened area on the skin that, when pressed, is "non-blanchable" (does not turn white). This indicates that a pressure ulcer is starting to develop.

Stage II: The skin blisters or forms an open sore. The area around the sore may be red and irritated.

Stage III: The skin breakdown now looks like a crater where there is damage to the tissue below the skin.

Stage IV: The pressure ulcer has become so deep that there is damage to the muscle and bone, and sometimes tendons and joints.

Once a pressure ulcer is identified, certain basic steps are taken. This includes relieving the pressure to the affected area. Pillows, special foam cushions, and sheepskin are used to help reduce the pressure. Treating the sore is based on the stage of the ulcer. Pressure ulcers are rinsed with a salt-water rinse that removes the loose, dead tissue. The sore is then covered with special gauze dressing made for pressure ulcers. Avoiding further trauma or friction is important, and powdering the sheets lightly can help decrease friction in bed.

Infection may occur, and can lead to serious problems because the infection can become systemic.

Eczema

Eczema, which is also called atopic or contact dermatitis (see Figure 3–20), is a chronic skin disorder characterized by scaly and itching rashes. People with eczema often have a family history of eczema, or allergic conditions like asthma and hay fever. Eczema is most common in infants, and at least half of those cases clear by age 3. In adults, it is generally a chronic condition.

Eczema results from a hypersensitivity reaction (similar to an allergy) that occurs in the skin, causing chronic inflammation. The inflammation causes the skin to become itchy and scaly. Chronic irritation and scratching causes the skin to thicken and become a leathery texture. Symptoms can be worsened by exposure to environmental irritants, dryness of the skin, exposure to water, temperature changes, and stress.

Treatment depends on the appearance or stage of the lesions. For example, acute "weeping" lesions, dry scaly lesions, or chronic dry, thickened lesions are each treated differently. Weeping lesions may be treated with moisturizers, mild soaps, or wet dressings. Less severe cases and dry, scaly lesions may be treated with mild anti-itch lotions or low-potency topical corticosteroids. Chronic thickened areas may be treated with ointments or creams that contain tar compounds, medium to very high potency corticosteroids, and lubricating ingredients. In severe cases, systemic corticosteroids may be prescribed to reduce inflammation. The most promising treatment for eczema is a new class of nonsteroidal skin medications called topical immunomodulators (TIMs).

People who suffer from eczema should avoid anything that aggravates the symptoms, including any food allergens and irritants such as wool and lanolin. Dry skin often makes the condition worse, so patients are encouraged to use a mild soap when washing or bathing, and to use as little soap as possible. After bathing, it is important that patients trap the moisture in the skin by applying a moisturizer on the skin while it is damp. Temperature changes and stress may cause sweating and aggravate the condition.

Psoriasis

Psoriasis is a common skin condition that is characterized by frequent episodes of redness, itching, and thick, dry, scales on the skin (see Figure 3–49). It is a very common condition that affects approximately 3 million Americans. The condition may affect people of any age, but it most commonly begins between ages 15 and 35. It is believed be an inherited disorder, related to an inflammatory response in which the immune system targets the body's own cells. Normally, it takes about a month for new skin cells to move up from the lower layers to the surface. In psoriasis, this process takes only a few days, resulting in a build-up of dead skin cells and formation of thick scales. The condition is most commonly seen on the trunk, elbows, knees, scalp, skin folds, or fingernails, but it may affect any (or all) parts of the skin.

Psoriasis can appear suddenly or gradually. In many cases, it goes away and then flares up again repeatedly over time. Medications, viral or bacterial infections, excessive alcohol consumption, obesity, lack of sunlight, sunburn, stress, general poor health, cold climate, and frequent friction on the skin are also associated with psoriasis flare-ups. The condition is not contagious.

Treatment varies with the extent and severity of the disorder. Psoriasis lesions that cover all or most of the body may require hospitalization, and may be acutely painful. In such severe cases, the body loses vast quantities of fluid and is susceptible to severe secondary infections that can become systemic, involve internal organs, and can even progress to septic shock and death. Treatment includes analgesics, sedation, intravenous fluids, retinoids (such as Retin-A), and antibiotics (such as cyclosporine).

Mild cases are usually treated at home with topical medications such as prescription or nonprescription dandruff shampoos, cortisone or other corticosteroids, and antifungal medications.

Nonpharmacologic treatments may include moderate exposure to sunlight or phototherapy. In phototherapy, the skin is sensitized by the application of coal tar ointment or by taking

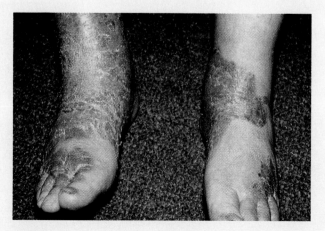

FIGURE 3–49

Psoriasis, lower extremities. (Courtesy of Jason L. Smith, MD.)

oral medications that cause the skin to become sensitive to light. The person is then exposed to ultraviolet light.

 Skin Cancer

Skin cancer is a disease in which malignant cells are found in the epidermis. The epidermis contains three kinds of cells: flat, scaly cells on the surface called squamous cells; round cells called basal cells, and cells called melanocytes, which give the skin its color.

The most common types of skin cancer are basal cell cancer and squamous cell cancer. Skin cancer is more common in persons with light-colored skin who have spent a lot of time in the sunlight. Skin cancer can occur anywhere on the body, but it is most common in places that have been exposed to more sunlight, such as the face, neck, hands, and arms.

The most common sign of skin cancer is a change on the skin, such as a growth or a sore that will not heal. Sometimes there may be a small lump. This lump can be smooth, shiny and waxy looking, or it can be red or reddish brown. Skin cancer may also appear as a flat red spot that is rough or scaly. Not all changes in the skin are cancer, but it is very important to have a dermatologist evaluate any change that occurs in one's skin.

It is recommended that one check his/her skin on a regular basis and to have a skin examination every three years if between the ages of 20 and 40 and every year after age 40.

Cancer that develops in the pigment cells is called **melanoma** (see Figures 3–50 and 3–51). It usually occurs in adults, but may occasionally be found in children and adolescents. Melanoma strikes more than 50,000 Americans annually and causes an estimated 7,800 deaths.

Often the first sign of melanoma is change in the size, shape, or color of a mole. The ABCDs of melanoma describe the changes that can occur in a mole using the letters:

A—asymmetry; the shape of one half does not match the other.

B—border; the edges are ragged, notched, or blurred.

C—color; is uneven. Shades of black, brown, or tan are present. Areas of white, red, or blue may be seen.

D—diameter; there is a change in size.

Scientists have pinpointed a genetic marker that may serve as an early indicator for melanoma. Protein produced by the gene, known as Id1, was found in tissue samples of early-stage melanoma. If this research holds up, then a physician can biopsy a mole and if it is positive for Id1, it can be surgically removed. This is very important because the disease is curable if caught early, but is usually fatal if not.

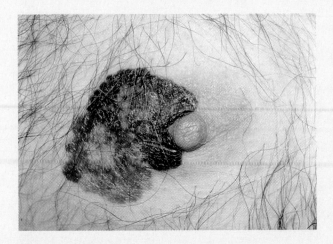

FIGURE 3–50

Melanoma. (Courtesy of Jason L. Smith, MD.)

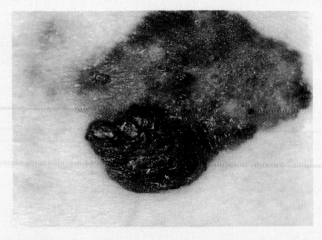

FIGURE 3–51

Melanoma, forearm. (Courtesy of Jason L. Smith, MD.)

Melanoma is a more serious type of cancer than basal cell or squamous cell cancers. Like most cancers, melanoma is best treated when it is found early. Melanoma can metastasize quickly to other parts of the body through the lymph system or through the blood.

Skin Signs

Skin signs are objective evidence of an illness or disorder. They can be seen, measured, or felt. They may be described as lesions that are circumscribed areas of pathologically altered tissue. Types of skin signs are shown and described in Figure 3–52.

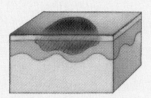

A macule is a discolored spot on the skin; freckle

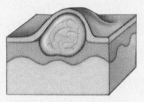

A pustule is a small, elevated, circumscribed lesion of the skin that is filled with pus; varicella (chickenpox)

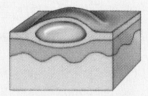

A wheal is a localized, evanescent elevation of the skin that is often accompanied by itching; urticaria

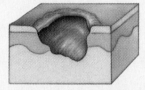

An erosion or ulcer is an eating or gnawing away of tissue; decubitus ulcer

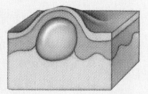

A papule is a solid, circumscribed, elevated area on the skin; pimple

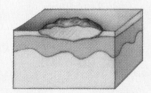

A crust is a dry, serous or seropurulent, brown, yellow, red, or green exudation that is seen in secondary lesions; eczema

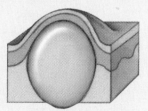

A nodule is a larger papule; acne vulgaris

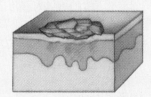

A scale is a thin, dry flake of cornified epithelial cells; psoriasis

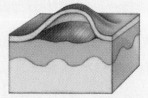

A vesicle is a small fluid filled sac; blister. A bulla is a large vesicle.

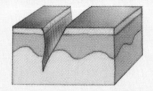

A fissure is a crack-like sore or slit that extends through the epidermis into the dermis; athlete's foot

---

FIGURE 3–52

Skin signs are objective evidence of an illness or disorder. They can be seen, measured, or felt.

✔ PATHOLOGY CHECKPOINT

Following is a concise list of the pathology-related terms that you've seen in the chapter. Review this checklist to make sure that you are familiar with the meaning of each term before moving on to the next section.

Conditions and Symptoms

- ❏ acne
- ❏ acrochordon
- ❏ actinic dermatitis
- ❏ albinism
- ❏ alopecia
- ❏ anhidrosis
- ❏ avulsion
- ❏ basal cell carcinoma
- ❏ bite
- ❏ boil
- ❏ bulla
- ❏ burn
- ❏ callus
- ❏ candidiasis
- ❏ carbuncle
- ❏ causalgia
- ❏ cellulites
- ❏ cicatrix
- ❏ comedo
- ❏ corn
- ❏ cyst
- ❏ decubitus
- ❏ dehiscence
- ❏ dermatitis
- ❏ dermomycosis
- ❏ ecchymosis
- ❏ eczema
- ❏ erythema
- ❏ erythroderma

- ❏ eschar
- ❏ excoriation
- ❏ exudate
- ❏ folliculitis
- ❏ herpes simplex
- ❏ hidradenitis
- ❏ hives
- ❏ hyperhydrosis
- ❏ icteric
- ❏ impetigo
- ❏ jaundice
- ❏ keloid
- ❏ lentigo
- ❏ leukoderma
- ❏ leukoplakia
- ❏ lupus
- ❏ melanocarcinoma
- ❏ melanoma
- ❏ miliaria
- ❏ mole
- ❏ onychitis
- ❏ onychomycosis
- ❏ pachyderma
- ❏ paronychia
- ❏ pediculosis
- ❏ petechiae
- ❏ pruritus
- ❏ psoriasis
- ❏ purpura
- ❏ roseola

- ❏ rubella
- ❏ rubeola
- ❏ scabies
- ❏ scar
- ❏ scleroderma
- ❏ seborrhea
- ❏ senile keratosis
- ❏ striae
- ❏ telangiectasia
- ❏ thermanesthesia
- ❏ tinea
- ❏ trichomycosis
- ❏ ulcer
- ❏ varicella
- ❏ vitiligo
- ❏ wart
- ❏ wound
- ❏ xanthoderma
- ❏ xanthoma
- ❏ xeroderma
- ❏ xerosis

Diagnosis and Treatment

- ❏ autograft
- ❏ dermatome
- ❏ hypodermic (injection)
- ❏ intradermal (injection)
- ❏ subcutaneous (injection)
- ❏ subungual
- ❏ rhytidoplasty

DRUG HIGHLIGHTS

Drugs that are used for dermatologic diseases or disorders include emollient, keratolytic, local anesthetic, antipruritic, antibiotic, antifungal, antiviral, anti-inflammatory, and antiseptic agents. Other drugs include Retin-A, Rogaine, and Botulinum toxin type A.

Emollients

Substances that are generally oily in nature. These substances are used for dry skin caused by aging, excessive bathing, and psoriasis.

Examples: Dermassage and Desitin.

Keratolytics

Agents that cause or promote loosening of horny (keratin) layers of the skin. These agents may be used for acne, warts, psoriasis, corns, calluses, and fungal infections.

Examples: Duofilm, Keralyt, and Compound W.

Local Anesthetic Agents

Agents that inhibit the conduction of nerve impulses from sensory nerves and thereby reduce pain and discomfort. These agents may be used topically to reduce discomfort associated with insect bites, burns, and poison ivy.

Examples: Solarcaine, Xylocaine, and Dyclone.

Antipruritic Agents

Agents that prevent or relieve itching.

Examples: Topical—PBZ (tripelennamine HCl); Oral—Benadryl (diphenhydramine HCl) and Atarax (hydroxyzine HCl).

Antibiotic Agents

Agents that destroy or stop the growth of microorganisms. These agents are used to prevent infection associated with minor skin abrasions and to treat superficial skin infections and acne. Several antibiotic agents are combined in a single product to take advantage of the different antimicrobial spectrum of each drug.

Examples: Neosporin, Polysporin, and Mycitracin.

Antifungal Agents

Agents that destroy or inhibit the growth of fungi and yeast. These agents are used to treat fungus and/or yeast infection of the skin, nails, and scalp.

Examples: Fungizone (amphotericin B), Lotrimin (clotrimazole) and Lamisil (terbinafine).

Antiviral Agents

Agents that combat specific viral diseases. *Zovirax (acyclovir)* is used in the treatment of herpes simplex virus types 1 and 2, varicella-zoster, Epstein-Barr, and cytomegalovirus. *Relenza (zanamivir)* has antiviral activity against influenza A and B viruses.

Anti-inflammatory Agents

Agents used to relieve the swelling, tenderness, redness, and pain of inflammation. Topically applied corticosteroids are used in the treatment of dermatitis and psoriasis.

Examples: Hydrocortisone, Decadron (dexamethasone), and Temovate (clobetasol propionate).

Oral corticosteroids are used in the treatment of contact dermatitis, such as in poison ivy, when the symptoms are severe.

Example: Sterapred (prednisone) 12-day unipak.

Antiseptic Agents

Agents that prevent or inhibit the growth of pathogens. Antiseptics are generally applied to the surface of living tissue.

Examples: Isopropyl alcohol and Zephrian (benzalkonium chloride)

Other Drugs

Retin-A (tretinoin) is available as a cream, gel, or liquid. It is used in the treatment of acne vulgaris. *Rogaine (minoxidil)* is available as a topical solution to stimulate hair growth. It was first approved as a treatment of male pattern baldness.

Botulinum Toxin Type A (Botox Cosmetic) is approved by the FDA to temporarily improve the appearance of moderate to severe frown lines between the eyebrows (glabellar lines). Small doses of a sterile, purified botulinum toxin are injected into the affected muscles and block the release of the chemical acetylcholine that would otherwise signal the muscle to contract. The toxin thus paralyzes or weakens the injected muscle.

DIAGNOSTIC & LAB TESTS

TEST	DESCRIPTION
tuberculosis skin tests (tū-bĕr″ kū-lō′ sĭs)	Tests performed to identify the presence of the *Tubercle bacilli*. The tine, Heaf, or Mantoux test may be used. The tine test and Heaf test are intradermal tests performed using a sterile, disposable, multiple-puncture lancet. The tuberculin is on metal tines that are pressed into the skin. A hardened raised area at the test site 48 to 72 hours later indicates the presence of the pathogens in the blood. In the **Mantoux** test 0.1 mL of purified protein derivative (PPD) tuberculin is intradermally injected. Test results are read 48 to 72 hours after administration.
sweat test (chloride) (swĕt)	A test performed on **sweat** to determine the level of chloride concentration on the skin. In **cystic fibrosis**, there is an increase in skin chloride.
Tzanck test (tsănk)	A microscopic examination of a small piece of tissue that has been surgically scraped from a pustule. The specimen is placed on a slide and stained, and the type of viral infection can be identified.
wound culture (woond)	A test done on wound exudate to determine the presence of microorganisms. An effective antibiotic can be prescribed for identified microbes.
biopsy (skin) (bī′ ŏp-sē)	Any skin lesion that exhibits signs or characteristics of malignancy may be excised and examined microscopically to establish a diagnosis. Usually only a small piece of living tissue is needed for examination.

ABBREVIATIONS

ABBREVIATION	MEANING	ABBREVIATION	MEANING
decub	decubitus	SLE	systemic lupus erythematosus
derm	dermatology	staph	staphylococcus
FB	foreign body	STD	skin test done
FUO	fever of undetermined origin	strep	streptococcus
H	hypodermic	STSG	split thickness skin graft
Hx	history	subcu, subq	subcutaneous
ID	intradermal	T	temperature
I&D	incision and drainage	TIMS	topical immunomodulators
NPUAP	National Pressure Ulcer Advisory Panel	TTS	transdermal therapeutic system
PUVA	psoralen-ultraviolet light	ung	ointment
SG	skin graft	UV	ultraviolet

STUDY AND REVIEW

Anatomy and Physiology

Write your answers to the following questions. Do not refer to the text.

1. Name the primary organ of the integumentary system. _____

2. Name the four accessory structures of the integumentary system.

    a. _____   b. _____

    c. _____   d. _____

3. State the four main functions of the skin.

    a. _____   b. _____

    c. _____   d. _____

4. The skin is essentially composed of two layers, the _____ and the

    _____.

5. Name the four strata of the epidermis.

    a. _____   b. _____

    c. _____   d. _____

6. _____ is a protein substance found in the dead cells of the epidermis.

7. _____ is a pigment that gives color to the skin.

8. The _____ is known as the corium or true skin.

9. Name the two layers of the part of the skin described in question 8.

    a. _____   b. _____

10. The crescent-shaped white area of the nail is the _____.

Word Parts

1. In the spaces provided, write the definition of these prefixes, roots, combining forms, and suffixes. Do not refer to the listings of medical words. Leave blank those words you cannot define.

2. After completing as many as you can, refer back to the medical word listings to check your work. For each word missed or left blank, write the word and its

definition several times on the margins of these pages or on a separate sheet of paper.

3. To maximize the learning process, it is to your advantage to do the following exercises as directed. To refer to the word building section before completing these exercises invalidates the learning process.

PREFIXES

Give the definitions of the following prefixes:

1. a-, an- _____

2. auto- _____

3. ec- _____

4. de- _____

5. ex- _____

6. hyper- _____

7. hypo- _____

8. intra- _____

9. par- _____

10. sub- _____

ROOTS AND COMBINING FORMS

Give the definitions of the following roots and combining forms:

1. acr/o _____

2. actin _____

3. aden _____

4. albin _____

5. carcin _____

6. caus _____

7. chym _____

8. coriat _____

9. cutane _____

10. derm _____

11. derm/a _____

12. dermat _____

13. dermat/o _____

14. derm/o _____

15. lopec _____

16. erythr/o _____

17. hidr _____

18. icter _____

19. kel _____

20. kerat _____

21. leuk/o _____

22. log _____

23. melan _____

24. melan/o _____

25. myc _____

26. onych _____

27. cellul _____

28. onych/o _____

29. pachy _____

30. pedicul _____

31. chord _____   32. rhytid/o _____

33. scler/o _____   34. seb/o _____

35. senile _____   36. therm _____

37. vuls _____   38. trich/o _____

39. ungu _____   40. xanth/o _____

41. xer/o _____   42. cubit _____

43. follicul _____   44. integument _____

45. jaund _____   46. plak _____

47. miliar _____   48. prurit _____

49. tel _____   50. ang/i _____

SUFFIXES

Give the definitions of the following suffixes:

1. -al _____   2. -algia _____

3. -on _____   4. -us _____

5. -derma _____   6. -ary _____

7. -esthesia _____   8. -graft _____

9. -ia _____   10. -ic _____

11. -ion _____   12. -ism _____

13. -ist _____   14. -itis _____

15. -logy _____   16. -ectasia _____

17. -oid _____   18. -oma _____

19. -osis _____   20. -ous _____

21. -plasty _____   22. -rrhea _____

23. -tome _____

Identifying Medical Terms

In the spaces provided, write the medical terms for the following meanings:

1. _____ Inflammation of the skin caused by exposure to actinic rays

2. _____ Pertaining to the skin

3. _____ Inflammation of the skin

4. _____ The study of the skin

5. _____ Severe itching

6. _____ Condition of excessive sweating

7. _____ Pertaining to under the skin

8. _____ Pertaining to jaundice

9. _____ Inflammation of the nail

10. _____ Thick skin

11. _____ Inability to distinguish between the sensations of heat and cold

12. _____ Yellow skin

Spelling

In the spaces provided, write the correct spelling of these misspelled terms.

1. caualgia _____

2. dermomcosis _____

3. echymosis _____

4. exoriation _____

5. hyprhidrosis _____

6. melnoma _____

7. onychomyosis _____

8. rhytdoplasty _____

9. sleroderma _____

10. sebrrhea _____

Matching

Select the appropriate lettered meaning for each word listed below.

_____ 1. acne

_____ 2. alopecia

_____ 3. cicatrix

_____ 4. comedo

_____ 5. decubitus

_____ 6. dehiscence

_____ 7. exudate

_____ 8. leukoplakia

_____ 9. petechiae

_____ 10. pruritus

a. Small, pinpoint, purplish hemorrhagic spots on the skin

b. The production of pus or serum

c. A severe itching

d. An inflammatory condition of the sebaceous gland and the hair follicles

e. The scar left after the healing of a wound

f. Loss of hair, baldness

g. White spots or patches formed on the mucous membrane of the tongue or cheek

h. Blackhead

i. The separation or bursting open of a surgical wound

j. A bedsore

k. A slough, scab

Abbreviations

Place the correct word, phrase, or abbreviation in the space provided.

1. fever of undetermined origin _____

2. transdermal therapeutic system _____

3. H _____

4. incision and drainage _____

5. skin graft _____

6. ID _____

7. temperature _____

8. ultraviolet _____

9. FB _____

10. PUVA _____

Diagnostic and Laboratory Tests

Select the best answer to each multiple choice question. Circle the letter of your choice.

1. The _____ _____ is an intradermal test performed using a sterile, disposable, multiple puncture lancet.
   a. sweat test
   b. Mantoux test
   c. tine test
   d. Tzanck test

2. A test done on wound exudate to determine the presence of microorganisms is:
   a. sweat test
   b. biopsy
   c. Tzanck test
   d. wound culture

3. A microscopic examination of a small piece of tissue that has been surgically scraped from a pustule is:
   a. Tzanck test
   b. sweat test
   c. biopsy
   d. wound culture

4. Tests performed to identify the presence of the *Tubercle bacilli* include the:
   a. tine, Heaf, and sweat
   b. tine, Heaf, and Mantoux
   c. tine, Tzanck, and Mantoux
   d. tine, Mantoux, and sweat

5. The _____ test may be used to determine the level of chloride concentration on the skin.
   a. sweat
   b. Tzanck
   c. tine
   d. Mantoux

CASE STUDY

CONTACT DERMATITIS, POISON IVY

Read the following case study and then answer the questions that follow.

A 42-year-old male was seen by a dermatologist; the following is a synopsis of his visit.

Present History: The patient states that he apparently came into contact with poison ivy while working in the yard.

Signs and Symptoms: Moderate itching at first and then severe (pruritus); small blisters (vesicles) on right and left forearms; redness of skin (erythroderma) with moderate to severe swelling (edema) of surrounding tissue.

Diagnosis: Contact Dermatitis Poison Ivy. See Figure 3–21 and Figure 3–53.

Treatment: Antipruritic agent—hydroxyzine HCl 25 mg Tab; corticosteroid therapy—Temovate 0.05% cream—apply twice a day to affected area; and Sterapred 12 day unipak—take as directed.

Prevention: Stay away from poison ivy. When working outside in the yard, wear clothing that covers arms and legs. After working in the yard, immediately take a bath or shower to remove any possible contamination of skin with poison ivy.

FIGURE 3–53

Poison ivy. (Source: Pearson Education/PH College.)

CASE STUDY QUESTIONS

1. When the patient states that his itching has become severe, you would note this in his chart as _____.

2. It is noted in the chart that small blisters appear on the right and left forearms. What is the medical term for blisters? _____

3. A person who is sensitive to poison ivy may develop what condition? _____

4. An _____ agent is used to help relieve itching.

5. Temovate 0.05% cream is a form of _____ therapy.

6. Prevention is a key concept in today's health care delivery system. List three preventive measures that this patient might have to use to help and/or prevent his condition.
   a. _____
   b. _____
   c. _____

7. What is the medical term for redness of the skin? _____

8. What medical term do you use to chart "moderate to severe swelling of surrounding tissue"? _____

MedMedia Wrap-Up

www.prenhall.com/rice

Additional interactive resources and activities for this chapter can be found on the Companion Website. For animations, videos, audio glossary, and review, access the accompanying CD-ROM in this book.

Audio Glossary
Medical Terminology Exercises & Activities
Pathology Spotlights
Terminology Translator
Animations
Videos

Objectives
Medical Terminology Exercises & Activities
Audio Glossary
Drug Updates
Medical Terminology in the News

THE SKELETAL SYSTEM $\quad$ 4

OBJECTIVES

On completion of this chapter, you will be able to:

- Describe the skeletal system.
- Describe various types of body movement.
- Describe the vertebral column.
- Identify abnormal curvatures of the spine.
- Describe the male and female pelvis.
- Describe various types of fractures.
- Describe skeletal differences of the child and the older adult.
- Analyze, build, spell, and pronounce medical words.
- Describe each of the conditions presented in the Pathology Spotlights.
- Complete the Pathology Checkpoint.
- Review Drug Highlights presented in this chapter.
- Provide the description of diagnostic and laboratory tests related to the skeletal system.
- Identify and define selected abbreviations.
- Successfully complete the study and review section.

MedMedia
www.prenhall.com/rice

Additional interactive resources and activities for this chapter can be found on the Companion Website. For Terminology Translator, animations, videos, audio glossary, and review, access the accompanying CD-ROM in this book.

Anatomy and Physiology Overview

T he skeletal system is composed of 206 **bones** that, together with **cartilage** and **ligaments**, make up the **framework** or skeleton of the body. The skeleton can be divided into two main groups of bones: the **axial skeleton** consisting of 80 bones and the **appendicular skeleton** with the remaining 126 bones (see Fig. 4–1). The principal bones of the axial skeleton are the skull, spine, ribs, and sternum. The shoulder girdle, arms, and hands and the pelvic girdle, legs, and feet are the primary bones of the appendicular skeleton.

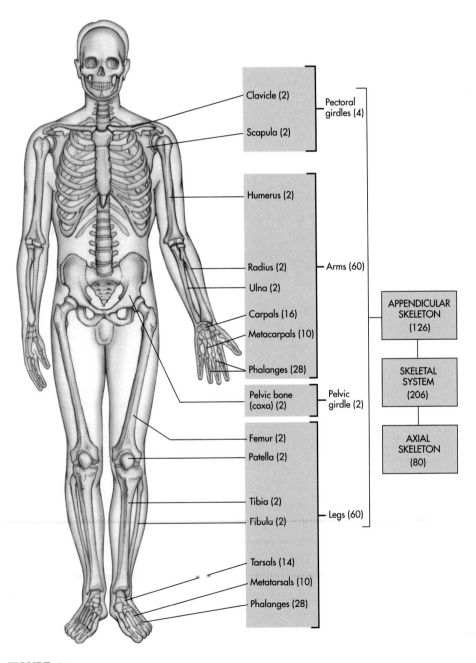

FIGURE 4–1

The principal bones of the appendicular skeleton.

THE SKELETAL SYSTEM

Organ/Structure	Primary Functions
Bones	Provide shape, support, protection, and the framework of the body
	Serve as a storage place for mineral salts, calcium, and phosphorus
	Play an important role in the formation of blood cells
	Provide areas for the attachment of skeletal muscles
	Help make movement possible
Cartilages	Form the major portion of the embryonic skeleton and part of the skeleton in adults
Ligaments	Connect the articular ends of bones, binding them together and facilitating or limiting motion
	Connect cartilage and other structures
	Serve to support or attach fascia or muscles

BONES

The **bones** are the primary organs of the skeletal system and are composed of about 50% water and 50% solid matter. The solid matter in bone is a calcified, rigid substance known as **osseous tissue**.

Classification of Bones

Bones are classified according to their shapes. See Figure 4–2. Table 4–1 classifies the bones and gives an example of each type.

Functions of Bones

The following are the main functions of bones:

1. Provide shape, support, and the framework of the body
2. Provide protection for internal organs
3. Serve as a storage place for mineral salts, calcium, and phosphorus
4. Play an important role in the formation of blood cells as **hemopoiesis** takes place in the bone marrow
5. Provide areas for the attachment of skeletal muscles
6. Help to make movement possible through **articulation**

The Structure of a Long Bone

Long bones, such as the tibia, femur, humerus, or radius, have most of the features found in all bones. These features are shown in Figure 4–3.

TABLE 4–1   CLASSIFICATIONS OF BONE

Shape	Example of This Classification
Flat	Ribs, scapula, parts of the pelvic girdle, bones of the skull
Long	Tibia, femur, humerus, radius
Short	Carpal, tarsal
Irregular	Vertebrae, ossicles of the ear
Sesamoid	Patella
Sutural or Wormian	Between the flat bones of the skull

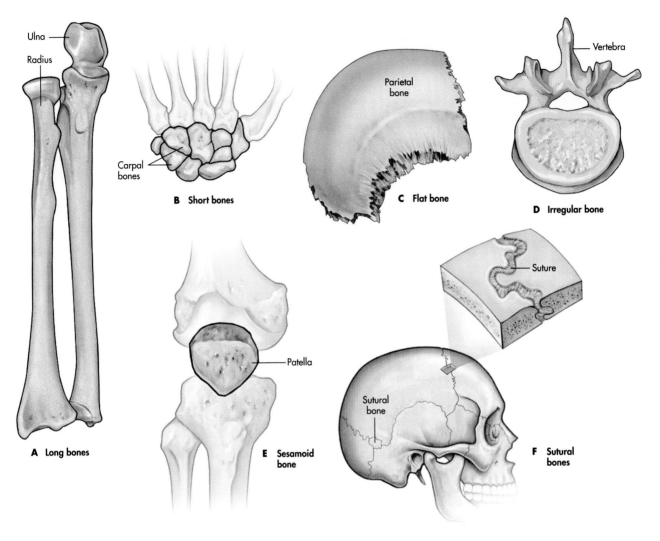

FIGURE 4–2

Classification of bones by shape.

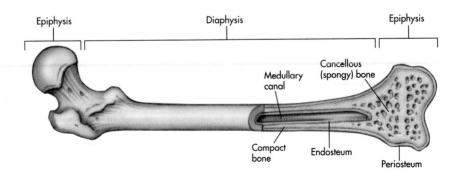

FIGURE 4–3

The features found in a long bone.

Epiphysis. The ends of a developing bone

Diaphysis. The shaft of a long bone

Periosteum. The membrane that forms the covering of bones except at their articular surfaces

Compact bone. The dense, hard layer of bone tissue

Medullary canal. A narrow space or cavity throughout the length of the diaphysis

Endosteum. A tough, connective tissue membrane lining the medullary canal and containing the bone marrow

Cancellous or spongy bone. The reticular tissue that makes up most of the volume of bone

Bone Markings

There are certain commonly used terms that describe the **markings of bones**. These markings are listed for your better understanding of their role in joining bones together, providing areas for muscle attachments, and serving as a passageway for blood vessels, ligaments, and nerves See Table 4–2.

JOINTS AND MOVEMENT

A **joint** is an articulation, a place where two or more bones connect. See Figure 4–4. The manner in which bones connect determines the type of movement allowed at the joint. Joints are classified as:

Synarthrosis. Does not permit movement. The bones are in close contact with each other and there is no joint cavity. An example is the *cranial sutures*.

Amphiarthrosis. Permits very slight movement. An example of this type of joint is the *vertebrae*.

Diarthrosis. Allows free movement in a variety of directions. Examples of this type of joint are the *knee, hip, elbow, wrist,* and *foot.*

TABLE 4–2 BONE MARKINGS

Marking	Description of the Bone Structure
Condyle	A rounded process that enters into the formation of a joint, articulation
Crest	A ridge on a bone
Fissure	A slit-like opening between two bones
Foramen	An opening in the bone for blood vessels, ligaments, and nerves
Fossa	A shallow depression in or on a bone
Head	The rounded end of a bone
Meatus	A tube-like passage or canal
Process	An enlargement or protrusion of a bone
Sinus	An air cavity within certain bones
Spine	A pointed, sharp, slender process
Sulcus	A groove, furrow, depression, or fissure
Trochanter	A very large process of the femur
Tubercle	A small, rounded process
Tuberosity	A large, rounded process

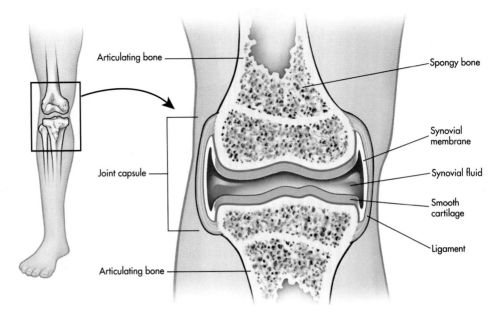

Articulating bone

Spongy bone

Synovial membrane

Joint capsule

Synovial fluid

Smooth cartilage

Articulating bone

Ligament

FIGURE 4–4

Typical joint.

The following terms describe types of body movement that occur at the **diarthrotic joints** (Fig. 4–5):

Abduction. The process of moving a body part away from the middle

Adduction. The process of moving a body part toward the middle

Circumduction. The process of moving a body part in a circular motion

Dorsiflexion. The process of bending a body part backward

Eversion. The process of turning outward

Extension. The process of straightening a flexed limb

Flexion. The process of bending a limb

Inversion. The process of turning inward

Pronation. The process of lying prone or face downward; also the process of turning the hand so the palm faces downward

Protraction. The process of moving a body part forward

Retraction. The process of moving a body part backward

Rotation. The process of moving a body part around a central axis

Supination. The process of lying supine or face upward; also the process of turning the palm or foot upward

THE VERTEBRAL COLUMN

The **vertebral column** is composed of a series of separate bones (**vertebrae**) connected in such a way as to form four spinal curves. These curves have been identified as the cervical, thoracic, lumbar, and sacral. The cervical curve consists of the first 7 verte-

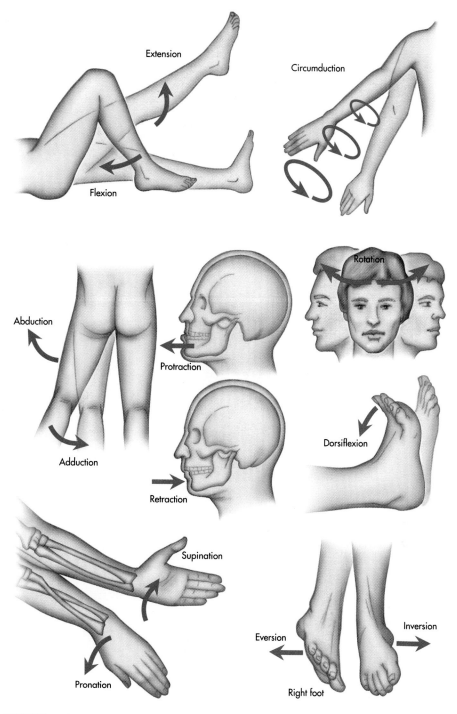

FIGURE 4–5

Types of body movements.

brae, the *thoracic curve* consists of the next 12 vertebrae, the *lumbar curve* consists of the next 5 vertebrae, and the *sacral curve* consists of the sacrum and coccyx (tailbone) (Fig. 4–6).

It is known that a curved structure has more strength than a straight structure. The spinal curves of the human body are most important, as they help support the weight of the body and provide the balance that is necessary to walk on two feet.

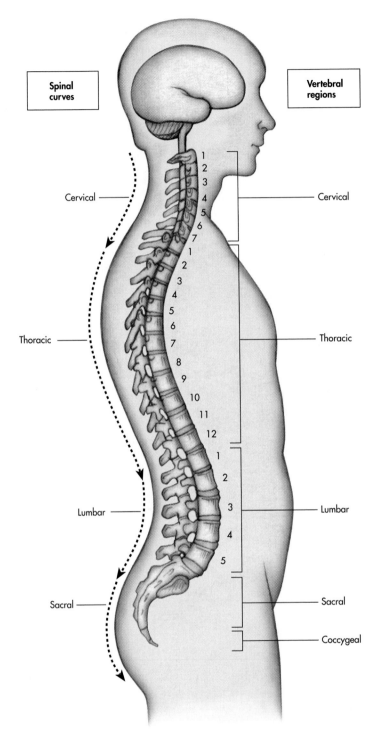

FIGURE 4–6

Vertebral regions, showing the four spinal curves.

THE MALE AND FEMALE PELVIS

The **pelvis** is the lower portion of the trunk of the body. It forms a basin bound anteriorly and laterally by the hip bones and posteriorly by the sacrum and coccyx.

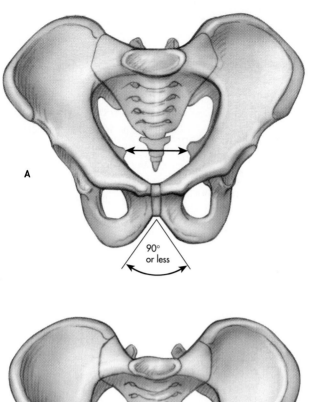

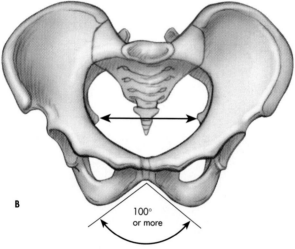

FIGURE 4–7

(A) The male pelvis is shaped like a funnel, forming a narrower outlet than the female. (B) The female pelvis is shaped like a basin.

The bony pelvis is formed by the sacrum, the coccyx, and the bones that form the hip and pubic arch, the ilium, pubis, and ischium. These bones are separate in the child, but become fused in adulthood.

The Male Pelvis

The **male pelvis** is shaped like a *funnel,* forming a narrower outlet than the female. It is heavier and stronger than the female pelvis; therefore, it is more suited for lifting and running. See Figure 4–7A.

The Female Pelvis

The **female pelvis** is shaped like a *basin.* It may be oval to round, and it is wider than the male pelvis. The female pelvis is constructed to accommodate the fetus during pregnancy and to facilitate its downward passage through the pelvic cavity in childbirth. In general the female pelvis is broader and lighter than the male pelvis. See Figure 4–7B.

L I F E S P A N
CONSIDERATIONS

■ THE CHILD

Bone begins to develop during the second month of fetal life as cartilage cells enlarge, break down, disappear, and are replaced by bone-forming cells called **osteoblasts**. Most bones of the body are formed by this process, known as **endochondral ossification**. In this process, the bone cells deposit organic substances in the spaces vacated by cartilage to form bone matrix. As this process proceeds, blood vessels form within the bone and deposit salts such as calcium and phosphorus that serve to harden the developing bone.

The **epiphyseal plate** is the center for longitudinal bone growth in children. See Figure 4–8. It is possible to determine the biological age of a child from the development of epiphyseal ossification centers as shown radiographically.

About 3 years from the onset of puberty the ends of the long bones (**epiphyses**) knit securely to their shafts (**diaphysis**), and further growth can no longer take place.

The bones of children are more resilient, tend to bend, and before breaking may become deformed. Fracture healing occurs more quickly in children because there is a rich blood supply to bones and their periosteum is thick and osteogenic activity is high.

Calcium is critical to the strength of bones. The daily recommendations of calcium by age group are:

1 to 3 years	500 mg
4 to 8 years	800 mg
9 to 13 years	1300 mg
14 to 18 years	1300 mg

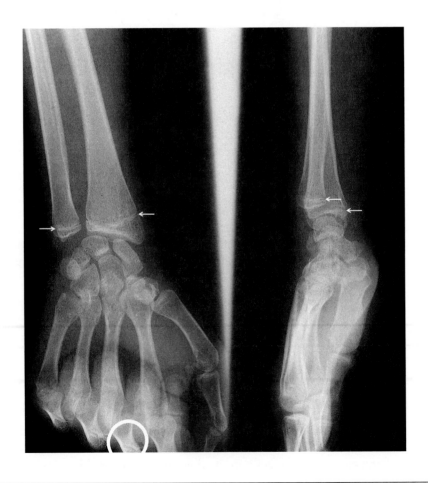

FIGURE 4–8

Epiphyseal plate (arrows). (Courtesy of Teresa Resch.)

■ THE OLDER ADULT

Women build bone until about age 35, then begin to lose about 1% of bone mass annually. Men usually start losing bone mass 10 to 20 years later. Most of the skeletal system changes that take place during the aging process involve changes in connective tissue. There is a loss of bone mass and bone strength due to the loss of bone mineral content during later life. Calcium salts may be deposited in the matrix and cartilage becomes hard and brittle.

Age-related **osteoporosis**, loss of bone mass, is often seen in older women and men. Other changes that may occur involve the joints as there is diminished viscosity of the synovial fluid, degeneration of collagen and elastin cells, outgrowth of cartilaginous clusters in response to continuous wear and tear, and formation of scar tissues and calcification in the joint capsules.

Low levels of calcium can make people more susceptible to osteoporosis and stress fractures, especially those that are commonly seen in the older adult. Bone healing in the older adult is slower and impaired due to osteoblasts being less able to use calcium to restructure bone tissue. The National Academy of Sciences suggests that people 51 and older consume 1200 mg of calcium per day to help strengthen their bones. See Table 4–3 for good sources of calcium.

TABLE 4–3 GOOD SOURCES OF CALCIUM

1 cup skim milk	300 mg
1 cup yogurt	450 mg
1 cup calcium-fortified orange juice	300 mg
1 ounce cheddar cheese	205 mg
1 ounce Swiss cheese	270 mg
1 cup tofu (processed with calcium sulfate)	520 mg
1 cup turnip greens, cooked	200 mg
3 ounces canned salmon (with bones)	205 mg
7-inch homemade waffle	179 mg
1 cup broccoli, cooked	90 mg

Dairy foods supply 75% of all the calcium in the U.S. food supply. People who get 2 to 3 servings of dairy products a day are most likely meeting the recommended requirements. For those who do not like milk or dairy products, there are other ways of getting enough calcium per day.

BUILDING YOUR MEDICAL VOCABULARY

This section provides the foundation for learning medical terminology. Medical words can be made up of four different types of word parts:

- Prefixes (P)
- Roots (R)
- Combining forms (CF)
- Suffixes (S)

By connecting various word parts in an organized sequence, thousands of words can be built and learned. In this text the word list is alphabetized so one can see the variety of meanings created when common prefixes and suffixes are repeatedly applied to certain word roots and/or combining forms. Words shown in pink are additional words related to the content of this chapter that are not built from word parts. These words are included to enhance your vocabulary. Note: an asterisk icon ✱ indicates terms that are covered in the Pathology Spotlights section in this chapter.

MEDICAL WORD	WORD PARTS (WHEN APPLICABLE)			DEFINITION
	Part	Type	Meaning	
acetabular (ăs″ ĕ-tăb′ ū-lăr)	acetabul -ar	R S	vinegar cup pertaining to	The cup-shaped socket of the hipbone into which the thighbone fits
achondroplasia (ă-kŏn″ drō-plā′ sĭ-ă)	a chondr/o -plasia	P CF S	without cartilage formation	A defect in the formation of cartilage at the epiphyses of long bones
acroarthritis (ăk″ rō-ăr-thrī′ tĭs)	acr/o arthr -itis	CF R S	extremity joint inflammation	Inflammation of the joints of the hands or feet
acromion (ă-krō′ mĭ-ŏn)	acr -omion	R S	extremity, point shoulder	The projection of the spine of the scapula that forms the point of the shoulder and articulates with the clavicle
ankylosis (ăng″ kĭ-lō′ sĭs)	ankyl -osis	R S	stiffening, crooked condition of	A condition of stiffening of a joint
arthralgia (ăr-thrăl′ jĭ-ă)	arthr -algia	R S	joint pain	Pain in a joint
arthritis (ăr-thrī′ tĭs)	arthr -itis	R S	joint inflammation	Inflammation of a joint. ✳ See Pathology Spotlight: Arthritis.
arthrocentesis (ăr″ thrō-sĕn-tē′ sĭs)	arthr/o -centesis	CF S	joint surgical puncture	Surgical puncture of a joint for removal of fluid
arthroplasty (ăr″ thrō-plăs′ tē)	arthr/o -plasty	CF S	joint surgical repair	Surgical repair of a joint
arthroscope (ăr-thrŏs′ kōp)	arthr/o -scope	CF S	joint instrument	An instrument used to examine the interior of a joint
bone marrow transplant (bōn măr′ ō trăns′ plănt)				The surgical process of transferring bone marrow from a donor to a patient
bursa (bŭr′ sah)				A small space between muscles, tendons, and bones that is lined with synovial membrane and contains a fluid, *synovia*
bursitis (bŭr-sī′ tĭs)	burs -itis	R S	a pouch inflammation	Inflammation of a bursa
calcaneal (kăl-kā′ nē-ăl)	calcan/e -al	CF S	heel bone pertaining to	Pertaining to the heel bone

MEDICAL WORD	WORD PARTS (WHEN APPLICABLE)			DEFINITION
	Part	**Type**	**Meaning**	
calcium (kăl′ sĭ-ŭm)				A mineral that is essential for bone growth, teeth development, blood coagulation, and many other functions
carpal (kär′ pəl)	carp -al	R S	wrist pertaining to	Pertaining to the wristbone
carpal tunnel syndrome (kär′ pĕl tŭn′ ĕl sĭn′ drōm)				A condition caused by compression of the median nerve by the carpal ligament; symptoms: soreness, tenderness, weakness, pain, tingling, and numbness at the wrist. ✷ See Figure 4–14 in Pathology Spotlight: Carpal Tunnel Syndrome.
cartilage (kär′ tĭ-lĭj)	cartil -age	R S	gristle related to	A specialized type of fibrous connective tissue present in adults, which forms the major portion of the embryonic skeleton
cast (kăst)				A type of material, made of plaster of paris, sodium silicate, starch, or dextrin used to immobilize a fractured bone, a dislocation, or a sprain
chondral (kŏn′ drăl)	chondr -al	R S	cartilage pertaining to	Pertaining to cartilage
chondrocostal (kŏn″ drō-kŏs′ tăl)	chondr/o cost -al	CF R S	cartilage rib pertaining to	Pertaining to the rib cartilage
clavicular (klă-vĭk′ ū-lăr)	clavicul -ar	R S	little key pertaining to	Pertaining to the clavicle
coccygeal (kŏk-sĭj′ ĭ-ăl)	coccyg/e -al	CF S	tailbone pertaining to	Pertaining to the coccyx
coccygodynia (kŏk-sĭ-gō-dĭn′ ĭ-ă)	coccyg/o -dynia	CF S	tailbone pain	Pain in the coccyx
collagen (kŏl′ă-jĕn)	coll/a -gen	CF S	glue formation, produce	A fibrous insoluble protein found in the connective tissue, skin, ligaments, and cartilage
connective (kə′ nĕk′ tĭv)	connect -ive	R S	to bind together nature of	That which connects or binds together
costal (kăst′ əl)	cost -al	R S	rib pertaining to	Pertaining to the rib

MEDICAL WORD	WORD PARTS (WHEN APPLICABLE)			DEFINITION
	Part	**Type**	**Meaning**	
costosternal (kŏs″ tō-stěr′ năl)	cost/o stern -al	CF R S	rib sternum pertaining to	Pertaining to a rib and the sternum
craniectomy (krā″ nĭ-ĕk′ tŏ-mē)	cran/i -ectomy	CF S	skull excision	Surgical excision of a portion of the skull
craniotomy (krā″ nĭ-ŏt′ ō-mē)	crani/o -tomy	CF S	skull incision	Incision into the skull
dactylic (dăk′ tĭl′ ĭk)	dactyl -ic	R S	finger or toe pertaining to	Pertaining to the finger or toe
dactylogram (dăk-til′ə grăm)	dactyl/o -gram	CF S	finger or toe mark, record	A fingerprint
dislocation (dĭs″ lō-kā′ shŭn)	dis locat -ion	P R S	apart to place process	The displacement of a bone from a joint
femoral (fĕm′ ŏr-ăl)	femor -al	R S	femur pertaining to	Pertaining to the femur; the thighbone
fibular (fĭb′ ū-lăr)	fibul -ar	R S	fibula pertaining to	Pertaining to the fibula
fixation (fĭks-ā′ shŭn)	fixat -ion	R S	fastened process	The process of holding or fastening in a fixed position; making rigid, immobilizing
flatfoot (flăt fŭt)				An abnormal flatness of the sole and arch of the foot; also known as *pes planus*
genu valgum (jē′ nū văl gŭm)				Knock-knee
genu varum (jē′ nū vā′ rŭm)				Bowleg
gout (gowt)				A hereditary metabolic disease that is a form of acute arthritis; usually begins in the knee or foot but can affect any joint. ✳ See Pathology Spotlight: Arthritis.
hallux (hăl″ ŭks)				The big or great toe
hammertoe (hăm′ er-tō)				An acquired flexion deformity of the interphalangeal joint

MEDICAL WORD	WORD PARTS (WHEN APPLICABLE)			DEFINITION
	Part	**Type**	**Meaning**	
humeral (hū′ mĕr-ăl)	humer -al	R S	humerus pertaining to	Pertaining to the humerus
hydrarthrosis (hi″ drăr-thrō′ sĭs)	hydr arthr -osis	P R S	water joint condition of	Condition of fluid in a joint
iliac (ĭl′ ē-ăk)	ili -ac	R S	ilium pertaining to	Pertaining to the ilium
iliosacral (ĭl″ ĭ-ō-sā′ krăl)	ili/o sacr -al	CF R S	ilium sacrum pertaining to	Pertaining to the ilium and the sacrum
intercostal (ĭn″ tēr-kŏs′ tăl)	inter cost -al	R R S	between rib pertaining to	Pertaining to between the ribs
ischial (ĭs′ kĭ-al)	isch/i -al	CF S	ischium, hip pertaining to	Pertaining to the ischium, hip
ischialgia (ĭs″ kĭ-ăl′ jĭ-ă)	isch/i -algia	CF S	ischium, hip pain	Pain in the ischium, hip
kyphosis (kī-fō′ sĭs)	kyph -osis	R S	a hump condition of	Humpback
laminectomy (lăm″ ĭ-nĕk′ tō-mē)	lamin -ectomy	R S	lamina (thin plate) excision	Surgical excision of a vertebral posterior arch
ligament (lĭg′ ă-mĕnt)				A band of fibrous connective tissue that connects bones, cartilages, and other structures; also serves as a place for the attachment of fascia or muscle
lordosis (lŏr-dō′ sĭs)	lord -osis	R S	bending condition of	Abnormal anterior curvature of the spine
lumbar (lŭm′ băr)	lumb -ar	R S	loin pertaining to	Pertaining to the loins
lumbodynia (lŭm″ bō-dĭn′ ĭ-ă)	lumb/o -dynia	CF S	loin pain	Pain in the loins
mandibular (măn-dĭb′ ū-lăr)	mandibul -ar	R S	lower jawbone pertaining to	Pertaining to the lower jawbone
maxillary (măk′ sĭ-lĕr″ ē)	maxill -ary	R S	jawbone pertaining to	Pertaining to the upper jawbone

MEDICAL WORD	WORD PARTS (WHEN APPLICABLE)			DEFINITION
	Part	**Type**	**Meaning**	
meniscus (měn-ĭs′ kŭs)	menisc -us	R S	crescent pertaining to	Crescent-shaped interarticular fibrocartilage found in certain joints, especially the lateral and medial *menisci* (semilunar cartilages) of the knee joint
metacarpal (mět″ ă-kär′ pəl)	meta carp -al	P R S	beyond wrist pertaining to	Pertaining to the bones of the hand
metacarpectomy (mět″ ă-kär-pěk′ tō-mē)	meta carp -ectomy	P R S	beyond wrist excision	Surgical excision of one or more bones of the hand
myelitis (mī-ě-li′ tĭs)	myel -itis	R S	marrow inflammation	Inflammation of the bone marrow
myeloma (mī-ē-lō′ mă)	myel -oma	R S	marrow tumor	A tumor of the bone marrow
myelopoiesis (mī′ ěl-ō-poy-ē′ sĭs)	myel/o -poiesis	CF S	marrow formation	The formation of bone marrow
olecranal (ō-lěk′ răn-ăl)	olecran -al	R S	elbow pertaining to	Pertaining to the elbow
osteoarthritis (ŏs″ tē-ō-ăr-thrī′ tĭs)	oste/o arthr -itis	CF R S	bone joint inflammation	Inflammation of the bone and joint. ✳ See Pathology Spotlight: Arthritis.
osteoblast (ŏs′ tē-ō-blăst″)	oste/o -blast	CF S	bone immature cell, germ cell	A bone-forming cell
osteocarcinoma (ŏs″ tē-ō-kăr″ sĭn-ō mă)	oste/o carcin -oma	CF R S	bone cancer tumor	A cancerous tumor of a bone; new growth of epithelial tissue
osteochondritis (ŏs″ tē-ō-kŏn-drī′ tĭs)	oste/o chondr -itis	CF R S	bone cartilage inflammation	Inflammation of the bone and cartilage
osteogenesis (ŏs″ tē-ō-jěn′ ě-sĭs)	oste/o -genesis	CF S	bone formation, produce	The formation of bone
osteomalacia (ŏs″ tē-ō-măl-ā′ shĭ-ă)	oste/o -malacia	CF S	bone softening	Softening of the bones
osteomyelitis (ŏs″ tē-ō-mī″ ěl-ī′ tĭs)	oste/o myel -itis	CF R S	bone marrow inflammation	Inflammation of the bone marrow. See Figure 4–9.

MEDICAL WORD	WORD PARTS (WHEN APPLICABLE)			DEFINITION
	Part	Type	Meaning	
osteopenia (ŏs″ tē-ō-pē′ nĭ-ă)	oste/o -penia	CF S	bone lack of	A lack of bone tissue
osteoporosis (ŏs″ tē-ō-por-ō′ sĭs)	oste/o por -osis	CF R S	bone a passage condition of	A condition that results in reduction of bone mass. ✱ See Figure 4–17 in Pathology Spotlight: Osteoporosis.
osteosarcoma (ŏs″ tē-ō-săr-kō′ mă)	oste/o sarc -oma	CF R S	bone flesh tumor	A malignant tumor of the bone; cancer arising from connective tissue
osteotome (ŏs′ tē-ō-tōm″)	oste/o -tome	CF S	bone instrument to cut	An instrument used for cutting bone
patellar (pă-tĕl′ ăr)	patell -ar	R S	kneecap pertaining to	Pertaining to the patella
pedal (pĕd′l)	ped -al	R S	foot pertaining to	Pertaining to the foot
periosteoedema (pĕr″ ĭ-ŏs″ tē-ō-ĕ-dē′ mă)	peri oste/o -edema	P CF S	around bone swelling	Swelling around a bone
phalangeal (fă-lăn′ jē-ăl)	phalang/e -al	CF S	closely knit row pertaining to	Pertaining to the bones of the fingers and the toes
phosphorus (fŏs′ fō-rŭs)	phos phor -us	R R S	light carrying pertaining to	A mineral that is essential in bone formation, muscle contraction, and many other functions
polyarthritis (pŏl″ ē-ăr-thrī′ tĭs)	poly arthr -itis	P R S	many, much joint inflammation	Inflammation of more than one joint
rachigraph (rā′ kĭ-grăf)	rach/i -graph	CF S	spine to write	An instrument used to measure the curvature of the spine
radial (rā′ dĭ-ăl)	rad/i -al	CF S	radius pertaining to	Pertaining to the radius
radiograph (rā′ dĭ-ō-grăf)	radi/o -graph	CF S	ray record	An x-ray photograph of a body part
reduction (rē-dŭk′ shŭn)	re duct -ion	P R S	back to lead process	The manipulative or surgical procedure used to correct a fracture or hernia

MEDICAL WORD	WORD PARTS (WHEN APPLICABLE)			DEFINITION
	Part	**Type**	**Meaning**	
rheumatoid arthritis (roo′ mă-toyd ăr-thrī′ tĭs)	rheumat -oid arthr -itis	R S R S	discharge resemble joint inflammation	A chronic systemic disease characterized by inflammation of the joints, stiffness, pain, and swelling that results in crippling deformities. ✴ See Pathology Spotlight: Arthritis.
rickets (rĭk′ ĕts)				A deficiency condition in children primarily caused by a lack of vitamin D; may also result from inadequate intake or excessive loss of calcium
scapular (skăp′ ū-lăr)	scapul -ar	R S	shoulder blade pertaining to	Pertaining to the shoulder blade
scoliosis (skō″ lĭ-ō′ sĭs)	scoli -osis	R S	curvature condition of	A condition of lateral curvature of the spine. ✴ See Pathology Spotlight: Abnormal Curvatures of the Spine.
spinal (spī′ năl)	spin -al	R S	spine pertaining to	Pertaining to the spine
splint (splĭnt)				An appliance used for fixation, support, and rest of an injured body part
spondylitis (spŏn-dĭl-ī′ tĭs)	spondyl -itis	R S	vertebra inflammation	Inflammation of one or more vertebrae
sprain (sprān)				Twisting of a joint that causes pain and disability
spur (spər)				A sharp or pointed projection, as on a bone
sternal (stēr′ năl)	stern -al	R S	sternum pertaining to	Pertaining to the sternum
sternotomy (stĕr-nŏt′ ō-mē)	stern/o -tomy	CF S	sternum incision	Surgical incision of the sternum
subclavicular (sŭb″ klă-vĭk′ ū-lăr)	sub clavicul -ar	P R S	under, beneath a little key pertaining to	Pertaining to beneath the clavicle
subcostal (sŭb-kŏs′ tăl)	sub cost -al	P R S	under, beneath rib pertaining to	Pertaining to beneath the ribs
submaxilla (sŭb″ măk-sĭl′ ă)	sub maxilla	P R	under, beneath jaw	The lower jaw or mandible

MEDICAL WORD	WORD PARTS (WHEN APPLICABLE)			DEFINITION
	Part	**Type**	**Meaning**	
symphysis (sĭm′ fĭ-sĭs)	sym -physis	P S	together growth	A growing together
tennis elbow (tĕn′ ĭs ĕl′ bō)				A chronic condition characterized by pain caused by excessive pronation and supination activities of the forearm; usually caused by strain, as in playing tennis
tenonitis (tĕn″ ō-nī′ tĭs)	tenon -itis	R S	tendon inflammation	Inflammation of a tendon
tibial (tĭb′ ĭ-ăl)	tibi -al	R S	tibia pertaining to	Pertaining to the tibia
traction (trăk′ shŭn)	tract -ion	P S	to draw process	The process of drawing or pulling on bones or muscles to relieve displacement and facilitate healing
ulnar (ŭl′ năr)	uln -ar	R S	elbow pertaining to	Pertaining to the elbow
ulnocarpal (ŭl″ nō-kăr′ păl)	uln/o carp -al	CF R S	elbow wrist pertaining to	Pertaining to the ulna side of the wrist
vertebral (vĕr′ tĕ-brăl)	vertebr -al	R S	vertebra pertaining to	Pertaining to a vertebra
vertebrosternal (vĕr″ tĕ-brō-ster′ năl)	vertebr/o stern -al	CF R S	vertebra sternum pertaining to	Pertaining to a vertebra and the sternum
xiphoid (zĭf′ oyd)	xiph -oid	R S	sword resemble	Resembling a sword

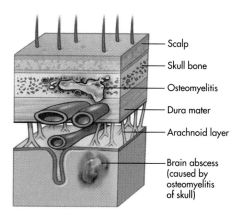
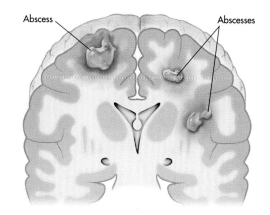

FIGURE 4–9

Abscess of the brain due to osteomyelitis.

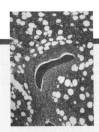

PATHOLOGY SPOTLIGHTS

Abnormal Curvatures of the Spine

Abnormal curvatures of the spine include scoliosis, lordosis, and kyphosis.

In scoliosis, there is an abnormal lateral curvature of the spine. This condition usually appears in adolescence, during periods of rapid growth. Treatment modalities may include the application of a cast, brace, traction, electrical stimulation, and/or surgery. See Figure 4–10C.

In lordosis, there is an abnormal anterior curvature of the spine. This condition may be referred to as "swayback" as the abdomen and buttocks protrude due to an exaggerated lumbar curvature. See Figure 4–10B.

In kyphosis, the normal thoracic curvature becomes exaggerated, producing a "hump-back" appearance. This condition may be caused by a congenital defect, a disease process such as tuberculosis and/or syphilis, a malignancy, compression fracture, faulty posture, osteoarthritis, rheumatoid arthritis, rickets, osteoporosis, or other conditions. See Figure 4–10A.

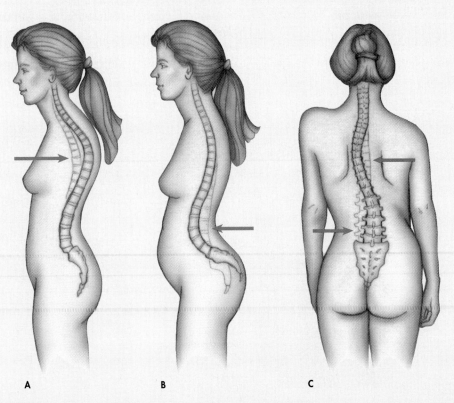

A   B   C

FIGURE 4–10

Abnormal curvatures of the spine: (A) kyphosis; (B) lordosis; and (C) scoliosis.

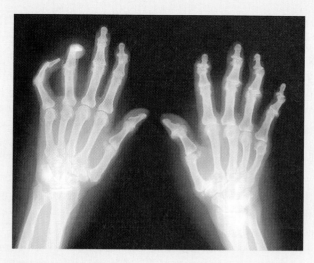

FIGURE 4–11

X-ray showing typical joint changes associated with osteoarthritis.
(Source: Vince Michaels/Getty Images/Stone Allstock.)

Arthritis

Arthritis is a disease that involves inflammation of one or more joints. Joint inflammation can result from various disease processes. Some of the most common include injury to a joint (including fracture), an attack on the joints by the body itself (an autoimmune disease), or "wear and tear" on joints.

Osteoarthritis is the most common type of arthritis in the United States. Osteoarthritis often results from years of accumulated "wear and tear" on joints, and tends to occur in the elderly in hips, knees, and finger joints. See Figure 4–11. In people over 55 years of age, women are more likely to suffer from osteoarthritis. Obesity, a history of trauma, and various genetic and metabolic diseases also increase the risk of osteoarthritis.

Gout, which is seen most often in men over 40 years of age, is caused by the formation of crystals in the joints, which leads to inflammation. See Figure 4–12. Autoimmune disorders, such as **rheumatoid arthritis** (see Figure 4–13), lupus, and scleroderma, can cause arthritis as well. In these diseases, the immune system attacks the joints.

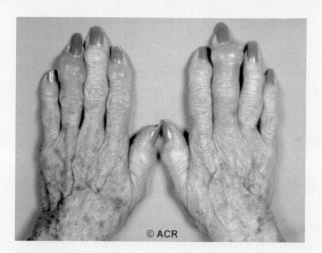

FIGURE 4–12

Gout of the finger joint. (Source: Reprinted from the Clinical Slide Collection on the Rheumatic Diseases, © 1991, 1995. Used by permission of the American College of Rheumatology.)

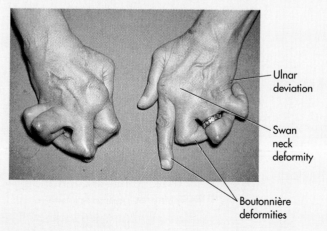

Ulnar deviation

Swan neck deformity

Boutonnière deformities

FIGURE 4–13

Typical hand deformities associated with rheumatoid arthritis.
(Source: Biophoto Associates/Photo Researchers, Inc.)

Arthritis can occur in both males and females of all ages. About 37 million people in America, almost 1 in 7 people, have arthritis of some kind. Symptoms of arthritis may include joint pain and swelling, morning stiffness, warmth around a joint, redness of the skin around a joint, and reduced ability to move a joint.

Arthritis treatment varies, depending on the particular cause, how severe the disease is, which joints are affected, to what degree the patient is affected, and the person's age, occupation, and daily activities. Treatment aims at reducing pain and discomfort and preventing further disability. Simple modifications in daily activities, along with adequate rest and appropriate forms of exercise may help to relieve some of the symptoms. For example, low impact aerobic exercise (such as swimming) can relieve joint strain. In other cases, more extensive therapies are needed. Treatment usually consists of exercise, heat or cold treatments, methods to protect the joints, various medications, and possibly surgery.

Medications to reduce joint pain and joint swelling in all types of arthritis may include acetaminophen, aspirin, nonsteroidal anti-inflammatory drugs (NSAIDs), corticosteroids, and other immunosuppressive drugs (drugs that suppress the immune system). The most recent breakthrough in rheumatoid arthritis treatment has been the development of "anti-biologic" medications that target individual molecules to reduce inflammation. These medications, which include etanercept (Enbrel) and infliximab (Remicade), are administered by injection or intravenously.

Carpal Tunnel Syndrome

Bounded by bones and ligaments, the carpal tunnel is a narrow passageway about as big around as one's thumb and located on the palm side of the wrist. This tunnel protects a main nerve to the hand and nine tendons that bend the fingers. When pressure is put on the median nerve it produces the numbness, pain and, eventually, hand weakness that characterize carpal tunnel syndrome. See Figure 4–14.

Injury or trauma to the area, including repetitive movement of the wrists, can cause swelling of the tissues and carpal tunnel syndrome. This type of repetitive-action injury may be caused by sports such as tennis and racquetball, or may occur during sewing, keyboarding, driving, assembly-line work, painting, writing, use of tools (especially hand tools or tools that vibrate), or similar activities. Some of the jobs associated with carpal tunnel syndrome include those that involve data entry or use of vibrating tools; mining; and professional musicians.

The condition occurs most often in people 30 to 60 years old, and is five times more common in women than men. Certain conditions, such as obesity, diabetes, and rheumatoid arthritis, have been associated with an increased risk of carpal tunnel syndrome.

Fortunately, for most people who develop carpal tunnel syndrome, proper treatment usually can relieve the pain and numbness and restore normal use of the wrists and hand. Treatment may include having the patient wear night splints for the wrist for several weeks. If unsuccessful, the splints are worn during the day and heat or cold compresses may be added. Other types of treatment include modifications in the work area. This may include ensuring that the keyboard is low enough so that the wrists aren't bent upwards during keyboarding, and modifying work duties or recreational activities. There are many specialized devices designed for the workplace to reduce the stress placed on the wrist and improve carpal tunnel syndrome.

Medications used in the treatment of carpal tunnel syndrome include NSAIDs such as ibuprofen or naproxen. The carpal tunnel may also be injected with corticosteroids. Surgery, called carpal tunnel release, may help those with carpal tunnel syndrome. This procedure cuts into the ligament to relieve pressure on the median nerve. Surgery has about an 85 percent success rate, depending on the severity of the problem. Surgery reduces the pressure on the nerve, but the damaged nerve must heal for the symptoms to improve. This can take months and in some cases the nerve may not fully heal. In severe cases, electromyography or nerve conduction studies may be used to follow the recovery of the nerve.

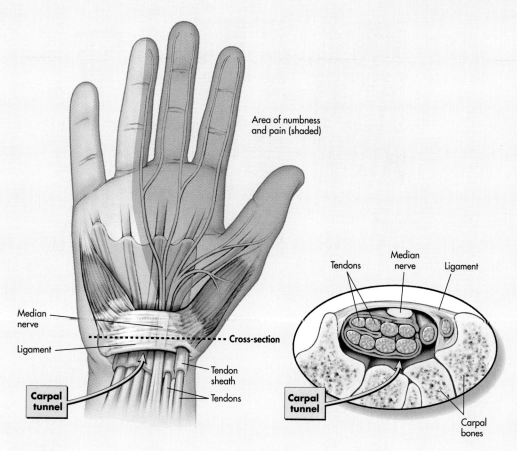

Area of numbness and pain (shaded)

Median nerve

Ligament

Cross-section

Carpal tunnel

Tendon sheath

Tendons

Tendons

Median nerve

Ligament

Carpal tunnel

Carpal bones

FIGURE 4–14

Cross-section of wrist showing tendons and nerves involved in carpal tunnel syndrome.

Fractures

Fractures are classified according to their external appearance, the site of the fracture, and the nature of the crack or break in the bone. Important fracture types are indicated in Figure 4–15 and several have been paired with representative x-rays. Many fractures fall in more than one category. For example, Colles' fracture is a transverse fracture, but depending on the injury it may also be a comminuted fracture that can be either open or closed. The following list provides a summary of the types of fractures:

- **Closed,** or **simple,** fractures do not involve a break in the skin; they are completely internal.
- **Open,** or **compound,** fractures are more dangerous because the fracture projects through the skin and there is a possibility of infection or hemorrhage. See Figure 4–16.
- **Comminuted** fractures shatter the affected part into a multitude of bony fragments.
- **Transverse** fractures break the shaft of a bone across its longitudinal axis.
- **Greenstick** fractures usually occur in children whose long bones have not fully ossified; only one side of the shaft is broken, and the other is bent (like a greenstick).
- **Spiral** fractures are spread along the length of a bone and are produced by twisting stresses.
- **Colles'** fracture is often the result of reaching out to cushion a fall; there is a break in the distal portion of the radius.
- **Pott's** fracture occurs at the ankle and affects both bones of the lower leg (fibula and tibia).

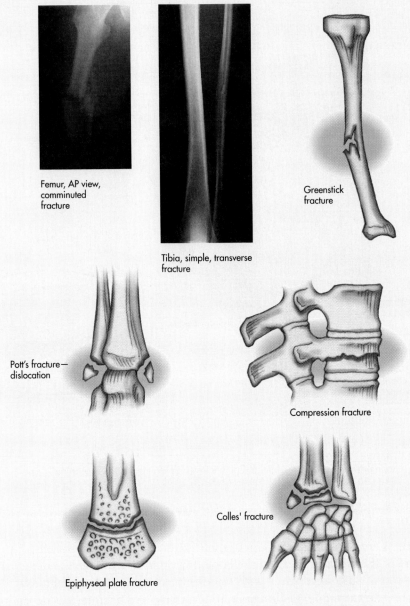

Femur, AP view, comminuted fracture

Tibia, simple, transverse fracture

Greenstick fracture

Pott's fracture— dislocation

Compression fracture

Epiphyseal plate fracture

Colles' fracture

FIGURE 4–15

Various types of fractures.

- **Compression** fractures occur in vertebrae subjected to extreme stresses, as when one falls and lands on his/her bottom.
- **Epiphyseal** fractures usually occur where the matrix is undergoing calcification and chondrocytes (cartilage cells) are dying; this type of fracture is seen in children.

Osteoporosis

Osteoporosis is a condition characterized by the progressive loss of bone density and thinning of bone tissue. See Figure 4–17. Osteoporosis occurs when the body fails to form enough new bone, or when too much old bone is reabsorbed by the body, or both. Osteoporosis frequently occurs when there is not enough calcium in the diet. The body then uses calcium stored in bones, weakening them and making them vulnerable to breaking. See Table 4–2 for good sources of calcium. Sufficient intake of vitamin D is also important for calcium absorption.

Vitamin D is absorbed through the skin from sunlight, and is also found in fatty fish, fish oils, and eggs from hens that have been fed vitamin D. Older adults are more prone to vitamin D deficiency.

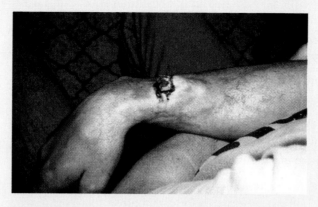

FIGURE 4–16

An open fracture of the wrist. (Source: Pearson Education/PH College.)

Osteoporosis affects more than 25 million Americans, most of them women 50 to 70 years of age. Each year, the disease leads to 1.4 million bone fractures, including more than 500,000 vertebral fractures, 300,000 hip fractures, and 200,000 wrist fractures.

There are some risk factors involved in developing osteoporosis and these are:

- Family history of osteoporosis
- Lack of exercise, especially weight-bearing exercise, which stimulates bone growth

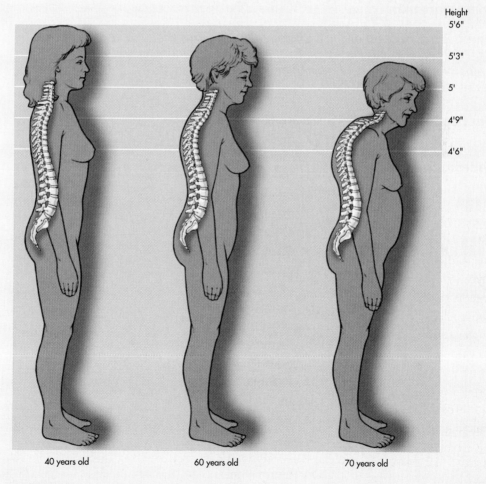

FIGURE 4–17

Spinal changes caused by osteoporosis.

- Thin, petite build
- Never been pregnant
- Early menopause (before 45 years)
- Prone to fractures, and loss of height in the past few years
- Avoided dairy products as a child
- Smoking, drinking alcoholic beverages
- Diet high in salt, caffeine, or fat
- Insufficient intake of vitamin D

Tests such as bone mineral density (BMD) testing are most frequently used for diagnosis and evaluation of osteoporosis. Treatments for osteoporosis focus on slowing down or stopping bone loss, preventing bone fractures by minimizing the risk of falls, and controlling pain associated with the disease. Hormone deficiencies (estrogen in women and testosterone in men) are the leading cause of osteoporosis. For this reason, estrogen replacement therapy is frequently used as a treatment for osteoporosis in women. Other drug treatments include biphosphonates such as alendronate (Fosamax).

✓PATHOLOGY CHECKPOINT

Following is a concise list of the pathology-related terms that you've seen in the chapter. Review this checklist to make sure that you are familiar with the meaning of each term before moving on to the next section.

Conditions and Symptoms

- ❑ achondroplasia
- ❑ acroarthritis
- ❑ ankylosis
- ❑ arthralgia
- ❑ arthritis
- ❑ bursitis
- ❑ carpal tunnel syndrome
- ❑ coccygodynia
- ❑ dislocation
- ❑ flatfoot
- ❑ genu valgum
- ❑ genu varum
- ❑ gout
- ❑ hammertoe
- ❑ hydrarthrosis
- ❑ ischialgia
- ❑ kyphosis
- ❑ lordosis
- ❑ lumbodynia

- ❑ myelitis
- ❑ myeloma
- ❑ osteoarthritis
- ❑ osteocarcinoma
- ❑ osteochondritis
- ❑ osteomalacia
- ❑ osteomyelitis
- ❑ osteopenia
- ❑ osteoporosis
- ❑ osteosarcoma
- ❑ periosteoedema
- ❑ polyarthritis
- ❑ rheumatoid arthritis
- ❑ rickets
- ❑ scoliosis
- ❑ spondylitis
- ❑ sprain
- ❑ spur
- ❑ tenonitis
- ❑ tennis elbow

Diagnosis and Treatment

- ❑ arthrocentesis
- ❑ arthroplasty
- ❑ arthroscope
- ❑ bone marrow transplant
- ❑ cast
- ❑ craniectomy
- ❑ craniotomy
- ❑ fixation
- ❑ laminectomy
- ❑ metacarpectomy
- ❑ osteotome
- ❑ rachigraph
- ❑ radiograph
- ❑ reduction
- ❑ splint
- ❑ sternotomy
- ❑ traction

DRUG HIGHLIGHTS

DRUG HIGHLIGHTS

Drugs that are generally used for skeletal system diseases and disorders include anti-inflammatory agents, disease-modifying antirheumatic drugs (DMARDs), COX-2 inhibitors, antitumor necrosis factor drugs, agents used to treat gout, agents used to treat or prevent postmenopausal osteoporosis, and analgesics. Fractures, arthritis, rheumatoid arthritis, bursitis, carpal tunnel syndrome, dislocation, osteoporosis, and pain are some of the conditions involving the skeletal system and the need for pharmacologic therapy.

Anti-inflammatory Agents	Relieve the swelling, tenderness, redness, and pain of inflammation. These agents may be classified as steroidal (corticosteroids) and nonsteroidal.
Corticosteroids (Glucocorticoids)	Steroid substance with potent anti-inflammatory effects. *Examples: Depo-Medrol (methylprednisolone acetate), Aristocort (triamcinolone), Celestone (betamethasone), and Decadron (dexamethasone).*
Nonsteroidal (NSAIDs)	Agents that are used in the treatment of arthritis and related disorders. *Examples: Bayer Aspirin (acetylsalicylic acid), Motrin (ibuprofen), Feldene (piroxicam), Orudis (ketoprofen), and Naprosyn (naproxen).*
Disease-modifying Antirheumatic Drugs (DMARDs)	May influence the course of the disease progression; therefore, their introduction in early rheumatoid arthritis is recommended to limit irreversible joint damage. *Examples: gold preparations Ridaura (auranofin) and Solganol (aurothioglucose); antimalarial Plaquenil Sulfate (hydroxychloroquine sulfate); a chelating agent Cuprimine (penicillamine) and the immunosuppressants Rheumatrex (methotrexate), Imuran (azathioprine), and Cytoxan (cyclophosphamide).*
COX-2 Inhibitors	Cyclooxygenase (COX) is an enzyme involved in many aspects of normal cellular function and also in the inflammatory response. COX-2 is found in joints and other areas affected by inflammation, such as occurs with osteoarthritis and rheumatoid arthritis. Inhibition of COX-2 reduces the production of compounds associated with inflammation and pain. *Examples: Celebrex (celecoxib), Vioxx (rofecoxib), and Mobic (meloxicam).*
Antitumor Necrosis Factor (Anti-TNF) Drugs	These drugs have evolved out of the biotechnology industry and seem to slow, if not halt altogether, the destruction of the joints by disrupting the activity of tumor necrosis factor (TNF), a substance involved in the body's immune response. *Example: Enbrel (etanercept).*
Agents Used to Treat Gout	Acute attacks of gout are treated with colchicine. Once the acute attack of gout has been controlled, drug therapy to control hyperuricemia can be initiated. *Example: Benemid (probenecid), Anturane (sulfinpyrazone), and Zyloprim (allopurinol).*
Agents Used to Treat or Prevent Postmenopausal Osteoporosis	Include *Fosamax (alendronate sodium)* and *Actonel (risedronate).* Fosamax reduces the activity of the cells that cause bone loss and increases the amount of bone in most patients. Actonel inhibits osteoclast-mediated bone resorption and modulates bone metabolism. To receive the clinical benefits of either of these drugs the patient must be informed and follow the prescribed drug regimen.
Analgesics	Agents that relieve pain without causing loss of consciousness. They are classified as narcotic or non-narcotic.
Narcotic	*Examples: Demerol (meperidine HCl) and morphine sulfate.*
Non-narcotic	*Examples: Tylenol (acetaminophen), aspirin, ibuprofen (Advil, Motrin, Nuprin), and Naprosyn (naproxen).*

DIAGNOSTIC & LAB TESTS

DIAGNOSTIC & LAB TESTS

TEST	DESCRIPTION
arthrography (ăr-thrŏg′ ră-fē)	A diagnostic examination of a joint (usually the knee) in which air and then a radiopaque contrast medium are injected into the joint space, x-rays are taken, and internal injuries of the meniscus, cartilage, and ligaments may be seen, if present.
arthroscopy (ăr-thrŏs′ kō-pē)	The process of examining internal structures of a joint via an arthroscope; usually done after an arthrography and before joint surgery.
goniometry (gō″ nē-ŏm′ ĕt-rē)	The measurement of joint movements and angles via a goniometer.
photon absorptiometry (fō′ tŏn ăb-sorp′ shē-ŏm′ ĕt-rē)	A bone scan that uses a low beam of radiation to measure bone-mineral density and bone loss in the lumbar vertebrae; useful in monitoring osteoporosis.
thermography (thĕr-mŏg′ ră-fē)	The process of recording heat patterns of the body's surface; can be used to investigate the pathophysiology of rheumatoid arthritis.
x-ray (ĕks′ rā)	The examination of bones by use of an electromagnetic wave of high energy produced by the collision of a beam of electrons with a target in a vacuum tube; used to identify fractures and pathologic conditions of the bones and joints such as rheumatoid arthritis, spondylitis, and tumors.
alkaline phosphatase blood test (ăl′ kă-līn fŏs′ fă-tās)	A blood test to determine the level of alkaline phosphatase; increased in osteoblastic bone tumors, rickets, osteomalacia, and during fracture healing.
antinuclear antibodies (ANA) (ăn″ tĭ-nū′ klē-ăr ăn′ tĭ-bŏd″ ēs)	Present in a variety of immunologic diseases; positive result may indicate rheumatoid arthritis.
calcium (Ca) blood test (kăl′ sē-ŭm)	The calcium level of the blood may be increased in metastatic bone cancer, acute osteoporosis, prolonged immobilization, and during fracture healing; may be decreased in osteomalacia and rickets.
C-Reactive protein blood test (sē-rē-ăk″ tĭv prō′ tē-in)	Positive result may indicate rheumatoid arthritis, acute inflammatory change, and widespread metastasis.
phosphorus (P) blood test (fŏs′ fō-rŭs)	Phosphorus level of the blood may be increased in osteoporosis and fracture healing.
serum rheumatoid factor (RF) (sē′ rŭm roo′ mă-toyd făk′ tōr)	An immunoglobulin present in the serum of 50 to 95% of adults with rheumatoid arthritis.
uric acid blood test (ū′ rĭk ăs′ ĭd)	Uric acid is increased in gout, arthritis, multiple myeloma, and rheumatism.

ABBREVIATIONS

ABBREVIATIONS

ABBREVIATION	MEANING
ACL	anterior cruciate ligament
AP	anteroposterior
BMD	bone mineral density (test)
CDH	congenital dislocation of hip
C 1	cervical vertebra, first
C 2	cervical vertebra, second
C 3	cervical vertebra, third
Ca	calcium
DJD	degenerative joint disease
Fx	fracture
JRA	juvenile rheumatoid arthritis
jt	joint
KJ	knee jerk
L 1	lumbar vertebra, first
L 2	lumbar vertebra, second
L 3	lumbar vertebra, third
LAC	long arm cast
lig	ligament

ABBREVIATION	MEANING
LLC	long leg cast
LLCC	long leg cylinder cast
OA	osteoarthritis
ORTHO	orthopedics, orthopaedics
PCL	posterior cruciate ligament
PEMFs	pulsing electromagnetic fields
PWB	partial weight bearing
RA	rheumatoid arthritis
SAC	short arm cast
SLC	short leg cast
SPECT	single photon emission computed tomography
T 1	thoracic vertebra, first
T 2	thoracic vertebra, second
T 3	thoracic vertebra, third
TMJ	temporomandibular joint
Tx	traction

STUDY AND REVIEW

Anatomy and Physiology

Write your answers to the following questions. Do not refer to the text.

1. The skeletal system is composed of _____ bones.

2. Name the two main divisions of the skeletal system.

    a. _____   b. _____

3. Name five classifications of bone and give an example of each.

    a. _____   Example _____

    b. _____   Example _____

    c. _____   Example _____

    d. _____   Example _____

    e. _____   Example _____

4. State the six main functions of the skeletal system.

    a. _____   b. _____

    c. _____   d. _____

    e. _____   f. _____

5. Define the following features of a long bone:

    a. Epiphysis _____

    b. Diaphysis _____

    c. Periosteum _____

    d. Compact bone _____

    e. Medullary canal _____

    f. Endosteum _____

    g. Cancellous or spongy bone _____

6. Match the term in column one with its definition from column two. Place the correct number from column two in the space provided in column one.

_____ a. Meatus	1. An air cavity within certain bones
_____ b. Head	2. A shallow depression in or on a bone
_____ c. Tuberosity	3. A pointed, sharp, slender process
_____ d. Process	4. A large, rounded process
_____ e. Condyle	5. A groove, furrow, depression, or fissure
_____ f. Tubercle	6. A tube-like passage or canal
_____ g. Crest	7. An opening in the bone for blood vessels, ligaments, and nerves
_____ h. Trochanter	8. A rounded process that enters into the formation of a joint, articulation
_____ i. Sinus	9. A ridge on a bone
_____ j. Fissure	10. A small, rounded process
_____ k. Fossa	11. The rounded end of a bone
_____ l. Spine	12. A slit-like opening between two bones
_____ m. Foramen	13. An enlargement or protrusion of a bone
_____ n. Sulcus	14. A very large process of the femur

7. Name the three classifications of joints.

a. _____   b. _____

c. _____

8. _____ is the process of moving a body part away from the middle.

9. Adduction is _____.

10. _____ is the process of moving a body part in a circular motion.

11. Dorsiflexion is _____.

12. _____ is the process of turning outward.

13. Extension is _____.

14. _____ is the process of bending a limb.

15. Inversion is _____.

16. _____ is the process of lying face downward.

17. Protraction is _____.

18. _____ is the process of moving a body part backward.

19. Rotation is _____.

20. _____ is the process of lying face upward.

Word Parts

1. In the spaces provided, write the definition of these prefixes, roots, combining forms, and suffixes. Do not refer to the listings of medical words. Leave blank those words you cannot define.

2. After completing as many as you can, refer back to the medical word listings to check your work. For each word missed or left blank, write the word and its definition several times on the margins of these pages or on a separate sheet of paper.

3. To maximize the learning process, it is to your advantage to do the following exercises as directed. To refer to the word building section before completing these exercises invalidates the learning process.

PREFIXES

Give the definitions of the following prefixes:

1. a- _____   2. dis- _____

3. hydr- _____   4. inter- _____

5. meta- _____   6. peri- _____

7. poly- _____   8. sub- _____

9. sym- _____   10. re- _____

ROOTS AND COMBINING FORMS

Give the definitions of the following roots and combining forms:

1. acetabul _____   2. cartil _____

3. acr _____   4. acr/o _____

5. ankyl _____   6. arthr _____

7. arthr/o _____   8. burs _____

9. calcan/e _____   10. locat _____

11. carcin _____   12. carp _____

13. carp/o _____   14. chondr _____

15. chondr/o _____

16. clavicul _____

17. fixat _____

18. coccyg/e _____

19. coccyg/o _____

20. coll/a _____

21. duct _____

22. connect _____

23. cost _____

24. cost/o _____

25. menisc _____

26. phos _____

27. cran/i _____

28. crani/o _____

29. dactyl _____

30. dactyl/o _____

31. femor _____

32. phor _____

33. fibul _____

34. radi/o _____

35. humer _____

36. ili _____

37. ili/o _____

38. isch/i _____

39. kyph _____

40. lamin _____

41. lord _____

42. lumb _____

43. lumb/o _____

44. mandibul _____

45. maxill _____

46. maxilla _____

47. myel _____

48. myel/o _____

49. rheumat _____

50. olecran _____

51. oste/o _____

52. patell _____

53. tract _____

54. ped _____

55. phalang/e _____

56. por _____

57. rachi _____

58. radi _____

59. sacr _____

60. sarc _____

61. scapul _____

62. scoli _____

63. scoli/o _____

64. spin _____

65. spondyl _____

66. stern _____

67. stern/o _____

68. tenon _____

69. tibi _____

70. uln _____

71. uln/o _____

72. vertebr _____

73. vertebr/o _____

74. xiph _____

SUFFIXES

Give the definitions of the following suffixes:

1. -ac _____

2. -al _____

3. -algia _____

4. -ar _____

5. -ary _____

6. -blast _____

7. -centesis _____

8. -age _____

9. -ion _____

10. -dynia _____

11. -ectomy _____

12. -edema _____

13. -gen _____

14. -genesis _____

15. -gram _____

16. -graph _____

17. -ic _____

18. -itis _____

19. -ive _____

20. -scope _____

21. -malacia _____

22. -us _____

23. -oid _____

24. -oma _____

25. -omion _____

26. -osis _____

27. -penia _____

28. -physis _____

29. -plasia _____

30. -plasty _____

31. -poiesis _____

32. -tome _____

33. -tomy _____

Identifying Medical Terms

In the spaces provided, write the medical terms for the following meanings:

1. _____ Inflammation of the joints of the hands or feet

2. _____ The condition of stiffening of a joint

3. _____ Inflammation of a joint

4. _____ Pertaining to the heel bone

5. _____ Pertaining to cartilage

6. _____ Pain in the coccyx

7. _____ Pertaining to the rib

8. _____ Surgical excision of a portion of the skull

9. _____ Pertaining to the finger or toe

10. _____ Condition of fluid in a joint

11. _____ Pertaining to between the ribs

12. _____ Pain in the hip

13. _____ Pertaining to the loins

14. _____ A tumor of the bone marrow

15. _____ Inflammation of the joint and bone

16. _____ Inflammation of the bone marrow

17. _____ A lack of bone tissue

18. _____ Pertaining to the foot

19. _____ Resembling a sword

Spelling

In the spaces provided, write the correct spelling of these misspelled terms:

1. acrmoin _____

2. arthrscope _____

3. buritis _____

4. chondblast _____

5. conective _____

6. cranplasty _____

7. dislocaton _____

8. ischal _____

9. melyitis _____

10. ostchonditis _____

11. phosphous _____

12. patelar _____

13. phalangal _____

14. rachgraph _____

15. scolosis _____

16. spondlitis _____

17. symphsis _____

18. tenonis _____

19. ulncarpal _____

20. vertbral _____

Matching

Select the appropriate lettered meaning for each word listed below.

_____ 1. arthroscope

_____ 2. carpal tunnel syndrome

_____ 3. fixation

_____ 4. gout

_____ 5. hammertoe

_____ 6. kyphosis

_____ 7. metacarpal

_____ 8. rickets

_____ 9. tennis elbow

_____10. ulnar

a. A deficiency condition in children primarily caused by a lack of vitamin D

b. An acquired flexion deformity of the interphalangeal joint

c. A hereditary metabolic disease that is a form of acute arthritis

d. A chronic condition characterized by pain that is caused by excessive pronation and supination activities of the forearm

e. Making rigid, immobilizing

f. Pertaining to the elbow

g. Pertaining to the bones of the hand

h. Humpback

i. An instrument used to examine the interior of a joint

j. A condition caused by compression of the median nerve by the carpal ligament

k. Pertaining to the knee

Abbreviations

Place the correct word, phrase, or abbreviation in the space provided.

1. congenital dislocation of hip _____

2. degenerative joint disease _____

3. LLC _____

4. OA _____

5. pulsing electromagnetic fields _____

6. RA _____

7. single photon emission computed tomography _____

8. T1 _____

9. TMJ _____

10. traction _____

Diagnostic and Laboratory Test

Select the best answer to each multiple choice question. Circle the letter of your choice.

1. _____ is a diagnostic examination of a joint in which air and, then, a radiopaque contrast medium are injected into the joint space, x-rays are taken, and internal injuries of the meniscus, cartilage, and ligaments may be seen, if present.
   a. Arthroscopy
   b. Goniometry
   c. Arthrography
   d. Thermography

2. The process of recording heat patterns of the body's surface is:
   a. arthrography
   b. arthroscopy
   c. goniometry
   d. thermography

3. _____ is increased in gout, arthritis, multiple myeloma, and rheumatism.
   a. Calcium
   b. Phosphorus
   c. Uric acid
   d. Alkaline phosphatase

4. _____ level of the blood may be increased in osteoporosis and fracture healing.
   a. Antinuclear antibodies
   b. Phosphorus
   c. Uric acid
   d. Alkaline phosphatase

5. _____ is/are present in a variety of immunologic diseases.
   a. Alkaline phosphatase
   b. Antinuclear antibodies
   c. C-Reactive protein
   d. Uric acid

CASE STUDY   OSTEOPOROSIS

Read the following case study and then answer the questions that follow.

A 62-year-old female was seen by a physician; the following is a synopsis of her visit.

Present History: The patient states that she seems to be shorter, her back "hurts" all the time, and she has developed a humpback.

Signs and Symptoms: Loss of height, kyphosis, and pain in the back.

Diagnosis: Osteoporosis (postmenopausal)

Treatment: Actonel (risedronate sodium); one 5mg tablet orally, taken daily. Begin a regular exercise program, a diet rich in calcium, phosphorus, magnesium, and vitamins A, C, D, the B-complex vitamins, and analgesics for pain.

Prevention: Know the risk factors involved in developing osteoporosis, follow a regular exercise program, and include a diet rich in calcium, phosphorus, magnesium, and vitamins A, C, D, and the B-complex vitamins. For more information on osteoporosis you can call the National Osteoporosis Foundation at 1–202–223–2226.

Good sources of **vitamin A** are dairy products, fish liver oils, animal liver, green and yellow vegetables. Good sources of **vitamin D** are ultraviolet rays, dairy products, and commercial foods that contain supplemental vitamin D (milk and cereals). Good sources of **vitamin C** are citrus fruits, tomatoes, melons, fresh berries, raw vegetables, and sweet potatoes. Good sources of the **B-complex vitamins** are organ meats, dried beans, poultry, eggs, yeast, fish, whole grains, and dark-green vegetables. Good sources of **calcium** are dairy products, beans, cauliflower, egg yolk, molasses, leafy green vegetables, tofu, sardines, clams, and oysters. Good sources of **phosphorus** are dairy products, eggs, fish, poultry, meats, dried peas and beans, whole grain cereals, and nuts. Good sources of **magnesium** are whole grain cereals, fruits, milk, nuts, vegetables, seafood, and meats.

CASE STUDY QUESTIONS

1. Signs and symptoms of osteoporosis include loss of height, kyphosis, and pain in the back. What is kyphosis? _____

2. What is the prescribed dosage of Actonel (risedronate sodium)? _____

3. Good sources of _____ are dairy products, fish liver oils, animal liver, and green and yellow vegetables.

4. Good sources of _____ are citrus fruits, tomatoes, melons, fresh berries, raw vegetables, and sweet potatoes.

5. Milk, yogurt, cheese, tofu, turnip greens, canned salmon, sardines, beans, egg yolk, molasses, and broccoli are examples of good sources of _____.

  **MedMedia— Wrap-Up**
www.prenhall.com/rice

Additional interactive resources and activities for this chapter can be found on the Companion Website. For animations, videos, audio glossary, and review, access the accompanying CD-ROM in this book.

Audio Glossary
Medical Terminology Exercises & Activities
Pathology Spotlights
Terminology Translator
Animations
Videos

 Objectives
Medical Terminology Exercises & Activities
Audio Glossary
Drug Updates
Medical Terminology in the News

THE MUSCULAR SYSTEM

5

OUTLINE

OBJECTIVES

On completion of this chapter, you will be able to:

- Describe the muscular system.
- Describe types of muscle tissue.
- Provide the functions of muscles.
- Describe muscular differences of the child and the older adult.
- Analyze, build, spell, and pronounce medical words.
- Describe each of the conditions presented in the Pathology Spotlights.
- Complete the Pathology Checkpoint.
- Review Drug Highlights presented in this chapter.
- Provide the description of diagnostic and laboratory tests related to the muscular system.
- Identify and define selected abbreviations.
- Successfully complete the study and review section.

MedMedia
www.prenhall.com/rice

Additional interactive resources and activities for this chapter can be found on the Companion Website. For Terminology Translator, animations, videos, audio glossary, and review, access the accompanying CD-ROM in this book.

Anatomy and Physiology Overview

The muscular system is composed of all the **muscles** in the body. This overview will describe the three basic types of muscles and some of their functions. The muscles are the primary tissues of the system. They make up approximately 42% of a person's body weight and are composed of long, slender cells known as **fibers**. Muscle fibers are of different lengths and shapes and vary in color from white to deep red. Each muscle consists of a group of fibers held together by connective tissue and enclosed in a fibrous sheath or **fascia**. See Figure 5–1. Each fiber within a muscle receives its own nerve impulses and has its own stored supply of glycogen, which it uses as fuel for energy. Muscle has to be supplied with proper nutrition and oxygen to perform properly; therefore, blood and lymphatic vessels permeate its tissues.

TYPES OF MUSCLE TISSUE

Skeletal muscle, smooth muscle, and **cardiac muscle** are the three basic types of muscle tissue classed according to their functions and appearance (Fig. 5–2).

Skeletal Muscle

Also known as **voluntary** or **striated** muscles, **skeletal muscles** are controlled by the conscious part of the brain and attach to the bones. There are 600 skeletal muscles that, through contractility, extensibility, and elasticity, are responsible for the movement of the body. These muscles have a cross-striped appearance and thus are known as striated muscles. They vary in size, shape, arrangement of fibers, and means of attachment to bones. Selected skeletal muscles are listed with their functions in Tables 5–1 and 5–2 and shown in Figures 5–3 and 5–4.

Skeletal muscles have two or more attachments. The more fixed attachment is known as the **origin**, and the point of attachment of a muscle to the part that it moves is the **insertion**. The means of attachment is called a **tendon**, which can vary in length from less than 1 inch to more than 1 foot. A wide, thin, sheet-like tendon is known as an **aponeurosis**.

THE MUSCULAR SYSTEM

Organ/ Structure	Primary Functions
Muscles	Responsible for movement, help to maintain posture, and produce heat
Skeletal	Through contractility, extensibility, and elasticity, are responsible for the movement of the body
Smooth	Produce relatively slow contraction with greater degree of extensibility in the internal organs, especially organs of the digestive, respiratory, and urinary tract, plus certain muscles of the eye and skin, and walls of blood vessels
Cardiac	Muscle of the heart, controlled by the autonomic nervous system and specialized neuromuscular tissue located within the right atrium that is capable of causing cardiac muscle to contract rhythmically. The neuromuscular tissue of the heart comprises the sinoatrial node, the atrioventricular node, and the atrioventricular bundle
Tendons	A band of connective tissue serving for the attachment of muscles to bones

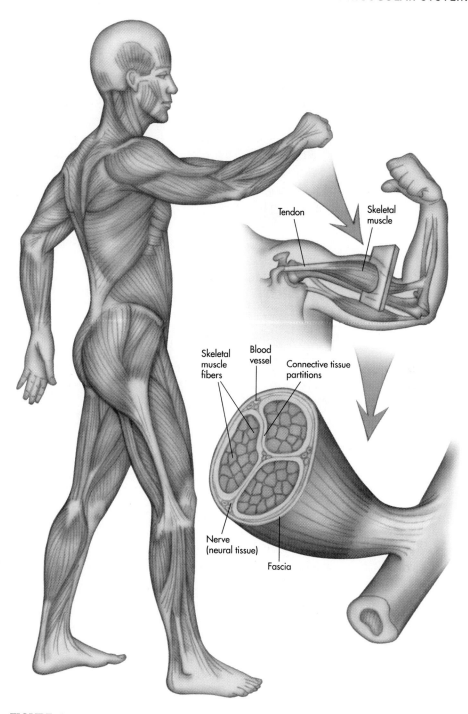

FIGURE 5–1

A skeletal muscle consists of a group of fibers held together by connective tissue. It is enclosed in a fibrous sheath (fascia).

A muscle has three distinguishable parts: the **body** or main portion, an **origin**, and an **insertion**. The skeletal muscles move body parts by pulling from one bone across its joint to another bone with movement occurring at the diarthrotic joint. The types of body movement occurring at the diarthrotic joints are described in Chapter 4, The Skeletal System.

Muscles and nerves function together as a motor unit. For skeletal muscles to contract, it is necessary to have stimulation by impulses from motor nerves. Muscles perform in groups and are classified as:

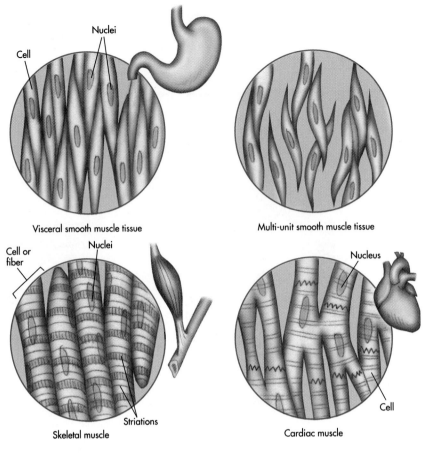

FIGURE 5–2

Types of muscle tissue.

- **Antagonist**—a muscle that counteracts the action of another muscle
- **Prime mover**—a muscle that is primary in a given movement. Its contraction produces the movement.
- **Synergist**—a muscle that acts with another muscle to produce movement

TABLE 5–1 SELECTED SKELETAL MUSCLES (ANTERIOR VIEW)

Muscle	Action
Sternocleidomastoid	Rotates and laterally flexes neck
Trapezlus	Draws head back and to the side, rotates scapula
Deltoid	Raises and rotates arm
Rectus femoris	Extends leg and assists flexion of thigh
Sartorius	Flexes and rotates the thigh and leg
Tibialis anterior	Dorsiflexes foot and increases the arch in the beginning process of walking
Pectoralis major	Flexes, adducts, and rotates arm
Biceps brachii	Flexes arm and forearm and supinates forearm
Rectus abdominis	Compresses or flattens abdomen
Gastrocnemius	Plantar flexes foot and flexes knee
Soleus	Plantar flexes foot

TABLE 5–2 SELECTED SKELETAL MUSCLES (POSTERIOR VIEW)

Muscle	Action
Trapezius	Draws head back and to the side, rotates scapula
Deltoid	Raises and rotates arm
Triceps	Extends forearm
Latissimus dorsi	Adducts, extends, and rotates arm. Used during swimming
Gluteus maximus	Extends and rotates thigh
Biceps femoris	Flexes knee and rotates it outward
Gastrocnemius	Plantar flexes foot and flexes knee
Semitendinosus	Flexes and rotates leg, extends thigh

Smooth Muscle

Also called *involuntary*, *visceral*, or *unstriated*, **smooth muscles** are not controlled by the conscious part of the brain. They are under the control of the autonomic nervous system and, in most cases, produce relatively slow contraction with greater degree of extensibility. These muscles lack the cross-striped appearance of skeletal muscle and are smooth. Included in this type are the muscles of internal organs of the digestive, respiratory, and urinary tract, plus certain muscles of the eye and skin.

Cardiac Muscle

The muscle of the heart (**myocardium**) is *involuntary* but *striated* in appearance. It is controlled by the autonomic nervous system and specialized neuromuscular tissue located within the right atrium.

FUNCTIONS OF MUSCLES

The following is a list of the primary functions of muscles:

1. Muscles are responsible for movement. The types of movement are locomotion, propulsion of substances through tubes as in circulation and digestion, and changes in the size of openings as in the contraction and relaxation of the iris of the eye.
2. Muscles help to maintain posture through a continual partial contraction of skeletal muscles. This process is known as **tonicity**.
3. Muscles help to produce heat through the chemical changes involved in muscular action.

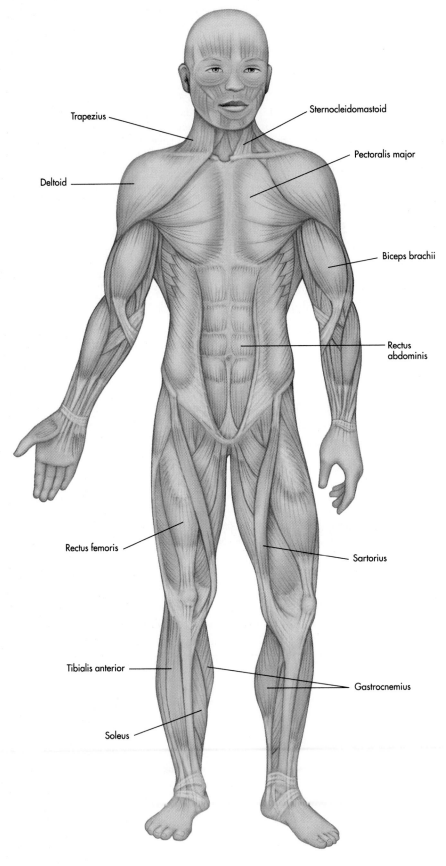

FIGURE 5–3

Selected skeletal muscles (anterior view).

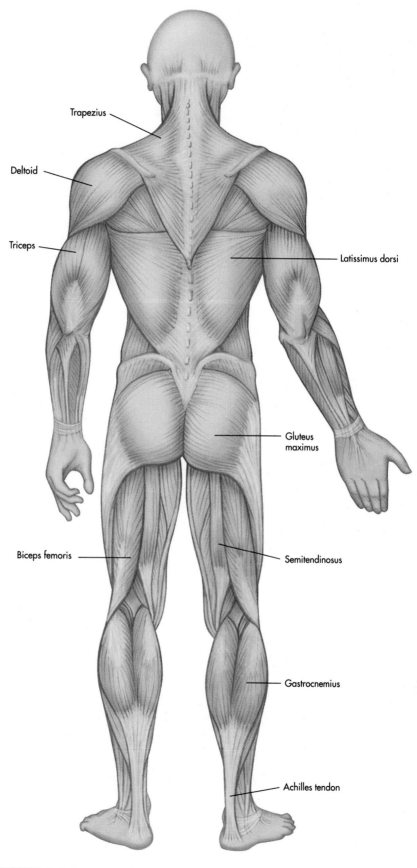

FIGURE 5–4

Selected skeletal muscles and the Achilles tendon (posterior view).

LIFE SPAN CONSIDERATIONS

■ THE CHILD

At about 6 weeks the size of the embryo is 12 mm (0.5 inch). The limb buds are extending and the skeletal and muscular systems are developing. At about 7 weeks the **diaphragm**, a partition of muscles and membranes that separates the chest cavity and the abdominal cavity, is completely developed. At the end of 8 weeks, the embryo is now known as the **fetus**. Fetal growth proceeds from head to tail (**cephalo** to **caudal**), with the head being larger in comparison to the rest of the body.

During fetal development the bones and muscles continue growing and developing. At about 32 weeks the developed skeletal system is soft and flexible. Muscle and fat accumulate and the fetus weighs approximately 2000 g (4 lb, 7 oz). At about 40 weeks the fetus is ready for birth and extrauterine life.

The movements of the newborn are uncoordinated and random. Muscular development proceeds from head to foot and from the center of the body to the periphery. Head and neck muscles are the first ones that can be controlled by the baby. A baby can hold his head up before he can sit erect. The baby needs freedom of movement. The bath is an excellent time for the newborn to exercise.

■ THE OLDER ADULT

With aging, changes related to mobility are most significant. There is a decrease in muscle strength, endurance, range of motion, coordination and elasticity, and flexibility of connective tissue. There is an actual loss in the number of muscle fibers due to **myofibril atrophy** with fibrous tissue replacement, which begins in the fourth decade of life.

To prevent loss of strength, muscles need to be exercised. Regular exercise strengthens muscles and keeps joints, tendons, and ligaments more flexible, allowing active people to move freely and carry out routine activities easily. Exercises such as aerobic dance, brisk walking, and bicycling improve muscle tone and heart and lung function. To maintain aerobic fitness one needs to participate in such activities for 20 minutes or more at least three times a week and work at one's target heart rate. The target range declines with age; the following table shows the correct range during exercise for women between 45 and 65 years old.

Age	Target Heart Rate (Beats per Minute)
45 years old	108 to 135
50 years old	102 to 127
55 years old	99 to 123
60 years old	96 to 120
65 years old	93 to 116

BUILDING YOUR MEDICAL VOCABULARY

This section provides the foundation for learning medical terminology. Medical words can be made up of four different types of word parts:

- Prefixes (P)
- Roots (R)
- Combining forms (CF)
- Suffixes (S)

By connecting various word parts in an organized sequence, thousands of words can be built and learned. In this text the word list is alphabetized so one can see the variety of meanings created when common prefixes and suffixes are repeatedly applied to certain word roots and/or combining forms. Words shown in pink are additional words related to the content of this chapter that are not built from word parts. These words are included to enhance your vocabulary. Note: an asterisk icon ✱ indicates words that are covered in the Pathology Spotlights section in this chapter.

MEDICAL WORD	WORD PARTS (WHEN APPLICABLE)			DEFINITION
	Part	Type	Meaning	
abductor (ăb-dŭk′tōr)	ab	P	away from	A muscle that, on contraction, draws away from the middle
	duct	R	to lead	
	-or	S	a doer	
adductor (ă-dŭk′tōr)	ad	P	toward	A muscle that draws a part toward the middle
	duct	R	to lead	
	-or	S	a doer	
amputation (ăm″pū-tā′shŭn)	amputat	R	to cut through	The removal of a limb, part, or other appendage. See Figure 5–5.
	-ion	S	process	
antagonist (ăn-tăg′ō-nĭst)	ant	P	against	A muscle that counteracts the action of another muscle
	agon	R	agony, a contest	
	-ist	S	agent	
aponeurosis (ăp″ō-nū-rō′sĭs)	apo	P	separation	A fibrous sheet of connective tissue that serves to attach muscle to bone or to other tissues
	neur	R	nerve	
	-osis	S	condition of	
ataxia (ă-tăks′ĭ-ă)	a	P	lack of	A lack of muscular coordination
	-taxia	S	order	
atonic (ă-tŏn′ĭk)	a	P	lack of	Pertaining to a lack of normal tone or tension
	ton	R	tone, tension	
	-ic	S	pertaining to	
atrophy (ăt′rō-fē)	a	P	lack of	A lack of nourishment; a wasting of muscular tissue that may be caused by lack of use. ✱ See Pathology Spotlight: Atrophy.
	-trophy	S	nourishment, development	
biceps (bī′sĕps)	bi	P	two	A muscle with two heads or points of origin
	-ceps	S	head	
brachialgia (brā″ki-ăl′jĭ-ă)	brach/i	CF	arm	Pain in the arm
	-algia	S	pain	
bradykinesia (brăd″ĭ-kĭ-nē′sĭ-ă)	brady	P	slow	Slowness of motion or movement
	-kinesia	S	motion	
clonic (klŏn′ĭk)	clon	R	turmoil	Pertaining to alternate contraction and relaxation of muscles
	-ic	S	pertaining to	

MEDICAL WORD	WORD PARTS (WHEN APPLICABLE)			DEFINITION
	Part	Type	Meaning	
contraction (kŏn-trăk′shŭn)	con tract -ion	P R S	with, together to draw process	The process of drawing up and thickening of a muscle fiber
contracture (kŏn-trăk′chūr)	con tract -ure	P R S	with, together to draw process	A condition in which a muscle shortens and renders the muscle resistant to the normal stretching process. See Figure 5–6.
dactylospasm (dăk′tĭ-lō-spăzm)	dactyl/o -spasm	CF S	finger or toe tension, spasm	Cramp of a finger or toe
dermatomyositis (dĕr″ mă-tō-mī″ ō-sī′tĭs)	dermat/o my/os -itis	CF CF S	skin muscle inflammation	Inflammation of the muscles and the skin; a connective tissue disease characterized by edema, dermatitis, and inflammation of the muscles. See Figure 5–7.
diaphragm (dī′ă-frăm)	dia -phragm	P S	through a fence, partition	The partition of muscles and membranes that separates the chest cavity and the abdominal cavity
diathermy (dī′ă-thĕr″ mē)	dia therm -y	P R S	through hot, heat pertaining to	Treatment using high-frequency current to produce heat within a part of the body; used to increase blood flow and should not be used in acute stage of recovery from trauma. Types: **Microwave.** Electromagnetic radiation is directed to specified tissues **Short-wave.** High-frequency electric current (wavelength of 3–30 m) is directed to specified tissues **Ultrasound.** High-frequency sound waves (20,000–10 billion cycles/sec) are directed to specified tissues
dystonia (dĭs′tō′nĭ-ă)	dys ton -ia	P R S	difficult tone, tension condition	A condition of impaired muscle tone
dystrophin (dĭs-trŏf′ĭn)	dys troph -in	P R S	difficult a turning chemical	A protein found in muscle cells; when the gene that is responsible for this protein is defective and sufficient dystrophin is not produced, muscle wasting occurs
dystrophy (dĭs′trō-fē)	dys -trophy	P S	difficult nourishment, development	Faulty muscular development caused by lack of nourishment

MEDICAL WORD	WORD PARTS (WHEN APPLICABLE)			DEFINITION
	Part	**Type**	**Meaning**	
exercise (ĕk'sĕr-sīz)				Performed activity of the muscles for improvement of health or correction of deformity. Types: **Active.** The patient contracts and relaxes his or her muscles **Assistive.** The patient contracts and relaxes his or her muscles with the assistance of a therapist **Isometric.** Active muscular contraction performed against stable resistance, thereby not shortening the muscle length **Passive.** Exercise is performed by another individual without the assistance of the patient **Range of Motion.** Movement of each joint through its full range of motion. Used to prevent loss of motility or to regain usage after an injury or fracture **Relief of Tension.** Technique used to promote relaxation of the muscles and provide relief from tension
fascia (făsh'ĭ-ă)	fasc -ia	R S	a band condition	A thin layer of connective tissue covering, supporting, or connecting the muscles or inner organs of the body
fascitis (fă-sī'tĭs)	fasc -itis	R S	a band inflammation	Inflammation of a fascia
fatigue (fă-tēg')				A state of tiredness or weariness occurring in a muscle as a result of repeated contractions
fibromyalgia (fī" brō-mī-ăl'jē-ă)	fibr/o my -algia	CF R S	fiber muscle pain	A condition with widespread muscular pain and debilitating fatigue. ✷ See Pathology Spotlight: Fibromyalgia.
fibromyitis (fī" brō-mī-ī'tĭs)	fibr/o my -itis	CF R S	fiber muscle inflammation	Inflammation of muscle and fibrous tissue

First Aid Treatment—RICE
  Rest
  Ice
  Compression
  Elevation
				Cryotherapy (use of cold) is the treatment of choice for soft tissue injuries and muscle injuries. It causes vasoconstriction of blood vessels and is effective in diminishing bleeding and edema. Ice should not be placed directly onto the skin.

MEDICAL WORD	WORD PARTS (WHEN APPLICABLE)			DEFINITION
	Part	**Type**	**Meaning**	
				Compression by an elastic bandage is generally determined by the type of injury and the preference of the physician. Some experts disagree on the use of elastic bandages. When used, the bandage should be 3 to 4 inches wide and applied firmly, and toes or fingers should be periodically checked for blue or white discoloration, indicating that the bandage is too tight. **Elevation** is used to reduce swelling. The injured part should be elevated on two or three pillows.
flaccid (flăk′sĭd)				Lacking muscle tone; *weak, soft,* and *flabby*
heat (hēt)				**Thermotherapy.** The treatment using scientific application of heat may be used 48 to 72 hours after the injury. Types: heating pad, hot water bottle, hot packs, infrared light, and immersion of body part in warm water. Extreme care should be followed when using or applying heat.
hydrotherapy (hī-drō-thĕr′ă-pē)	hydro -therapy	P S	water treatment	Treatment using scientific application of water; types: hot tub, cold bath, whirlpool, and vapor bath
insertion (ĭn″ sûr′shŭn)	in sert -ion	P R S	into to gain process	The point of attachment of a muscle to the part that it moves
intramuscular (ĭn″ tră-mŭs′kū-lər)	intra muscul -ar	P R S	within muscle pertaining to	Pertaining to within a muscle
isometric (ī″ sō-mĕt′rĭk)	is/o metr -ic	CF R S	equal to measure pertaining to	Pertaining to having equal measure
isotonic (ī″ sō-tŏn′ĭk)	is/o ton -ic	CF R S	equal tone, tension pertaining to	Pertaining to having the same tone or tension
levator (lē-vā′tər)	levat -or	R S	lifter a doer	A muscle that raises or elevates a part

MEDICAL WORD	WORD PARTS (WHEN APPLICABLE)			DEFINITION
	Part	**Type**	**Meaning**	
massage (măh-săhzh)				To knead, apply pressure and friction to external body tissues
muscular dystrophy (mŭs'kū-lār dĭs'trō-fē)				A chronic, progressive wasting and weakening of muscles. ✳ See Pathology Spotlight: Muscular Dystrophy.
myalgia (mī-ăl'jĭ-ă)	my -algia	R S	muscle pain	Pain in the muscle
myasthenia gravis (mī-ăs-thē'nĭ-ă gră vĭs)	my -asthenia gravis	R S R	muscle weakness grave	A chronic disease characterized by progressive muscular weakness
myitis (mī-ī'tĭs)	my -itis	R S	muscle inflammation	Inflammation of a muscle
myoblast (mī'ō blăst)	my/o -blast	CF S	muscle immature cell, germ cell	An embryonic cell that develops into a cell of muscle fiber
myofibroma (mī"ō fĭ-brō'mă)	my/o fibr -oma	CF R S	muscle fiber tumor	A tumor that contains muscle and fiber
myograph (mī'ō-grăf)	my/o -graph	CF S	muscle to write, record	An instrument used to record muscular contractions
myokinesis (mī"ō-kĭn-ē'sĭs)	my/o -kinesis	CF S	muscle motion	Muscular motion or activity
myology (mĭ-ōl ō-jē)	my/o -logy	CF S	muscle study of	The study of muscles
myoma (mī-ō' mă)	my -oma	R S	muscle tumor	A tumor containing muscle tissue
myomalacia (mī"ō-mă-lā'sĭ-ă)	my/o -malacia	CF S	muscle softening	Softening of muscle tissue
myoparesis (mī"ō-păr' ĕ-sĭs)	my/o -paresis	CF S	muscle weakness	Weakness or slight paralysis of a muscle
myopathy (mī-ŏp' ă-thē)	my/o -pathy	CF S	muscle disease	Muscle disease
myoplasty (mī' ō-plăs" tē)	my/o -plasty	CF S	muscle surgical repair	Surgical repair of a muscle
myorrhaphy (mī-ȯr' ă-fē)	my/o -rrhaphy	CF S	muscle suture	Suture of a muscle wound

MEDICAL WORD	WORD PARTS (WHEN APPLICABLE)			DEFINITION
	Part	Type	Meaning	
myosarcoma (mī″ ō-sar-kō′ mă)	my/o sarc -oma	CF R S	muscle flesh tumor	A malignant tumor derived from muscle tissue
myosclerosis (mī″ ō-sklĕr-ō′ sĭs)	my/o scler -osis	CF R S	muscle hardening condition of	A condition of hardening of muscle
myospasm (mī″ ō-spăzm)	my/o -spasm	CF S	muscle tension, spasm	Spasmodic contraction of a muscle
myotome (mī′ ō-tōm)	my/o -tome	CF S	muscle instrument to cut	An instrument used to cut muscle
myotomy (mī″ ŏt′ ō-mē)	my/o -tomy	CF S	muscle incision	Incision into a muscle
neuromuscular (nū″ rō-mŭs′ kū-lăr)	neur/o muscul -ar	CF R S	nerve muscle pertaining to	Pertaining to both nerves and muscles
neuromyopathic (nū″ rō-mī″ ō-păth′ ĭk)	neur/o my/o path -ic	CF CF R S	nerve muscle disease pertaining to	Pertaining to disease of both nerves and muscles
polyplegia (pŏl″ ē-plē′ jĭ-ă)	poly -plegia	P S	many stroke, paralysis	Paralysis affecting many muscles
position (pō-zĭsh′ ŭn)				Bodily posture or attitude; the manner in which a patient's body may be arranged for examination. See Table 5–3.
prosthesis (prŏs′ thē-sĭs)	prosth/e -sis	CF S	an addition condition of	An artificial device, organ, or part such as a hand, arm, leg, or tooth
quadriceps (kwŏd′ rĭ-sĕps)	quadri -ceps	P S	four head	A muscle that has four heads or points of origin
relaxation (rē-lăk-sā′ shŭn)	relaxat -ion	R S	to loosen process	The process in which a muscle loosens and returns to a resting stage
rhabdomyoma (răb″ dō-mī-ō′ mă)	rhabd/o my -oma	CF R S	rod muscle tumor	A tumor of striated muscle tissue
rheumatism (roo′mă-tĭzm)	rheumat -ism	R S	discharge condition of	A general term used to describe conditions characterized by inflammation, soreness, and stiffness of muscles, and pain in joints

MEDICAL WORD	WORD PARTS (WHEN APPLICABLE)			DEFINITION
	Part	Type	Meaning	
rigor mortis (rĭg' ur mȯr tĭs)				Stiffness of skeletal muscles seen in death
rotation (rō-tā' shŭn)	rotat -ion	R S	to turn process	The process of moving a body part around a central axis
rotator cuff (rō-tā' tor kŭf)				A term used to describe the muscles immediately surrounding the shoulder joint. They stabilize the shoulder joint while the entire arm is moved.
sarcolemma (sar″ kō-lĕm' ă)	sarc/o lemma	CF R	flesh a rind	A plasma membrane surrounding each striated muscle fiber
spasticity (spăs-tĭs' ĭ-tē)	spastic -ity	R S	convulsive condition	A condition of increased muscular tone causing stiff and awkward movements
sternocleidomastoid (stur″ nō-klī″ dō-măs' toyd)	stern/o cleid/o mast -oid	CF CF R S	sternum clavicle breast resemble	Muscle arising from the sternum and clavicle with its insertion in the mastoid process
strain (strān)				Excessive, forcible stretching of a muscle or the musculotendinous unit
synergetic (sin″ ĕr-jĕt' ĭk)	syn erget -ic	P R S	with, together work pertaining to	Pertaining to certain muscles that work together
synovitis (sĭn″ ȯ-vī' tĭs)	synov -itis	R S	joint fluid inflammation	Inflammation of a synovial membrane
tendon (tĕn' dŭn)				A band of fibrous connective tissue serving for the attachment of muscles to bones; a giant cell tumor of a tendon sheath is a benign, small, yellow, tumor-like nodule. See Figure 5–8.
tenodesis (tĕn-ōd' ĕ-sĭs)	ten/o -desis	CF S	tendon binding	Surgical binding of a tendon
tenodynia (tĕn″ ō-dĭn-ĭ-ă)	ten/o -dynia	CF S	tendon pain	Pain in a tendon
tonic (tŏn' ĭk)	ton -ic	R S	tone, tension pertaining to	Pertaining to tone, especially muscular tension

MEDICAL WORD	WORD PARTS (WHEN APPLICABLE)			DEFINITION
	Part	**Type**	**Meaning**	
torsion (tor' shŭn)	tors -ion	R S	twisted process	The process of being twisted
torticollis (tor" tĭ-kŏl' ĭs)	tort/i -collis	CF R	twisted neck	Stiff neck caused by spasmodic contraction of the muscles of the neck; wryneck
triceps (trī' sĕps)	tri -ceps	P S	three head	A muscle having three heads with a single insertion
voluntary (vŏl' ŭn-tĕr" ē)	volunt -ary	R S	will pertaining to	Pertaining to under the control of one's will

Terminology Translator

Medicine Medicina Médecine Medizin

This feature, found on the accompanying CD-ROM, provides an innovative tool to translate medical words into Spanish, French, and German.

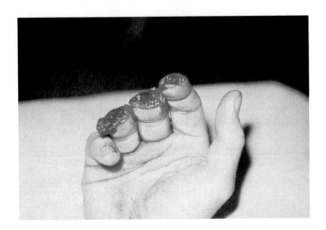

FIGURE 5–5

Amputation of three fingers. (Source: Pearson Education/PH College.)

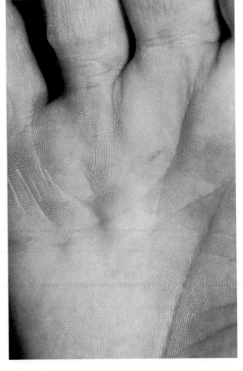

FIGURE 5–6

Dupuytren's contracture. (Courtesy of Jason L. Smith, MD.)

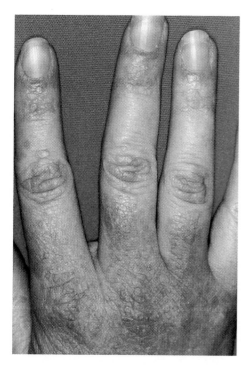

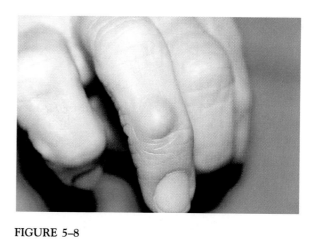

FIGURE 5–8

Giant cell tumor of tendon sheath. (Courtesy of Jason L. Smith, MD.)

FIGURE 5–7

Dermatomyositis. (Courtesy of Jason L. Smith, MD.)

TABLE 5–3 TYPES OF POSITIONS

Position	Description
Anatomic	Body is erect, head facing forward, arms by the sides with palms to the front; used as the position of reference in designating the site or direction of a body structure
Dorsal recumbent	Patient is on back with lower extremities flexed and rotated outward; used in application of obstetric forceps, vaginal and rectal examination, and bimanual palpation
Fowler's	The head of the bed or examining table is raised about 18 inches or 46 cm, and the patient sits up with knees also elevated
Knee-chest	Patient on knees, thighs upright, head and upper part of chest resting on bed or examining table, arms crossed and above head; used in sigmoidoscopy, displacement of prolapsed uterus, rectal exams, and flushing of intestinal canal
Lithotomy	Patient is on back with lower extremities flexed and feet placed in stirrups; used in vaginal examination; Pap smear, vaginal operations, and diagnosis and treatment of diseases of the urethra and bladder
Orthopneic	Patient sits upright or erect; used for patients with dyspnea
Prone	Patient lying face downward; used in examination of the back, injections, and massage
Sims'	Patient is lying on left side, right knee and thigh flexed well up above left leg that is slightly flexed, left arm behind the body, and right arm forward, flexed at elbow; used in examination of rectum, sigmoidoscopy, enema, and intrauterine irrigation after labor
Supine	Patient lying flat on back with face upward and arms at the sides; used in examining the head, neck, chest, abdomen, and extremities and in assessing vital signs
Trendelenburg	Patient's body is supine on a bed or examining table that is tilted at about 45° angle with the head lower than the feet; used to displace abdominal organs during surgery and in treating cardiovascular shock; also called the "shock position"

PATHOLOGY SPOTLIGHTS

Atrophy

Atrophy occurs with the disuse of muscles over a long period of time. Bedrest and immobility can cause loss of muscle mass and strength. When immobility is due to a treatment mode, such as casting or traction, one can decrease the effects of immobility by isometric exercise of the muscles of the immobilized part. Isometric exercise involves active muscular contraction performed against stable resistance, such as tightening the muscles of the thigh and/or tightening the muscles of the buttocks. Active exercise of uninjured parts of the body helps prevent muscle atrophy.

Other benefits of exercise:

- It may slow down the progression of osteoporosis.
- It reduces the levels of triglycerides and raises the "good" cholesterol (high-density lipoproteins).
- It can lower systolic and diastolic blood pressure.
- It may improve blood glucose levels in the diabetic person.
- Combined with a low-fat, low-calorie diet, it is effective in preventing obesity and helping individuals maintain a proper body weight.
- It can elevate one's mood and reduce anxiety and tension.

Lipoatrophy is atrophy of fat tissue. This condition may occur at the site of an insulin and/or corticosteroid injection. It is also known as lipodystrophy. See Figure 5–9.

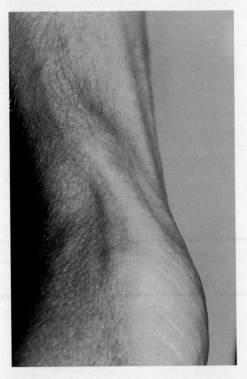

FIGURE 5–9

Lipoatrophy, wrist. (Courtesy of Jason L. Smith, MD.)

Fibromyalgia

Fibromyalgia, or fibromyalgia syndrome (FMS), is a widespread musculoskeletal pain and fatigue disorder. An estimated 3 million are affected in the United States. It affects women more than men, but occurs in those of all ages.

Symptoms include mild to severe muscle pain and fatigue, sleep disorders, irritable bowel syndrome, depression, and chronic headaches. Although the exact cause is still unknown, fibromyalgia is often traced to an injury or physical or emotional trauma. Some doctors feel that many causes contribute to the development of the syndrome, including bacterial, fungal, or viral infection, and hormonal changes. Researchers have found that people with fibromyalgia may have abnormal levels of several chemicals, such as substance P and serotonin, used by the body to transmit and respond to pain signals.

The American College of Rheumatology (ACR) has identified specific criteria for fibromyalgia. The ACR classifies a patient with fibromyalgia if at least 11 of 18 specific areas of the body are painful under pressure. These specific areas are often called "trigger points." See Figure 5–10. Another criterion is that the patient must have had widespread pain lasting at least three months. The location of some of these trigger points includes the inside of the elbow joint, the front of the collarbone, and the base of the skull.

Treatments are geared toward improving the quality of sleep, as well as reducing pain. Because deep sleep is so crucial for many body functions, such as tissue repair and antibody

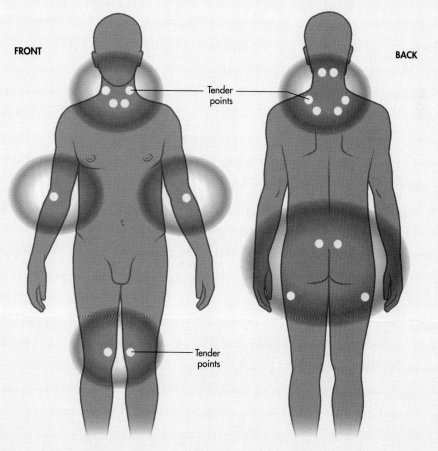

FIGURE 5–10

The 18 tender points of fibromyalgia.

production, the sleep disorders that frequently occur in fibromyalgia are thought to be a major contributing factor to the symptoms. Medications that boost the body's level of serotonin and norepinephrine—neurotransmitters that modulate sleep, pain, and immune system function—are commonly prescribed. Examples of drugs in this category would include cyclobenzaprine (Flexeril), paroxetine (Paxil), and alprazolam (Xanax). In addition, nonsteroidal, anti-inflammatory drugs (NSAIDs) like ibuprofen may also be beneficial. Most patients will probably need to use other treatment methods as well, such as trigger point injections with lidocaine, physical therapy, acupuncture, acupressure, relaxation techniques, chiropractic care, therapeutic massage, or a gentle exercise program.

Myasthenia Gravis

Myasthenia gravis (MG) is a chronic autoimmune neuromuscular disease characterized by varying degrees of weakness of the skeletal (voluntary) muscles of the body. The name *myasthenia gravis*, which is Latin and Greek in origin, literally means "grave muscle weakness." With current therapies, however, most cases of myasthenia gravis are not as "grave" as the name implies. For the majority of individuals with myasthenia gravis, life expectancy is not lessened by the disorder.

The primary symptom of myasthenia gravis is muscle weakness that increases during periods of activity and improves after periods of rest. Certain muscles such as those that control eye and eyelid movement, facial expression, chewing, talking, and swallowing are often, but not always, involved in the disorder. The muscles that control breathing and neck and limb movements may also be affected.

Myasthenia gravis is caused by a defect in the transmission of nerve impulses to muscles. It occurs when normal communication between the nerve and muscle is interrupted at the neuromuscular junction—the place where nerve cells connect with the muscles they control.

Normally when impulses travel down the nerve, the nerve endings release a neurotransmitter substance called acetylcholine. Acetylcholine travels through the neuromuscular junction and binds to acetylcholine receptors which are activated and generate a muscle contraction.

In myasthenia gravis, antibodies block, alter, or destroy the receptors for acetylcholine at the neuromuscular junction, which prevents the muscle contraction from occurring. These antibodies are produced by the body's own immune system. Thus, myasthenia gravis is an autoimmune disease because the immune system—which normally protects the body from foreign organisms—mistakenly attacks itself.

Myasthenia gravis occurs in all ethnic groups and both genders. It most commonly affects young adult women (under 40) and older men (over 60), but it can occur at any age.

Treatment may include lifestyle adjustments that may enable continuation of many activities, including planning activity to allow for scheduled rest periods, and avoiding stress and excessive heat exposure. Some medications, such as neostigmine or pyridostigmine, improve the communication between the nerve and the muscle. Prednisone and other medications that suppress the immune response (such as azathioprine or cyclosporine) may be used if symptoms are severe and there is inadequate response to other medications.

Muscular Dystrophy

Muscular dystrophy (MD) refers to a group of genetic diseases characterized by progressive weakness and degeneration of the skeletal or voluntary muscles which control movement. The muscles of the heart and some other involuntary muscles are also affected in some forms of MD, and a few forms involve other organs as well.

The major forms of MD include myotonic, Duchenne, Becker, limb-girdle, facioscapulo-humeral, congenital, oculopharyngeal, distal and Emery-Dreifuss. Duchenne is the most common form of MD affecting children, and myotonic MD is the most common form affecting adults. MD can affect people of all ages. Although some forms first become apparent in infancy or childhood, others may not appear until middle age or later.

The prognosis of MD varies according to the type of MD and the progression of the disorder. Some cases may be mild and very slowly progressive, with normal lifespan, while other cases may have more marked progression of muscle weakness, functional disability and loss of ambulation. Life expectancy may depend on the degree of progression and late respiratory deficit. In Duchenne MD, death usually occurs in the late teens to early twenties.

There is no specific treatment for any of the forms of MD. Physical therapy to prevent contractures (a condition in which shortened muscles around joints cause abnormal and sometimes painful positioning of the joints), orthoses (orthopedic appliances used for support) and corrective orthopedic surgery may be needed to improve the quality of life in some cases. The cardiac problems that occur with Emery-Dreifuss MD and myotonic MD may require a pacemaker. The myotonia (delayed relaxation of a muscle after a strong contraction) occurring in myotonic MD may be treated with medications such as phenytoin or quinine.

✔ PATHOLOGY CHECKPOINT

Following is a concise list of the pathology-related terms that you've seen in the chapter. Review this checklist to make sure that you are familiar with the meaning of each term before moving on to the next section.

Conditions and Symptoms

- ❑ amputation
- ❑ ataxia
- ❑ atonic
- ❑ atrophy
- ❑ brachialgia
- ❑ bradykinesia
- ❑ contracture
- ❑ dactylospasm
- ❑ dermatomyositis
- ❑ dystonia
- ❑ dystrophy
- ❑ fascitis
- ❑ fatigue
- ❑ fibromyalgia
- ❑ fibromyitis
- ❑ flaccid
- ❑ muscular dystrophy
- ❑ myalgia
- ❑ myasthenia

- ❑ myasthenia gravis
- ❑ myitis
- ❑ myofibroma
- ❑ myokinesis
- ❑ myoma
- ❑ myomalacia
- ❑ myoparesis
- ❑ myopathy
- ❑ myosarcoma
- ❑ myosclerosis
- ❑ myospasm
- ❑ neuromyopathic
- ❑ polyplegia
- ❑ rhabdomyoma
- ❑ rheumatism
- ❑ rigor mortis
- ❑ spasticity
- ❑ strain
- ❑ synovitis
- ❑ tenodynia

- ❑ torsion
- ❑ torticollis

Diagnosis and Treatment

- ❑ diathermy
- ❑ exercise
- ❑ First Aid—RICE
- ❑ heat
- ❑ hydrotherapy
- ❑ massage
- ❑ myograph
- ❑ myoplasty
- ❑ myorrhaphy
- ❑ myotome
- ❑ myotomy
- ❑ position
- ❑ prosthesis
- ❑ tenodesis

DRUG HIGHLIGHTS

Drugs that are generally used for muscular system diseases and disorders include skeletal muscle relaxants and stimulants, neuromuscular blocking agents, anti-inflammatory agents, and analgesics. See Chapter 4, The Skeletal System, Drug Highlights for a description of anti-inflammatory agents and analgesics.

Skeletal Muscle Relaxants

Used to treat painful muscle spasms that may result from strains, sprains, and musculo-skeletal trauma or disease. Centrally acting muscle relaxants act by depressing the central nervous system (CNS) and can be administered either orally or by injection. The patient must be informed of the sedative effect produced by these drugs. Drowsiness, dizziness, and blurred vision may diminish the patient's ability to drive a vehicle, operate equipment, or climb stairs.

Examples: Lioresal (baclofen), Flexeril (cyclobenzaprine HCl), and Robaxin (methocarbamol).

Skeletal Muscle Stimulants

Used in the treatment of myasthenia gravis. This disease is characterized by progressive weakness of skeletal muscles and their rapid fatiguing. Skeletal muscle stimulants act by inhibiting the action of acetylcholinesterase, the enzyme that halts the action of acetylcholine at the neuromuscular junction. By slowing the destruction of acetylcholine, these drugs foster accumulation of higher concentrations of this neurotransmitter and increase the number of interactions between acetylcholine and the available receptors on muscle fibers.

Examples: Tensilon (edrophonium chloride), Prostigmin Bromide (neostigmine bromide), and Mestinon (pyridostigmine bromide).

Neuromuscular Blocking Agents

Used to provide muscle relaxation. These agents are used in patients undergoing surgery and/or electroconvulsive therapy, endotracheal intubation, and to relieve laryngospasm.

Examples: Tracrium (atracurium besylate), Flaxedil (gallamine triethiodide), and Norcuron (vecuronium).

DIAGNOSTIC & LAB TESTS

TEST	DESCRIPTION
aldolase (ALD) blood test (ăl′ dō-lāz blod test)	A test performed on serum that measures ALD enzyme present in skeletal and heart muscle. It is helpful in the diagnosis of Duchenne's muscular dystrophy before symptoms appear.
calcium blood test (kăl′ sē-ŭm blod test)	A test performed on serum to determine levels of calcium. Calcium is essential for muscular contraction, nerve transmission, and blood clotting.
creatine phosphokinase (CPK) (krē′ ă-tĭn fŏs″ fō-kīn′ āz)	A blood test to determine the level of CPK. It is increased in necrosis or atrophy of skeletal muscle, traumatic muscle injury, strenuous exercise, and progressive muscular dystrophy.
electromyography (EMG) (ē-lĕk″ trō-mī-ŏg′ ră-fē)	A test to measure electrical activity across muscle membranes by means of electrodes that are attached to a needle that is inserted into the muscle. Electrical activity can be heard over a loudspeaker, viewed on an oscilloscope, or printed on a graph (electromyogram). Abnormal results may indicate myasthenia gravis, amyotrophic lateral sclerosis, muscular dystrophy, peripheral neuropathy, and anterior poliomyelitis.
lactic dehydrogenase (LDH) (lăk′ tĭk dē-hī-drŏj′ ĕ-nāz)	A blood test to determine the level of LDH enzyme. It is increased in muscular dystrophy, damage to skeletal muscles, after a pulmonary embolism, and during skeletal muscle malignancy.
muscle biopsy (mŭs′ ĕl bī′ ŏp-sē)	An operative procedure in which a small piece of muscle tissue is excised and then stained for microscopic examination. Lower motor neuron disease, degeneration, inflammatory reactions, or involvement of specific muscle fibers may indicate myopathic disease.
serum glutamic oxaloacetic transaminase (SGOT) (sē′ rŭm gloo-tăm′ ĭk ŏks″ ăl-ō-ă-sē′ tĭk trăns ăm′ ĭn-āz)	A blood test to determine the level of SGOT enzyme. It is increased in skeletal muscle damage and muscular dystrophy. This test is also called aspartate aminotransferase (AST).
serum glutamic pyruvic transaminase (SGPT) (sē′ rŭm gloo-tăm′ ĭk pī-roo′ vĭk trăns-ăm′ ĭn-āz)	A blood test to determine the level of SGPT enzyme. It is increased in skeletal muscle damage. This test is also called alanine aminotransferase (ALT).

ABBREVIATIONS

ABBREVIATION	MEANING
ACR	American College of Rheumatology
ADP	adenosine diphosphate
AE	above elbow
AK	above knee
ALD	aldolase
AST	aspartate aminotransferase
ATP	adenosine triphosphate
BE	below elbow
BK	below knee
Ca	calcium
CPK	creatine phosphokinase
CPM	continuous passive motion
DTRs	deep tendon reflexes
EMG	electromyography
FMS	fibromyalgia syndrome
FROM	full range of motion
Ht	height
IM	intramuscular

ABBREVIATION	MEANING
LDH	lactic dehydrogenase
LOM	limitation or loss of motion
MD	muscular dystrophy
MG	myasthenia gravis
MS	musculoskeletal
NSAIDs	nonsteroidal anti-inflammatory drugs
PM	physical medicine
PMR	physical medicine and rehabilitation
ROM	range of motion
SGOT	serum glutamic oxaloacetic transaminase
SGPT	serum glutamic pyruvic transaminase
sh	shoulder
TBW	total body weight
TJ	triceps jerk
wt	weight

STUDY AND REVIEW

Anatomy and Physiology

Write your answers to the following questions. Do not refer to the text.

1. The muscular system is made up of three types of muscle tissue. Name the three types.

   a. _____   b. _____

   c. _____

2. Muscles make up approximately _____ percent of a person's body weight.

3. Name the two essential ingredients that are needed for a muscle to perform properly.

   a. _____   b. _____

4. Name the two points of attachment for a skeletal muscle.

   a. _____   b. _____

5. Skeletal muscle is also known as _____ or _____.

6. A wide, thin, sheet-like tendon is known as an _____.

7. Name the three distinguishable parts of a muscle.

   a. _____   b. _____

   c. _____

8. Define the following:

   a. Antagonist _____

   b. Prime mover _____

   c. Synergist _____

9. Smooth muscle is also called _____, _____, or

   _____.

10. Smooth muscles are found in the internal organs. Name five examples of these locations.

    a. _____   b. _____

    c. _____   d. _____

    e. _____

11. _____ is the muscle of the heart.

12. Name the three primary functions of the muscular system.

    a. _____   b. _____

    c. _____

Word Parts

1. In the spaces provided, write the definition of these prefixes, roots, combining forms, and suffixes. Do not refer to the listings of medical words. Leave blank those words you cannot define.

2. After completing as many as you can, refer to the medical word listings to check your work. For each word missed or left blank, write the word and its definition several times on the margins of these pages or on a separate sheet of paper.

3. To maximize the learning process, it is to your advantage to do the following exercises as directed. To refer to the word building section before completing these exercises invalidates the learning process.

PREFIXES

Give the definitions of the following prefixes:

1. a- _____   2. ab- _____

3. ad- _____   4. ant- _____

5. apo- _____   6. bi- _____

7. brady- _____   8. con- _____

9. dia- _____   10. dys- _____

11. in- _____   12. intra- _____

13. hydro- _____   14. quadri- _____

15. syn- _____   16. tri- _____

ROOTS AND COMBINING FORMS

Give the definitions of the following roots and combining forms:

1. agon _____

2. brach\i _____

3. cleid/o _____

4. amputat _____

5. collis _____

6. dactyl/o _____

7. duct _____

8. erget _____

9. fasc _____

10. dermat/o _____

11. rheumat _____

12. fibr _____

13. fibr/o _____

14. is/o _____

15. lemma _____

16. levat _____

17. prosth/e _____

18. mast _____

19. therm _____

20. metr _____

21. muscul _____

22. my _____

23. my/o _____

24. my/os _____

25. neur _____

26. neur/o _____

27. path _____

28. relaxat _____

29. rhabd/o _____

30. rotat _____

31. troph _____

32. sarc/o _____

33. scler _____

34. sert _____

35. spastic _____

36. stern/o _____

37. teno _____

38. ton _____

39. torti _____

40. tract _____

41. volunt _____

42. synov _____

43. tors _____

SUFFIXES

Give the definitions of the following suffixes:

1. -algia _____

2. -ar _____

3. -ary _____

4. -asthenia _____

5. -blast _____

6. -ceps _____

7. -desis _____

8. -dynia _____

9. -in _____

10. -therapy _____

11. -graph _____

12. -ia _____

13. -ic _____

14. -ion _____

15. -ist _____

16. -itis _____

17. -ity _____

18. -kinesia _____

19. -kinesis _____

20. -logy _____

21. -ure _____

22. -malacia _____

23. -oid _____

24. -oma _____

25. -or _____

26. -osis _____

27. -paresis _____

28. -pathy _____

29. -phragm _____

30. -plasty _____

31. -plegia _____

32. -rrhaphy _____

33. -y _____

34. -spasm _____

35. -taxia _____

36. -tome _____

37. -tomy _____

38. -trophy _____

39. -sis _____

40. -ism _____

Identifying Medical Terms

In the spaces provided, write the medical terms for the following meanings:

1. _____ Pertaining to a lack of normal tone or tension

2. _____ Slowness of motion or movement

3. _____ Cramp of a finger or toe

4. _____ Faulty muscular development caused by lack of nourishment

5. _____ Pertaining to within a muscle

6. _____ A muscle that raises or elevates a part

7. _____ Muscle weakness

8. _____ Study of muscles

9. _____ Weakness or slight paralysis of a muscle

10. _____ Surgical repair of a muscle

11. _____ A malignant tumor derived from muscle tissue

12. _____ Incision into a muscle

13. _____ Paralysis affecting many muscles

14. _____ Surgical binding of a tendon

15. _____ Pertaining to certain muscles that work together

16. _____ A muscle having three heads with a single insertion

Spelling

In the spaces provided, write the correct spelling of these misspelled terms:

1. facia _____

2. mykinesis _____

3. dermatomyoitis _____

4. rhadomyoma _____

5. sarclemma _____

6. sterncleidomastoid _____

7. dystropin _____

8. torticolis _____

Matching

Select the appropriate lettered meaning for each ward listed below.

_____ 1. dermatomyositis

_____ 2. fibromyalgia

_____ 3. muscular dystrophy

_____ 4. flaccid

_____ 5. prosthesis

_____ 6. rotator cuff

_____ 7. strain

_____ 8. tenodynia

_____ 9. torsion

_____10. voluntary

a. A term used to describe the muscles immediately surrounding the shoulder joint

b. The process of being twisted

c. Pain in a tendon

d. Inflammation of the muscles and the skin

e. Lacking muscle tone

f. Pertaining to under the control of one's will

g. A chronic, progressive wasting and weakening of muscles

h. Excessive, forcible stretching of a muscle or the musculotendinous unit

i. A condition with widespread muscular pain and debilitating fatigue

j. An artificial device, organ, or part

k. Pain in a joint

Abbreviations

Place the correct word, phrase, or abbreviation in the space provided.

1. AE _____

2. AST _____

3. calcium _____

4. electromyography _____

5. FROM _____

6. MS _____

7. range of motion _____

8. shoulder _____

9. TBW _____

10. TJ _____

Diagnostic and Laboratory Tests

Select the best answer to each multiple choice question. Circle the letter of your choice.

1. A diagnostic test to help diagnose Duchenne's muscular dystrophy before symptoms appear.
   a. creatine phosphokinase
   b. aldolase blood test
   c. calcium blood test
   d. muscle biopsy

2. A test to measure electrical activity across muscle membranes by means of electrodes that are attached to a needle that is inserted into the muscle.
   a. muscle biopsy
   b. lactic dehydrogenase
   c. creatine phosphokinase
   d. electromyography

3. This test is also called aspartate aminotransferase.
   a. lactic dehydrogenase
   b. serum glutamic oxaloacetic transaminase
   c. serum glutamic pyruvic transaminase
   d. creatine phosphokinase

4. This test is also called alanine aminotransferase.
   a. lactic dehydrogenase
   b. serum glutamic oxaloacetic transaminase
   c. serum glutamic pyruvic transaminase
   d. creatine phosphokinase

5. For a/an _____, a small piece of muscle tissue is excised and then stained for microscopic examination.
   a. muscle biopsy
   b. electromyography
   c. bone biopsy
   d. electrocardiography

CASE STUDY

DUCHENNE'S MUSCULAR DYSTROPHY

Read the following case study and then answer the questions that follow.

A 3-year-old male child was seen by a physician; the following is a synopsis of the visit.

Present History: The mother states that she noticed that her son has been falling a lot and seems to be very clumsy. She says that he has a waddling gait, is very slow in running and climbing, and walks on his toes. She is most concerned as she is at risk for carrying the gene that causes muscular dystrophy.

Signs and Symptoms: A waddling gait, very slow in running and climbing, walks on his toes, frequent falling, clumsy.

Diagnosis: Duchenne's muscular dystrophy. The diagnosis was determined by the characteristic symptoms, family history, a muscle biopsy, an electromyography, and an elevated serum creatine kinase level.

Treatment: Physical therapy, deep breathing exercises to help delay muscular weakness, supportive measures such as splints and braces to help minimize deformities and to preserve mobility. Counseling and referral

services are essential. For more information you may contact the Muscular Dystrophy Association at: 3561 E. Sunrise Drive, Tucson, AZ 85718. Telephone: 1-602-529-2000 or 1-800-572-1717. E-mail: mda@mdausa.org

CASE STUDY QUESTIONS

1. Signs and symptoms of Duchenne's muscular dystrophy include a _____ gait, frequent falls, clumsiness, slowness in running and climbing, and walking on toes.

2. The diagnosis was determined by the characteristic symptoms, family history, a muscle biopsy, an _____, and an elevated serum creatine kinase level.

3. As part of the treatment for Duchenne's muscular dystrophy, the use of splints and braces help to: a. _____ and b. _____.

  **MedMedia— Wrap-Up**

www.prenhall.com/rice

Additional interactive resources and activities for this chapter can be found on the Companion Website. For animations, videos, audio glossary, and review, access the accompanying CD-ROM in this book.

Audio Glossary
Pathology Spotlights
Medical Terminology Exercises & Activities
Terminology Translator
Animations
Videos

 Objectives
Medical Terminology Exercises & Activities
Audio Glossary
Drug Updates
Medical Terminology in the News

THE DIGESTIVE SYSTEM 6

OBJECTIVES

On completion of this chapter, you will be able to:

- Describe the digestive system.
- Describe the primary organs of the digestive system and state their functions.
- Describe the two sets of teeth that man is provided with.
- Describe the three main portions of a tooth.
- Describe the accessory organs of the digestive system and state their functions.
- Describe digestive differences of the child and the older adult.
- Analyze, build, spell, and pronounce medical words.
- Describe each of the conditions presented in the Pathology Spotlights.
- Complete the Pathology Checkpoint.
- Review Drug Highlights presented in this chapter.
- Provide the description of diagnostic and laboratory tests related to the digestive system.
- Identify and define selected abbreviations.
- Successfully complete the study and review section.

MedMedia
www.prenhall.com/rice

Additional interactive resources and activities for this chapter can be found on the Companion Website. For Terminology Translator, animations, videos, audio glossary, and review, access the accompanying CD-ROM in this book.

Anatomy and Physiology Overview

A general description of the digestive system is that of a continuous tube beginning with the mouth and ending at the anus. This tube is known as the **alimentary canal** and/or **gastrointestinal tract**. It measures about 30 feet in adults and contains both primary and accessory organs for the conversion of food and fluids into a semiliquid that can be absorbed for use by the body. The three main functions of the digestive system are **digestion, absorption,** and **elimination**. Each of the various organs commonly associated with digestion is described in this chapter. The organs of digestion are shown in Figure 6–1.

THE MOUTH

The **mouth** is the cavity formed by the palate or roof, the lips and cheeks on the sides, and the tongue at its floor. Contained within are the teeth and salivary glands. The cheeks form the lateral walls and are continuous with the lips. The vestibule includes the space between the cheeks and the teeth. The **gingivae** (gums) surround the necks of the teeth. The hard and soft palates provide a roof for the oral cavity, with the tongue at its floor. The free portion of the tongue is connected to the underlying epithelium by a thin fold of mucous membrane, the **lingual frenulum**. The **tongue** is made of skeletal muscle and is covered with mucous membrane. The tongue can be divided into a blunt rear portion called the **root**, a pointed **tip**, and a central **body**. Located on the surface of the tongue are **papillae** (elevations) and **taste buds** (sweet,

THE DIGESTIVE SYSTEM

Organ	Functions
Mouth	Breaks food apart by the action of the teeth, moistens and lubricates food with saliva; food formed into a bolus
Teeth	Serve as organs of mastication
Pharynx	Common passageway for both respiration and digestion; muscular constrictions move the bolus into the esophagus
Esophagus	Peristalsis moves the food down the esophagus into the stomach
Stomach	Reduces food to a digestible state, converts the food to a semiliquid form
Small Intestine	Digestion and absorption take place. Nutrients are absorbed into tiny capillaries and lymph vessels in the walls of the small intestine and transmitted to body cells by the circulatory system
Large Intestine	Removes water from the fecal material, stores, and then eliminates waste from the body via the rectum and anus
Salivary Glands	Secrete saliva to moisten and lubricate food
Liver	Changes glucose to glycogen and stores it until needed; changes glycogen back to glucose; desaturates fats, assists in protein catabolism, manufactures bile, fibrinogen, prothrombin, heparin, and blood proteins, stores vitamins, produces heat, and detoxifies substances
Gallbladder	Stores and concentrates bile
Pancreas	Secretes pancreatic juice into the small intestine, contains cells that produce digestive enzymes, secretes insulin and glucagon

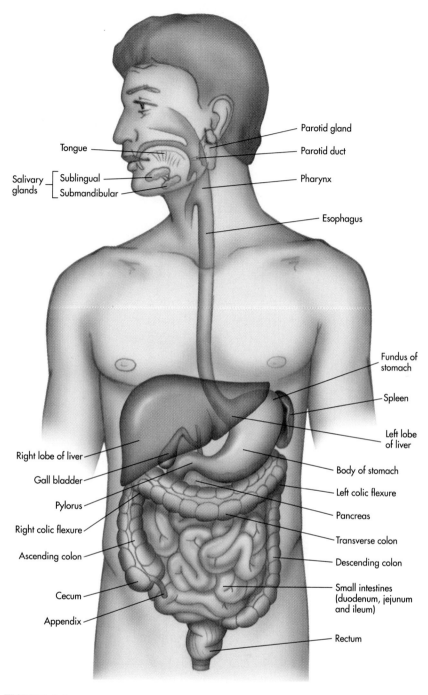

FIGURE 6–1

The digestive system.

salt, sour, and bitter). Three pairs of salivary glands secrete fluids into the oral cavity. These glands are the **parotid**, **sublingual**, and **submandibular**. The posterior margin of the soft palate supports the dangling uvula and two pairs of muscular pharyngeal arches. On either side, a palatine tonsil lies between an anterior palatoglossal arch and a posterior palatopharyngeal arch. A curving line that connects the palatoglossal arches and uvula forms the boundaries of the fauces, the passageway between the oral cavity and the pharynx (Fig. 6–2). Digestion begins as food is broken apart by the action of the teeth, moistened and lubricated by saliva, and formed into a **bolus**. A bolus is a small mass of masticated food ready to be swallowed.

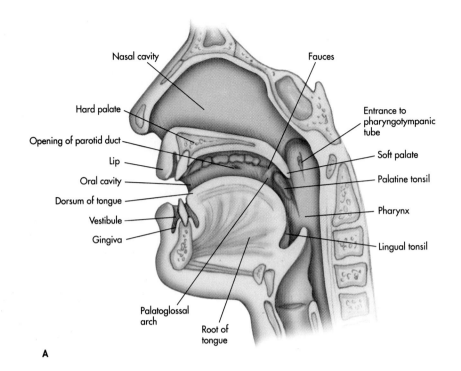

Nasal cavity

Fauces

Hard palate

Entrance to pharyngotympanic tube

Opening of parotid duct

Soft palate

Lip

Palatine tonsil

Oral cavity

Pharynx

Dorsum of tongue

Vestibule

Lingual tonsil

Gingiva

Palatoglossal arch

Root of tongue

A

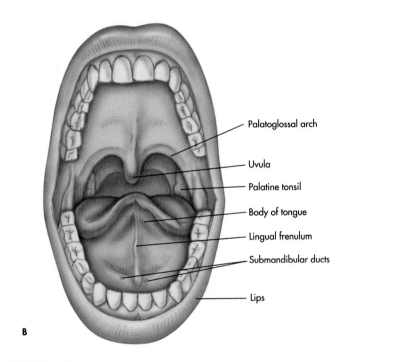

Palatoglossal arch

Uvula

Palatine tonsil

Body of tongue

Lingual frenulum

Submandibular ducts

Lips

B

FIGURE 6–2

The oral cavity: (A) sagittal section; (B) anterior view as seen through the open mouth.

THE TEETH

Man is provided with two sets of teeth. There are twenty **deciduous** teeth: eight incisors, four canines (cuspids), and eight molars. There are thirty-two **permanent** teeth: eight incisors, four canines, eight premolars, and twelve molars. See Figure 6–3.

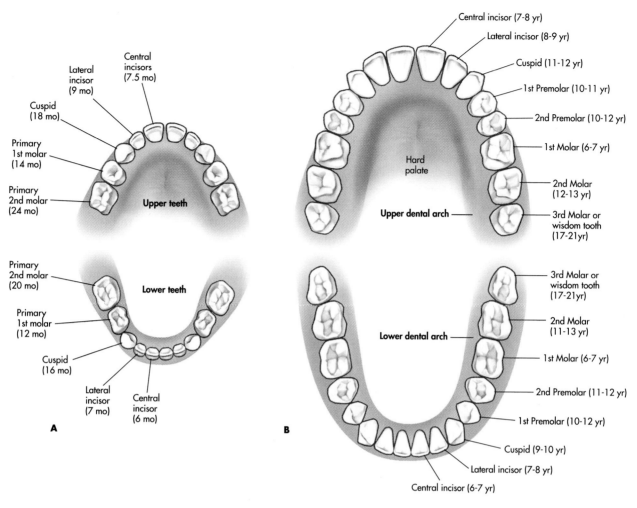

FIGURE 6–3

Deciduous and permanent teeth. (A) The deciduous teeth, with the age of eruption given in months; (B) the permanent teeth, with the age at eruption given in years.

The **incisors** are so named from their presenting a sharp cutting edge, adapted for biting the food. They form the four front teeth in each dental arch. The upper incisors are larger and stronger than the lower.

The **canine** or **cuspid** teeth are larger and stronger than the incisors, and their roots sink deeply into the bones, and cause well-marked prominences upon the surface. The upper canine teeth are called "eye teeth" and are larger and longer than the lower. The lower canine teeth, called "stomach teeth," are placed nearer the middle line than the upper.

The **premolars** or **bicuspid** teeth are situated lateral to and behind the canine teeth. They are eight in number, four in each arch and are smaller and shorter than the canine teeth.

The **molar** teeth are the largest of the permanent set, and their broad crowns are adapted for grinding and pounding the food. They are twelve in number: six in each arch, three being placed posterior to each of the second premolars.

The deciduous teeth are smaller than, but generally resemble in form, the teeth which bear the same names in the permanent set.

Each tooth consists of three main portions: the **crown**, projecting above the gum; the **root**, imbedded in the alveolus; and the **neck**, the constricted portion between the crown and root. The roots of the teeth are firmly implanted in depressions within the alveoli; these depressions are lined with periosteum, which invests the tooth as far as the neck. At the margins of the alveoli, the periosteum is continuous with the fibrous structure of the gums.

On making a vertical section of a tooth, a cavity will be found in the interior of the crown and the center of each root; it opens by a minute orifice at the extremity of the latter. See Figure 6–4. This is called the **pulp cavity**, and contains the dental pulp, a loose connective tissue richly supplied with vessels and nerves, which enter the cavity through the small aperture at the point of each root. The pulp cavity receives blood vessels and nerves from the **root canal**, a narrow tunnel located at the **root**, or base, of the tooth. Blood vessels and nerves enter the root canal through an opening called the **apical foramen** to supply the pulp cavity.

The root of each tooth sits in a bony socket called an alveolus. Collagen fibers of the **periodontal ligament** extend from the dentin of the root to the bone of the alveolus, creating a strong articulation known as a gomphosis (that binds the teeth to bony sockets in the maxillary bone and mandible). A layer of **cementum** covers the dentin of the root, providing protection and firmly anchoring the periodontal ligament.

The solid portion of the tooth consists of the **dentin**, which forms the bulk of the tooth; the **enamel**, which covers the exposed part of the crown and is the hardest and most compact part of a tooth; and a thin layer of bone, the **cementum**, which is disposed on the surface of the root.

The neck of the tooth marks the boundary between the root and the crown, the exposed portion of the tooth that projects above the soft tissue of the **gingiva**. A shallow groove called the **gingival sulcus** surrounds the neck of each tooth.

When the calcification of the different tissues of the tooth is sufficiently advanced to enable it to bear the pressure to which it will be afterward subjected, eruption takes place, the tooth making its way through the gums. The eruption of the deciduous teeth commences about the seventh month after birth, and is completed about the end of the second year, the teeth of the lower jaw preceding those of the upper. At the age of 2½ years a child should have 20 teeth.

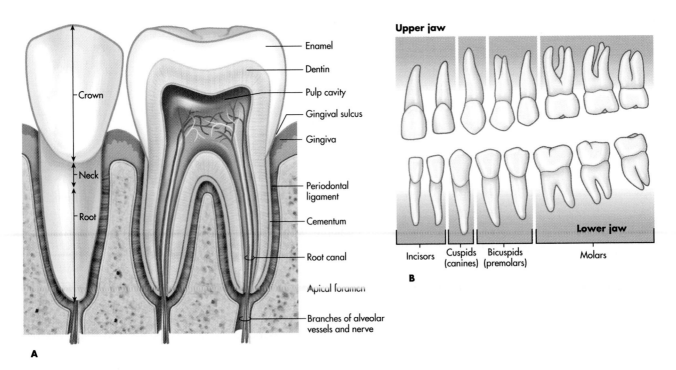

FIGURE 6–4

Teeth. (A) A diagrammatic section through a typical adult tooth; (B) the adult teeth.

The eruption of the permanent teeth takes place around the following time periods:

Upper Dental Arch

First molars	6th to 7th year
Two central incisors	7th to 8th year
Two lateral incisors	8th to 9th year
First premolars	10th to 11th year
Second premolars	10th to 12th year
Canines	11th to 12th year
Second molars	12th to 13th year
Third molars	17th to 21st year

THE PHARYNX

Just beyond the mouth, at the beginning of the tube leading to the stomach, is the **pharynx**. Simply put, the pharynx is a common passageway for both respiration and digestion. Both the **larynx**, or voicebox, and the esophagus begin in the pharynx. Food that is swallowed passes through the pharynx into the esophagus reflexively. Muscular constrictions move the ball of food into the esophagus while, at the same time, blocking the opening to the larynx and preventing the food from entering the airway leading to the trachea or windpipe.

THE ESOPHAGUS

The **esophagus** is a collapsible tube about 10 inches long that leads from the pharynx to the stomach. Food passes down the esophagus and into the stomach. Food is carried along the esophagus by a series of wave-like muscular contractions called **peristalsis**.

THE STOMACH

The **stomach** is a large sac-like organ into which food passes from the esophagus for storage while undergoing the early processes of digestion. In the stomach, food is further reduced to a digestible state. Hydrochloric acid and gastric juices convert the food to a semiliquid state, which is passed, at intervals, into the small intestine.

THE SMALL INTESTINE

The **small intestine** is about 21 feet long and 1 inch in diameter. It extends from the pyloric orifice at the base of the stomach to the entrance of the large intestine. The small intestine is considered to have three parts: the **duodenum**, the **jejunum**, and the

ileum. The duodenum is the first 12 inches just beyond the stomach. The jejunum is the next 8 feet or so, and the ileum is the remaining 12 feet of the tube. Semiliquid food (called **chyme**) is received from the stomach through the pylorus and mixed with bile from the liver and gallbladder along with pancreatic juice from the pancreas. Digestion and absorption take place chiefly in the small intestine. Nutrients are absorbed into tiny capillaries and lymph vessels in the walls of the small intestine and transmitted to body cells by the circulatory system.

THE LARGE INTESTINE

The **large intestine** is about 5 feet long and 2.5 inches in diameter. It extends from the ileocecal orifice at the small intestine to the anus. The large intestine may be divided into the **cecum**, the **colon**, the **rectum**, and the **anal canal**. The cecum is a pouch-like structure forming the beginning of the large intestine. It is about 3 inches long and has the appendix attached to it. The **colon** makes up the bulk of the large intestine and is divided into several parts—the ascending colon, the transverse colon, the descending colon, and, at its end, the sigmoid colon. Digestion and absorption continue in the large intestine on a reduced scale. The waste products of digestion are eliminated from the body via the rectum and the anus.

ACCESSORY ORGANS

The **salivary glands**, the **liver**, the **gallbladder**, and the **pancreas** are not actually part of the digestive tube; however, they are closely related to it in their functions.

The Salivary Glands

Located in or near the mouth, the **salivary glands** secrete **saliva** in response to the sight, smell, taste, or mental image of food. The various salivary glands are the **parotid**, located on either side of the face slightly below the ear; the **submandibular**, located in the floor of the mouth; and the **sublingual**, located below the tongue. All salivary glands secrete through openings into the mouth to moisten and lubricate food.

The Liver

The largest glandular organ in the body, the **liver** weighs about 3½ lb and is located in the upper right part of the abdomen. The liver plays an essential role in the normal metabolism of carbohydrates, fats, and proteins. In carbohydrate metabolism, it changes glucose to glycogen and stores it until needed by body cells. It also changes glycogen back to glucose. In fat metabolism, the liver serves as a storage place and acts to desaturate fats before releasing them into the bloodstream. In protein metabolism, the liver acts as a storage place and assists in protein catabolism.

The liver manufactures the following important substances:

- **Bile**—a digestive juice
- **Fibrinogen and prothrombin**—coagulants essential for blood clotting
- **Heparin**—an anticoagulant that helps to prevent the clotting of blood
- **Blood proteins**—albumin, gamma globulin

Additionally, the liver stores iron and vitamins B_{12}, A, D, E, and K. It also produces body heat and detoxifies many harmful substances such as drugs and alcohol.

The Gallbladder

The **gallbladder** is a membranous sac attached to the liver in which excess bile is stored and concentrated. Bile leaving the gallbladder is 6 to 10 times as concentrated as that which comes to it from the liver. Concentration is accomplished by absorption of water from the bile into the mucosa of the gallbladder.

The Pancreas

The **pancreas** is a large, elongated gland situated behind the stomach and secreting pancreatic juice into the small intestine. The pancreas is 6 to 9 inches long and contains cells that produce digestive **enzymes**. Other cells in the pancreas secrete the hormones insulin and glucagon directly into the bloodstream.

LIFE SPAN CONSIDERATIONS

■ THE CHILD

The primitive digestive tract is formed by the embryonic membrane (yolk sac) and is divided into three sections. The **foregut** evolves into the pharynx, lower respiratory tract, esophagus, stomach, duodenum, and beginning of the common bile duct. The **midgut** elongates in the fifth week to form the primary intestinal loop. The remainder of the large colon is derived from the primitive **hindgut**. The liver, pancreas, and biliary tract evolve from the **foregut**. At 8 weeks, the anal membrane ruptures, forming the anal canal and opening.

Normally the functioning of the gastrointestinal tract begins after birth. Food is prepared for absorption and absorbed, and waste products are eliminated. **Meconium**, the first stool, is a mixture of amniotic fluid and secretions of the intestinal glands. It is thick and sticky, and dark green in color. It is usually passed 8 to 24 hours following birth. The stools change during the first week and become loose and greenish-yellow. The stools of a breast-fed baby are bright yellow, soft, and pasty. The stools of a bottle-fed baby are more solid than those of the breast-fed baby and they vary from yellow to brown in color.

The infant's stomach is small and empties rapidly. Newborns produce very little saliva until they are 3 months of age. Swallowing is a reflex action for the first 3 months. The hepatic efficiency of the newborn is often immature, thereby, causing **jaundice**. Fat absorption is poor because of a decreased level of bile production.

■ THE OLDER ADULT

With aging, the digestive system becomes less motile, as muscle contractions become weaker. Glandular secretions decrease, thus causing a drier mouth and a lower volume of gastric juices. Nutrient absorption is mildly reduced due to **atrophy** of the mucosal lining. The teeth are mechanically worn down with age and begin to recede from the gums. There is a loss of tastebuds, and food preferences change. Gastric motor activity slows; as a result, gastric emptying is delayed and hunger contractions diminish. There are no significant changes in the small intestine, but in the large intestine, the muscle layer and mucosa atrophy. Smooth muscle tone and blood flow decrease, and connective tissue increases.

Constipation is a frequent problem among older adults. It is believed that constipation is not a normal age-related change, but is caused by low fluid intake, lack of dietary fiber, inactivity, medicines, depression, and other health-related conditions.

BUILDING YOUR MEDICAL VOCABULARY

This section provides the foundation for learning medical terminology. Medical words can be made up of four different types of word parts:

- Prefixes (P)
- Roots (R)
- Combining forms (CF)
- Suffixes (S)

By connecting various word parts in an organized sequence, thousands of words can be built and learned. In this text the word list is alphabetized so one can see the variety of meanings created when common prefixes and suffixes are repeatedly applied to certain word roots and/or combining forms. Words shown in pink are additional words related to the content of this chapter that are not built from word parts. These words are included to enhance your vocabulary. Note: an asterisk icon ✱ indicates words that are covered in the Pathology Spotlights section in this chapter.

MEDICAL WORD	WORD PARTS (WHEN APPLICABLE)			DEFINITION
	Part	Type	Meaning	
absorption (ăb-sōrp′ shŭn)	absorpt -ion	R S	to suck in process	The process whereby nutrient material is taken into the bloodstream or lymph
amylase (ăm′ ĭ-lās)	amyl -ase	R S	starch enzyme	An enzyme that breaks down starch
anabolism (ă-năb′ ō-lĭzm)	ana bol -ism	P R S	up to cast, throw condition of	Literally "a throwing upward"; the building up of the body substance
anorexia (ăn″ ō-rĕks′ ĭ-ă)	an -orexia	P S	lack of appetite	Lack of appetite
appendectomy (ăp″ ĕn-dĕk′ tō-mē)	append -ectomy	R S	appendix excision	Surgical excision of the appendix
appendicitis (ă-pĕn″ di-sī′ tis)	appendic -itis	R S	appendix inflammation	Inflammation of the appendix
ascites (ă-sī′ tēz)				An accumulation of serous fluid in the peritoneal cavity
biliary (bĭl′ ĭ-ār″ ē)	bil/i -ary	CF S	gall, bile pertaining to	Pertaining to or conveying bile

MEDICAL WORD	WORD PARTS (WHEN APPLICABLE)			DEFINITION
	Part	**Type**	**Meaning**	
bilirubin (bĭl″ ĭ-rōō′ bĭn)				The orange-colored bile pigment produced by the separation of hemoglobin into parts that are excreted by the liver cells
black hairy tongue				A condition in which the tongue is covered by hair-like papillae, entangled with threads produced by *Aspergillus niger* or *Candida albicans* fungi. This condition may be caused by poor oral hygiene and/or overgrowth of fungi due to antibiotic therapy. See Figure 6–5.
bowel (bou′əl)				The intestine, gut, entrail
buccal (bək′ əl)	bucc -al	R S	cheek pertaining to	Pertaining to the cheek
bulimia (bū-lĭm′ē-ă)				A condition of episodic binge eating with or without self-induced vomiting. ✳ See Pathology Spotlight: Eating Disorders.
catabolism (kă-tăb′ ō-lĭzm)	cata bol -ism	P R S	down to cast, throw condition of	Literally "a throwing down"; a breaking of complex substances into more basic elements
celiac (sē′ lĭ-ăk)	celi -ac	R S	abdomen, belly pertaining to	Pertaining to the abdomen
cheilosis (kī-lō′ sĭs)	cheil -osis	R S	lip condition of	An abnormal condition of the lip as seen in riboflavin and other B-complex deficiencies
cholecystectomy (kō″ lē-sĭs-tĕk′ tō-mē)	chol/e cyst -ectomy	CF R S	gall, bile bladder excision	Surgical excision of the gallbladder; with laparoscopic cholecystectomy, the gallbladder is removed through a small incision near the navel
cholecystitis (kō″ lē-sĭs-tī′ tĭs)	chol/e cyst -itis	CF R S	gall, bile bladder inflammation	Inflammation of the gallbladder
choledochotomy (kō-lĕd″ ō-kŏt′ ō-mē)	choledoch/o -tomy	CF S	common bile duct incision	Surgical incision of the common bile duct
chyle (kīl)				The milky fluid of intestinal digestion, composed of lymph and emulsified fats

MEDICAL WORD	WORD PARTS (WHEN APPLICABLE)			DEFINITION
	Part	**Type**	**Meaning**	
cirrhosis (sĭ-rō′ sĭs)	cirrh -osis	R S	orange-yellow condition of	A chronic degenerative liver disease characterized by changes in the lobes; parenchymal cells and the lobules are infiltrated with fat. See Figure 6–6.
colectomy (kō-lĕk′ tō-mē)	col -ectomy	R S	colon excision	Surgical excision of part of the colon
colon cancer (kō-lŏn kăn′ ser)				A malignancy of the colon; sometimes called "colorectal cancer"
colonic (kō-lŏn′ ĭk)	colon -ic	R S	colon pertaining to	Pertaining to the colon
colonoscopy (kō-lŏn-ŏs′ kō-pē)	colon/o -scopy	CF S	colon to view, examine	Examination of the upper portion of the colon
colostomy (kō-lŏs′ tō-mē)	col/o -stomy	CF S	colon new opening	The creation of a new opening into the colon
constipation (kon″ stĭ-pā′ shŭn)	constipat -ion	R S	to press together process	Infrequent passage of unduly hard and dry feces; *difficult defecation*
Crohn's disease (krōnz dĭ-zez′)				A chronic autoimmune disease that can affect any part of the gastrointestinal tract but most commonly occurs in the ileum
defecation (dĕf-ĕ-kā′ shŭn)	defecat -ion	R S	to remove dregs process	The evacuation of the bowel
deglutition (dē″ glōō-tĭsh′ ŭn)				The act or process of swallowing
dentalgia (dĕn-tăl′ jĭ-ă)	dent -algia	R S	tooth pain	Pain in a tooth; *toothache*
dentist (dĕn′ təst)	dent -ist	R S	tooth one who specializes	One who specializes in dentistry
diarrhea (dī′ ă-rē′ ă)	dia -rrhea	P S	through flow	Frequent passage of unformed watery stools
digestion (dī-jĕst′ chŭn)	di gest -ion	P R S	through to carry process	The process by which food is changed in the mouth, stomach, and intestines by chemical, mechanical, and physical action so that it can be absorbed by the body

MEDICAL WORD	WORD PARTS (WHEN APPLICABLE)			DEFINITION
	Part	**Type**	**Meaning**	
diverticulitis (dĭ″ vĕr-tĭk″ ū-lī′ tĭs)	diverticul -itis	R S	diverticula inflammation	Inflammation of the diverticula in the colon. ✶ See Figure 6–10 in Pathology Spotlight: Diverticulitis.
duodenal (dū″ ō-dē′ năl)	duoden -al	R S	duodenum pertaining to	Pertaining to the duodenum; the first part of the small intestine
dysentery (dĭs′ ĕn-tĕr″ ē)	dys enter -y	P R S	difficult intestine pertaining to	An intestinal disease characterized by inflammation of the mucous membrane
dyspepsia (dĭs-pĕp′ sĭ-ă)	dys -pepsia	P S	difficult to digest	Difficulty in digestion; *indigestion*
dysphagia (dĭs-fā′ jĭ-ă)	dys -phagia	P S	difficult to eat	Difficulty in swallowing
eating disorder (ē′ tĭng dĭs-ōr′ dĕr)				A health condition characterized by a preoccupation with weight that results in severe disturbances in eating behavior; anorexia nervosa and bulimia are the most common types. ✶ See Pathology Spotlight: Eating Disorders.
emesis (ĕm′ ĕ-sĭs)	eme -sis	R S	to vomit condition of	Vomiting
enteric (ĕn-tĕr′ ĭk)	enter -ic	R S	intestine pertaining to	Pertaining to the intestine
enteritis (ĕn″ tĕr-ī′ tĭs)	enter -itis	R S	intestine inflammation	Inflammation of the intestine
enzyme (ĕn′ zīm)				A protein substance capable of causing chemical changes in other substances without being changed itself
epigastric (ĕp′ ĭ-găs′ trĭc)	epi gastr -ic	P R S	above stomach pertaining to	Pertaining to the region above the stomach
eructation (ē-rk-tā′ shŭn)	eructat -ion	R S	a breaking out process	Belching
esophageal (ē-sŏf″ ă-jē′ ăl)	esophag/e -al	CF S	esophagus pertaining to	Pertaining to the esophagus
feces (fē′ sēz)				Body waste expelled from the bowels; *stools, excreta*

MEDICAL WORD	WORD PARTS (WHEN APPLICABLE)			DEFINITION
	Part	Type	Meaning	
fibroma (fĭ-brō′ mă)	fibr -oma	R S	fibrous tissue tumor	A fibrous, encapsulated connective tissue tumor. See Figure 6–7.
flatus (flā′ tŭs)				Gas in the stomach or intestines
gastrectomy (găs-trĕk′ tō-mē)	gastr -ectomy	R S	stomach excision	Surgical excision of a part or the whole stomach
gastric (găs′ trĭk)	gastr -ic	R S	stomach pertaining to	Pertaining to the stomach
gastroenterology (găs″ trō-ĕn″ tĕr-ŏl′ ō-jē)	gastr/o enter/o -logy	CF CF S	stomach intestine study of	Study of the stomach and the intestines
gastroesophageal (găs′ trō ē-sŏf″ ă-jē-ăl)	gastr/o esophag/e -al	CF CF S	stomach esophagus pertaining to	Pertaining to the stomach and esophagus
gastroesophageal reflux (găs′ trō ē-sŏf″ ă-jē-ăl rē′ flŭcks)				Occurs when the muscle between the esophagus and the stomach, the lower esophageal sphincter, is weak or relaxes inappropriately, allowing the stomach's contents to back up ("reflux") into the esophagus. ✳ See Pathology Spotlight: Gastroesophageal Reflux Disease.
gavage (gă-văzh′)				To feed liquid or semiliquid food via a tube (stomach or nasogastric)
gingivitis (jĭn″ jĭ-vī′ tĭs)	gingiv -itis	R S	gums inflammation	Inflammation of the gums
glossotomy (glŏ-sŏt′ ō-mē)	gloss/o -tomy	CF S	tongue incision	Surgical incision into the tongue
glycogenesis (glī″ kŏ-jĕn′ ĕ-sĭs)	glyc/o -genesis	CF S	sweet, sugar formation, produce	The formation of glycogen from glucose
halitosis (hăl″ ĭ-tō′ sĭs)	halit -osis	R S	breath condition of	Bad breath
hematemesis (hĕm″ ăt-ēm′ ĕ-sĭs)	hemat -emesis	R S	blood vomiting	Vomiting of blood
hemorrhoid (hĕm′ ō-royd)	hemorrh -oid	R S	vein liable to bleed resemble	A mass of dilated, tortuous veins in the anorectum; may be internal or external

MEDICAL WORD	WORD PARTS (WHEN APPLICABLE)			DEFINITION
	Part	Type	Meaning	
hepatitis (hĕp″ ă-tī′ tĭs)	hepat -itis	R S	liver inflammation	Inflammation of the liver
hepatoma (hĕp″ ă-tŏ′ mă)	hepat -oma	R S	liver tumor	A tumor of the liver
hernia (hĕr′ nē-ă)				The abnormal protrusion of an organ or a part of an organ through the wall of the body cavity that normally contains it. ✱ See Figure 6–12 in Pathology Spotlight: Hernia.
herniotomy (hĕr″ nĭ-ŏt′ ō-mē)	herni/o -tomy	CF S	hernia incision	Surgical incision for the repair of a hernia
hyperalimentation (hī″ pĕr-ăl″ ĭ mĕn-tā′ shŭn)	hyper alimentat -ion	P R S	excessive nourishment process	An intravenous infusion of a hypertonic solution to sustain life; used in patients whose gastrointestinal tracts are not functioning properly
hyperemesis (hī″ pĕr-ĕm′ ĕ-sĭs)	hyper -emesis	P S	excessive, above vomiting	Excessive vomiting
hypogastric (hī″ pō-găs′ trĭk)	hypo gastr -ic	P R S	deficient, below stomach pertaining to	Pertaining to below the stomach
ileitis (ĭl″ ē-ī′ tis)	ile -itis	R S	ileum inflammation	Inflammation of the ileum
ileostomy (ĭl″ ē-ŏs′ tō-mē)	ile/o -stomy	CF S	ileum new opening	The creation of a new opening through the abdominal wall into the ileum
irritable bowel syndrome (IBS) (ĭr′ ă-tă-bl bŏu′ ĕl sĭn′ drōm)				A disorder that interferes with the normal functions of the large intestine (colon). It is characterized by a group of symptoms, including crampy abdominal pain, bloating, constipation, and diarrhea. ✱ See Pathology Spotlight: Irritable Bowel Syndrome.
labial (lā′ bĭ-ăl)	labi -al	R S	lip pertaining to	Pertaining to the lip
laparotomy (lăp″ ăr-ŏt′ ō-mē)	lapar/o -tomy	CF S	flank, abdomen incision	Surgical incision into the abdomen
lavage (lă-văzh′)				To wash out a cavity

MEDICAL WORD	WORD PARTS (WHEN APPLICABLE)			DEFINITION
	Part	Type	Meaning	
laxative (lăk′ să-tĭv)	laxat -ive	R S	to loosen nature of, quality of	A substance that acts to loosen the bowels
lingual (lĭng′ gwal)	lingu -al	R S	tongue pertaining to	Pertaining to the tongue
lipolysis (lĭp-ŏl′ ĭ-sĭs)	lip/o -lysis	CF S	fat destruction, to separate	The destruction of fat
liver transplant (lĭv′ ĕr trăns′ plănt)				The surgical process of transferring the liver from a donor to a patient
malabsorption (măl″ ăb-sōrp′ shŭn)	mal absorpt -ion	P R S	bad to suck in process	The process of bad or inadequate absorption of nutrients from the intestinal tract
mastication (măs″ tĭ-kā′ shŭn)	masticat -ion	R S	to chew process	Chewing
melena (mĕl′ ĕ-nă)				Black feces caused by the action of intestinal juices on blood
mesentery (mĕs′ ĕn-tĕr″ ē)	mes enter -y	R R S	middle intestine pertaining to	Pertaining to the peritoneal fold encircling the small intestines and connecting the intestines to the abdominal wall
nausea (naw′ sē-ă)				The feeling of the inclination to vomit
pancreas transplant (păn′ krē-ăs trăns plănt)				The surgical process of transferring the pancreas from a donor to a patient
pancreatitis (păn″ krē-ă-tī′ tĭs)	pancreat -itis	R S	pancreas inflammation	Inflammation of the pancreas
paralytic ileus (păr″ ă-lĭt′ ĭk ĭl′ ē-ŭs)	paralyt -ic ile -us	R S R S	to disable; paralysis pertaining to a twisting pertaining to	A paralysis of the intestines that causes distention and symptoms of acute obstruction and prostration
peptic (pĕp′ tĭk)	pept -ic	R S	to digest pertaining to	Pertaining to gastric digestion
periodontal (pĕr″ ē-ō-dŏn′ tăl)	peri odont -al	P R S	around tooth pertaining to	Pertaining to the area around the tooth

MEDICAL WORD	WORD PARTS (WHEN APPLICABLE)			DEFINITION
	Part	**Type**	**Meaning**	
periodontal disease (pĕr″ ē-ō-dŏn′ tăl dĭ-zēz′)				Inflammation and degeneration of the gums and surrounding bone, which frequently causes loss of the teeth
peristalsis (pĕr″ ĭ-stăl′ sĭs)	peri -stalsis	P S	around contraction	A wave-like contraction that occurs involuntarily in hollow tubes of the body, especially the alimentary canal
pharyngeal (făr-ĭn′ jē-ăl)	pharyng/e -al	CF S	pharynx pertaining to	Pertaining to the pharynx
pilonidal cyst (pī″ lō-nī′ dăl sĭst)	pil/o nid -al cyst	CF R S R	hair nest pertaining to sac	A closed sac in the crease of the sacrococcygeal region caused by a developmental defect that permits epithelial tissue and hair to be trapped below the skin
postprandial (pōst-prăn′ dĭ-ăl)	post prand/i -al	P CF S	after meal pertaining to	Pertaining to after a meal
proctologist (prŏk-tŏl′ ō-jĭst)	proct/o log -ist	CF R S	rectum, anus study of one who specializes	One who specializes in the study of the anus and the rectum
proctoscope (prŏk′ tō-scōp)	proct/o -scope	CF S	rectum, anus instrument	An instrument used to view the anus and rectum
pyloric (pī-lōr′ ĭk)	pylor -ic	R S	pylorus, gatekeeper pertaining to	Pertaining to the gatekeeper, the opening between the stomach and the duodenum
rectocele (rĕk′ tō-sēl)	rect/o -cele	CF S	rectum hernia	A hernia of part of the rectum into the vagina
sialadenitis (sī″ ăl-ăd″ ĕ-nī′ tĭs)	sial aden -itis	R R S	saliva gland inflammation	Inflammation of the salivary gland
sigmoidoscope (sĭg-moy′ dō-skōp)	sigmoid/o -scope	CF S	sigmoid instrument	An instrument used to view the sigmoid
splenomegaly (splē″ nō-mĕg′ ă-lē)	splen/o -megaly	CF S	spleen enlargement, large	Enlargement of the spleen
stomatitis (stō″ mă-tī′ tĭs)	stomat -itis	R S	mouth inflammation	Inflammation of the mouth

MEDICAL WORD	WORD PARTS (WHEN APPLICABLE)			DEFINITION
	Part	**Type**	**Meaning**	
sublingual (sŭb-lĭng′ gwăl)	sub lingu -al	P R S	below tongue pertaining to	Pertaining to below the tongue. See Figure 6–8.
ulcer (ŭl′ sĕr)				An open lesion or sore of the epidermis or mucous membrane. A peptic ulcer forms in the mucosal wall of the stomach, the pylorus, the duodenum, or the esophagus. It is referred to as a *gastric, duodenal,* or *esophageal ulcer,* depending on the location. ✳ See Figure 6–13 in Pathology Spotlight: Peptic Ulcer Disease.
ulcerative colitis (ŭl′ sĕr-ă-tĭv kō-lī′ tĭs)				A disease that causes inflammation and ulcers in the lining of the large intestine. The inflammation usually occurs in the rectum and lower part of the colon, but it may affect the entire colon. May also be called colitis or proctitis.
vermiform (vēr′ mĭ-form)	verm/i -form	CF S	worm shape	Shaped like a worm
volvulus (vŏl′ vū-lŭs)	volvul -us	R S	to roll pertaining to	A twisting of the bowel on itself that causes an obstruction. See Figure 6–9.
vomit (vŏm′ ĭt)				To eject stomach contents through the mouth

Terminology Translator

Medicine Medicina Médecine Medizin   **This feature, found on the accompanying CD-ROM, provides an innovative tool to translate medical words into Spanish, French, and German.**

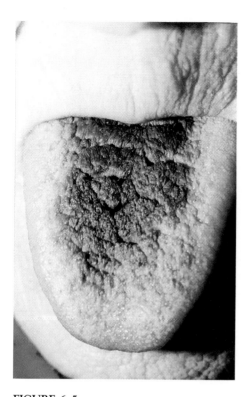

FIGURE 6–5

Black hairy tongue. (Courtesy of Jason L. Smith, MD.)

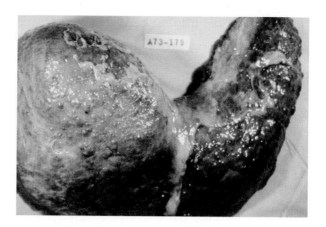

FIGURE 6–6

Cirrhosis of the liver. (Source: Pearson Education/PH College.)

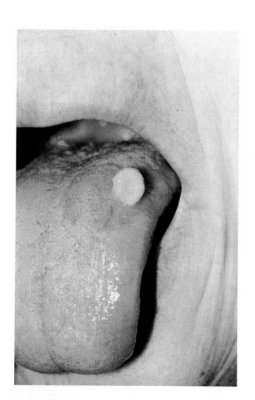

FIGURE 6–7

Fibroma. (Courtesy of Jason L. Smith, MD.)

FIGURE 6–8

Sublingual drug administration. (Source: Pearson Education/PH College.)

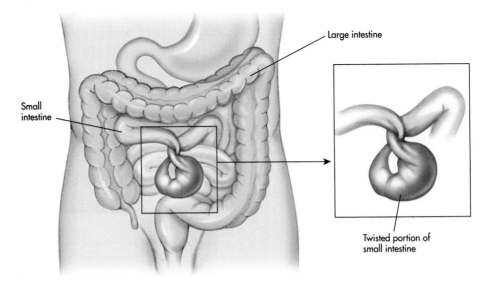

Large intestine

Small intestine

Twisted portion of small intestine

FIGURE 6–9

Volvulus.

PATHOLOGY SPOTLIGHTS

Diverticulitis

Diverticulitis is an inflammation of the diverticula in the colon. Pain is a common symptom of diverticulitis. Diverticulitis occurs when a **diverticulum** (a pouch or sac in the walls of an organ or canal) becomes inflamed or infected. See Figure 6–10. The exact cause of this condition is unknown, but it generally begins when stool lodges in the diverticula. Infection can lead to complications such as swelling or rupturing of the diverticula. Symptoms include pain, fever, chills, cramping, bloating, constipation, or diarrhea. Treatment depends upon the severity of the condition. A liquid diet and oral antibiotics are used for mild conditions, generally, followed by a high-fiber diet (see Table 6–1). If the condition is severe, hospitalization, bedrest, IV antibiotics and fluids, and/or surgery are recommended.

Eating Disorders

Eating disorders are health conditions characterized by a preoccupation with weight that results in severe disturbances in eating behavior. These disorders include anorexia nervosa and bulimia.

Anorexia nervosa essentially is self-starvation, in which a person refuses to maintain a normal body weight. It is a complex psychological disorder in which the individual refuses to eat or has an aberrant eating pattern. People with eating disorders may engage in self-induced vomiting and abuse of laxatives, diuretics or exercise in order to control their weight. The condition may lead them to become thin or even emaciated. In severe cases, anorexia can be life-threatening. See Figure 6–11.

Bulimia involves repeated episodes of binge eating, followed by inappropriate ways of trying to rid the body of the food or of the expected weight gain. A person with bulimia may consume large, high-calorie meals, and then induce vomiting or take laxatives to try to rid the body of the food before the body absorbs calories and weight gain occurs. People may have this condition and be of normal weight.

The incidence of anorexia and bulimia is higher among teenage girls and young women than in other groups of Americans. Males can develop either disorder, and the disorders may be more common among males than previously thought. Females account for about 90 percent

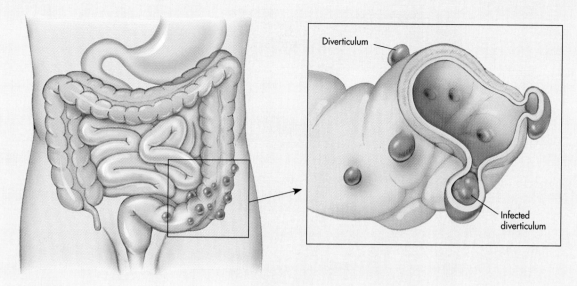

FIGURE 6–10

Diverticulitis.

of eating disorders in the United States. According to the American Psychiatric Association, between 0.5 percent and 3.7 percent of females experience anorexia, and between 1.1 and 4.2 percent of females experience bulimia in their lifetime.

Gastroesophageal Reflux Disease (GERD)

Gastroesophageal reflux disease (GERD) occurs when the muscle between the esophagus and the stomach, the lower esophageal sphincter, is weak or relaxes inappropriately. This allows the stomach's contents to back up ("reflux") into the esophagus. It is also called esophageal reflux or reflux esophagitis. Symptoms include heartburn, belching, and regurgitation of food.

TABLE 6–1 GOOD CHOICES OF HIGH-FIBER FOODS

One needs 25 to 30 grams of fiber each day to keep the colon working at its best. The following are selected good choices of high-fiber foods.

Fruits

1 medium apple	4 grams
1 medium pear	4 grams
1 medium orange	3 grams
1 cup strawberries	3 grams
5 dried prunes (uncooked)	3 grams

Vegetables

1 baked potato (with skin)	5 grams
1/2 cup cooked frozen peas	4 grams
1/2 cup cooked fresh spinach	3 grams
1/2 cup cooked frozen corn	2 grams

Beans

1/2 cup cooked lentils	8 grams
1/2 cup cooked kidney beans	6 grams
1/2 cup cooked green beans	2 grams

Whole-Grain Cereals

1/3 cup all-bran cereal	10 grams
1/3 cup wheat flakes	3 grams
1/3 cup shredded wheat	3 grams

Whole-Bran Breads and Rice

2 slices whole-wheat bread	4 grams
2 slices rye bread	4 grams
1/2 cup cooked brown rice	2 grams

Pure Bran

3 T unprocessed wheat bran	6 grams
3 T unprocessed oat bran	3 grams

T = tablespoon

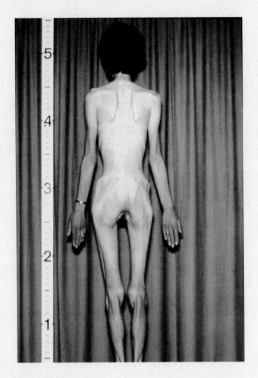

FIGURE 6–11

An emaciated young woman with anorexia nervosa.
(Source: Custom Medical Stock Photo, Inc.)

Most GERD sufferers have frequent, severe heartburn. This tears down and damages the cell wall lining of the esophagus. Without treatment, GERD can lead to the following conditions: Barrett's esophagus, a precancerous change in the cells lining the esophagus; esophageal cancer; esophageal perforation, or a hole in the esophagus; esophageal ulcers, which damage the lining further; esophagitis, inflammation of the esophagus and/or esophageal stricture, or narrowing of the esophagus that interferes with eating. When deemed necessary, a surgical procedure known as **dilation** is done to correct esophageal stricture. The surgeon passes a series of dilators down the esophagus. The dilators gently stretch the narrowed opening apart.

Dietary and lifestyle choices may contribute to GERD. Certain foods and beverages, such as chocolate, peppermint, fried or fatty foods, coffee, or alcoholic beverages, may weaken the lower esophageal sphincter (LES) and cause reflux and heartburn. Studies show that cigarette smoking relaxes the lower esophageal sphincter. Obesity and pregnancy can also cause GERD. Some doctors believe a **hiatal hernia** may weaken the LES and cause reflux.

Decreasing the size of portions at mealtime may help control symptoms. Eating meals at least 2 to 3 hours before bedtime may lessen reflux by allowing the acid in the stomach to decrease and the stomach to empty partially. In addition, being overweight often worsens symptoms. Many overweight people find relief when they lose weight.

Some of the medical and surgical treatments for GERD include: **fundoplication**, a surgical reduction of the opening into the fundus of the stomach, and suturing of the previously removed end of the esophagus to the opening; medications: H_2 blockers, such as cimetidine (Tagamet), ranitidine (Zantac), famotidine (Pepcid), and nizatidine (Axid) and proton-pump inhibitors, such as esomeprazole (Nexium), omeprazole (Prilosec), lansoprazole (Prevacid), rabeprazole (Aciphex), or pantoprazole (Protonix).

Hernia

A **hernia** is the abnormal protrusion of an organ or a part of an organ through the wall of the body cavity that normally contains it. Most often, the term hernia refers to an abdominal hernia. The two most common types of abdominal hernia are hiatal and inguinal.

Hiatal hernia occurs when the upper part of the stomach moves up into the chest through a small opening in the diaphragm. See Figure 6–12. Studies show that the opening in the diaphragm acts as an additional sphincter around the lower end of the esophagus. Studies also show that hiatal hernia results in retention of acid and other contents above this opening. These substances can reflux easily into the esophagus.

Coughing, vomiting, straining, or sudden physical exertion can cause increased pressure in the abdomen that results in hiatal hernia. Obesity and pregnancy also contribute to this condition. Many otherwise healthy people age 50 and over have a small hiatal hernia. Although considered a condition of middle age, hiatal hernias affect people of all ages.

Hiatal hernias usually do not require treatment. However, treatment may be necessary if the hernia is in danger of becoming strangulated (twisted in a way that cuts off blood supply) or is complicated by severe GERD or esophagitis. The physician may perform surgery to reduce the size of the hernia or to prevent strangulation.

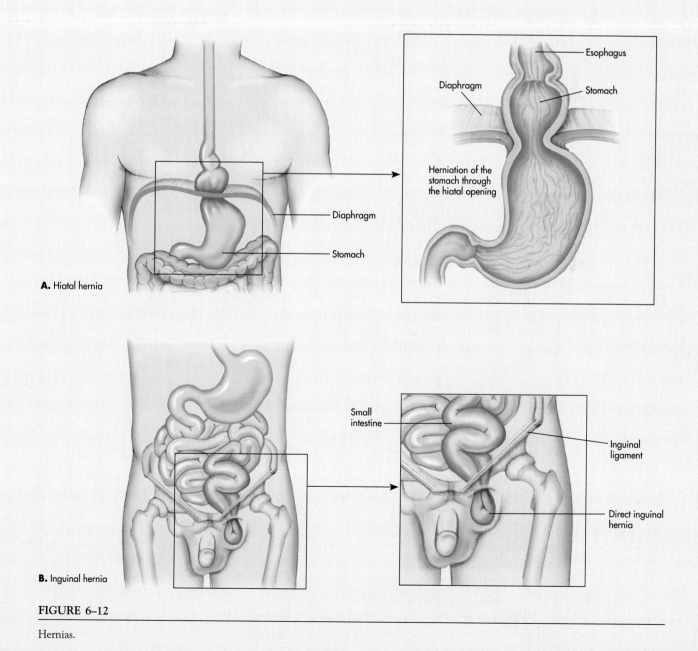

A. Hiatal hernia

B. Inguinal hernia

FIGURE 6–12

Hernias.

An **inguinal hernia** occurs when a loop of intestine enters the inguinal canal, a tubular passage through the lower layers of the abdominal wall. Symptoms include groin discomfort or pain, and in the male, a scrotum lump.

This type of hernia is sometimes associated with heavy lifting. In men, an inguinal hernia can develop in the groin near the scrotum. A direct inguinal hernia creates a bulge in the groin area, and an indirect hernia descends into the scrotum. Inguinal hernias occur more often in men than in women. A family history of hernias increases the risk.

Infants and children may also develop inguinal hernias. In these populations, hernias can occur when a portion of the peritoneum (the lining around all the organs in the abdomen) does not close properly before birth. This causes a small portion of the intestine to push out into the opening (a bulge might be seen in the groin or scrotum). According to the American Academy of Pediatrics, 5 out of 100 children have inguinal hernias (more boys than girls). Some may not have symptoms until adulthood.

Diagnosis is typically made through a physical examination in which the hernia mass is palpated, and may increase in size when coughing, bending, lifting, or straining. The hernia (bulge) may not be obvious in infants and children, except when the child is crying or coughing. Treatment is usually done through a hernia repair surgery, in which the hernia is pushed back into the abdominal cavity.

Irritable Bowel Syndrome (IBS)

Irritable bowel syndrome (IBS) is a disorder that interferes with the normal functions of the large intestine (colon). It is characterized by a group of symptoms, including crampy abdominal pain, bloating, constipation, and diarrhea. The cause is not known, but the symptoms are often worsened by emotional stress.

Symptoms of irritable bowel syndrome may include: abdominal distress that is often relieved with a bowel movement; bloating, or feeling like the stomach is inflated; excess gas and changes in stool. Some people with IBS may have painful, loose stools, or diarrhea, while others may have painful hard stools, or constipation. Some people may alternate between diarrhea and constipation.

One in five Americans has IBS, making it one of the most common disorders diagnosed by doctors. It occurs more often in women than in men, and it usually begins between the ages of 20 and 30. Predisposing factors may include a low-fiber diet, emotional stress, and use of laxatives.

IBS causes a great deal of discomfort and distress, but it does not permanently harm the intestines and does not lead to intestinal bleeding or to any serious disease such as cancer. Treatment of irritable bowel syndrome often focuses on treating the symptoms and preventing flare-ups. Most people can control their symptoms with diet, stress management, and medications prescribed by their physician. Increasing dietary fiber and eliminating stimulants such as caffeine may be beneficial. See Table 6–1. Exercise and counseling for anxiety may be helpful, as well. But for some people, IBS can be disabling. They may be unable to work, go to social events, or travel even short distances.

Peptic Ulcer Disease

Peptic ulcer disease occurs when the lining of the esophagus, stomach, or duodenum is worn away. See Figure 6–13. Peptic ulcer disease most commonly occurs in the upper part of the small intestine, called the duodenum. It also occurs in the stomach. Ulcers less commonly occur in the esophagus.

Symptoms of peptic ulcer disease include abdominal pain, nausea, vomiting, and weight loss. Peptic ulcers may also cause no symptoms. An esophageal ulcer may also cause chest pain. Other common symptoms include: black, tarlike, or maroon-colored stools; blood in the stool; and/or burning or gnawing pain in the stomach, the chest, or the back.

Peptic ulcers are caused by an imbalance between acid and pepsin (an enzyme) secretion and the defenses of the mucosal lining. This leads to inflammation, which may also be caused

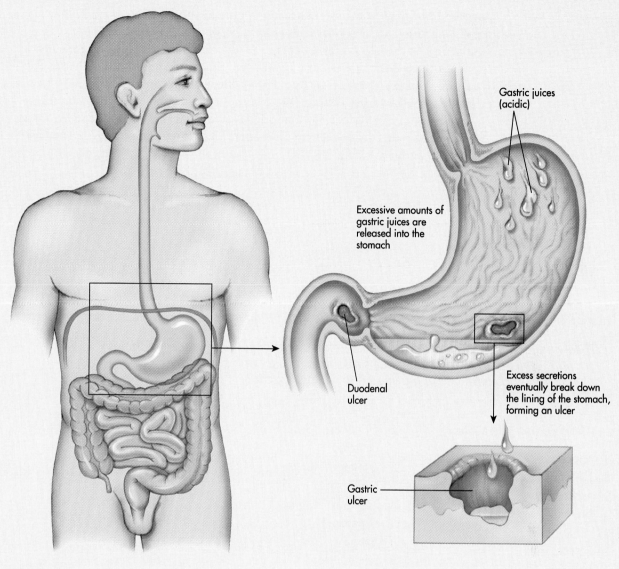

Gastric juices (acidic)

Excessive amounts of gastric juices are released into the stomach

Duodenal ulcer

Excess secretions eventually break down the lining of the stomach, forming an ulcer

Gastric ulcer

FIGURE 6–13

Peptic ulcer disease (PUD).

by aspirin and nonsteroidal anti-inflammatory medications (NSAIDs). Contrary to popular belief, ulcers are not caused by spicy foods or stress but rather are aggravated by them. The erosion of the mucosa that characterizes peptic ulcers is often caused by infection with a bacterium called *Helicobacter pylori*. Approximately 90 percent of duodenal ulcers and 70 percent of peptic ulcers are associated with *Helicobacter pylori*. The bacteria settle in the lining of the duodenum or stomach, opening a wound that is then made worse by digestive juices and stomach acids. The wound is said to resemble a flattened volcano or a white-centered, red-rimmed, painful canker sore. By killing the bacteria with antibiotics, it is estimated that 90 percent of the ulcers caused by *H. pylori* can be cured.

Prevention of peptic ulcer disease includes avoiding alcohol and tobacco; avoiding or limiting use of aspirin and nonsteroidal anti-inflammatory drugs (NSAIDs); taking enteric-coated aspirin with meals, if aspirin is needed daily.

The medical history and physical examination may be sufficient for diagnosis. X-ray tests or endoscopy can confirm the diagnosis. **Endoscopy** is a procedure that involves putting a thin telescope into the mouth. This telescope can be moved down into the stomach and intestines. This procedure allows the physician to directly see any ulcers. The physician may take samples of the stomach contents to test for *H. pylori* infection.

Untreated peptic ulcer disease may cause a hole in the digestive tract. It may also cause bleeding, inflammation, or abnormal connections between abdominal organs.

Treatment of peptic ulcer disease depends on the cause. If aspirin or other medications are the cause, then these medications must be stopped. Smoking and drinking alcohol should be stopped as well, because they can delay healing. Medications are given to help protect the stomach lining and allow faster healing. Most of these medications work by neutralizing stomach acid or preventing its production. If an infection with *H. pylori* is present, antibiotics are given. Surgery may be needed for severe ulcers that bleed, are unresponsive to medication, or that cause a hole in the stomach.

✓ PATHOLOGY CHECKPOINT

Following is a concise list of the pathology-related terms that you've seen in the chapter. Review this checklist to make sure that you are familiar with the meaning of each term before moving on to the next section.

Conditions and Symptoms

- ❑ anorexia
- ❑ appendicitis
- ❑ ascites
- ❑ bulimia
- ❑ cheilosis
- ❑ cholecystitis
- ❑ cirrhosis
- ❑ colon cancer
- ❑ constipation
- ❑ Crohn's disease
- ❑ dentalgia
- ❑ diarrhea
- ❑ diverticulitis
- ❑ dysentery
- ❑ dyspepsia
- ❑ dysphagia
- ❑ eating disorder
- ❑ emesis
- ❑ enteritis
- ❑ eructation
- ❑ flatus
- ❑ gastroesophageal reflux
- ❑ gastroesophageal reflux disease (GERD)

- ❑ gingivitis
- ❑ halitosis
- ❑ hematemesis
- ❑ hemorrhoid
- ❑ hepatitis
- ❑ hepatoma
- ❑ hernia
- ❑ hiatal hernia
- ❑ hyperemesis
- ❑ ileitis
- ❑ inguinal hernia
- ❑ irritable bowel syndrome (IBS)
- ❑ malabsorption
- ❑ melena
- ❑ nausea
- ❑ pancreatitis
- ❑ paralytic ileus
- ❑ peptic ulcer disease
- ❑ periodontal disease
- ❑ pilonidal cyst
- ❑ rectocele
- ❑ sialadentitis
- ❑ splenomegaly
- ❑ stomatitis

- ❑ ulcer
- ❑ ulcerative colitis
- ❑ volvulus
- ❑ vomit

Diagnosis and Treatment

- ❑ appendectomy
- ❑ cholecystectomy
- ❑ choledochotomy
- ❑ colectomy
- ❑ colonoscopy
- ❑ colostomy
- ❑ gastrectomy
- ❑ gavage
- ❑ glossotomy
- ❑ herniotomy
- ❑ hyperalimentation
- ❑ ileostomy
- ❑ laparotomy
- ❑ lavage
- ❑ laxative
- ❑ liver transplant
- ❑ pancreas transplant
- ❑ proctoscope
- ❑ sigmoidscope

DRUG HIGHLIGHTS

Drugs that are generally used for digestive system diseases and disorders include antacids, antacid mixtures, histamine H_2-receptor antagonists, mucosal protective medications, gastric acid pump inhibitors (proton pump inhibitor), other ulcer medications, laxatives, antidiarrheal agents, antiemetics, and emetics. See Figure 6–14.

Antacids

Neutralize hydrochloric acid in the stomach. Antacids are classified as nonsystemic and systemic.

Nonsystemic

Examples: Amphojel (aluminum hydroxide), Tums (calcium carbonate), Riopan (magaldrate), and Milk of Magnesia (magnesium hydroxide).

Systemic

Example: sodium bicarbonate.

Antacid Mixtures

Products that combine aluminum (may cause constipation) and/or calcium compounds with magnesium (may cause diarrhea) salts. By combining the antacid properties of two single-entity agents, these products provide the antacid action of both, yet tend to counter the adverse effects of each other.

Examples: Gaviscon, Gelusil, Maalox Plus, and Mylanta.

Histamine H_2-Receptor Antagonists

Inhibit both daytime and nocturnal basal gastric acid secretion and inhibit gastric acid stimulated by food, histamines, caffeine, insulin, and pentagastrin. These drugs are used in the treatment of active duodenal ulcer.

Examples: Tagamet (cimetidine), Pepcid (famotidine), Axid (nizatidine), and Zantac (ranitidine).

Mucosal Protective Medications

These medicines protect the stomach's mucosal lining from acids, but they do not inhibit the release of acid.

Examples: Carafate (sucralfate) and Cytotec (misoprostol).

Gastric Acid Pump Inhibitors (Proton Pump Inhibitor—PPI)

These are antiulcer agents that suppress gastric acid secretion by specific inhibition of the H + /K + ATPase enzyme at the secretory surface of the gastric parietal cell. Because this enzyme system is regarded as the acid (proton) pump within the gastric mucosa, gastric acid pump inhibitors are so classified, as they block the final step of acid production.

Examples: Prilosec (omeprazole), Aciphex (rabeprazole sodium), Prevacid (lansoprazole), and Protonix (pantoprazole).

Other Ulcer Medications

The treatment regimen for active duodenal ulcers associated with H. pylori may involve a two- or three-drug program.

Examples: a two-drug program—Biaxin (clarithromycin) and Prilosec (omeprazole); and a three-drug program—Flagyl (metronidazole) and either tetracycline or amoxicillin and Pepto Bismol.

Note: For the treatment program to be effective, the patient has to complete the full treatment program that involves taking 15 pills a day for a total of at least 2 weeks.

Laxatives

Used to relieve constipation and to facilitate the passage of feces through the lower gastrointestinal tract.

Examples: Dulcolax (bisacodyl), Milk of Magnesia (magnesium hydroxide), Metamucil (psyllium hydrophilic muciloid), and Ex-Lax (phenolphthalein).

Antidiarrheal Agents

Used to treat diarrhea.

Examples: Pepto-Bismol (bismuth subsalicylate), Kaopectate (kaolin mixture with pectin), and Imodium (loperamide HCl).

| Antiemetics | Prevent or arrest vomiting. These drugs are also used in the treatment of vertigo, motion sickness, and nausea. |

Examples: Dramamine (dimenhydrinate), Phenergan (promethazine HCl), Tigan (trimethobenzamide HCl), and Transderm Scop (scopolamine).

| Emetics | Are used to induce vomiting in people who have taken an overdose of oral drugs or who have ingested certain poisons. An emetic agent should not be given to a person who is unconscious, in shock, or in a semicomatose state. Emetics are also contraindicated in individuals who have ingested strongly caustic substances, such as lye or acid, since their use could result in additional injury to the person's esophagus. |

Example: Ipecac syrup.

DIAGNOSTIC & LAB TESTS

TEST	DESCRIPTION
alcohol toxicology (ethanol and ethyl) (ăl′ kō-hōl tŏks″ ĭ-kŏl′ ō-jē)	A test performed on blood serum or plasma to determine levels of alcohol. Legally, 0.05% or 50 mg/dL is considered not under the influence. Increased values indicate alcohol consumption that may lead to cirrhosis of the liver, gastritis, malnutrition, vitamin deficiencies, and other gastrointestinal disorders.
ammonia (NH$_4$) (ă-mō′ nē-ă)	A test performed on blood plasma to determine the level of ammonia (end product of protein breakdown). Increased values may indicate hepatic failure, hepatic encephalopathy, portacaval anastomosis, high protein diet in hepatic failure, and Reye's syndrome.
barium enema (BE) (bă′ rē-ūm ĕn′ ĕ-mă)	A test performed by administering barium via the rectum to determine the condition of the colon. X-rays are taken to ascertain the structure and to check the filling of the colon. Abnormal results may indicate cancer of the colon, polyps, fistulas, ulcerative colitis, diverticulitis, hernias, and intussusception.
bilirubin blood test (total) (bĭl-ĭ-rōō′ bĭn blod test)	A test done on blood serum to determine if bilirubin is conjugated and excreted in the bile. Abnormal results may indicate obstructive jaundice, hepatitis, and cirrhosis.
carcinoembryonic antigen (CEA) (kăr″ sĭn-ō-ĕm″ brē-ōn′ ĭk ăn′ tĭ-jĕn)	A test performed on whole blood or plasma to determine the presence of CEA (antigens originally isolated from colon tumors). Increased values may indicate stomach, intestinal, rectal, and various other cancers and conditions. This test is nonspecific and must be combined with other tests for a final diagnosis. It is being used to monitor the course of cancer therapy.
cholangiography (kō-lăn″ jē-ŏg′ ră-fē)	X-ray examination of the common bile duct, cystic duct, and hepatic ducts. A radiopaque dye is injected, and then films are taken. Abnormal results may indicate obstruction, stones, and tumors.
cholecystography (kō″ lē-sĭs-tŏg′ ră-fē)	X-ray examination of the gallbladder. A radiopaque dye is injected, and then films are taken. Abnormal results may indicate cholecystitis, cholelithiasis, and tumors.

TEST	DESCRIPTION
colonofiberoscopy (kŏ′ lō-nŏ-fī″ bĕr-ŏs′ kō-pē)	Fiberoptic colonoscopy. The direct visual examination of the colon via a flexible colonoscope; used as a diagnostic aid, for removal of foreign bodies, polyps, and tissue.
endoscopic retrograde cholangiopancreatography (ERCP) (ĕn′ dō-skōp-ĭk rĕt′ rō-grād kō-lăn″ jē-ō-păn″ krē-ă-tŏg′ ră-fē)	X-ray examination of the biliary and pancreatic ducts. A contrast medium is injected, and then films are taken. Abnormal results may indicate fibrosis, biliary or pancreatic cysts, strictures, stones, and chronic pancreatitis.
esophagogastroduodenoscopy (ĕ-sŏf″ ă-gō′ găs″ trō-dū″ ō-dĕ-nŏs′ kō-pē)	An endoscopic examination of the esophagus, stomach, and small intestine. During the procedure, photographs, biopsy, or brushings may be done.
gamma-glutamyl transferase (GGT) (găm′ ă glōō tŭm′ ĭl trăns′ fĕr-ās)	A test performed on blood serum to determine the level of GGT (enzyme found in the liver, kidney, prostate, heart, and spleen). Increased values may indicate cirrhosis, liver necrosis, hepatitis, alcoholism, neoplasms, acute pancreatitis, acute myocardial infarction, nephrosis, and acute cholecystitis.
gastric analysis (găs′ trĭk ă-năl′ ĭ sĭs)	A test performed to determine quality of secretion, amount of free and combined HCl, and absence or presence of blood, bacteria, bile, and fatty acids. Increased level of HCl may indicate peptic ulcer disease, Zollinger-Ellison syndrome, and hypergastremia. Decreased level of HCl may indicate stomach cancer, pernicious anemia, and atrophic gastritis.
gastrointestinal (GI) series (găs″ trō-ĭn-tes′ tĭn″ ăl sēr′ ēz)	Fluoroscopic examination of the esophagus, stomach, and small intestine. Barium is given orally, and it is observed as it flows through the GI system. See Figure 6–15. Abnormal results may indicate esophageal varices, ulcers, gastric polyps, malabsorption syndrome, hiatal hernias, diverticuli, pyloric stenosis, and foreign bodies.
hepatitis-associated antigen (HAA) (hĕp″ ă-tī-tĭs ă-sō′ shē-āt′ ĕd ăn′ tĭ-jĕn)	A test performed to determine the presence of the hepatitis B virus.
liver biopsy (lĭv′ ĕr bī-ŏp-sē)	Microscopic examination of liver tissue. Abnormal results may indicate cirrhosis, hepatitis, and tumors
occult blood (ŭ-kŭlt blod)	A test performed on feces to determine gastrointestinal bleeding that is invisible (hidden). Positive results may indicate gastritis, stomach cancer, peptic ulcer, ulcerative colitis, bowel cancer, bleeding esophageal varices, portal hypertension, pancreatitis, and diverticulitis.
ova and parasites (O & P) (o′ vă păr′ ă-sīts)	A test performed on stool to identify ova and parasites. Positive results indicate protozoa infestation.
stool culture (stool kŭl′ tūr)	A test performed on stool to identify the presence of organisms.
ultrasonography, gallbladder (ŭl-tră-sŏn-ŏg′ ră-fē găl″ blăd′ dĕr)	A test to visualize the gallbladder by using high-frequency sound waves. The echoes are recorded on an oscilloscope and film. See Figure 6–16. Abnormal results may indicate biliary obstruction, cholelithiasis, and acute cholecystitis.

ultrasonography, liver
(ŭl-tră-sŏn-ŏg′ ră-fē lĭv′ ēr)

A test to visualize the liver by using high-frequency sound waves. The echoes are recorded on an oscilloscope and film. See Figure 6–17. Abnormal results may indicate hepatic tumors, cysts, abscess, and cirrhosis.

upper gastrointestinal fiberoscopy
(ŭp′ ir găs′ trō-ĭn-tĕs′ tĭn″ ăl fī′ bĕr-ŏs′ kō-pē)

The direct visual examination of the gastric mucosa via a flexible fiberscope. Colored photographs or motion pictures can be taken during the procedure; used when gastric neoplasm is suspected.

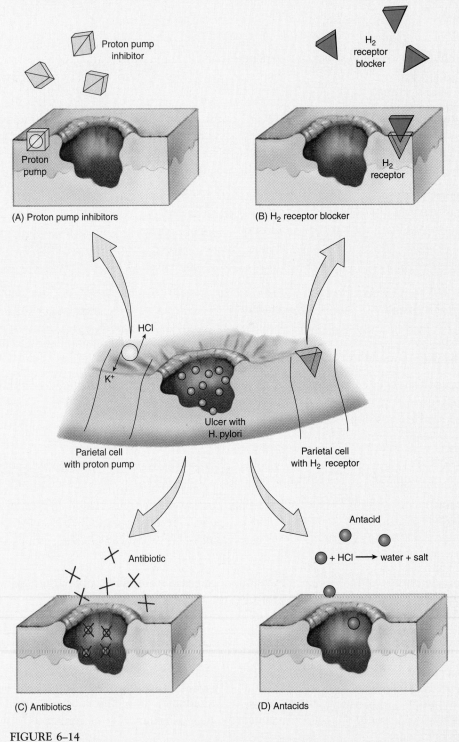

FIGURE 6–14

Mechanisms of action of antiulcer drugs. (Source: Pearson Education/PH College.)

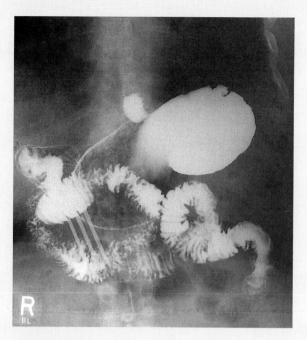

FIGURE 6–15

Upper GI series. (Courtesy of Teresa Resch.)

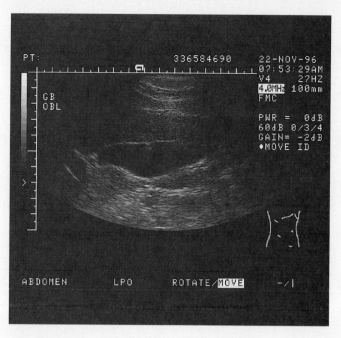

FIGURE 6–16

Gallbladder ultrasound. (Courtesy of Teresa Resch.)

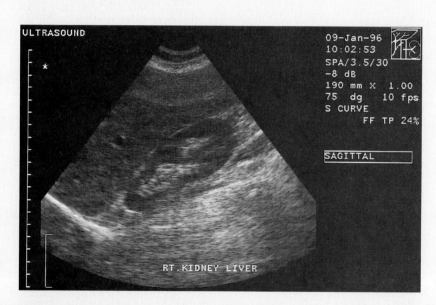

FIGURE 6–17

Ultrasound liver and right kidney. (Courtesy of Teresa Resch.)

ABBREVIATIONS

ABBREVIATION	MEANING	ABBREVIATION	MEANING
ac	before meals (ante cibum)	HBV	hepatitis B virus
A/G	albumin/globulin (ratio)	HCl	hydrochloric acid
Ba	barium	*H. pylori*	*Helicobacter pylori*
BE	barium enema	IBS	irritable bowel syndrome
BM	bowel movement	LES	lower esophageal sphincter
BRP	bathroom privileges	NANBH	non-A, non-B hepatitis virus
BS	bowel sounds	NG	nasogastric (tube)
BSP	bromsulphalein	NH_4	ammonia
CEA	carcinoembryonic antigen	npo, NPO	nil per os (nothing by mouth)
CHO	carbohydrate	N&V	nausea and vomiting
chol	cholesterol	O & P	ova and parasites
cib	food (cibus)	pc	after meals (post cibum)
CUC	chronic ulcerative colitis	PEG	percutaneous endoscopic
E. coli	*Escherichia coli*		gastrostomy
ERCP	endoscopic retrograde	po, PO	per os (by mouth)
	cholangiopancreatography	PP	postprandial (after meals)
GB	gallbladder	PTC	percutaneous transhepatic
GERD	gastroesophageal reflux disease		cholangiography
GGT	gamma-glutamyl transferase	PPI	proton pump inhibitor
GI	gastrointestinal	PUD	peptic ulcer disease
GTT	glucose tolerance test	RDA	recommended dietary or daily
HAA	hepatitis-associated antigen		allowance
HAV	hepatitis A virus	TPN	total parenteral nutrition
HBIG	hepatitis B immune globulin	UGI	upper gastrointestinal

STUDY AND REVIEW

Anatomy and Physiology

Write your answers to the following questions. Do not refer to the text.

1. Name the primary organs commonly associated with digestion.

   a. _____   b. _____

   c. _____   d. _____

   e. _____   f. _____

2. Name four accessory organs of digestion.

   a. _____   b. _____

   c. _____   d. _____

3. State the three main functions of the digestive system.

   a. _____

   b. _____

   c. _____

4. Define bolus. _____

   _____

5. Define peristalsis. _____

   _____

6. _____ _____ and _____ _____ convert the food into a semiliquid state.

7. The _____ is the first portion of the small intestine.

8. Semiliquid food is called _____.

9. The _____ _____ transports nutrients to body cells.

10. The large intestine can be divided into four distinct sections called the

    _____, the _____, the _____, and the

    _____.

11. The _____ is the largest glandular organ in the body.

12. State the function of the gallbladder. _____

13. Name an important function of the pancreas. _____

14. State three functions of the liver.

    a. _____   b. _____

    c. _____

15. Where does digestion and absorption chiefly take place? _____

16. The salivary glands located in and about the mouth are called the

    _____, the _____, and the _____.

17. Name the two hormones secreted into the bloodstream by the pancreas.

    a. _____   b. _____

Word Parts

1. In the spaces provided, write the definition of these prefixes, roots, combining forms, and suffixes. Do not refer to the listings of medical words. Leave blank those words you cannot define.

2. After completing as many as you can, refer to the medical word listings to check your work. For each word missed or left blank, write the word and its definition several times on the margins of these pages or on a separate sheet of paper.

3. To maximize the learning process, it is to your advantage to do the following exercises as directed. To refer to the word building section before completing these exercises invalidates the learning process.

PREFIXES

Give the definitions of the following prefixes:

1. an- _____   2. ana- _____

3. cata- _____   4. dys- _____

5. epi- _____   6. hyper- _____

7. hypo _____   8. mal _____

9. di- _____   10. peri- _____

11. post- _____   12. dia- _____

13. sub- _____

ROOTS AND COMBINING FORMS

Give the definitions of the following roots and combining forms:

1. absorpt _____

2. aden _____

3. amyl _____

4. cirrh _____

5. append _____

6. appendic _____

7. bil/i _____

8. bol _____

9. bucc _____

10. celi _____

11. cheil _____

12. chol/e _____

13. choledoch/o _____

14. col _____

15. col/o _____

16. colon _____

17. colon/o _____

18. cyst _____

19. dent _____

20. constipat _____

21. diverticul _____

22. duoden _____

23. enter _____

24. defecat _____

25. esophag/e _____

26. gest _____

27. gastr _____

28. gastr/o _____

29. gingiv _____

30. gloss/o _____

31. glyc/o _____

32. hemat _____

33. hepat _____

34. hepat/o _____

35. herni/o _____

36. ile _____

37. ile/o _____

38. labi _____

39. lapar/o _____

40. laxat _____

41. lingu _____

42. lip/o _____

43. log _____

44. mes _____

45. pancreat _____

46. pept _____

47. pharyng/e _____

48. prand/i _____

49. eme _____

50. proct/o _____

51. pylor _____

52. rect/o _____

53. sial _____

54. sigmoid/o _____

55. splen/o _____

56. stomat _____

57. tox _____

58. eructat _____

59. verm/i _____

60. halit _____

61. hemorrh _____

62. alimentat _____

63. masticat _____

64. paralyt _____

65. pil/o _____

66. nid _____

67. volvul _____

68. odont _____

SUFFIXES

Give the definitions of the following suffixes:

1. -ac _____

2. -al _____

3. -algia _____

4. -ary _____

5. -ase _____

6. -cele _____

7. -oid _____

8. -sis _____

9. -ectomy _____

10. -emesis _____

11. -form _____

12. -genesis _____

13. -ic _____

14. -in _____

15. -ion _____

16. -ism _____

17. -ist _____

18. -itis _____

19. -ive _____

20. -logy _____

21. -lysis _____

22. -megaly _____

23. -oma _____

24. -orexia _____

25. -osis _____

26. -rrhea _____

27. -pepsia _____

28. -us _____

29. -phagia _____

30. -scope _____

31. -scopy _____

32. -stalsis _____

33. -stomy _____

34. -tomy _____

35. -y _____

Identifying Medical Terms

In the spaces provided, write the medical terms for the following meanings:

1. _____ An enzyme that breaks down starch

2. _____ The building up of the body substances

3. _____ Lack of appetite

4. _____ Surgical excision of the appendix

5. _____ Inflammation of the appendix

6. _____ Pertaining to or conveying bile

7. _____ Pertaining to the abdomen

8. _____ Difficulty in swallowing

9. _____ Inflammation of the liver

10. _____ Surgical incision for the repair of a hernia

11. _____ Pertaining to after meals

12. _____ Enlargement of the spleen

13. _____ Instrument used to view the sigmoid

Spelling

In the spaces provided, write the correct spelling of these misspelled terms:

1. bilery _____

2. colonscopy _____

3. degultition _____

4. gastorentreology _____

5. haltosis _____

6. laxtive _____

7. persitalsis _____

8. salademitis _____

9. peridontal _____

10. verimform _____

Matching

Select the appropriate lettered meaning for each word listed below.

_____ 1. cirrhosis

_____ 2. constipation

_____ 3. diarrhea

_____ 4. gavage

_____ 5. hemorrhoid

_____ 6. hernia

_____ 7. hyperalimentation

_____ 8. lavage

_____ 9. pilonidal cyst

_____10. volvulus

a. To wash out a cavity
b. To feed liquid or semiliquid food via a tube
c. A twisting of the bowel on itself
d. Frequent passage of unformed watery stools
e. A chronic degenerative liver disease
f. Infrequent passage of unduly hard and dry feces
g. A closed sac in the crease of the sacrococcygeal region
h. The abnormal protrusion of an organ or a part of an organ through the wall of the body cavity that normally contains it
i. A mass of dilated, tortuous veins in the anorectum
j. An intravenous infusion of a hypertonic solution to sustain life
k. The evacuation of the bowel

Abbreviations

Place the correct word, phrase, or abbreviation in the space provided.

1. before meals _____

2. BM _____

3. BS _____

4. food _____

5. gallbladder _____

6. hepatitis A virus _____

7. NG _____

8. NPO, npo _____

9. after meals _____

10. total parenteral nutrition _____

Diagnostic and Laboratory Tests

Select the best answer to each multiple choice question. Circle the letter of your choice.

1. X-ray examination of the common bile duct, cystic duct, and hepatic ducts.
   a. cholangiography
   b. cholecystography
   c. cholangiopancreatography
   d. ultrasonography

2. The direct visual examination of the colon via a flexible colonoscope.
   a. cholangiography
   b. ultrasonography
   c. colonofiberoscopy
   d. cholecystography

3. Fluoroscopic examination of the esophagus, stomach, and small intestine.
   a. barium enema
   b. ultrasonography
   c. cholangiography
   d. gastrointestinal series

4. An endoscopic examination of the esophagus, stomach, and small intestine.
   a. cholangiography
   b. gastroduodenoesophagoscopy
   c. esophagogastroduodenoscopy
   d. gastric analysis

5. A test performed to determine the presence of the hepatitis B virus.
   a. occult blood test
   b. stool culture
   c. hepatic antigen
   d. ova and parasites test

CASE STUDY

PEPTIC ULCER DISEASE (PUD)

Read the following case study and then answer the questions that follow.

A 35-year-old male was seen by a physician; the following is a synopsis of the visit.

Present History: The patient states that he has been under a lot of pressure at work lately and has noticed a dull, aching pain in his stomach and back. He states that he has heartburn and "belches" a lot.

Signs and Symptoms: Dull, gnawing pain and a burning sensation in the midepigastrium. Pyrosis (heartburn) and sour eructation (belching).

Diagnosis: Acute gastric ulcer; peptic ulcer disease. Diagnosis determined by a gastrointestinal (GI) series, gastric analysis, and histology with culture to determine presence of *Helicobacter pylori*. No *H. pylori* were found in the culture.

Treatment: Goal is to manage and reduce gastric acidity. This may be accomplished through various treatment regimens such as stress management, rest, diet, avoidance of tobacco, caffeine, and alcohol, and medication. The patient is placed on Mylanta 2 tablets every 2 to 4 hours between meals and at bedtime, and Zantac 300 mg at bedtime.

Prevention: Avoid substances that produce gastric acidity. Stress management, rest, diet, avoidance of tobacco, caffeine, and alcohol are recommended.

CASE STUDY QUESTIONS

1. Signs and symptoms of a gastric ulcer include a dull, gnawing pain and a burning sensation in the midepigastrium. Other indications are: _____, which is heartburn, and sour eructation.

2. The diagnosis of acute gastric ulcer was determined by a gastric analysis and a _____ series.

3. The goal of treatment for acute gastric ulcer is to manage and reduce gastric _____.

4. The medication regimen prescribed included _____ 2 tablets every 2 to 4 hours between meals and at bedtime and,

5. Zantac _____ mg at bedtime.

MedMedia Wrap-Up

www.prenhall.com/rice

Additional interactive resources and activities for this chapter can be found on the Companion Website. For animations, videos, audio glossary, and review, access the accompanying CD-ROM in this book.

Audio Glossary
Medical Terminology Exercises & Activities
Pathology Spotlights
Terminology Translator
Animations
Videos

Objectives
Medical Terminology Exercises & Activities
Audio Glossary
Drug Updates
Medical Terminology in the News

THE CARDIOVASCULAR SYSTEM

7

OBJECTIVES

On completion of this chapter, you will be able to:

- Describe the cardiovascular system.
- Describe and state the functions of arteries, veins, and capillaries.
- Describe cardiovascular differences of the child and the older adult.
- Identify the commonly used pulse checkpoints of the body.
- Describe blood pressure.
- Analyze, build, spell, and pronounce medical words.
- Describe each of the conditions presented in the Pathology Spotlights.
- Complete the Pathology Checkpoint.
- Review Drug Highlights presented in this chapter.
- Provide the description of diagnostic and laboratory tests related to the cardiovascular system.
- Identify and define selected abbreviations.
- Successfully complete the study and review section.

MedMedia
www.prenhall.com/rice

Additional interactive resources and activities for this chapter can be found on the Companion Website. For Terminology Translator, animations, videos, audio glossary, and review, access the accompanying CD-ROM in this book.

Anatomy and Physiology Overview

Through the cardiovascular system, blood is circulated to all parts of the body by the action of the heart. This process provides the body's cells with oxygen and nutritive elements and removes waste materials and carbon dioxide. The **heart**, a muscular pump, is the central organ of the system, which also includes **arteries**, **veins**, and **capillaries**. The various organs and components of the cardiovascular system are described in this chapter, along with some of their functions.

THE HEART

The **heart** is a four-chambered, hollow muscular pump that circulates blood throughout the cardiovascular system. The heart is the center of the cardiovascular system from which the various blood vessels originate and later return. It is slightly larger than a man's fist and weighs approximately 300 g in the average adult male. It lies slightly to the left of the midline of the body and is shaped like an inverted cone with its apex downward. The heart has three layers or linings; see Figure 7–1.

Endocardium. The inner lining of the heart
Myocardium. The muscular middle layer of the heart
Pericardium. The outer membranous sac surrounding the heart

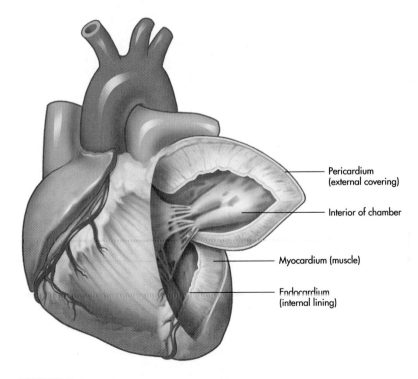

Pericardium (external covering)

Interior of chamber

Myocardium (muscle)

Endocardium (internal lining)

FIGURE 7–1

Tissues of the heart.

Chambers of the Heart

The human heart acts as a double pump and is divided into the right and left heart by a partition called the **septum**. Each side contains an upper and lower chamber. The **atria** or upper chambers are separated by the interatrial septum. The **ventricles** or lower chambers are separated by the interventricular septum. The atria receive blood from the various parts of the body, whereas the ventricles pump blood to body parts. A description of the heart's four chambers and some of their functions is given below.

THE RIGHT ATRIUM

The right upper portion of the heart is called the **right atrium**. It is a thin-walled space that receives blood from all body parts except the lungs. Two large veins bring the blood into the right atrium and are known as the superior and inferior vena cavae.

THE CARDIOVASCULAR SYSTEM

Organ/Structure	Primary Functions
Heart	Hollow muscular pump that circulates blood throughout the cardiovascular system
Arteries	Branching system of vessels that transports blood from the right and left ventricles of the heart to all body parts
Veins	Vessels that transport blood from peripheral tissues to the heart
Capillaries	Microscopic blood vessels that connect arterioles with venules; facilitate passage of life-sustaining fluids containing oxygen and nutrients to cell bodies and the removal of accumulated waste and carbon dioxide

THE RIGHT VENTRICLE

The right lower portion of the heart is called the **right ventricle**. It receives blood from the right atrium through the atrioventricular valve and pumps it through a semilunar valve to the lungs.

THE LEFT ATRIUM

The left upper portion of the heart is called the **left atrium**. It receives blood rich in oxygen as it returns from the lungs via the left and right pulmonary veins.

THE LEFT VENTRICLE

The left lower portion of the heart is called the **left ventricle**. It receives blood from the left atrium through an atrioventricular valve and pumps it through a semilunar valve to a large artery known as the aorta and from there to all parts of the body except the lungs.

Heart Valves

The **valves** of the heart are located at the entrance and exit of each ventricle. See Figure 7–2. The functions of each of the four heart valves are described in the following section.

THE TRICUSPID VALVE

The **right atrioventricular** or **tricuspid valve** guards the opening between the atrium and the right ventricle. The tricuspid valve allows the flow of blood into the ventricle and prevents its return to the right atrium.

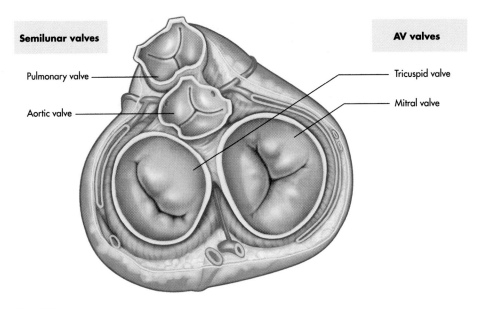

Semilunar valves

Pulmonary valve

Aortic valve

AV valves

Tricuspid valve

Mitral valve

FIGURE 7–2

Heart valves in closed position viewed from the top.

THE PULMONARY SEMILUNAR VALVE

The exit point for blood leaving the right ventricle is called the **pulmonary semilunar valve.** Located between the right ventricle and the pulmonary artery, it allows blood to flow from the right ventricle through the pulmonary artery to the lungs.

THE BICUSPID OR MITRAL VALVE

The left atrioventricular valve between the left atrium and ventricle is called the **bicuspid** or **mitral valve.** It allows blood to flow to the left ventricle and closes to prevent its return to the left atrium.

THE AORTIC SEMILUNAR VALVE

Blood exits from the left ventricle through the **aortic semilunar valve.** Located between the left ventricle and the aorta, it allows blood to flow into the aorta and prevents its return to the ventricle.

Vascular System of the Heart

Due to the membranous lining of the heart (**endocardium**) and the thickness of the myocardium, it is essential that the heart have its own vascular system. The coronary arteries supply the heart with blood, and the cardiac veins, draining into the coronary sinus, collect the blood and return it to the right atrium (Fig. 7–3).

THE FLOW OF BLOOD

Blood flows through the heart, to the lungs, back to the heart, and on to the various body parts as indicated in Figure 7–4. Blood from the superior and inferior vena cavae enters the right atrium and subsequently passes through the tricuspid valve and into

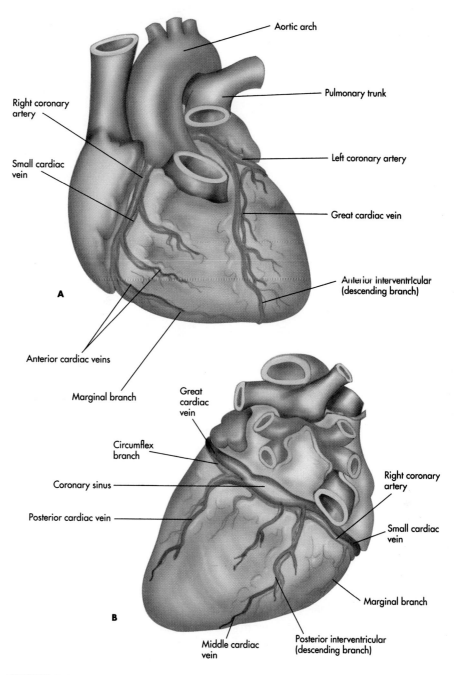

Aortic arch

Pulmonary trunk

Left coronary artery

Great cardiac vein

Anterior interventricular (descending branch)

Right coronary artery

Small cardiac vein

A

Anterior cardiac veins

Marginal branch

Great cardiac vein

Circumflex branch

Coronary sinus

Posterior cardiac vein

Right coronary artery

Small cardiac vein

Marginal branch

B

Middle cardiac vein

Posterior interventricular (descending branch)

FIGURE 7–3

Coronary circulation. (A) Coronary vessels portraying the complexity and extent of the coronary circulation. (B) Coronary vessels that supply the anterior surface of the heart.

the right ventricle, which pumps it through the pulmonary semilunar valve into the left and right pulmonary arteries, which carry it to the lungs. In the lungs, the blood gives up wastes and takes on oxygen as it passes through capillaries into veins. Blood leaves the lungs through the left and right pulmonary veins, which carry it to the heart's left atrium. The oxygenated blood then passes through the bicuspid or mitral valve into the left ventricle, which pumps it out through the aortic valve and into the **aorta**. This large artery supplies a branching system of smaller arteries that connect to tiny capillaries throughout the body.

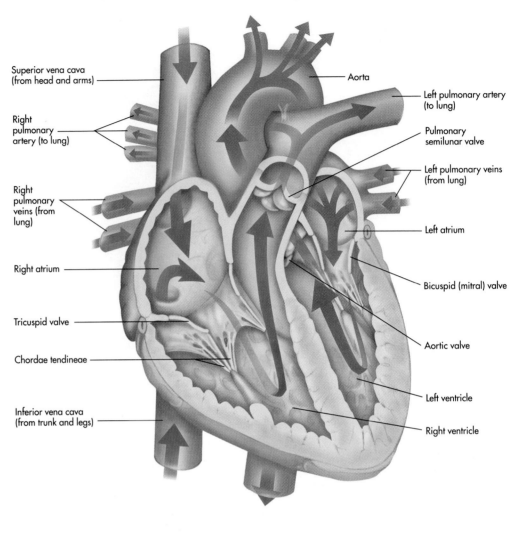

Superior vena cava
(from head and arms)

Aorta

Left pulmonary artery
(to lung)

Right
pulmonary
artery (to lung)

Pulmonary
semilunar valve

Left pulmonary veins
(from lung)

Right
pulmonary
veins (from
lung)

Left atrium

Right atrium

Bicuspid (mitral) valve

Tricuspid valve

Aortic valve

Chordae tendineae

Left ventricle

Inferior vena cava
(from trunk and legs)

Right ventricle

FIGURE 7–4

The flow of blood through the heart.

Capillaries are microscopic blood vessels with thin walls that allow the passage of oxygen and nutrients to the body and let the blood pick up waste and carbon dioxide. Veins lead away from the capillaries as tiny vessels and increase in size until they join the superior and inferior vena cavae as they return to the heart.

The Heartbeat

The **heartbeat** is controlled by the autonomic nervous system. It is normally generated by specialized neuromuscular tissue of the heart that is capable of causing cardiac muscle to contract rhythmically. The neuromuscular tissue of the heart comprises the **sinoatrial node**, the **atrioventricular node**, and the **atrioventricular bundle** (Fig. 7–5).

SINOATRIAL NODE (SA NODE)

Often called the **pacemaker of the heart**, the **SA node** is located in the upper wall of the right atrium, just below the opening of the superior vena cava. It consists of a dense network of **Purkinje fibers** (*atypical muscle fibers*) considered to be the source of impulses initiating the heartbeat. Electrical impulses discharged by the SA node are distributed to the right and left atria and cause them to contract.

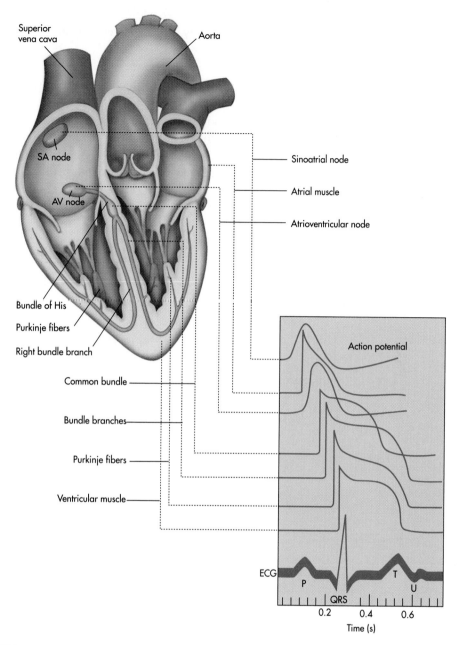

FIGURE 7–5

The conduction system of the heart. Action potentials for the SA and AV nodes, other parts of the conduction system, and the atrial and ventricular muscles are shown along with the correlation to recorded electrical activity (electrocardiogram ECG [EKG]).

ATRIOVENTRICULAR NODE (AV NODE)

Located beneath the endocardium of the right atrium, the **AV node** transmits electrical impulses to the **bundle of His** (*atrioventricular bundle*).

ATRIOVENTRICULAR BUNDLE (BUNDLE OF HIS)

The **bundle of His** forms a part of the conducting system of the heart. It extends from the AV node into the intraventricular septum, where it divides into two branches within the two ventricles. The **Purkinje system** includes the bundle of His and the peripheral fibers. These fibers end in the ventricular muscles, where the excitation of muscle is initiated, causing contraction. The average heartbeat (*pulse*) is between 60 and 100 beats per minute for the average adult. The rate of heartbeat may be affected by emotions, smoking, disease, body size, age, stress, the environment, and many other factors.

Electrocardiogram

An **electrocardiogram** (ECG, EKG) records the electrical activity of the heart. A standard electrocardiogram consists of 12 different leads. With electrodes placed on the patient's arms, legs, and six positions on the chest, a 12-lead ECG can be recorded. There are six unipolar chest leads that record electrical activity of different parts of the heart. An ECG provides valuable information in the diagnosing of cardiac abnormalities, such as myocardial damage and arrhythmias (Fig. 7–6).

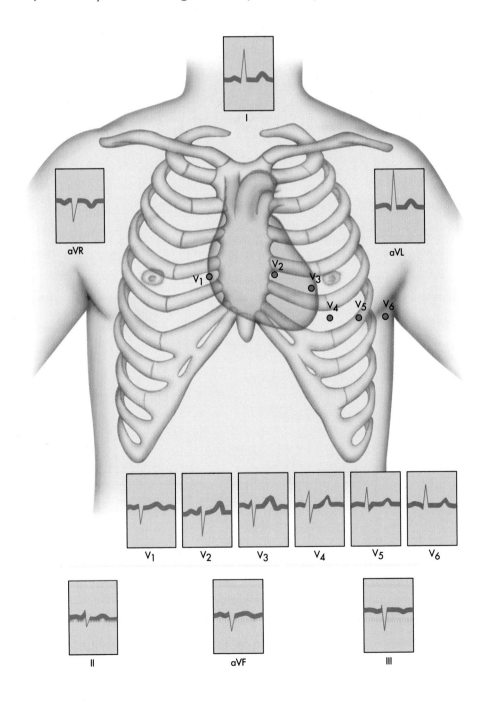

FIGURE 7–6

A normal electrocardiogram (ECG [EKG]).

ARTERIES

The **arteries** constitute a branching system of vessels that transports blood from the right and left ventricles of the heart to all body parts (Table 7–1, and Fig. 7–7). In a normal state, arteries are elastic tubes that recoil and carry blood in pulsating waves. See Figure 7–8. All arteries have a pulse, reflecting the rhythmical beating of the heart; however, certain points are commonly used to check the rate, rhythm, and condition of the arterial wall. These checkpoints are listed below and shown in Figure 7–9.

Radial. Located on the radial (*thumb side*) of the wrist. This is the most common site for taking a pulse.

Brachial. Located in the antecubital space of the elbow. This is the most common site used to check blood pressure.

Carotid. Located in the neck. In an emergency (*cardiac arrest*), this site is the most readily accessible.

Temporal. Located at the temple.

Femoral. Located in the groin.

Popliteal. Located behind the knee.

Dorsalis Pedis. Located on the upper surface of the foot.

BLOOD PRESSURE

Blood pressure, generally speaking, is the pressure exerted by the blood on the walls of the vessels. The term most commonly refers to the pressure exerted in large arteries at the peak of the pulse wave. This pressure is measured with a **sphygmomanometer** used

TABLE 7–1 SELECTED ARTERIES

Artery	Tissue Supplied
Right common carotid	Right side of the head and neck
Left common carotid	Left side of the head and neck
Left subclavian	Left upper extremity
Brachiocephalic	Head and arm
Aortic arch	Branches to head, neck, and upper extremities
Celiac	Stomach, spleen, and liver
Renal	Kidneys
Superior mesenteric	Lower half of large intestine
Inferior mesenteric	Small intestines and first half of the large intestine
Axillary	Axilla
Brachial	Arm
Radial	Lateral side of the hand
Ulnar	Medial side of the hand
Internal iliac	Pelvic viscera and rectum
External iliac	Genitalia and lower trunk muscles
Deep femoral	Deep thigh muscles
Femoral	Thigh
Popliteal	Leg and foot
Anterior tibial	Leg
Dorsalis pedis	Foot

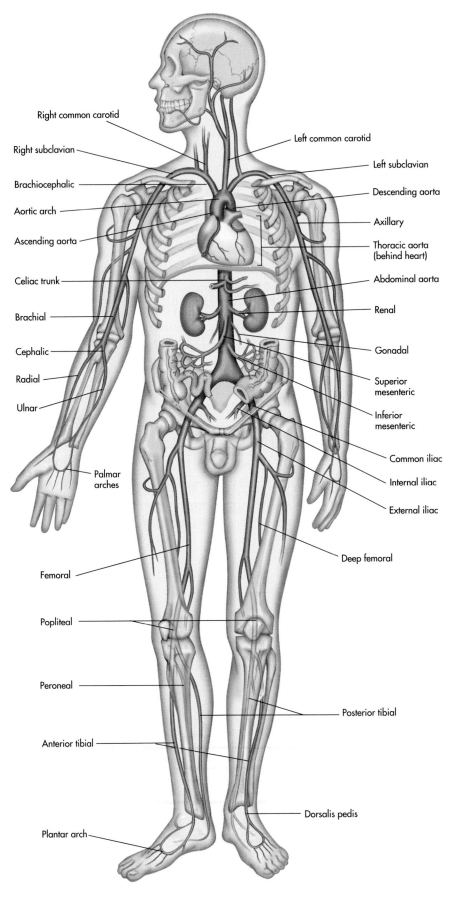

Right common carotid

Right subclavian

Brachiocephalic

Aortic arch

Ascending aorta

Celiac trunk

Brachial

Cephalic

Radial

Ulnar

Palmar arches

Femoral

Popliteal

Peroneal

Anterior tibial

Plantar arch

Left common carotid

Left subclavian

Descending aorta

Axillary

Thoracic aorta (behind heart)

Abdominal aorta

Renal

Gonadal

Superior mesenteric

Inferior mesenteric

Common iliac

Internal iliac

External iliac

Deep femoral

Posterior tibial

Dorsalis pedis

FIGURE 7–7

An overview of the arterial system.

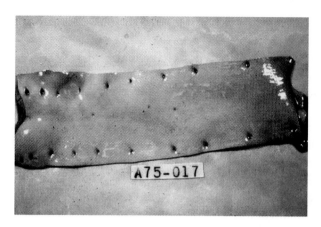

FIGURE 7–8

Inside surface of a normal artery. (Source: Pearson Education/PH College.)

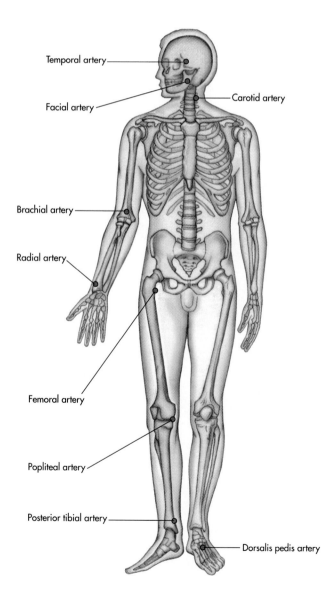

FIGURE 7–9

The primary pulse points of the body.

in concert with a **stethoscope**. Pressure is reported in millimeters of mercury as observed on a graduated column. With the use of a pressure cuff, circulation is interrupted in the brachial artery just above the elbow. Pressure from the cuff is shown on the graduated column of the sphygmomanometer, and as the pressure is released, blood again flows past the cuff. At this point, using a stethoscope, one hears a heartbeat and records the systolic pressure. Continued release of pressure results in a change in the heartbeat sound from loud to soft, at which point one records the diastolic pressure. This method results in a ratio of systolic over diastolic readings expressed in millimeters of mercury (mm Hg). In the average adult, the systolic pressure usually ranges from 100 to 140 mm Hg and the diastolic from 60 to 90 mm Hg. A typical blood pressure showing systolic over diastolic readings might be expressed as 120/80. Two types of sphygmomanometers are shown in Figure 7–10.

Pulse Pressure

The **pulse pressure** is the difference between the systolic and diastolic readings. This reading is an indication of the tone of the arterial walls. The normal pulse pressure is found when the systolic pressure is about 40 points higher than the diastolic reading. For example, if the blood pressure is 120/80, the pulse pressure would be 40. A pulse pressure over 50 points or under 30 points is considered abnormal.

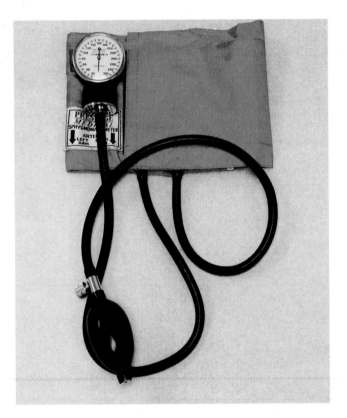 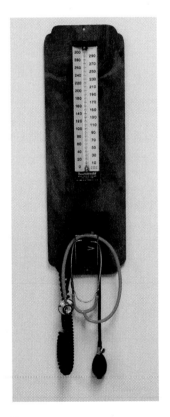

A

B

FIGURE 7–10

Sphygmomanometers: (A) aneroid type, (B) mercury type.

VEINS

The vessels that transport blood from peripheral tissues to the heart are the *veins* (see Table 7–2, and Fig. 7–11). In a normal state, veins have thin walls and valves that prevent the backflow of blood. Veins are the vessels used when blood is removed for analysis. The process of removing blood from a vein is called **venipuncture**.

CAPILLARIES

The **capillaries** are microscopic blood vessels with single-celled walls that connect **arterioles** (*small arteries*) with **venules** (*small veins*). Blood, passing through capillaries, gives up the oxygen and nutrients carried to this point by the arteries and picks up waste and carbon dioxide as it enters veins. The extremely thin walls of capillaries facilitate passage of life-sustaining fluids containing oxygen and nutrients to cell bodies and the removal of accumulated waste and carbon dioxide.

TABLE 7–2 SELECTED VEINS

Vein	*Tissue Drained*
External jugular	Superficial tissues of the head and neck
Internal jugular	Sinuses of the brain
Subclavian	Upper extremities
Superior vena cava	Head, neck, and upper extremities
Inferior vena cava	Lower body
Hepatic	Liver
Hepatic portal	Liver and gallbladder
Superior mesenteric	Small intestine and most of the colon
Inferior mesenteric	Descending colon and rectum
Cephalic	Lateral arm
Axillary	Axilla and arm
Basilic	Medial arm
External iliac	Lower limb
Internal iliac	Pelvic viscera
Femoral	Thigh
Great saphenous	Leg
Popliteal	Lower leg
Peroneal	Foot
Anterior tibial	Deep anterior leg and dorsal foot

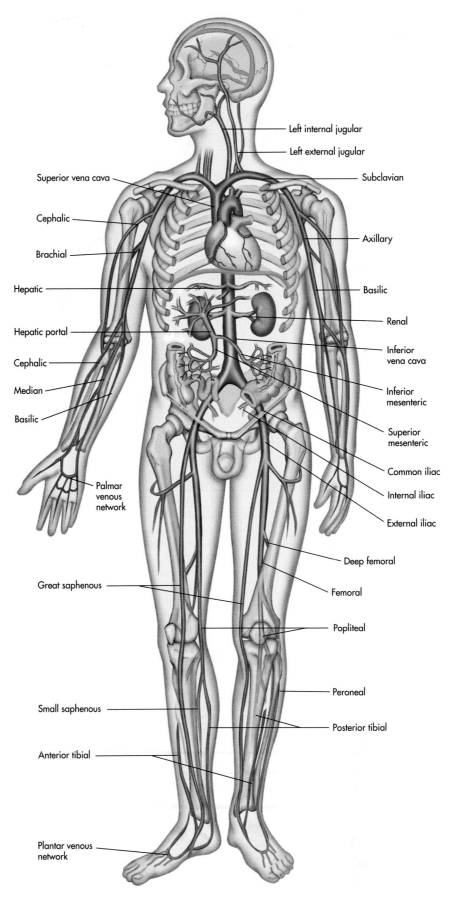

Left internal jugular

Left external jugular

Superior vena cava

Subclavian

Cephalic

Axillary

Brachial

Basilic

Hepatic

Renal

Hepatic portal

Inferior
vena cava

Cephalic

Inferior
mesenteric

Median

Superior
mesenteric

Basilic

Common iliac

Internal iliac

Palmar
venous
network

External iliac

Deep femoral

Great saphenous

Femoral

Popliteal

Peroneal

Small saphenous

Posterior tibial

Anterior tibial

Plantar venous
network

FIGURE 7–11

An overview of the venous system.

LIFE SPAN
CONSIDERATIONS

■ THE CHILD

The development of the fetal heart is usually completed during the first 2 months of intrauterine life. It is completely formed and functioning by 10 weeks. At 16 weeks fetal heart tones can be heard with a **fetoscope**. Oxygenated blood is transported by the umbilical vein from the placenta to the fetus. Fetal circulation is terminated at birth when the umbilical cord is clamped. The newborn's circulation begins to function shortly after birth and if proper adaptations do not take place, congenital heart disease may occur. Most congenital heart defects develop before the 10th week of pregnancy. Pediatric cardiologists have recognized more than 50 congenital heart defects. If the left side of the heart is not completely separated from the right side, various septal defects develop. If the four chambers of the heart do not

occur normally, complex anomalies form, such as tetralogy of Fallot, a congenital heart defect involving pulmonary stenosis, ventricular septal defect, dextroposition of the aorta, and hypertrophy of the right ventricle.

The **pulse**, **blood pressure**, and **respirations** will vary according to the age of the child. A newborn's pulse rate is irregular and rapid, varying from 120 to 140 beats/minute. Blood pressure is low and may vary with the size of the cuff used. The average blood pressure at birth is 80/46. The respirations are approximately 35 to 50 per minute.

■ THE OLDER ADULT

Current evidence indicates that cardiac changes that were once attributed to the aging process may be minimized by modifying lifestyle and personal habits, such

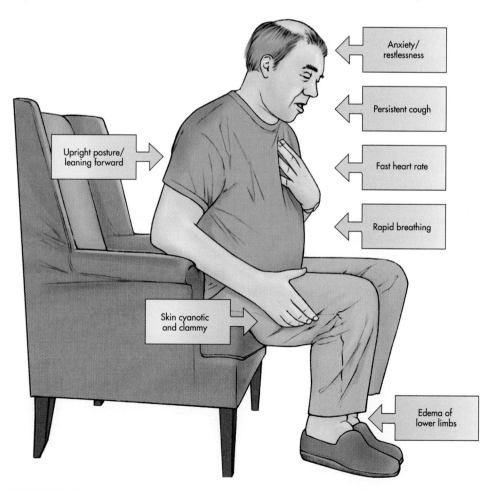

Upright posture/
leaning forward

Skin cyanotic
and clammy

Anxiety/
restlessness

Persistent cough

Fast heart rate

Rapid breathing

Edema of
lower limbs

FIGURE 7–12

Signs and symptoms of the patient with heart failure.

as following a low-sodium, low-fat diet, not smoking, drinking in moderation, managing stress, and exercising regularly. Studies have shown that the normal aging heart is able to provide an adequate cardiac output. But in some older adults, the heart must work harder to pump blood because of hardening of the arteries (**arteriosclerosis**) and a buildup of fatty plaques in the arterial walls (**atherosclerosis**). Arteries may gradually become stiff and lose their elastic recoil. The aorta and arteries supplying the heart and brain are generally affected first. Reduced blood flow, elevated blood lipids, and defective endothelial repair that can be seen in aging accelerate the course of cardiovascular disease.

Heart failure (HF) is one of the most common types of cardiovascular disease seen in the older adult.

It is the inability of the ventricles to pump enough blood to meet the needs of the body and may involve either the left or right side of the heart or both sides. Left-sided failure leads to a buildup of fluid in the lungs, or **pulmonary edema**, which causes **dyspnea** and shortness of breath. Right-sided failure is a result of a buildup of blood flowing into the right side of the heart which causes edema of the ankles, distention of the neck veins, and enlargement of the spleen and/or liver.

Heart failure may be caused by coronary artery disease, diabetes, chronic hypertension, myocardial infarction, infection, and valvular disorders such as mitral stenosis. Left-sided heart failure is commonly called congestive heart failure (CHF). See Figure 7–12 for some signs and symptoms of a patient with heart failure.

BUILDING YOUR MEDICAL VOCABULARY

This section provides the foundation for learning medical terminology. Medical words can be made up of four different types of word parts:

- Prefixes (P)
- Roots (R)
- Combining forms (CF)
- Suffixes (S)

By connecting various word parts in an organized sequence, thousands of words can be built and learned. In this text the word list is alphabetized so one can see the variety of meanings created when common prefixes and suffixes are repeatedly applied to certain word roots and/or combining forms. Words shown in pink are additional words related to the content of this chapter that are not built from word parts. These words are included to enhance your vocabulary. Note: an asterisk (✱) indicates words that are covered in the Pathology Spotlights section in this chapter.

MEDICAL WORD	WORD PARTS (WHEN APPLICABLE)			DEFINITION
	Part	Type	Meaning	
anastomosis (ă-năs″ tō-mō′ sĭs)	anastom	R	opening	A surgical connection between blood vessels or the joining of one hollow or tubular organ to another
	-osis	S	condition of	
aneurysm (ăn′ ū-rĭzm)				A sac formed by a local widening of the wall of an artery or a vein; usually caused by injury or disease

MEDICAL WORD	WORD PARTS (WHEN APPLICABLE)			DEFINITION
	Part	**Type**	**Meaning**	
anginal (ăn′ jĭ-năl)	angin -al	R S	to choke, quinsy pertaining to	Pertaining to attacks of choking or suffocative pain
angioblast (ăn′ jĭ-ō-blăst)	angi/o -blast	CF S	vessel immature cell, germ cell	The germ cell from which blood vessels develop
angiocardiography (ăn″ jĭ-ō-kăr″ dĭ-ŏg′ ră-fē)	angi/o cardi/o -graphy	CF CF S	vessel heart recording	The process of recording the heart and vessels after an intravenous injection of a radiopaque solution
angiocarditis (ăn″ jĭ-ō-kăr-dī′ tĭs)	angi/o card -itis	CF R S	vessel heart inflammation	Inflammation of the heart and its great vessels
angioma (ăn″ jĭ-ō′ mă)	ang/i -oma	CF S	vessel tumor	A tumor of a blood vessel. See Figure 7–13.
angioplasty (ăn′ jĭ-ō-plăs″ tē)	angi/o -plasty	CF S	vessel surgical repair	Surgical repair of a blood vessel or vessels
angiostenosis (ăn″ jĭ-ō-stĕ-nō′ sĭs)	angi/o sten -osis	CF R S	vessel narrowing condition of	A condition of narrowing of a blood vessel
aortomalacia (ā-ōr″ tō-mă-lā′ shĭ-ă)	aort/o -malacia	CF S	aorta softening	Softening of the walls of the aorta
arrhythmia (ă-rĭth′ mĭ-ă)	a rrhythm -ia	P R S	lack of rhythm condition	A condition in which there is a lack of rhythm of the heartbeat
arterial (ăr-tē′ rĭ-ăl)	arter/i -al	CF S	artery pertaining to	Pertaining to an artery
arteriosclerosis (ăr-tē″ rĭ-ō-sklĕ-rō′ sĭs)	arteri/o scler -osis	CF R S	artery hardening condition of	A condition of hardening of an artery
arteritis (ăr″ tĕ-rī′ tĭs)	arter -itis	R S	artery inflammation	Inflammation of an artery. See Figure 7–14.
artificial pacemaker (ăr tĭ-fĭsh′ ăl pās′ māk-ĕr)				An electronic device that stimulates impulse initiation within the heart
atheroma (ăth″ ĕr-ō mă)	ather -oma	R S	fatty substance, porridge tumor	Tumor of an artery containing a fatty substance

MEDICAL WORD	WORD PARTS (WHEN APPLICABLE)			DEFINITION
	Part	Type	Meaning	
atherosclerosis (ăth″ ĕr-ō-sklĕ-rō′ sĭs)	ather/o	CF	fatty substance, porridge	A condition of the arteries characterized by the buildup of fatty substances and hardening of the walls. ✱ See Pathology Spotlight: Coronary Heart Disease, and Figures 7–27—7–29.
	scler	R	hardening	
	-osis	S	condition of	
atrioventricular (ăt″ rĭ-ō-vĕn-trĭk′ ū-lăr)	atri/o	CF	atrium	Pertaining to the atrium and the ventricle
	ventricul	R	ventricle	
	-ar	S	pertaining to	
auscultation (ŏs″ kool-tā′ shŭn)	auscultat	R	listen to	A method of physical assessment using a stethoscope to listen to sounds within the chest, abdomen, and other parts of the body
	-ion	S	process	
bicuspid (bī-kŭs′ pĭd)	bi	P	two	Having two points or cusps; pertaining to the mitral valve
	-cuspid	S	point	
bradycardia (brăd″ ĭ-kăr′ dĭ-ă)	brady	P	slow	A condition of slow heartbeat
	card	R	heart	
	-ia	S	condition	
bruit (brōōt)				Noise; a sound of venous or arterial origin heard on auscultation
cardiac (kăr′ dĭ-ăk)	card/i	CF	heart	Pertaining to the heart
	-ac	S	pertaining to	
cardiocentesis (kăr″ dĭ-ō-sĕn-tē′ sĭs)	cardi/o	CF	heart	Surgical puncture of the heart
	-centesis	S	surgical puncture	
cardiologist (kăr-dē-ŏl′ ō-jĭst)	cardi/o	CF	heart	One who specializes in the study of the heart
	log	R	study of	
	-ist	S	one who specializes	
cardiology (kăr″ dĭ-ŏl′ ō-jē)	cardi/o	CF	heart	The study of the heart
	-logy	S	study of	
cardiomegaly (kăr″ dĭ-ō-mĕg′ ă-lē)	cardi/o	CF	heart	Enlargement of the heart
	-megaly	S	enlargement, large	
cardiometer (kăr″ dĭ-ōm′ ĕ-tĕr)	cardi/o	CF	heart	An instrument used to measure the action of the heart
	-meter	S	instrument to measure	

MEDICAL WORD	WORD PARTS (WHEN APPLICABLE)			DEFINITION
	Part	**Type**	**Meaning**	
cardiomyopathy (kăr″ dē-ō-mī-ŏp′ ă-thē)	cardi/o my/o -pathy	CF CF S	heart muscle disease	Disease of the heart muscle that may be caused by a viral infection, a parasitic infection, or overconsumption of alcohol. See Figure 7–15.
cardiopathy (kăr″ dĭ-ŏp′ ă-thē)	cardi/o -pathy	CF S	heart disease	Heart disease
cardiopulmonary (kăr″ dĭ-ō-pŭl′ mō-něr-ē)	cardi/o pulmonar -y	CF R S	heart lung pertaining to	Pertaining to the heart and lungs
cardiotonic (kăr″ dĭ-ō-tŏn′ ĭk)	cardi/o ton -ic	CF R S	heart tone pertaining to	Pertaining to increasing the tone of the heart; a type of medication
cardiovascular (kăr″ dĭ-ō-văs′ kū-lar)	cardi/o vascul -ar	CF R S	heart small vessel pertaining to	Pertaining to the heart and small blood vessels
carditis (kăr-dī′ tĭs)	card -itis	R S	heart inflammation	Inflammation of the heart
catheterization (kăth″ ĕ-tĕr-ĭ-zā′ shŭn)				The process of inserting a catheter into the heart or the urinary bladder
cholesterol (kō-lĕs′ tĕr-ŏl)	chol/e sterol	CF R	bile solid (fat)	A waxy, fat-like substance in the bloodstream of all animals. It is believed to be dangerous when it builds up on arterial walls and contributes to the risk of coronary heart disease.
circulation (sər″ -kyə lā′ shŭn)	circulat -ion	R S	circular process	The process of moving the blood in the veins and arteries throughout the body
claudication (klaw-dĭ-kā′ shŭn)	claudicat -ion	R S	to limp process	The process of lameness, limping; may result from inadequate blood supply to the muscles in the leg
constriction (kən-strĭk′ shŭn)	con strict -ion	P R S	together, with to draw, to bind process	The process of drawing together, as in the narrowing of a vessel
coronary bypass (kŏr′ ō-nă-rē bī′ păs)				A surgical procedure performed to increase blood flow to the myocardium by using a section of a saphenous vein or internal mammary artery to bypass the obstructed or occluded coronary artery

MEDICAL WORD	WORD PARTS (WHEN APPLICABLE)			DEFINITION
	Part	**Type**	**Meaning**	
coronary heart disease (CHD) (kŏr′ ō-nǎ-rē hart dĭ-zēz′)				Coronary heart disease (CHD), also referred to as coronary artery disease (CAD), refers to the narrowing of the coronary arteries sufficient to prevent adequate blood supply to the myocardium. ✱ See Pathology Spotlight: Coronary Heart Disease.
cyanosis (sī-ă n-ō′ sĭs)	cyan -osis	R S	dark blue condition of	A dark blue condition of the skin and mucous membranes caused by oxygen deficiency
diastole (dī-ǎs′ tō-lē)	diast -ole	R S	to expand small	The relaxation phase of the heart cycle during which the heart muscle relaxes and the heart chambers fill with blood
dysrhythmia (dĭs-rĭth′ mē-ă)	dys rhythm -ia	P R S	difficult rhythm condition	An abnormal, difficult, or bad rhythm. ✱ See Pathology Spotlight: Dysrythmias.
echocardiography (ĕk″ ō-kăr″ dē-ŏg′ rah-fē)	ech/o cardi/o -graphy	CF CF S	echo heart recording	A noninvasive ultrasound method for evaluating the heart for valvular or structural defects and coronary artery disease
electrocardiograph (ē-lĕk″ trō-kăr′ dĭ-ō-grăf)	electr/o cardi/o -graph	CF CF S	electricity heart to write, record	A device used for recording the electrical impulses of the heart muscle
electrocardio- phonograph (ē-lĕk″ trō-kăr″ dĭ-ō-fō′ nō-grăf)	electr/o cardi/o phon/o -graph	CF CF CF S	electricity heart sound to write, record	A device used to record heart sounds
embolism (ĕm′ bō-lĭzm)	embol -ism	R S	a throwing in condition of	A condition in which a blood clot obstructs a blood vessel; *a moving blood clot*
endarterectomy (ĕn″ dăr-tĕr-ĕk′ tō-mē)	end arter -ectomy	P R S	within artery excision	Surgical excision of the inner portion of an artery
endocarditis (ĕn″ dō-kăr-dī′ tĭs)	endo card -itis	P R S	within heart inflammation	Inflammation of the endocardium, See Figure 7–16.
endocardium (ĕn″ dō-kăr′ dē-ŭm)	endo card/i -um	P CF S	within heart tissue	The inner lining of the heart

MEDICAL WORD	WORD PARTS (WHEN APPLICABLE)			DEFINITION
	Part	Type	Meaning	
extracorporeal circulation (ĕks-tră-kor-pōr′ ē-ăl sər″ -kyə lā′ shŭn)	extra corpor/e -al circulat -ion	P CF S R S	outside body pertaining to circular process	Pertaining to the circulation of the blood outside the body via a heart–lung machine or hemodialyzer
fibrillation (fĭ″ brĭl-ā′ shŭn)	fibrillat -ion	R S	fibrils (small fibers) process	Quivering of muscle fiber; may be atrial or ventricular
flutter (flŭt′ ər)				A condition of the heartbeat in which the contractions become extremely rapid
heart failure				A disorder in which the heart loses its ability to pump blood efficiently. See Fig. 7–12.
heart–lung transplant (hart-lŭng trăns′ plănt)				The surgical process of transferring the heart and lungs from a donor to a patient
heart transplant (hart trăns′ plănt)				The surgical process of transferring the heart from a donor to a patient
hemangiectasis (hē″ măn-jĭ-ĕk′ tă-sĭs)	hem ang/i -ectasis	R CF S	blood vessel dilatation	Dilatation of a blood vessel
hemangioma (hē-măn″ jĭ-ō′ mă)	hem ang/i -oma	R CF S	blood vessel tumor	A benign tumor of a blood vessel. See Figures 7–17 and 7–18.
hemodynamic (hē″ mō-dī-năm′ ĭk)	hem/o dynam -ic	CF R S	blood power pertaining to	Pertaining to the study of the heart's ability to function as a pump; the movement of the blood and its pressure
hypertension (hī″ pĕr-tĕn′ shŭn)	hyper tens -ion	P R S	excessive, above pressure process	High blood pressure; a disease of the arteries caused by such pressure. ✳ See Pathology Spotlight: Hypertension.
hypotension (hī″ pō-tĕn′ shŭn)	hypo tens -ion	P R S	deficient, below pressure process	Low blood pressure
infarction (ĭn-fărk′ shŭn)	infarct -ion	R S	infarct (necrosis of an area) process	Process of development of an infarct, which is necrosis of tissue resulting from obstruction of blood flow

MEDICAL WORD	WORD PARTS (WHEN APPLICABLE)			DEFINITION
	Part	**Type**	**Meaning**	
ischemia (ĭs-kē′ mĭ-ă)	isch -emia	R S	to hold back blood condition	A condition in which there is a lack of blood supply to a part caused by constriction or obstruction of a blood vessel
lipoprotein (lĭp-ō-prō′ tēn)	lip/o prot/e -in	CF CF S	fat first chemical	*Fat (lipid)* and *protein molecules* that are bound together. They are classified as: **VLDL**—very-low-density lipoproteins; **LDL**—low-density lipoproteins; and **HDL**—high-density lipoproteins. High levels of VLDL and LDL are associated with cholesterol and triglyceride deposits in arteries, which could lead to coronary heart disease, hypertension, and atherosclerosis.
lubb-dupp (lŭb-dŭp)				The two separate heart sounds that can be heard with the use of a stethoscope
mitral stenosis (mī′ trăl stĕ-nō′ sĭs)	mitr -al sten -osis	R S R S	mitral valve pertaining to narrowing condition of	A condition of narrowing of the mitral valve
murmur (mər′ mər)				A soft blowing or rasping sound heard by auscultation of various parts of the body, especially in the region of the heart
myocardial (mī″ ō-kăr′ dĭ-ăl)	my/o card/i -al	CF CF S	muscle heart pertaining to	Pertaining to the heart muscle
myocardial infarction (MI) (mī″ ō-kăr′ dē-ăl ĭn-fărk′ shŭn)	my/o card/i -al infarct -ion	CF CF S R S	muscle heart pertaining to infarct (necrosis of an area) process	Occurs when an area of heart muscle dies or is permanently damaged because of an inadequate supply of oxygen to that area; also known as a heart attack. ✳ See Pathology Spotlight: Heart Attack.
myocarditis (mī″ ō-kăr-dī′ tĭs)	my/o card -itis	CF R S	muscle heart inflammation	Inflammation of the heart muscle
occlusion (ŏ-kloo′ zhŭn)	occlus -ion	R S	to shut up process	The process or state of being closed

MEDICAL WORD	WORD PARTS (WHEN APPLICABLE)			DEFINITION
	Part	Type	Meaning	
oximetry (ŏk-sĭm′ ĕ-trē)	ox/i -metry	CF S	oxygen measurement	The process of measuring the oxygen saturation of blood. A photoelectric device (oximeter) measures oxygen saturation of the blood by recording the amount of light transmitted or reflected by deoxygenated versus oxygenated hemoglobin. A pulse oximetry is a noninvasive method of indicating the arterial oxygen saturation of functional hemoglobin. See Figure 7–19.
oxygen (ŏk′ sĭ-jĕn)	oxy -gen	R S	sour, sharp, acid formation, produce	A colorless, odorless, tasteless gas essential to respiration in animals
palpitation (păl-pĭ-tā′ shŭn)	palpitat -ion	R S	throbbing process	Rapid throbbing or fluttering of the heart
percutaneous transluminal coronary angioplasty (pĕr″ kū-tā′ nē-ŭs trăns-lū′ mĭ-năl kŏr′ ō-nă-rē ăn′ jĭ-ō-plăs″ tē)				The use of a balloon-tipped catheter to compress fatty plaques against an artery wall. When successful, the plaques remain compressed, and this permits more blood to flow through the artery, thereby relieving the symptoms of heart disease.
pericardial (pĕr″ ĭ-kăr′ dĭ-ăl)	peri card/i -al	P CF S	around heart pertaining to	Pertaining to the pericardium, the sac surrounding the heart
pericarditis (pĕr″ ĭ-kăr-dī′ tĭs)	peri card -itis	P R S	around heart inflammation	Inflammation of the pericardium
phlebitis (flĕ-bī′ tĭs)	phleb -itis	R S	vein inflammation	Inflammation of a vein
phlebotomy (flĕ-bŏt′ ō-mē)	phleb/o -tomy	CF S	vein incision	Incision into a vein
Raynaud's phenomenon (rā-nōz fĕ-nŏm′ ĕ-nŏn)				A disorder that generally affects the blood vessels in the fingers and toes; it is characterized by intermittent attacks that cause the blood vessels in the digits to narrow. The attack is usually due to exposure to cold or occurs during emotional stress. Once the attack begins, the patient may experience pallor, cyanosis, and/or rubor in the affected part. See Figure 7–20.

MEDICAL WORD	WORD PARTS (WHEN APPLICABLE)			DEFINITION
	Part	Type	Meaning	
rheumatic heart disease (rōō-măt′ ĭk hart dĭ-zēz′)				Endocarditis or valvular heart disease as a result of complications of acute rheumatic fever
semilunar (sĕm″ ĭ-lū′ năr)	semi lun -ar	P R S	half moon pertaining to	Valves of the aorta and pulmonary artery
septum (sĕp′ tŭm)	sept -um	R S	a partition tissue	A wall or partition that divides or separates a body space or cavity
shock (shŏk)				A state of disruption of oxygen supply to the tissues and a return of blood to the heart. See Figure 7–21.
sinoatrial (sīn″ ō-ā ′ trĭ-ăl)	sin/o atri -al	CF R S	a curve atrium pertaining to	Pertaining to the sinus venosus and the atrium
sphygmomano- meter (sfĭg″ mō-măn-ōm ĕt-ĕr)	sphygm/o man/o -meter	CF CF S	pulse thin instrument to measure	An instrument used to measure the arterial blood pressure. See Figure 7–10.
spider veins (spī′ dĕr vāns)				Hemangioma in which numerous telangiectatic vessels radiate from a central point. See Figure 7–22.
stethoscope (stĕth′ ō-skōp)	steth/o -scope	CF S	chest instrument	An instrument used to listen to the sounds of the heart, lungs, and other internal organs
systole (sĭs′ tō-lē)	syst -ole	R S	contraction small	The contractive phase of the heart cycle during which blood is forced into the aorta and the pulmonary artery
tachycardia (tăk″ ĭ-kăr′ dĭ-ă)	tachy card -ia	P R S	fast heart condition	A fast heartbeat
telangiectasis (tĕl-ăn″ jē-ĕk-tă′ sĭs)	tel ang/i -ectasis	R CF S	end vessel dilatation	A vascular lesion formed by dilatation of a group of small blood vessels; it may appear as a birthmark or be caused by long-term exposure to the sun. See Figure 7–23.
thrombophlebitis (thrŏm″ bō-flē-bī′ tĭs)	thromb/o phleb -itis	CF R S	clot of blood vein inflammation	Inflammation of a vein associated with the formation of a thrombus. See Figure 7–24.

MEDICAL WORD	WORD PARTS (WHEN APPLICABLE)			DEFINITION
	Part	**Type**	**Meaning**	
thrombosis (thrŏm-bō′ sĭs)	thromb -osis	R S	clot of blood condition of	A condition in which there is a blood clot within the vascular system; *a stationary blood clot*. See Figure 7–25.
tricuspid (trī-kŭs′ pĭd)	tri -cuspid	P S	three a point	Having three points; pertaining to the tricuspid valve
triglyceride (trī-glĭs′ ĕr-īd)	tri glyc -er -ide	P R S S	three sweet, sugar relating to having a particular quality	Pertaining to a compound consisting of three molecules of fatty acids
varicose veins (văr′ ĭ-kōs vāns)				Swollen, distended, and knotted veins which usually occur in the lower leg(s). They result from a stagnated or sluggish flow of blood in combination with defective valves and weakened walls of the veins. See Figure 7–26.
vasoconstrictive (văs″ ō-kŏn-strĭk′ tĭv)	vas/o con strict -ive	CF P R S	vessel together to draw, to bind nature of, quality of	The drawing together, as in the narrowing of a blood vessel
vasodilator (văs″ ō-dī-lā′ tor)	vas/o dilat -or	CF R S	vessel to widen one who, a doer	A nerve or agent that causes dilation of blood vessels
vasospasm (văs′ ō-spăzm)	vas/o -spasm	CF S	vessel contraction, spasm	Contraction of a blood vessel
venipuncture (vĕn′ ĭ-pŭnk″ chūr)	ven/i -puncture	CF S	vein to pierce	To pierce a vein
ventricular (vĕn-trĭk′ ū-lăr)	ventricul -ar	R S	ventricle pertaining to	Pertaining to a ventricle

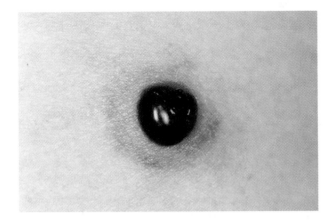

FIGURE 7–13

Infarction angioma. (Courtesy of Jason L. Smith, MD.)

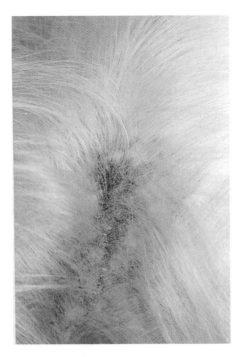

FIGURE 7–14

Temporal arteritis. (Courtesy of Jason L. Smith, MD.)

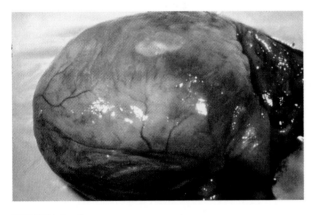

FIGURE 7–15

Cardiomyopathy. (Source: Pearson Education/PH College.)

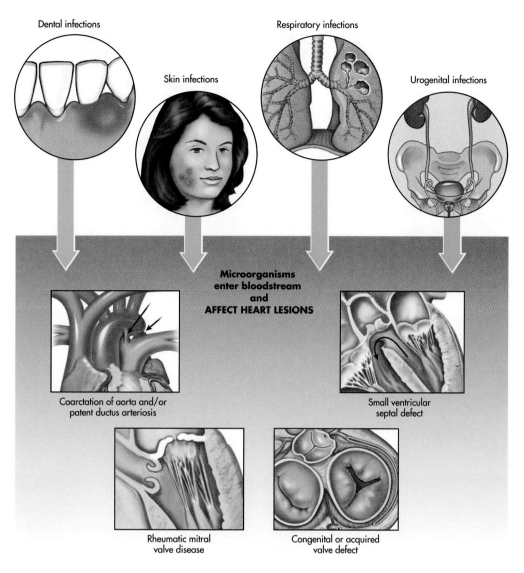

Dental infections

Skin infections

Respiratory infections

Urogenital infections

**Microorganisms
enter bloodstream
and
AFFECT HEART LESIONS**

Coarctation of aorta and/or
patent ductus arteriosis

Small ventricular
septal defect

Rheumatic mitral
valve disease

Congenital or acquired
valve defect

FIGURE 7–16

Infections resulting in bacterial endocarditis.

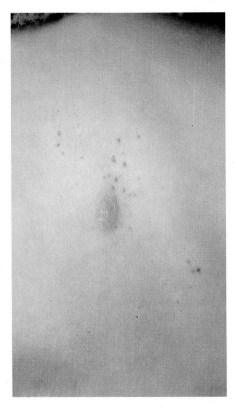

FIGURE 7–17

Hemangioma. (Courtesy of Jason L. Smith, MD.)

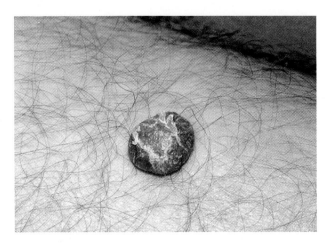

FIGURE 7–18

Sclerosing hemangioma. (Courtesy of Jason L. Smith, MD.)

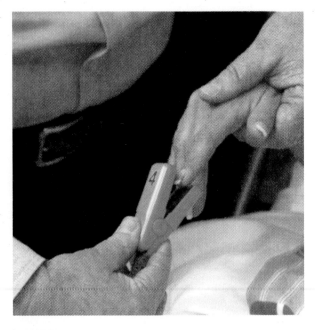

FIGURE 7–19

Pulse oximetry: the sensor probe is applied securely, flush with skin, making sure that both sensor probes are aligned directly opposite each other.

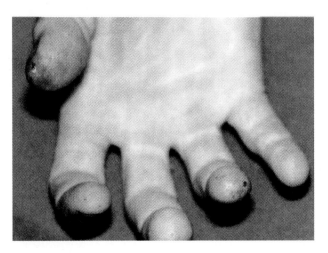

FIGURE 7–20

Raynaud's phenomenon. (Courtesy of Jason L. Smith, MD.)

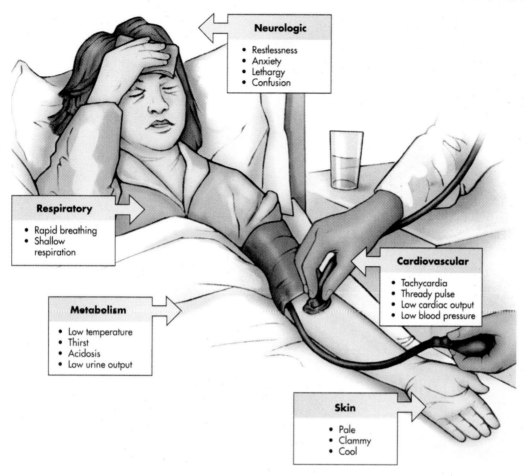

Neurologic
- Restlessness
- Anxiety
- Lethargy
- Confusion

Respiratory
- Rapid breathing
- Shallow respiration

Metabolism
- Low temperature
- Thirst
- Acidosis
- Low urine output

Cardiovascular
- Tachycardia
- Thready pulse
- Low cardiac output
- Low blood pressure

Skin
- Pale
- Clammy
- Cool

FIGURE 7–21

Symptoms of a patient in shock.

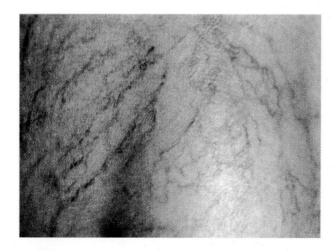

FIGURE 7–22

Spider veins. (Courtesy of Jason L. Smith, MD.)

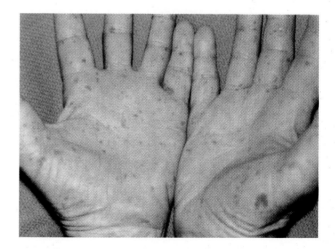

FIGURE 7–23

Telangiectasis. (Courtesy of Jason L. Smith, MD.)

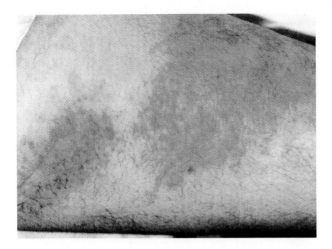

FIGURE 7–24

Thrombophlebitis. (Courtesy of Jason L. Smith, MD.)

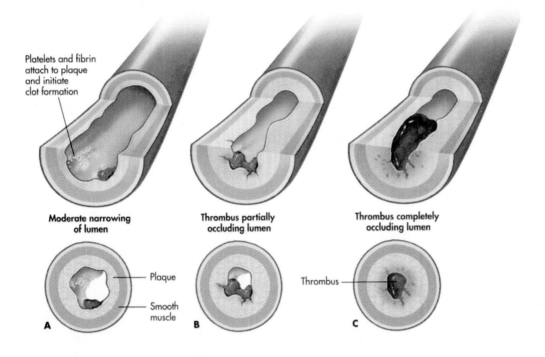

FIGURE 7–25

Thrombus formation in an atherosclerotic vessel. Depicted are the initial clot formation (A) and the varying degrees of occlusion (B) and (C).

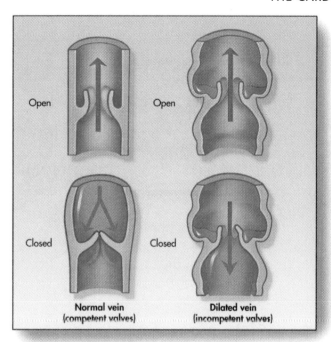

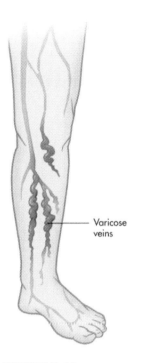

FIGURE 7–26

Development of varicose veins.

TERMINOLOGY TRANSLATOR

This feature, found on the accompanying CD-ROM, provides an innovative tool to translate medical words into Spanish, French, and German.

PATHOLOGY SPOTLIGHTS

Coronary Heart Disease (CHD)

Coronary heart disease (CHD) is the most common form of heart disease. It is also referred to as coronary artery disease (CAD) and refers to the narrowing of the coronary arteries that supply blood to the heart. It is a progressive disease that increases the risk of myocardial infarction (heart attack) and sudden death.

CHD usually results from the buildup of fatty material and plaque (**atherosclerosis**). See Figures 7–27, 7–28, and 7–29. As the coronary arteries narrow, the flow of blood to the heart can slow or stop. Blockage can occur in one or many coronary arteries.

Small blockages may not always affect the heart's performance. The person may not have symptoms until the heart needs more oxygen-rich blood than the arteries can supply. This commonly occurs during exercise or other activity. The pain that results is called stable angina.

If a blockage is large, angina pain can occur with little or no activity. This is known as unstable angina. In this case, the flow of blood to the heart is so limited that the person cannot

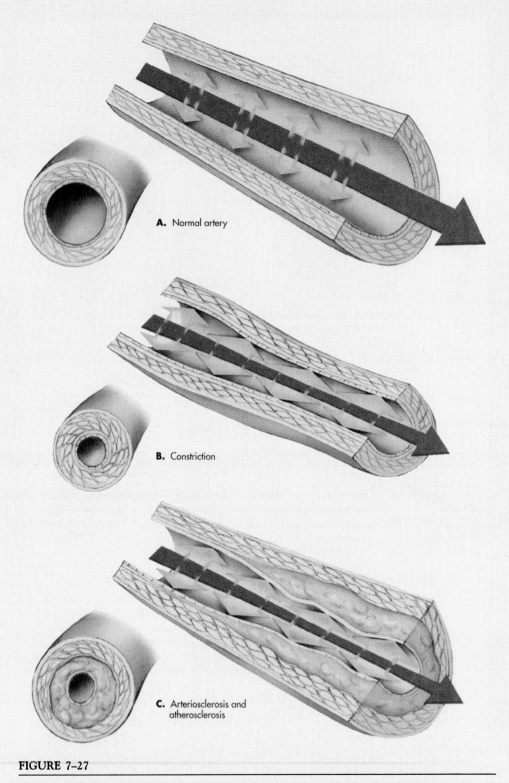

FIGURE 7–27

Blood vessels: (A) normal artery, (B) constriction, and (C) arteriosclerosis and atherosclerosis.

do daily tasks without bringing on an angina attack. When the blood flow to an area of the heart is completely blocked, a myocardial infarction (heart attack) occurs.

Symptoms of CHD vary widely. The classic indicator of CHD is angina, or chest pain. The pain may radiate to the neck, jaw, or left arm. It is often described as a crushing, burning, or squeezing sensation. The person may also have shortness of breath. This is usually a symptom of **heart failure**. The heart at this point is weak because of the long-term lack of blood and

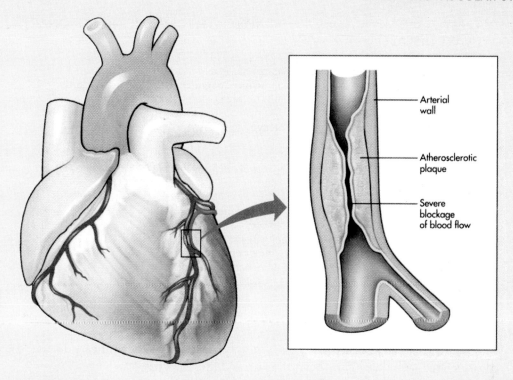

Arterial wall

Atherosclerotic plaque

Severe blockage of blood flow

FIGURE 7–28

An atherosclerotic artery.

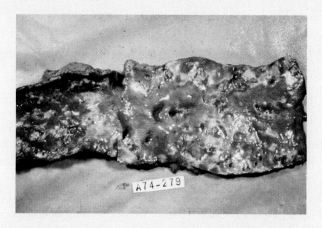

A74-279

FIGURE 7–29

Inside surface of a diseased artery showing atherosclerosis.
(Source: Pearson Education/PH College.)

oxygen, or sometimes from a recent or past heart attack. If the heart is not pumping enough blood to circulate in the body, shortness of breath may be accompanied by swollen feet and ankles. Sometimes, a person may have no symptoms at all until he or she suffers a heart attack.

CHD is the leading cause of death in the United States for men and women. According to the American Heart Association, about every 29 seconds someone in the United States suffers from a CHD-related event, and about every minute someone dies from such an event. The lifetime risk of having coronary heart disease after age 40 is 49 percent for men and 32 percent for women. As women get older, the risk increases almost to that of men.

One in ten American women 45 to 64 years of age has some form of heart disease, and this increases to one in four women over 65. The common misconception that heart disease is

TABLE 7–3 RISK FACTORS ASSOCIATED WITH DEVELOPING CORONARY HEART DISEASE

Male age 45 or older	Diabetes mellitus
Female age 55 or older	High-density lipoprotein (HDL) below 35 mg/dL
Female under age 55 with premature menopause	Family history of early heart disease (parent or sibling; male less than 55, female less than 65)
Smoker	Obesity
Hypertension	

Note: To help lower cholesterol one should limit intake of foods that are high in saturated fat:

Whole milk	Bacon
Dairy cream	Ribs
Cheese	Ground red meat
Butter	Cold cuts
Red meat, heavily marbled with fat	Poultry skin
Prime cuts	Coconut or palm oil
Sausage	Hydrogenated vegetable oil

a man's disease may cause many women to be misinformed about heart disease, the risk factors associated with developing heart disease, and lifestyle changes.

CHD affects people of all races. It can be caused by a combination of unhealthy lifestyle choices and genetics. High levels of VLDL and LDL lipoproteins are associated with cholesterol and **triglyceride** deposits in arteries, which could lead to coronary heart disease, hypertension, and atherosclerosis. One's total cholesterol level should be below 200 mg/dL and HDL (good cholesterol) above 35 mg/dL. See Table 7–3 for risk factors that increase the risk of CHD. The more risk factors that one has, the greater the possibility of developing coronary artery disease, a major cause of myocardial infarction.

Dysrhythmias

A **dysrhythmia** of the heart is an abnormality of the rhythm or rate of the heartbeat. The dysrhythmia is caused by a disturbance of the normal electrical activity within the heart. Dysrhythmias can be divided into 2 main groups: **tachycardias** and **bradycardias**. Tachycardias cause a rapid heartbeat, with over 100 beats per minute. Bradycardias cause a slow heartbeat, with less than 60 beats per minute. The rhythm of the heart may be regular during a dysrhythmia: each beat of the atria, or upper chambers of the heart, is followed by one beat of the ventricles, or lower chambers of the heart. The beat may also be irregular and may begin in an abnormal area of the heart.

TABLE 7–4 CONTRIBUTING FACTORS TO HYPERTENSION

Those That One Can Control:	
Smoking	Avoid the use of tobacco products
Overweight	Maintain a proper weight for age and body size
Lack of Exercise	Exercise regularly
Stress	Learn to manage stress
Alcohol	Limit intake of alcohol

Other Contributing Factors:	
Heredity	Family history of high blood pressure, heart attack, stroke, or diabetes
Race	There is a greater incidence of hypertension among African-Americans
Sex	Males have a greater chance of developing hypertension
Age	The likelihood of hypertension increases with age

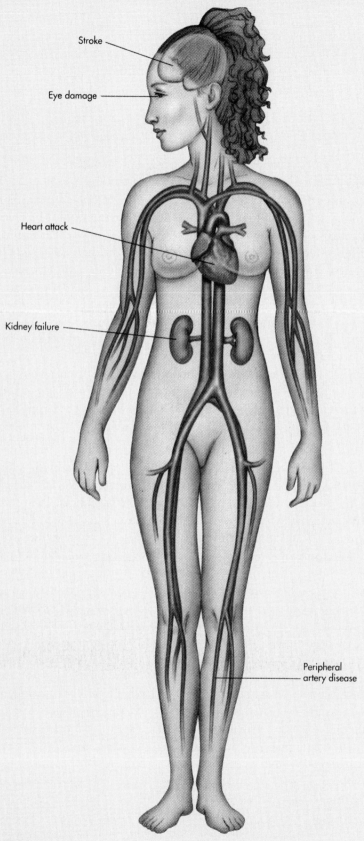

Stroke

Eye damage

Heart attack

Kidney failure

Peripheral
artery disease

FIGURE 7–30

Uncontrolled hypertension can lead to kidney failure, stroke, heart attack, peripheral artery disease, and eye damage.

Symptoms vary depending on the type of dysrhythmia, but may include: dizziness, or light-headedness, palpitations, shortness of breath, fatigue, weakness, **angina**, and fainting. Most dysrhythmias are caused by heart disease, including coronary heart disease, disease of the heart valves, including infections such as **endocarditis**, and **heart failure**.

Dysrhythmias can be life-threatening if they cause a severe decrease in the pumping function of the heart. When the pumping function is severely decreased for more than a few seconds, blood circulation is essentially stopped, and organ damage (such as brain damage) may occur within a few minutes.

Hypertension

Hypertension is a medical term that is used to describe a blood pressure higher than normal. Approximately 50 million adults in the United States are believed to have hypertension, a number expected to climb as the population ages. With hypertension (high blood pressure: HBP), the blood vessels can become tight and constricted. These changes can cause the blood to press on the vessel walls with extra force. When this force exceeds a certain level and remains there, one has high blood pressure. Hypertension often has no symptoms and is frequently called "the silent killer" because, if left untreated, it can lead to kidney failure, stroke, heart attack, peripheral artery disease, and eye damage. See Figure 7–29. There are various factors that can contribute to developing hypertension and it is important to know these factors (see Table 7–4).

Hypertension can be controlled by a variety of methods, such as taking blood pressure medications as prescribed, seeing a physician on a regular basis, establishing healthy eating habits, exercising, avoiding stress, and making lifestyle changes.

Prehypertension

Individuals aged 18 years and over with blood pressure ranging from 120/80 to 139/89 mm Hg belong to a new category designated as prehypertension, a high-risk precursor to hypertension, according to the Joint National Committee (JNC) seventh report. Because of this report, recently released by the National Heart, Lung, and Blood Institute (NHLBI), part of the National Institutes of Health (NIH), new blood pressure categories have become a part of the guidelines for the prevention and treatment of hypertension.

According to the report, adults at the upper end of the prehypertension blood pressure range (130/80 to 139/89 mm Hg) are twice as likely to progress to hypertension than those with lower blood pressure levels. The reporting panel of experts recommended lifestyle modification for patients with prehypertension. Therapeutic behavior changes identified as critical in the prevention of high blood pressure included reducing dietary fat and sodium, increasing exercise, and limiting alcohol consumption.

Other changes were made to the blood pressure classification system. While stage 1 hypertension (blood pressure range 140/90 to 159/99 mm Hg) remained a category, therapeutic recommendations were altered, identifying thiazide-type diuretics as treatment of choice for uncomplicated cases. The focus on diuretics for initial treatment of stage 1 hypertension is primarily associated with recently published results of the Antihypertensive and Lipid-Lowering Treatment to Prevent Heart Attack Trial (ALLHAT), suggesting that diuretics are as or more effective than other single drug therapies in the treatment of hypertension.

Former stages 2 and 3 hypertension were combined as stage 2, including patients with blood pressure above 160/100 mm Hg. Multi-drug therapy is recommended for these patients, in which a diuretic is combined with an angiotensin-converting enzyme (ACE) inhibitor, a beta-blocker, or calcium channel blocker. Public health, community, and school programs were identified as opportunities to promote public awareness and encourage healthy lifestyle behaviors. "The JNC 7th endorses the American Public Health Association resolution that the food manufacturers and restaurants reduce sodium in the food supply by 50% during the next decade," the report stated.

Heart Attack (Myocardial Infarction)

A **heart attack** (or **myocardial infarction**) occurs when the blood supply to part of the heart muscle (myocardium) is severely reduced or stopped. This occurs when one of the coronary arteries that supplies blood to the heart muscle is blocked. The blockage is usually from the buildup of plaque (deposits of fat-like substances) due to atherosclerosis. The plaque can eventually tear or rupture, triggering a blood clot that blocks the artery and leads to a heart attack. Such an event is called a coronary thrombosis or coronary occlusion.

If the blood supply is cut off severely or for a long time, muscle cells suffer irreversible injury and die. Disability or death can result, depending on how much heart muscle is damaged.

A recent study indicates that having a large "pot belly" or "spare tire" around the middle is associated with an increased risk for atherosclerosis. Experts explain that in addition to the fat one can see bulging around the middle, there are also fat deposits deep within the abdomen tucked around abdominal organs. The presence of this fat further increases the risk of having high cholesterol and insulin resistance, a precursor to diabetes.

The most common symptom of a heart attack is chest pain (angina). This pain is often described as a feeling of crushing, pressure, fullness, heaviness, or aching in the center of the chest. These sensations may extend into the neck, the jaw, and down the left arm. Angina is often associated with excessive sweating, feelings of apprehension, nausea, shortness of breath, and weakness.

Some heart attacks are sudden and intense, but most heart attacks start slowly, with mild pain or discomfort. Often the people affected are not sure of what is happening and wait too long before getting help. Heart attack and stroke are life-and-death emergencies; every second counts.

The American Heart Association lists the following as warning signs of heart attack:

- Pressure, fullness, squeezing pain in the center of the chest that lasts 2 minutes or longer
- Pain that spreads to the shoulders, neck, or arms
- Dizziness, fainting, sweating, nausea, or shortness of breath

Today heart attack and stroke victims can benefit from new medications and treatments. Clot-busting drugs can stop some heart attacks and strokes in progress, reducing disability and saving lives. But to be effective, these drugs must be given relatively quickly after heart attack or stroke symptoms first appear. It is said that the average heart attack victim waits 3 hours after symptoms occur to seek help. Many times they try to ignore the symptoms or say "it's just indigestion." It is imperative to seek medical help immediately. Calling 911 is almost always the fastest way to get lifesaving treatment.

✔ PATHOLOGY CHECKPOINT

Following is a concise list of the pathology-related terms that you've seen in the chapter. Review this checklist to make sure that you are familiar with the meaning of each term before moving on to the next section.

Conditions and Symptoms

- ❏ aneurysm
- ❏ anginal
- ❏ angiocarditis
- ❏ angioma
- ❏ angiostenosis
- ❏ aortomalacia
- ❏ arrhythmia
- ❏ arteriosclerosis
- ❏ arteritis
- ❏ atheroma
- ❏ atherosclerosis
- ❏ bradycardia
- ❏ bruit
- ❏ cardiomegaly
- ❏ cardiomyopathy
- ❏ cardiopathy
- ❏ carditis
- ❏ claudication
- ❏ constriction
- ❏ coronary heart disease (CHD)
- ❏ cyanosis
- ❏ dysrhythmia
- ❏ embolism
- ❏ endocarditis
- ❏ fibrillation
- ❏ flutter

- ❏ heart failure (HF)
- ❏ hemangiectasis
- ❏ hemangioma
- ❏ hypertension
- ❏ hypotension
- ❏ infarction
- ❏ ischemia
- ❏ mitral stenosis
- ❏ murmur
- ❏ myocardial infarction (MI)
- ❏ myocarditis
- ❏ occlusion
- ❏ palpitation
- ❏ pericarditis
- ❏ phlebitis
- ❏ Raynaud's phenomenon
- ❏ rheumatic heart disease
- ❏ shock
- ❏ spider veins
- ❏ tachycardia
- ❏ telangiectasis
- ❏ thrombophlebitis
- ❏ thrombosis
- ❏ vasoconstrictive
- ❏ vasospasm
- ❏ varicose veins

Diagnosis and Treatment

- ❏ anastomosis
- ❏ angiocardiography
- ❏ artificial pacemaker
- ❏ auscultation
- ❏ cardiocentesis
- ❏ cardiometer
- ❏ cardiotonic
- ❏ catheterization
- ❏ coronary bypass
- ❏ echocardiography
- ❏ electrocardiograph
- ❏ electrocardiophonograph
- ❏ endarterectomy
- ❏ extracorporeal circulation
- ❏ heart-lung transplant
- ❏ heart transplant
- ❏ oximetry
- ❏ percutaneous transluminal coronary angioplasty
- ❏ phlebotomy
- ❏ sphygmomanometer
- ❏ stethoscope
- ❏ vasodilator
- ❏ venipuncture

DRUG HIGHLIGHTS

Drugs that are generally used for cardiovascular diseases and disorders include digitalis preparations, antiarrhythmic agents, vasopressors, vasodilators, antihypertensive agents, antihyperlipidemic, antiplatelet drugs, and thrombolytic agents.

Digitalis Drugs

Strengthen the heart muscle, increase the force and velocity of myocardial systolic contraction, slow the heart rate, and decrease conduction velocity through the atrioventricular (AV) node. These drugs are used in the treatment of congestive heart failure, atrial fibrillation, atrial flutter, and paroxysmal atrial tachycardia. With the administration of digitalis, toxicity may occur. The most common early symptoms of digitalis toxicity are anorexia, nausea, vomiting, and arrhythmias.

Examples: Crystodigin (digitoxin), Lanoxin (digoxin), and Digitaline (digitoxin).

Antiarrhythmic Agents

Used in the treatment of cardiac arrhythmias.

Examples: Tambocor (flecainide acetate), Tonocard (tocainide HCl), Inderal (propranolol HCl), and Calan (verapamil).

Vasopressors

Cause contraction of the muscles associated with capillaries and arteries, thereby narrowing the space through which the blood circulates. This narrowing results in an elevation of blood pressure. Vasopressors are useful in the treatment of patients suffering from shock.

Examples: Intropin (dopamine HCl), Aramine (metaraminol bitartrate), and Levophed Bitartrate (norepinephrine).

Vasodilators

Cause relaxation of blood vessels and lower blood pressure. Coronary vasodilators are used for the treatment of angina pectoris.

Examples: Sorbitrate (isosorbide dinitrate), nitroglycerin, amyl nitrate, and Peritrate (pentaerythritol tetranitrate).

Antihypertensive Agents

Used in the treatment of hypertension.

Examples: Catapres (clonidine HCl), Aldomet (methyldopa), Lopressor (metoprolol tartrate), and Capoten (captopril).

Antihyperlipidemic Agents

Used to lower abnormally high blood levels of fatty substances (lipids) when other treatment regimens fail.

Examples: Nicolar or Nicobid (niacin), Mevacor (lovastatin), Lopid (gemfibrozil), Lipitor (atorvastatin calcium), Pravachol (pravastatin), and Zocor (simvastatin).

Antiplatelet Drugs

Help reduce the occurrence of and death from vascular events such as heart attacks and strokes. *Aspirin* is considered to be the reference standard antiplatelet drug and is recommended by the American Heart Association for use in patients with a wide range of cardiovascular disease. Aspirin helps keep platelets from sticking together to form clots. *Plavix (clopidogrel)* is approved by the Food and Drug Administration for many of the same indications as aspirin. It is recommended for patients for whom aspirin fails to achieve a therapeutic benefit.

Thrombolytic Agents

Act to dissolve an existing thrombus when administered soon after its occurrence. They are often referred to as **tissue plasminogen activators** (tPA, TPA) and may reduce the chance of dying after a myocardial infarction by 50 percent. Unless contraindicated, the drug should be administered within 6 hours of the onset of chest pain. In some hospitals the time period for administering thrombolytic agents has been extended to 12 and 24 hours. These agents dissolve the clot, reopen the artery, restore blood flow to the heart, and prevent further damage to the myocardium. Bleeding is the most common complication encountered during thrombolytic therapy.

Examples: Kabikinase and Streptase (streptokinase), Eminase (anistreplase), Activase (alteplase), and Abbokinase (urokinase).

DIAGNOSTIC & LAB TESTS

TEST	DESCRIPTION
angiogram (ăn′ jē-ō-grăm)	A test used to determine the size and shape of arteries and veins of organs and tissues. A radiopaque substance is injected into the blood vessel, and x-rays are taken.
angiography (ăn″ jē-ŏg′ ră-fē)	The x-ray recording of a blood vessel after the injection of a radiopaque substance. Used to determine the condition of the blood vessels, organ, or tissue being studied. Types: aortic, cardiac, cerebral, coronary, digital subtraction (use of a computer technique), peripheral, pulmonary, selective, and vertebral.
cardiac catheterization (kăr′ dĭ-ăk kăth″ ĕ-tĕr-ĭ-zā′ shŭn)	A test used in diagnosis of heart disorders. A tiny catheter is inserted into an artery in the arm or leg of the patient and is fed through this artery to the heart. Dye is then pumped through the catheter, enabling the physician to locate by x-ray any blockages in the arteries supplying the heart. See Figure 7–31.
cardiac enzymes (kar′ dĭ-ăk ĕn′-zīmz)	Blood tests performed to determine cardiac damage in an acute myocardial infarction.

alanine
  aminotransferase
  (ALT)
	Levels begin to rise 6 to 10 hours after an MI and peak at 24 to 48 hours.

aspartate
  aminotransferase
  (AST)
	Levels begin to rise 6 to 10 hours after an MI and peak at 24 to 48 hours.

creatine
  phosphokinase
  (CPK)
	Used to detect area of damage.

creatine kinase (CK)
  creatine kinase
  isoenzymes
	Level may be 5 to 8 times normal.
	Used to indicate area of damage; CK-MB heart muscle, CK-MM skeletal muscle, and CK-BB brain.

cholesterol (kŏl-lĕs′ tĕr-ŏl)	A blood test to determine the level of cholesterol in the serum. Elevated levels may indicate an increased risk of coronary heart disease. Any level greater than 200 mg/dL is considered too high for good heart health.
electrophysiology (ē-lĕk″ trō-fĭz″ ĭ-ŏl′ ō-jē)	A cardiac procedure that maps the electrical activity of the heart from within the heart itself.
Holter monitor (hōlt ər mŏn′ ĭ-tər)	A method of recording a patient's ECG for 24 hours. The device is portable and small enough to be worn by the patient during normal activity.

TEST	DESCRIPTION
lactic dehydrogenase (LDH) (lăk′ tĭk dē-hĭ-drŏj′ ĕ-nās)	Increased 6 to 12 hours after cardiac injury.
stress test (strĕs tĕst)	A method of evaluating cardiovascular fitness. The ECG is monitored while the patient is subjected to increasing levels of work. A treadmill or ergometer is used for this test.
triglycerides (trī-glĭs′ ĕr-īds)	A blood test to determine the level of triglycerides in the serum. Elevated levels (greater than 200 mg/dL) may indicate an increased risk of coronary heart disease and diabetes mellitus.
ultrasonography (ŭl-tră-sŏn-ŏg′ ră-fē)	A test used to visualize an organ or tissue by using high-frequency sound waves. It may be used as a screening test or as a diagnostic tool to determine abnormalities of the aorta, arteries and veins, and the heart.
ultrafast CT scan	Has begun to be used in the past few years to diagnose heart disease. Ultrafast CT can take multiple images of the heart within the time of a single heartbeat, thus providing much more detail about the heart's function and structures, while also greatly decreasing the amount of time required for a study. Ultrafast CT can detect very small amounts of calcium within the heart and the coronary arteries. This calcium has been shown to indicate that lesions which may eventually block off one or more coronary arteries and cause chest pain or even a heart attack are in the beginning stages of formation. Thus, ultrafast CT scanning is being used by many physicians as a means to diagnose early coronary artery disease in certain people, especially persons who have no symptoms of the disease.

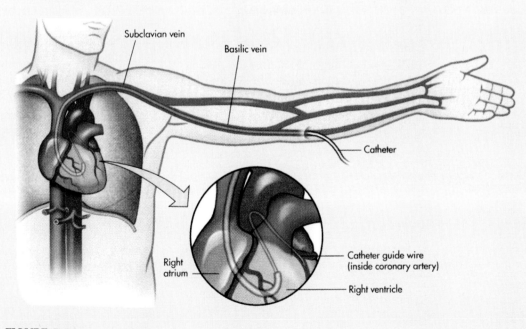

FIGURE 7–31

Cardiac catheterization.

ABBREVIATIONS

ABBREVIATION	MEANING	ABBREVIATION	MEANING
ACG	angiocardiography	Hgb	hemoglobin
AI	aortic insufficiency	H&L	heart and lungs
AMI	acute myocardial infarction	IHSS	idiopathic hypertrophic subaortic stenosis
AS	aortic stenosis	JNC	Joint National Committee
ASD	atrial septal defect	LA	left atrium
ASH	asymmetrical septal hypertrophy	LBBB	left bundle branch block
ASHD	arteriosclerotic heart disease	LD	lactic dehydrogenase
AST	aspartate aminotransferase	LDL	low-density lipoprotein
A-V, AV	atrioventricular; arteriovenous	LEDs	light-emitting diodes
BBB	bundle branch block	LV	left ventricle
BP	blood pressure	MI	myocardial infarction
CABG	coronary artery bypass graft	MS	mitral stenosis
CAD	coronary artery disease	MVP	mitral valve prolapse
CC	cardiac catheterization	NHLBI	National Heart, Lung, and Blood Institute
CCU	coronary care unit	NIH	National Institutes of Health
CHD	coronary heart disease	OHS	open heart surgery
CHF	congestive heart failure	PAT	paroxysmal atrial tachycardia
CK	creatine kinase	PMI	point of maximal impulse
CO	cardiac output	PTCA	percutaneous transluminal coronary angioplasty
CPR	cardiopulmonary resuscitation	PVC	premature ventricular contraction
CVP	central venous pressure	RA	right atrium
DVT	deep vein thrombosis	RV	right ventricle
ECC	extracorporeal circulation	S-A, SA	sinoatrial (node)
ECG	electrocardiogram	SCD	sudden cardiac death
EKG	electrocardiogram	tPA, TPA	tissue plasminogen activator
FHS	fetal heart sound	VLDL	very-low-density lipoprotein
HBP	high blood pressure	VSD	ventricular septal defect
HDL	high-density lipoprotein		
HF	heart failure		
Hg	mercury		

STUDY AND REVIEW

Anatomy and Physiology

Write your answers to the following questions. Do not refer to the text.

1. The cardiovascular system includes:

   a. _____   b. _____

   c. _____   d. _____

2. Name the three layers of the heart.

   a. _____   b. _____

   c. _____

3. The heart weighs approximately _____ grams.

4. The _____ or upper chambers of the heart are separated by the

   _____ septum.

5. The _____ or lower chambers of the heart are separated by the

   _____ septum.

6. By listing each cardiovascular part in the proper order, trace the flow of blood through the heart, to the lungs, back to the heart, and on to the various body parts.

   a. _____   b. _____

   c. _____   d. _____

   e. _____   f. _____

   g. _____   h. _____

   i. _____   j. _____

   k. _____   l. _____

   m. _____   n. _____

7. The _____ _____ _____ controls the heartbeat.

8. The _____ _____ is called the pacemaker of the heart.

9. The _____ _____ includes the bundle of His and the peripheral fibers.

10. Name the three primary pulse points and state their locations on the body.

a. _____ located _____

b. _____ located _____

c. _____ located _____

11. Define the following terms:

a. Blood pressure _____

b. Pulse pressure _____

12. The average adult heart is about the size of a _____ and normally

beats at a pulse rate of _____ to _____ beats per minute.

13. The average adult usually has a systolic pressure between _____ and

_____ mm Hg and a diastolic pressure between _____ and

_____ mm Hg.

14. Give the purpose and function of arteries. _____

_____

15. Give the purpose and function of veins. _____

_____

Word Parts

1. In the spaces provided, write the definition of these prefixes, roots, combining forms, and suffixes. Do not refer to the listing of medical words. Leave blank those words you cannot define.

2. After completing as many as you can, refer to the medical word listings to check your work. For each word missed or left blank, write the word and its definition several times on the margins of these pages or on a separate sheet of paper.

3. To maximize the learning process, it is to your advantage to do the following exercises as directed. To refer to the word building section before completing these exercises invalidates the learning process.

PREFIXES

Give the definitions of the following prefixes:

1. a- _____   2. bi- _____

3. brady- _____ 4. con- _____

5. end- _____   6. endo- _____

7. extra- _____

8. hyper- _____

9. hypo- _____

10. peri- _____

11. dys- _____

12. semi- _____

13. tachy- _____

14. tri- _____

ROOTS AND COMBINING FORMS

Give the definitions of the following roots and combining forms:

1. ang/i _____

2. angin _____

3. angi/o _____

4. anastom _____

5. aort/o _____

6. arter _____

7. arter/i _____

8. arteri/o _____

9. ather _____

10. ather/o _____

11. atri _____

12. atri/o _____

13. card _____

14. card/i _____

15. cardi/o _____

16. cyan _____

17. auscultat _____

18. dilat _____

19. electr/o _____

20. embol _____

21. glyc _____

22. hem _____

23. isch _____

24. chol/e _____

25. log _____

26. lun _____

27. man/o _____

28. mitr _____

29. my/o _____

30. circulat _____

31. oxy _____

32. phleb _____

33. phleb/o _____

34. phon/o _____

35. pulmonar _____

36. rrhythm _____

37. scler _____

38. sin/o _____

39. sphygm/o _____

40. sten _____

41. steth/o _____

42. strict _____

43. claudicat _____

44. tens _____

45. thromb _____

46. diast _____

47. vascul _____

48. vas/o _____

49. ech/o _____

50. ven/i _____

51. corpor/e _____

52. ventricul _____

53. fibrillat _____

54. hem/o _____

55. dynam _____

56. infarct _____

57. lip/o _____

58. prot/e _____

59. occlus _____

60. ox/i _____

61. palpitat _____

62. sept _____

63. syst _____

64. tel _____

65. thromb/o _____

66. sterol _____

SUFFIXES

Give the definitions of the following suffixes:

1. -ac _____

2. -al _____

3. -ar _____

4. -blast _____

5. -centesis _____

6. -ole _____

7. -cuspid _____

8. -metry _____

9. -ectasis _____

10. -ectomy _____

11. -emia _____

12. -er _____

13. -gen _____

14. -in _____

15. -graph _____

16. -graphy _____

17. -ia _____

18. -ic _____

19. -ide _____

20. -ion _____

21. -ism _____

22. -ist _____

23. -itis _____

24. -ive _____

25. -logy _____

26. -malacia _____

27. -megaly _____

28. -meter _____

29. -oma _____

30. -or _____

31. -osis _____

32. -pathy _____

33. -plasty _____

34. -puncture _____

35. -scope _____

36. -spasm _____

37. -tomy _____

38. -um _____

39. -y _____

Identifying Medical Terms

In the spaces provided, write the medical terms for the following meanings:

1. _____ A tumor of a blood vessel

2. _____ The germ cell from which blood vessels develop

3. _____ Surgical repair of a blood vessel or vessels

4. _____ A condition of narrowing of a blood vessel

5. _____ Incision into an artery

6. _____ Inflammation of an artery

7. _____ Having two points or cusps; pertaining to the mitral valve

8. _____ One who specializes in the study of the heart

9. _____ Enlargement of the heart

10. _____ Pertaining to the heart and lungs

11. _____ The process of drawing together as in the narrowing of a vessel

12. _____ A condition in which a blood clot obstructs a blood vessel

13. _____ Inflammation of a vein

14. _____ A fast heartbeat

15. _____ A widening of a blood vessel

Spelling

In the spaces provided, write the correct spelling of these misspelled terms:

1. astomosis _____

2. athrosclerosis _____

3. atriventrcular _____

4. endcarditis _____

5. extracoporal _____

6. iscemia _____

7. mycardial _____

8. oyxgen _____

9. phelebitis _____

10. palpitaiton _____

Matching

Select the appropriate lettered meaning for each word listed below.

_____ 1. cholesterol

_____ 2. claudication

_____ 3. dysrhythmia

_____ 4. diastole

_____ 5. fibrillation

_____ 6. lipoprotein

_____ 7. lubb-dupp

_____ 8. palpitation

_____ 9. percutaneous transluminal coronary angioplasty

_____ 10. systole

a. The two separate heart sounds that can be heard with the use of a stethocope

b. Quivering of muscle fiber

c. Fat and protein molecules that are bound together

d. A waxy, fat-like substance in the bloodstream of all animals

e. The process of lameness, limping

f. An abnormal, difficult, or bad rhythm

g. The relaxation phase of the heart cycle

h. The contraction phase of the heart cycle

i. Rapid throbbing or fluttering of the heart

j. The use of a balloon-tipped catheter to compress fatty plaques against an artery wall

k. The process of being closed

Abbreviations

Place the correct word, phrase, or abbreviation in the space provided.

1. acute myocardial infarction _____

2. atrioventricular _____

3. BP _____

4. CAD _____

5. cardiac catheterization _____

6. ECG, EKG _____

7. HDL _____

8. heart and lungs _____

9. MI _____

10. tPA, TPA _____

Diagnostic and Laboratory Tests

Select the best answer to each multiple choice question. Circle the letter of your choice.

1. _____ is a cardiac procedure that maps the electrical activity of the heart from within the heart itself.
   a. electrocardiogram
   b. electrocardiomyogram
   c. electrophysiology
   d. cardiac catheterization

2. Blood tests performed to determine cardiac damage in an acute myocardial infarction.
   a. cardiac enzymes
   b. cholesterol
   c. triglycerides
   d. angiogram

3. A method of recording a patient's ECG for 24 hours.
   a. stress test
   b. Holter monitor
   c. ultrasonography
   d. angiography

4. A test used to determine the size and shape of arteries and veins of organs and tissues.
   a. electrophysiology
   b. stress test
   c. angiogram
   d. cholesterol

5. The x-ray recording of a blood vessel after the injection of a radiopaque substance.
   a. angiogram
   b. angiography
   c. stress test
   d. cardiac catheterization

CASE STUDY

ANGINA PECTORIS

Read the following case study and then answer the questions that follow.

A 45-year-old male was seen by a cardiologist; the following is a synopsis of his visit.

Present History: The patient states that during a workout session he felt tightness in his chest, became short of breath, and felt very apprehensive. He states that this uncomfortable sensation went away after he stopped exercising.

Signs and Symptoms: Tightness in his chest, dyspnea, apprehension.

Diagnosis: Angina pectoris. Diagnosis was determined by a complete physical examination, an electrocardiogram, and blood enzyme studies.

Treatment: Nitroglycerin sublingual tablets 0.4 mg as needed for chest pain. The patient is instructed to seek medical attention without delay if the pain is not relieved by three tablets, taken one every 5 minutes over a 15-minute period.

Prevention: Teach the patient to avoid situations that precipitate angina attacks. Proper rest and diet, stress management, lifestyle changes, avoidance of alcohol and tobacco are recommended.

CASE STUDY QUESTIONS

1. Signs and symptoms of angina pectoris include tightness in the chest, _____ (shortness of breath), and apprehension.

2. The diagnosis of angina pectoris was determined by a complete physical examination, an _____ _____, and blood enzyme studies.

3. The medication regimen prescribed included _____ 0.4 mg as needed for chest pain.

4. If the patient follows the recommended medication regimen and it does not relieve the pain, he should _____.

MedMedia Wrap-Up

www.prenhall.com/rice

Additional interactive resources and activities for this chapter can be found on the Companion Website. For animations, videos, audio glossary, and review, access the accompanying CD-ROM in this book.

Audio Glossary
Medical Terminology Exercises & Activities
Pathology Spotlight
Terminology Translator
Animations
Videos

Objectives
Medical Terminology Exercises & Activities
Audio Glossary
Drug Updates
Medical Terminology in the News

BLOOD AND THE LYMPHATIC SYSTEM

8

OBJECTIVES

On completion of this chapter, you will be able to:

- Describe the blood.
- Describe the formed elements in blood.
- Name the four blood types.
- Describe and state the functions of the lymphatic system.
- Describe the accessory organs of the lymphatic system.
- Describe the immune system/response.
- Analyze, build, spell, and pronounce medical words.
- Describe each of the conditions presented in the Pathology Spotlights.
- Complete the Pathology Checkpoint.
- Review Drug Highlights presented in this chapter.
- Provide the description of diagnostic and laboratory tests related to blood and the lymphatic system.
- Identify and define selected abbreviations.
- Successfully complete the study and review section.

MedMedia
www.prenhall.com/rice

Additional interactive resources and activities for this chapter can be found on the Companion Website. For Terminology Translator, animations, videos, audio glossary, and review, access the accompanying CD-ROM in this book.

Anatomy and Physiology Overview

Blood and lymph are two of the body's main fluids and are circulated through two separate but interconnected vessel systems. **Blood** is circulated by the action of the heart, through the circulatory system consisting largely of arteries, veins, and capillaries. **Lymph** does not actually circulate. It is propelled in one direction, away from its source, through increasingly larger lymph vessels, to drain into large veins of the circulatory system located in the neck region. Numerous valves within the lymph vessels permit one-directional flow, opening and closing as a consequence of pressure caused by the massaging action of muscles on the vessels and the fluid they contain. The various organs and components of blood and the lymphatic system are described in this chapter.

BLOOD

Blood is a fluid consisting of formed elements and plasma, both of which are continuously produced by the body for the purpose of transporting respiratory gases (*oxygen and carbon dioxide*), chemical substances (*foods, salts, hormones*), and cells that act to protect the body from foreign substances. The blood volume within an individual depends on body weight. An individual weighing 154 lb (70 kg) has a blood volume of about 5 qt or 5 L.

Formed Elements

The formed elements in blood are the red blood cells or **erythrocytes**, **platelets** or **thrombocytes**, and white blood cells or **leukocytes**. Formed elements constitute about 45 percent of the total volume of blood and are sometimes referred to as whole blood (Table 8–1).

BLOOD AND THE LYMPHATIC SYSTEM

Organ/Structure	Primary Functions
Blood	Fluid consisting of formed elements and plasma that transport respiratory gases (oxygen and carbon dioxide), chemical substances (foods, salts, hormones), and cells that act to protect the body from foreign substances
Lymphatic System	A vessel system composed of lymphatic capillaries, lymphatic vessels, lymphatic ducts, and lymph nodes that convey lymph from the tissue to the blood. The three main functions of the lymphatic system are: 1. It transports proteins and fluids, lost by capillary seepage, back to the bloodstream 2. It protects the body against pathogens by phagocytosis and immune response 3. It serves as a pathway for the absorption of fats from the small intestines into the bloodstream
Spleen	Major site of erythrocyte destruction; serves as a reservoir for blood; acts as a filter, removing microorganisms from the blood
Tonsils	Filter bacteria and aid in the formation of white blood cells
Thymus	Essential role in the formation of antibodies and the development of the immune response in the newborn; manufactures infection-fighting T cells and helps distinguish normal T cells from those that attack the body's own tissue

TABLE 8–1 TYPES OF BLOOD CELLS AND FUNCTIONS

Blood Cell	*Function*
Erythrocyte (red blood cell)	Transports oxygen and carbon dioxide
Thrombocyte (platelet)	Blood clotting
Leukocyte (white blood cell)	Body's main defense against invasion of pathogens
Types of leukocytes	
Neutrophil	Protection against infection, phagocytosis
Eosinophil	Destroys parasitic organisms, plays a key role in allergic reactions
Basophil	Key role in releasing histamine and other chemicals that act on blood vessels, essential to nonspecific immune response to inflammation
Monocyte	One of the first lines of defense in the inflammatory process, phagocytosis
Lymphocyte	Provides the body with immune capacity
B lymphocyte	Identifies foreign antigens and differentiates into antibody-producing plasma cells (source for immunoglobulins–antibodies)
T lymphocyte	Essential for the specific immune response of the body

ERYTHROCYTES

Erythrocytes are doughnut-shaped cells without nuclei. They transport oxygen (most of which is bound to hemoglobin contained in the cell) and carbon dioxide. There are approximately 5 million erythrocytes per cubic millimeter, and they have a life span of 80 to 120 days. Erythrocytes are formed in the red bone marrow and are commonly called red blood cells (Fig. 8–1).

Thrombocytes

Thrombocytes are disk-shaped cells about half the size of erythrocytes. They play an important role in the clotting process by releasing *thrombokinase*, which, in the presence of calcium, reacts with *prothrombin* to form *thrombin*. There are approximately

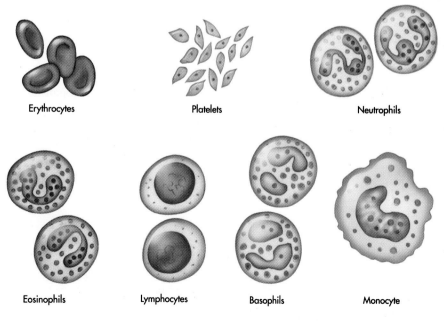

Erythrocytes   Platelets   Neutrophils

Eosinophils   Lymphocytes   Basophils   Monocyte

FIGURE 8–1

The formed elements of blood: erythrocytes, leukocytes (neutrophils, eosinophils, basophils, lymphocytes, and monocytes), and thrombocytes (platelets).

200,000 to 500,000 thrombocytes per cubic millimeter. Thrombocytes are fragments of certain giant cells called megakaryocytes, which are formed in the red bone marrow. Thrombocytes are commonly called **platelets** (Fig. 8–1).

Leukocytes

Leukocytes are sphere-shaped cells containing nuclei of varying shapes and sizes. Leukocytes are the body's main defense against the invasion of **pathogens**. At the time pathogens enter the tissue, the leukocytes leave the blood vessels through their walls and move in an amoeba-like motion to the area of infection, where they perform **phagocytosis**. There are approximately 8000 leukocytes per cubic millimeter. There are five types of leukocytes: **neutrophils, eosinophils, basophils, lymphocytes,** and **monocytes**.

Except for the lymphocytes, leukocytes are formed in the red bone marrow. Lymphocytes are formed in lymph nodes and other lymphoid tissue. Leukocytes are commonly called **white blood cells** (Fig. 8–1).

Blood Grouping

There are a number of human blood systems which are determined by a series of two or more genes closely linked on a single autosomal chromosome. The ABO system which was discovered in 1901 by Karl Landsteiner is of great significance in blood typing and blood transfusion. The four blood types identified in this system are types A, B, AB, and O. The differences in human blood are due to the presence or absence of certain protein molecules called antigens and antibodies. The antigens are located on the surface of the red blood cells and the antibodies are in the blood plasma. Individuals have different types and combinations of these molecules. Individuals in the A group have the A antigen on the surface of their red blood cells and anti-B antibody in the blood plasma; B group has the B antigen and the anti-A antibody; AB group has both A and B antigens and no anti-A or anti-B antibodies; and group O has neither A or B antigens and both anti-A and anti-B antibodies. Type AB blood group is known as the universal recipient and type O as the universal donor. See Table 8–2 and Figure 8–2.

Rh Factor

The presence of a substance called an **agglutinogen** in the red blood cells is responsible for what is known as the **Rh factor**. It was first discovered in the blood of the rhesus monkey from which the factor gets its name. About 85 percent of the population have the Rh factor and are called Rh positive. The other 15 percent lack the Rh factor and are designated Rh negative. There are more than 20 genetically determined blood group systems known today, but the ABO and Rh systems are the most important ones used for blood transfusions. Not all blood groups are compatible with each

TABLE 8–2 BLOOD GROUPS

Type	Antigen	Plasma Antibody	Percentage/Population
A	A	Anti-B	41
B	B	Anti-A	10
AB	Both A and B	No anti-A or anti-B	4
O	No A and B	Both anti-A and anti-B	45

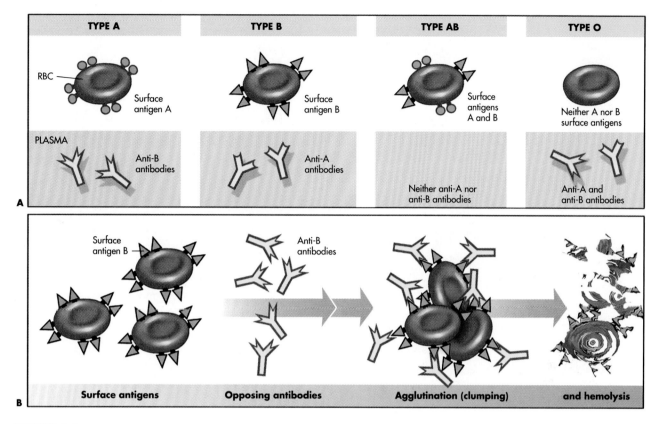

FIGURE 8–2

Blood-typing and cross-reactions: the blood type depends on the presence of surface antigens (agglutinogens) on RBC surfaces. (A) The plasma antibodies (agglutinins) that will react with foreign surface antigens. (B) In a cross-reaction, antibodies that encounter their target antigens lead to agglutination and hemolysis of the affected RBCs.

other. Mixing incompatible blood groups leads to blood clumping or agglutination, which is dangerous for individuals.

If an individual with Rh− blood receives a transfusion of Rh+ blood, it causes the formation of anti-Rh agglutinin. Subsequent transfusions of Rh+ blood may result in serious transfusion reactions (agglutination and hemolysis of red blood cells). A pregnant woman who is Rh− may become sensitized by blood of an Rh+ fetus. Sensitization can also occur if an Rh-negative woman has had a previous miscarriage, induced abortion, or ectopic pregnancy. There is also a slight chance that a woman may develop antibodies after having amniocentesis done later in pregnancy. These are all cases in which fetal blood (that might be Rh positive) could mix with maternal blood, resulting in the production of antibodies that could complicate a subsequent pregnancy. In subsequent pregnancies, if the fetus is Rh+, Rh antibodies produced in maternal blood may cross the placenta and destroy fetal cells, producing hemolytic disease of the newborn (HDN). See Figure 8–3. Today, hemolytic disease can for the most part be prevented if the Rh-negative woman has not already made antibodies against the Rh factor from an earlier pregnancy or blood transfusion. Rh immunoglobulin (Rhogam) is a product that can safely prevent sensitization of an Rh-negative mother. It suppresses her ability to respond to Rh-positive red cells. With its use, sensitization can be prevented almost all the time, although Rhogam is not helpful if the mother is already sensitized.

For a blood transfusion to be successful, ABO and Rh blood groups must be compatible between the donor and the recipient. If they are not, the red blood cells from

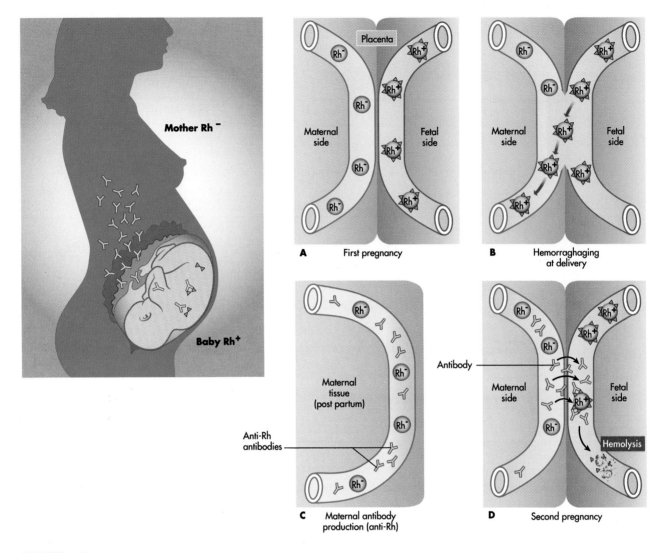

FIGURE 8–3

Rh factors and pregnancy: when an Rh-negative woman has her first Rh-positive child, fetal and maternal blood mix at delivery when the placenta breaks down. The appearance of Rh-positive blood cells in the maternal bloodstream sensitizes the mother, stimulating the production of anti-Rh antibodies. If another pregnancy occurs with an Rh-positive fetus, maternal anti-Rh antibodies can cross the placenta and attack fetal blood cells, producing hemolytic disease of the newborn (HDN).

the donated blood can clump or agglutinate and cause clogging of blood vessels and slow and/or stop the circulation of blood to various parts of the body. The agglutinated red blood cells may also hemolyze and their contents leak out in the body. The red blood cells contain hemoglobin which becomes toxic when outside the red blood cell, and this could lead to fatal consequences for the recipient.

Plasma

The fluid part of the blood is called **plasma**. It comprises about 55 percent of the total volume of blood, is clear and somewhat straw-colored, and is composed of water (91 percent) and chemical compounds (9 percent). Plasma is the medium for circulation of blood cells, it provides nutritive substances to various body structures, and it removes waste products of metabolism from body structures. There are four major plasma proteins: **albumin**, **globulin**, **fibrinogen**, and **prothrombin**.

THE LYMPHATIC SYSTEM

The **lymphatic system** is a vessel system apart from, but connected to, the circulatory system. The lymphatic system returns fluids from tissue spaces to the bloodstream. The lymphatic system is composed of *lymphatic capillaries, lymphatic vessels, lymphatic ducts,* and *lymph nodes*. The system conveys lymph from the tissues to the blood. Lymph is a clear, colorless, alkaline fluid that is about 95 percent water. The principal component of lymph is fluid from plasma that has seeped out of capillary walls into spaces among the body tissues. Lymph contains white blood cells, particularly lymphocytes. Figure

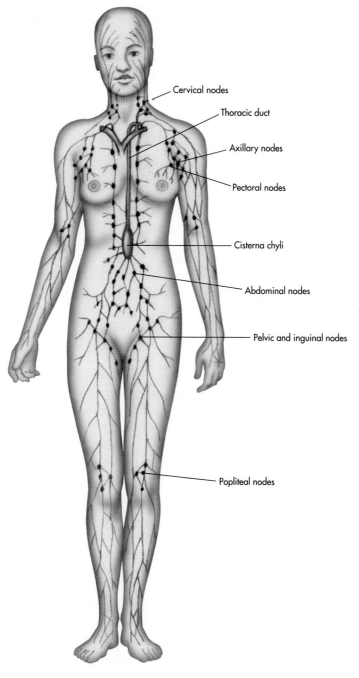

Cervical nodes

Thoracic duct

Axillary nodes

Pectoral nodes

Cisterna chyli

Abdominal nodes

Pelvic and inguinal nodes

Popliteal nodes

FIGURE 8–4

The lymphatic system.

8–4 shows the major lymphatics of the body. The three main functions of the lymphatic system are:

1. It transports proteins and fluids, lost by capillary seepage, back to the bloodstream.
2. It protects the body against pathogens by phagocytosis and immune response.
3. It serves as the pathway for the absorption of fats from the small intestines into the bloodstream.

ACCESSORY ORGANS

The **spleen**, the **tonsils**, and the **thymus** are not actually part of the lymphatic system; however, they are closely related to it in their functions. See Figure 8–5.

The Spleen

The **spleen** is a soft, dark red oval body lying in the upper left quadrant of the abdomen. The spleen is the major site of erythrocyte destruction. It serves as a reservoir for blood. The spleen plays an essential role in the immune response and acts as a filter, removing microorganisms from the blood.

The Tonsils

The **tonsils** are lymphoid masses located in depressions of the mucous membranes of the face and pharynx. They consist of the *palatine tonsil*, *pharyngeal tonsil* (adenoid), and the *lingual tonsil*. The tonsils filter bacteria and aid in the formation of white blood cells. See Figure 8–6.

The Thymus

The **thymus** is considered one of the endocrine glands, but because of its function and appearance, it is a part of the lymphoid system. It is located in the mediastinal cavity. The thymus plays an essential role in the formation of antibodies and the development of the immune response in the newborn. It manufactures infection-fighting **T cells** and helps distinguish normal T cells from those that attack the body's own tissue. T cells are important in the body's cellular immune response.

THE IMMUNE SYSTEM/RESPONSE

All of us live in a virtual "sea" of microorganisms, organisms so tiny that they cannot be seen with the naked eye. Many of these organisms are not harmful to humans, while others are **pathogenic**, capable of causing disease. Each day our bodies are faced with microorganisms, potentially harmful toxins in the environment, and even some of our own cells that may change into cancer. Fortunately, the average, healthy human body is equipped with natural defenses that assist the body in fighting off disease and cancer. These natural defenses are intact skin, the cleansing action of the body's secretions (such as tears, mucus), white blood cells, body chemicals (such as hormones, enzymes), and antibodies. As long as the immune system is intact and functioning properly, it can defend the body against invading foreign substances and cancer.

The **immune system** consists of the tissues, organs, and physiologic processes used by the body to identify abnormal cells, foreign substances, and foreign tissue cells that

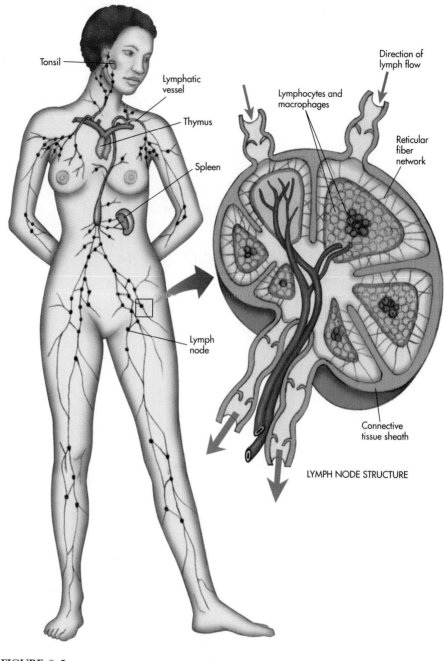

FIGURE 8–5

The tonsils, lymph nodes, thymus, spleen, and lymphatic vessels with an expanded view of a lymph node.

may have been transplanted into the body. Many of these tissues and organs are part of the lymphatic system.

THE IMMUNE RESPONSE

The **immune response** is the reaction of the body to foreign substances and the means by which it protects the body. The following is an overview of this response.

The immune response may be described as humoral immunity or antibody-mediated immunity, and cellular immunity or cell-mediated immunity.

Humoral (pertaining to body fluids or substances contained in them) **immunity** or **antibody-mediated immunity** involves the production of plasma lymphocytes (B cells)

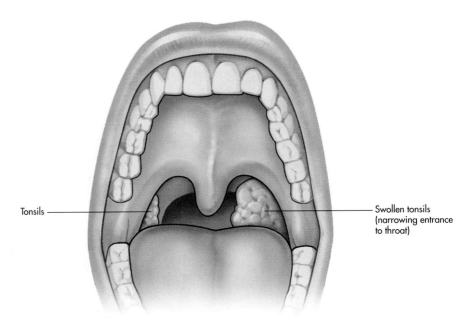

FIGURE 8–6

Tonsils—normal and enlarged.

in response to antigen exposure with subsequent formation of antibodies. **Antibodies** are protein substances that are developed in response to a specific antigen. An **antigen** is a substance such as bacteria, toxins, or certain allergens that induces the formation of antibodies. Humoral immunity is a major defense against bacterial infections.

Cellular immunity or **cell-mediated immunity** involves the production of lymphocytes (T cells) that responds to any form of injury and NK (natural killer) cells that attack foreign cells, normal cells infected with viruses, and cancer cells. Cellular immunity constitutes a major defense against infections caused by viruses, fungi, and a few bacteria, such as the tubercle bacillus that causes tuberculosis. It also helps defend against the formation of tumors, especially cancer.

There are four general phases associated with the body's immune response to a foreign substance and these are:

1. The first phase is the recognition of the foreign substance or the invader (enemy).
2. Activation of the body's defenses by producing more white blood cells that are designed to seek and destroy the invader(s), especially the macrophages that eat and engulf the foreign substances and lymphocytes, B cells, and T cells (see Table 8–3), constitutes the second phase.

    T cells of the helper type identify the enemy and rush to the spleen and lymph nodes, where they stimulate the production of other cells to aid in the fight of the foreign substance.

TABLE 8–3 SUMMARY OF FUNCTIONS OF LYMPHOCYTES

Type of Cell	Functions
T cells (thymus-dependent)	Cellular immunity
B cells (bone marrow-derived)	Humoral immunity
NK cells (natural killers)	Attack foreign cells, normal cells infected with viruses, and cancer cells

T cells of the natural killer (NK) type are large granular lymphocytes that also specialize in killing cells of the body that have been invaded by foreign substances and fighting cells that have turned cancerous.

The B cells reside in the spleen or lymph nodes and produce antibodies for specific antigens.

3. During the attack phase, the above defenders of the body produce antibodies and/or seek out to kill and/or remove the foreign invader. This is done by phagocytosis, where the macrophages squeeze out between the cells in the capillaries and crawl into the tissue to the site of the infection. Here they surround and eat the foreign substances that caused the infection. Other white blood cells respond to infection by producing antibodies. Antibodies are released into the bloodstream and carried to the site of the infection, where they surround and immobilize the invaders. Later, both antibody and invader may be eaten by the phagocytes.

4. In the slowdown phase, the number of defenders returns to normal, following victory over the foreign invader.

LIFE SPAN CONSIDERATIONS

■ THE CHILD

In the embryo, plasma and blood cells are formed about the 2nd week of life. At approximately the 5th week of development, blood formation occurs in the liver and later in the spleen, thymus, lymphatic system, and bone marrow. At 12 weeks the fetus is 11.5 cm (4.5 inches) from crown to head and weighs 45 g (1.6 oz). The fetal **liver** is the chief producer of red blood cells, and **bile** is secreted by the gallbladder. At 16 weeks blood vessels are visible through the now-transparent skin. Fetal circulation provides oxygenation and nutrition to the fetus and disposes of carbon dioxide and other waste products.

The **thymus gland** plays an important role in the development of the immune response in the newborn. At birth, the average weight of the thymus is 10 to 15 g. It attains a weight of 40 g at puberty, after which it begins to undergo involution, with the thymus being replaced with adipose and connective tissue.

■ THE OLDER ADULT

With advancing age, lymphatic tissue shrinks, the bone marrow becomes less productive, and the walls of peripheral vessels stiffen. There is also loss of elasticity in the peripheral vessels, which causes increases in peripheral resistance, impairs the flow of blood, and results in an increase in the workload of the left ventricle. As a result of these changes in the peripheral vascular system, the transportation of oxygen and nutrients to the tissues and the removal of wastes from the tissues are affected adversely. The transportation of oxygen may also be compromised by the decrease of **hemoglobin** of some older adults.

Immune response declines with age, limiting the body's ability to identify and fight foreign substances such as bacteria and viruses. With aging there is loss of the thymus cortex, which leads to a reduced production of T lymphocytes, including T cells, natural killer cells, and B lymphocytes. Persons at the extremes of the life span are more likely to develop immune-response problems than those in their middle years. Frequency and severity of infections are generally increased in elderly persons because of a decreased ability of the immune system to respond adequately to invading microorganisms. The incidence of **auto-immune diseases** also increases with aging, most likely due to a decreased ability of antibodies to differentiate between self and nonself. Failure of the immune response system to recognize mutant, or abnormal, cells may be the reason for the high incidence of cancer associated with increasing age.

BUILDING YOUR MEDICAL VOCABULARY

This section provides the foundation for learning medical terminology. Medical words can be made up of four different types of word parts:

- Prefixes (P)
- Roots (R)
- Combining forms (CF)
- Suffixes (S)

By connecting various word parts in an organized sequence, thousands of words can be built and learned. In this text the word list is alphabetized so one can see the variety of meanings created when common prefixes and suffixes are repeatedly applied to certain word roots and/or combining forms. Words shown in pink are additional words related to the content of this chapter that are not built from word parts. These words are included to enhance your vocabulary. Note: an asterisk icon ✳ indicates words that are covered in the Pathology Spotlights section in this chapter.

MEDICAL WORD	WORD PARTS (WHEN APPLICABLE)			DEFINITION
	Part	Type	Meaning	
acquired immuno-deficiency syndrome (AIDS) (ă-kwĭrd ĭm″ ū-nō dĕ-fĭsh′ ĕn-sē sĭn-drōm)				AIDS is a disease caused by the human immunodeficiency virus (HIV). This virus is transmitted through sexual contact, through exposure to infected blood or blood components, and perinatally from mother to infant. The HIV virus invades the T4 lymphocytes, and as the disease progresses the body's immune system becomes paralyzed. The patient becomes severely weakened, and potentially fatal infections can occur. *Pneumocystis carinii* pneumonia and Kaposi's sarcoma account for many of the deaths of AIDS patients. ✳ See Pathology Spotlight: AIDS.
agglutination (ă-gloo″ tĭ-nā′ shŭn)	agglutinat -ion	R S	clumping process	The process of clumping together, as of blood cells that are incompatible
albumin (ăl-bū′ mĭn)				One of a group of simple proteins found in blood plasma and serum
allergy (ăl′ ĕr-jē)	all -ergy	R S	other work	Individual hypersensitivity to a substance that is usually harmless. ✳ See Figure 8–18 in Pathology Spotlight: Rhinitis.

MEDICAL WORD	WORD PARTS (WHEN APPLICABLE)			DEFINITION
	Part	Type	Meaning	
anaphylaxis (ăn″ ă-fĭ-lăk′ sĭs)	ana -phylaxis	P S	up protection	An unusual or exaggerated allergic reaction to foreign proteins or other substances. ✱ See Figure 8–19 in Pathology Spotlight: Anaphylaxis.
anemia (ă-nē′ mĭ-ă)	an -emia	P S	lack of blood condition	A condition of a lack of red blood cells. ✱ See Figures 8–20 and 8–21 in Pathology Spotlight: Anemia.
anisocytosis (ăn-ī″ sō-sī-tō′ sĭs)	anis/o cyt -osis	CF R S	unequal cell condition of	A condition in which the erythrocytes are unequal in size and shape
antibody (ăn′ tĭ-bŏd″ ē)	anti -body	P S	against body	A protein substance produced in the body in response to an invading foreign substance (*antigen*). ✱ See Pathology Spotlight: Antibody.
anticoagulant (ăn″ tĭ-kō-ăg′ ū-lănt)	anti coagul -ant	P R S	against clots forming	An agent that works against the formation of blood clots
antigen (ăn′ tĭ-jĕn)	anti -gen	P S	against formation, produce	An invading foreign substance that induces the formation of antibodies
autoimmune disease (aw″ tō-ĭm-mūn dĭ-zēz)				A condition in which the body's immune system becomes defective and produces antibodies against itself. Hemolytic anemia, rheumatoid arthritis, myasthenia gravis, and scleroderma are considered as autoimmune diseases.
autotransfusion (aw″ tō-trăns-fū′ zhŭn)	auto trans fus -ion	P P R S	self across to pour process	The process of reinfusing a patient's own blood. Methods used are: "harvesting" the blood 1 to 3 weeks before elective surgery; "salvaging" intraoperative blood; and collecting blood from trauma or selected surgical patients for reinfusion within 4 hours.
basocyte (bā′ sō-sīt)	bas/o -cyte	CF S	base cell	A base cell leukocyte
basophil (bā′ sō-fĭl)	bas/o -phil	CF S	base attraction	A cell that has an attraction for a base dye
blood (blŭd)				The fluid that circulates through the heart, arteries, veins, and capillaries

MEDICAL WORD	WORD PARTS (WHEN APPLICABLE)			DEFINITION
	Part	Type	Meaning	
coagulable (kō-ăg′ ū-lăb-l)	coagul -able	R S	to clot capable	Capable of forming a clot
corpuscle (kŏr′ pŭs-ĕl)				A blood cell
creatinemia (krē″ ă-tĭn-ē′ mĭ-ă)	creatin -emia	R S	flesh, creatine blood condition	A condition of excess creatine in the blood
embolus (ĕm′ bō-lŭs)				A blood clot carried in the bloodstream
eosinophil (ē″ ŏ-sĭn′ ō-fĭl)	eosin/o -phil	CF S	rose-colored attraction	A cell that stains readily with the acid stain; attraction for the rose-colored stain
erythroblast (ĕ-rĭth′ rō-blăst)	erythr/o -blast	CF S	red immature cell, germ cell	An immature red blood cell
erythrocyte (ĕ-rĭth′ rō-sīt)	erythr/o -cyte	CF S	red cell	A red blood cell
erythrocytosis (ĕ-rĭth″ rō-sī-tō′ sĭs)	erythr/o cyt -osis	CF R S	red cell condition of	An abnormal condition in which there is an increase in red blood cells
erythropoiesis (ĕ-rĭth″ rō-poy-ē′ sĭs)	erythr/o -poiesis	CF S	red formation	Formation of red blood cells
erythropoietin (ĕ-rĭth″ rō-poy′ ĕ′-tĭn)	erythr/o poiet -in	CF R S	red formation chemical	A hormone that stimulates the production of red blood cells
extravasation (ĕks-tră″ vă-sā′ shŭn)	extra vas(at) -ion	P R S	beyond vessel process	The process whereby fluids and/or medications (IVs) escape into surrounding tissue
fibrin (fī′ brĭn)	fibr -in	R S	fiber chemical	An insoluble protein formed from fibrinogen by the action of thrombin in the blood-clotting process
fibrinogen (fī-brĭn′ ō-gĕn)	fibrin/o -gen	CF S	fiber formation	A blood protein converted to fibrin by the action of thrombin in the blood-clotting process
globulin (glŏb′ ū-lĭn)	globul -in	R S	globe chemical	An albuminous protein found in body fluids and cells
granulocyte (grăn′ ū-lō-sīt″)	granul/o -cyte	CF S	little grain, granular cell	A granular leukocyte

MEDICAL WORD	WORD PARTS (WHEN APPLICABLE)			DEFINITION
	Part	**Type**	**Meaning**	
hematocrit (hē-măt′ ō-krĭt)	hemat/o -crit	CF S	blood to separate	A blood test that separates solids from plasma in the blood by centrifuging the blood sample
hematologist (hē″ mă-tŏl′ ō-jĭst)	hemat/o log -ist	CF R S	blood study of one who specializes	One who specializes in the study of the blood
hematology (hē″ mă-tŏl′ ō-jē)	hemat/o -logy	CF S	blood study of	The study of the blood
hematoma (hē″ mă-tō′ mă)	hemat -oma	R S	blood tumor	A blood tumor. See Figure 8–7.
hemochromatosis (hē″ mō-krō″ mă-tō′ sĭs)	hem/o chromat -osis	CF R S	blood color condition of	A disease condition in which iron is not metabolized properly and it accumulates in body tissues. The skin has a bronze hue, the liver becomes enlarged, and diabetes and cardiac failure may occur.
hemoglobin (hē″ mō-glō′ bĭn)	hem/o -globin	CF S	blood globe, protein	Blood protein; the iron-containing pigment of red blood cells
hemolysis (hē-mŏl′ ĭ-sĭs)	hem/o -lysis	CF S	blood destruction	Destruction of red blood cells
hemophilia (hē″ mō-fĭl′ ĭ-ă)	hem/o -philia	CF S	blood attraction	A hereditary blood disease characterized by prolonged coagulation and tendency to bleed
hemorrhage (hěm′ ě-rĭj)	hem/o -rrhage	CF S	blood bursting forth	Excessive bleeding; bursting forth of blood. See Figure 8–8.
hemostasis (hē-mŏs′ tā-sĭs)	hem/o -stasis	CF S	blood control, stopping	The control or stopping of bleeding. See Figure 8–9.
heparin (hěp′ ă-rĭn)				A substance found in the liver, lungs, and other body tissues that inhibits blood clotting
hypercalcemia (hī″ pěr-kăl-sē′ mĭ-ă)	hyper calc -emia	P R S	excessive lime, calcium blood condition	A condition of excessive amounts of calcium in the blood
hyperglycemia (hī″ pěr-glī-sē′ mĭ-ă)	hyper glyc -emia	P R S	excessive sweet, sugar blood condition	A condition of excessive amounts of sugar in the blood

MEDICAL WORD	WORD PARTS (WHEN APPLICABLE)			DEFINITION
	Part	**Type**	**Meaning**	
hyperlipemia (hī″ pĕr-lĭp-ē′ mĭ-ă)	hyper lip -emia	P R S	excessive fat blood condition	A condition of excessive amounts of fat in the blood
hypoglycemia (hī″ pō-glĭ-sē′ mĭ-ă)	hypo glyc -emia	P R S	deficient sweet, sugar blood condition	A condition of deficient amounts of sugar in the blood
immunoglobulin (Ig) (ĭm″ ū-nō-glŏb′ ū-lĭn)	immun/o globul -in	CF R S	immunity globe chemical	A blood protein capable of acting as an antibody. The five major types are IgA, IgD, IgE, IgG, and IgM.
Kaposi's sarcoma (kăp′ ō-sēz săr-kō′ mă)				A malignant neoplasm that causes violaceous vascular lesions and general lymphadenopathy; it is the most common AIDS-related tumor. See Figures 8–10 and 8–11.
leukapheresis (loo″ kă-fĕ-rē′ sĭs)	leuk/a -pheresis	CF S	white removal	Removal of white blood cells from the circulation
leukemia (loo-kē′ mē-ă)	leuk -emia	R S	white blood condition	A disease of the blood characterized by overproduction of leukocytes. The disease may be malignant, acute, or chronic. ✳ See Figure 8–22 in Pathology Spotlight: Leukemia.
leukocyte (loo′ kō-sīt)	leuk/o -cyte	CF S	white cell	A white blood cell
leukocytopenia (loo″ kō-sī″ tō-pē′ nĭ-ă)	leuk/o cyt/o -penia	CF CF S	white cell lack of	A lack of white blood cells
lymph (lĭmf)				A clear, colorless, alkaline fluid found in the lymphatic vessels
lymphadenitis (lĭm-făd″ ĕn-ī′ tĭs)	lymph aden -itis	R R S	lymph gland inflammation	Inflammation of the lymph glands
lymphadenotomy (lĭm-făd″ ĕ-nō tō-mē)	lymph aden/o -tomy	R CF S	lymph gland incision	Incision into a lymph gland
lymphangiology (lĭm-făn″ jē-ŏl′ ō-jē)	lymph angi/o -logy	R CF S	lymph vessel study of	The study of the lymphatic vessels
lymphangitis (lĭm″ făn-jī′ tĭs)	lymph ang -itis	R R S	lymph vessel inflammation	Inflammation of lymphatic vessels. See Figure 8–12.

MEDICAL WORD	WORD PARTS (WHEN APPLICABLE)			DEFINITION
	Part	Type	Meaning	
lymphedema (lĭmf-ĕ-dē′ mă)	lymph -edema	R S	lymph swelling	An abnormal accumulation of lymph in the interstitial spaces. See Figures 8–13 and 8–14.
lymphoma (lĭm-fō′ mă)	lymph -oma	R S	lymph tumor	A lymphoid neoplasm, usually malignant. See Figures 8–15 and 8–16.
lymphostasis (lĭm-fō′ stā-sĭs)	lymph/o -stasis	CF S	lymph control, stopping	The control or stopping of the flow of lymph
macrocyte (măk′ rō-sīt)	macr/o -cyte	CF S	large cell	An abnormally large erythrocyte
monocyte (mŏn′ ō-sīt)	mono -cyte	P S	one cell	The largest leukocyte, which has one nucleus
mononucleosis (mŏn″ ō-nū″ klē-ō′ sĭs)	mono nucle -osis	P R S	one kernel, nucleus condition	A condition of excessive amounts of mononuclear leukocytes in the blood
neutrophil (nū′ trō-fĭl)	neutr/o -phil	CF S	neither attraction	A leukocyte that stains with neutral dyes
opportunistic infection (ŏp″ ŏr-too-nĭs′ tĭk ĭn-fĕk′ shŭn)				A protozoal, fungal, viral, or bacterial infection that occurs when one's immune system is compromised. AIDS patients are very vulnerable and develop one or more opportunistic infections.
pancytopenia (păn″ sī-tō-pē′ nĭ-ă)	pan cyt/o -penia	P CF S	all cell lack of	A lack of the cellular elements of the blood
phagocytosis (făg″ ō-sī-tō′ sĭs)	phag/o cyt -osis	CF R S	eat, engulf cell condition of	A condition of the engulfing and eating of bacteria by the phagocytes
plasma (plăz′ mă)				The fluid part of the blood
plasmapheresis (plăz″ mă-fĕr-ē′ sĭs)	plasma -pheresis	R S	a thing formed, plasma removal	Removal of blood from the body and centrifuging it to separate the plasma from the blood
Pneumocystis carinii (nū″ mō-sĭs′ tĭs kă-rī′ nē-ī)				A protozoan that causes *Pneumocystis carinii* pneumonia (PCP)

MEDICAL WORD	WORD PARTS (WHEN APPLICABLE)			DEFINITION
	Part	Type	Meaning	
Pneumocystis carinii **pneumonia** (nū″ mō-sĭs′ tĭs nū-mō′ nē-ă)				An opportunistic infection that is prevalent in AIDS patients. If not treated, the mortality rate is high.
polycythemia (pŏl″ ē-sī-thē′ mĭ-ă)	poly cyth -emia	P R S	many cell blood condition	A condition of too many red blood cells
prothrombin (prō-thrŏm′ bĭn)	pro thromb -in	P R S	before clot chemical	A chemical substance that interacts with calcium salts to produce thrombin
radioimmunoassay (rā″ dē-ō-ĭm″ ū-nō-ăs′ ā)				A method of determining the concentration of protein-bound hormones in the blood plasma
reticulocyte (rĕ-tĭk′ ū-lō-sīt)	reticul/o -cyte	CF S	net cell	A red blood cell containing a network of granules
septicemia (sĕp″ tĭ-sē′ mĭ-ă)	septic -emia	R S	putrefying blood condition	A condition in which pathogenic bacteria are present in the blood
seroculture (sē′ rō-kŭl″ chūr)	ser/o -culture	CF S	whey, serum cultivation	A bacterial culture of blood serum
serum (sē′ rŭm)	ser (a) -um	R S	whey tissue	The clear, yellowish fluid that separates from the clot when blood clots
sideropenia (sĭd″ ĕr-ō-pē′ nĭ-ă)	sider/o -penia	CF S	iron lack of	Lack of iron in the blood
splenomegaly (splē″ nō-mĕg′ ă-lē)	splen/o -megaly	CF S	spleen enlargement	Enlargement of the spleen
stem cell (stĕm sĕl)				A cell in the bone marrow that gives rise to various types of blood cells
thalassemia (thăl-ă-sē′ mĭ-ă)	thalass -emia	R S	sea blood condition	Hereditary anemias occurring in populations bordering the Mediterranean Sea and in Southeast Asia
thrombectomy (thrŏm bĕk′ tō mē)	thromb ectomy	R S	clot excision	Surgical excision of a blood clot
thrombin (thrŏm′ bĭn)	thromb -in	R S	clot chemical	A blood enzyme that causes clotting by forming fibrin
thrombocyte (thrŏm′ bō-sīt)	thromb/o -cyte	CF S	clot cell	A clotting cell; *a blood platelet*

MEDICAL WORD	WORD PARTS (WHEN APPLICABLE)			DEFINITION
	Part	Type	Meaning	
thromboplastin (thrŏm″ bō-plăs′ tĭn)	thromb plast -in	R R S	clot a developing chemical	An essential factor in the production of thrombin and blood clotting
thrombosis (thrŏm-bō′ sĭs)	thromb -osis	R S	clot condition of	Condition of a blood clot
thymoma (thī-mō′ mă)	thym -oma	R S	thymus tumor	A tumor of the thymus
tonsillectomy (tŏn″ sĭl-ĕk′ tō-mē)	tonsill -ectomy	R S	tonsil excision	Surgical excision of the tonsil
transfusion (trăns-fū″ zhŭn)	trans fus -ion	P R S	across to pour process	The process whereby blood is transferred from one individual to the vein of another
vasculitis (văs″ kŭ-lī′ tĭs)	vascul -itis	R S	small vessel inflammation	Inflammation of a lymph or blood vessel. See Figure 8–17.

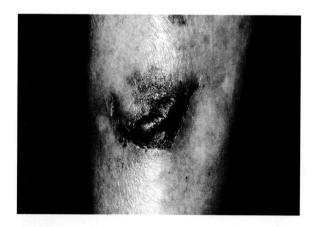

FIGURE 8–7

Traumatic hematoma. (Courtesy of Jason L. Smith, MD.)

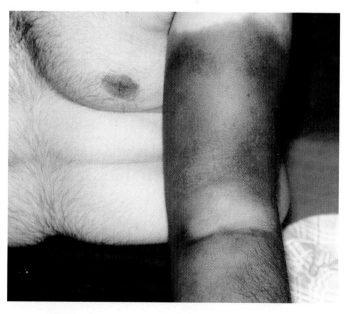

FIGURE 8–8

Hemorrhage, vein. (Courtesy of Jason L. Smith, MD.)

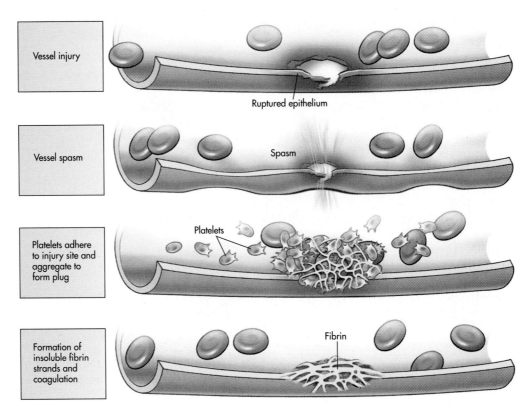

FIGURE 8–9

Basic steps in hemostasis.

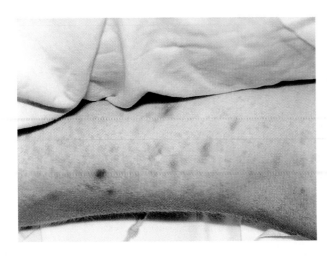

FIGURE 8–10

Kaposi's sarcoma. (Courtesy of Jason L. Smith, MD.)

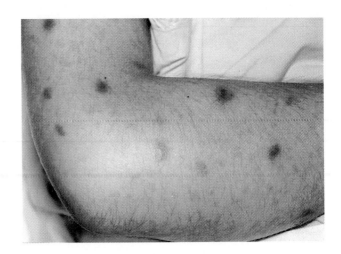

FIGURE 8–11

Kaposi's sarcoma. (Courtesy of Jason L. Smith, MD.)

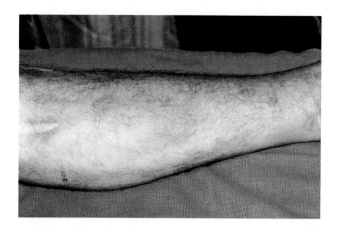

FIGURE 8–12

Lymphangitis. (Courtesy of Jason L. Smith, MD.)

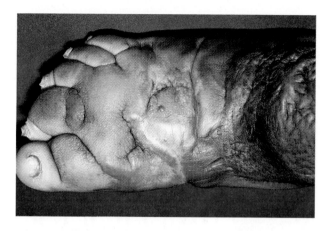

FIGURE 8–13

Congenital lymphedema. (Courtesy of Jason L. Smith, MD.)

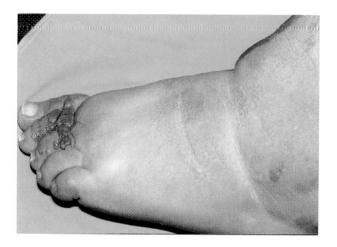

FIGURE 8–14

Chronic lymphedema. (Courtesy of Jason L. Smith, MD.)

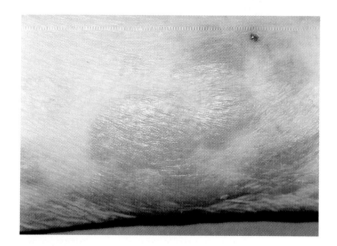

FIGURE 8–15

Lymphoma. (Courtesy of Jason L. Smith, MD.)

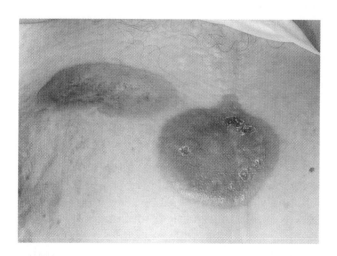

FIGURE 8–16

Cutaneous T-cell lymphoma. (Courtesy of Jason L. Smith, MD.)

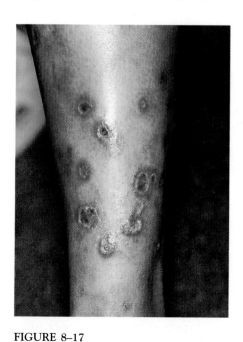

FIGURE 8–17

Vasculitis. (Courtesy of Jason L. Smith, MD.)

Terminology Translator

This feature, found on the accompanying CD-ROM, provides an innovative tool to translate medical words into Spanish, French, and German.

PATHOLOGY SPOTLIGHTS

Acquired Immunodeficiency Syndrome (AIDS)

AIDS is the final stage of human immunodeficiency virus (HIV) disease. AIDS is caused by the human immunodeficiency virus (HIV). The virus attacks the immune system and leaves the body vulnerable to a variety of life-threatening illnesses and cancers. Common bacteria, yeast, parasites, and viruses that ordinarily do not cause serious disease in people with healthy immune systems can cause serious or fatal illnesses in those with AIDS.

The Centers for Disease Control (CDC) defines AIDS as beginning when a person with HIV infection has a CD4 cell (also called a "T-cell", which is a type of immune cell) count below 200/mm^3. AIDS is also defined by the opportunistic infections and cancers that occur in someone with HIV infection. The statistics are sobering: AIDS is the fifth leading cause of death among persons between ages 25 and 44 in the United States. More than 47 million people worldwide have been infected with HIV since the start of the epidemic.

The symptoms of AIDS are the result of the opportunistic infections that do not normally develop in individuals with healthy immune systems. Common symptoms are flu-like and include fevers, sweats, swollen glands, chills, weakness, and weight loss. There may be no symptoms after initial infection, however. Some people with HIV infection remain without symptoms for years between the time of exposure and development of AIDS.

HIV has been found in such body fluids as saliva, tears, nervous system tissue, blood, semen, vaginal fluid, and breast milk. At this time, only blood, semen, vaginal secretions, and breast milk have been proven to transmit infection to others.

Transmission of the virus occurs in the following ways:

- Through sexual contact—including oral, vaginal, and anal sex
- Through blood, including blood transfusions (now extremely rare in the United States) or needle sharing
- From mother to child—a pregnant woman can passively transmit the virus to her fetus, or a nursing mother can transmit it to her baby

Although rare, HIV can be transmitted in other ways, including accidental needle injury, artificial insemination with donated semen, and through a donated organ.

HIV cannot be spread by casual contact such as hugging and touching, by touching dishes, doorknobs, or toilet seats previously touched by a person infected with the virus, during participation in sports, or by mosquitoes. It is not transmitted to a person who *donates* blood or organs in the United States because hospitals do not re-use syringes and sterilize all devices involved in these procedures. However, HIV can be transmitted to the person *receiving* blood or organs from an infected donor. This is the reason blood banks and organ donor programs screen donors, blood, and tissues thoroughly.

People who are at highest risk for HIV infection include homosexual or bisexual men who engage in unprotected sex, intravenous drug users who share needles, the sexual partners of those who participate in high-risk activities, infants born to mothers with HIV, and people who received blood transfusions or clotting products between 1977 and 1985 (prior to standard screening for the virus in the blood).

Although there is no cure for AIDS at this time, there are several treatments that can delay the progression of disease for many years and improve the quality of life of those who have developed symptoms.

The main form of treatment is through antiviral therapy, which suppresses the replication of the HIV virus. The newest form involves a combination of several antiretroviral agents, called highly active anti-retroviral therapy (HAART), and has been highly effective in reducing the number of HIV particles in the blood stream (as measured by a blood test called the viral load). This can help the immune system recover and improve T-cell counts.

Although HAART shows great promise, it is not a cure for HIV, and people on HAART with suppressed levels of HIV can still transmit the virus to others through sex or sharing of needles. There is good evidence that, if the levels of HIV remain suppressed and the CD4 count remains high (>200), life and quality of life can be significantly prolonged and improved. However, HIV tends to become resistant in patients who do not take their medications every day. Certain strains of HIV mutate easily and may become resistant to HAART especially quickly.

Other antiviral agents are in investigational stages and many new drugs are in the pipeline. Medications are also used to prevent opportunistic infections (such as *Pneumocystis carinii* pneumonia) and can keep AIDS patients healthier for longer periods of time. Opportunistic infections are treated as they occur.

Allergic Rhinitis

Allergic rhinitis is a collection of symptoms that typically occur in the nose and eyes after exposure to airborne particles of dust, dander, or the pollens of certain seasonal plants in people who are allergic to these substances. Symptoms include coughing, headache, sneezing, and itching nose, mouth, and eyes.

Allergies are common, and are caused by an oversensitive immune system. The immune system normally protects the body against harmful substances such as bacteria and viruses. Allergy occurs when the immune system reacts to substances (allergens) that are generally harmless and in most people do not cause an immune response. Heredity and environmental exposures may also contribute to a predisposition to allergies.

When the symptoms are caused by pollens, the allergic rhinitis is commonly known as hay fever. See Figure 8–18. This same reaction occurs with allergy to mold, animal dander, dust, and similar inhaled allergens.

When an allergen such as pollen or dust is inhaled by a person with a sensitized immune system, it triggers antibody production. See p. 275 for more information about antibodies. These antibodies bind to cells that contain histamine. When the antibodies are stimulated by pollen and dust, histamine (and other chemicals) are released. This causes itching, swelling, and mucus production. Symptoms vary in severity from person to person. Very sensitive individuals can experience hives or other rashes.

In order to diagnose allergic rhinitis, the history of the person's symptoms is important, including whether the symptoms vary according to time of day or the season, exposure to pets or other allergens, and diet.

Allergy testing may reveal the specific allergens to which the person is reacting. Skin testing is the most common method of allergy testing. This may include intradermal, scratch, patch, or other tests.

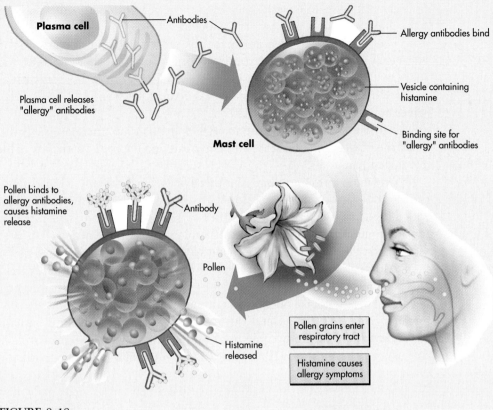

FIGURE 8-18

Allergic rhinitis.

The goal of treatment is to reduce the inflammation that causes allergy symptoms. The most effective treatment is avoidance of the allergens, or reducing exposure to allergens. Medication options include over-the-counter and prescription antihistamines, nasal corticosteroid sprays, and decongestants.

Allergy shots (immunotherapy) may be administered if the allergen cannot be avoided and if symptoms are hard to control. This includes regular injections of the allergen, given in increasing doses (each dose is slightly larger than the previous dose) that may help the body adjust to the allergen.

Anaphylaxis

Anaphylaxis is a type of allergic reaction that affects the whole body. It is a response to a substance to which a person has become very sensitive. This allergic response is sudden, severe, and involves the whole body.

During an anaphylactic allergic reaction, tissues in different parts of the body release histamine and other substances. This causes constriction of the airways, resulting in wheezing; difficulty breathing; and gastrointestinal symptoms such as abdominal pain, cramps, vomiting, and diarrhea. See Figure 8-19. Symptoms develop rapidly, often within seconds or minutes.

Shock may occur as a result of lowered blood pressure and blood volume. Hives and angioedema (hives on the lips, eyelids, throat, and/or tongue) often occur, and angioedema may be severe enough to cause obstruction of the airway. Prolonged anaphylaxis can cause heart arrhythmias.

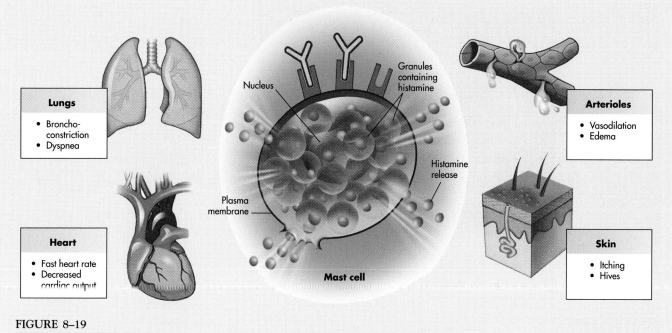

Lungs
- Broncho-
  constriction
- Dyspnea

Heart
- Fast heart rate
- Decreased
  cardiac output

Nucleus

Granules
containing
histamine

Histamine
release

Plasma
membrane

Mast cell

Arterioles
- Vasodilation
- Edema

Skin
- Itching
- Hives

FIGURE 8–19

Symptoms of anaphylaxis.

Some drugs such as morphine, x-ray dye, and others may cause an anaphylactic-like reaction on the first exposure. Anaphylaxis can occur in response to any allergen. Common causes include insect bites/stings, food allergies, and drug allergies. Pollens and other inhaled allergens, which commonly cause allergic rhinitis, rarely cause anaphylaxis. Some people have an anaphylactic reaction with no identifiable cause.

Although anaphylaxis occurs infrequently, it is life-threatening and can occur at any time. Risks include prior history of any type of allergic reaction.

Anaphylaxis is an emergency condition that requires immediate professional medical attention. Assessment of the ABCs (airway, breathing, and circulation, per Basic Life Support protocols) should be done in all suspected anaphylactic reactions. If indicated, CPR should be initiated. People with a history of severe allergic reactions may carry an Epi-Pen or other allergy kit, and should be assisted if necessary. Paramedics or physicians may place a tube through the nose or mouth into the airway (endotracheal intubation) or conduct emergency surgery to place a tube directly into the trachea (tracheostomy).

Epinephrine (or an Epi-Pen) should be given by injection without delay. Epinephrine opens the airways and raises the blood pressure by constricting blood vessels.

If the person is in shock, treatment includes intravenous fluids and medications that support the actions of the heart and circulatory system. Antihistamines (such as diphenhydramine) and corticosteroids (such as prednisone) may be given to further reduce symptoms after lifesaving measures and epinephrine are administered.

Anemia

Anemia is a condition that is characterized by a lower than normal number of red blood cells (erythrocytes) in the blood, usually measured by a decrease in the amount of hemoglobin. See Figure 8–20. Hemoglobin is a protein, and is the red pigment in red blood cells that transports oxygen.

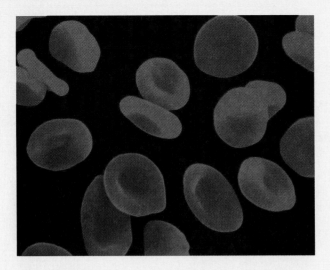

FIGURE 8–20

Normal red blood cells. (Source: Dr. Gopal Murti/Science Photo Library/
Custom Medical Stock Photo, Inc.)

There are many types and causes of anemia. Some common types include sickle cell anemia (see Figure 8–21), hemolytic anemia, and pernicious anemia. Anemia can also result from nutritional deficiencies, such as B_{12}, folate, and iron.

The cause varies with the type of anemia. Potential causes include blood loss, nutritional deficits, many diseases, medication reactions, and various problems with the bone marrow.

Possible symptoms include fatigue, angina (chest pain), and shortness of breath. Anemia can be confirmed by a red blood count or hemoglobin level test. Other tests depend on the type of anemia.

Treatment is directed at the cause of the anemia, and includes blood transfusions and the medication erythropoietin.

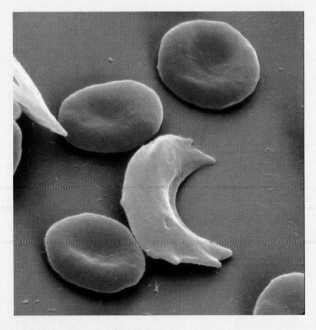

FIGURE 8–21

Iron deficiency anemia blood cells. (Source: Oliver Meckes & Nicole
Ottawa/Photo Researchers, Inc.)

TABLE 8–4 ANTIBODIES/IMMUNOGLOBULINS

Antibody	Functions
IgG	Crosses placenta to provide passive immunity for the newborn
	Opsonizing (coating) microorganisms to enhance phagocytosis
	Activates complement system (a group of proteins in the blood)
	Components of complement are labeled C1 through C9. Complement acts by directly killing organisms; by opsonizing an antigen; and by stimulating inflammation and the B-cell-mediated immune response.
IgM	Activates complement
	First antibody produced in response to bacterial and viral infections
IgA	Protects epithelial surfaces
	Activates complement
	Passed to breast-feeding newborn via the colostrum
IgE	Active in allergic reactions and some parasitic infections
	Trigger mast cells to release histamine, serotonin, kinins, slow-reacting substance of anaphylaxis, and the neutrophil factor. These mediators produce allergic skin reaction, asthma, and hay fever.
IgD	Role not clear; possibly influences B lymphocyte differentiation

Antibody

An antibody is also referred to as an immunoglobulin. It is a complex glycoprotein produced by B lymphocytes in response to the presence of an antigen. Antibodies neutralize or destroy antigens in several ways. They can initiate destruction of the antigen by activating the complement system, neutralizing toxins released by bacteria, opsonizing (coating) the antigen or forming a complex to stimulate phagocytosis, promoting antigen clumping, or preventing the antigen from adhering to host cells. See Table 8–4 for the five classes of antibodies: IgG, IgM, IgA, IgE, and IgD.

Leukemia

Leukemia is any of a group of diseases of the blood involving uncontrolled increase of white blood cells (leukocytes). Common types include chronic lymphocytic leukemia (CLL) and acute lymphocytic leukemia.

Chronic lymphocytic leukemia is a malignancy (cancer) of the white blood cells (lymphocytes) characterized by a slow, progressive increase of these cells in the blood and the bone marrow. Chronic lymphocytic leukemia (CLL) affects the B lymphocytes and causes immunosuppression, failure of the bone marrow, and invasion of malignant (cancerous) cells into organs.

Usually the symptoms develop gradually (see Figure 8–22). The incidence of CLL is about 2 per 100,000 and increases with age. 90 percent of cases are found in people over 50 years old. Many cases are detected by routine blood tests in people with no symptoms. The cause of CLL is unknown. No relationship to viruses, or exposure to radiation or carcinogenic chemicals has been determined. The disease is more common in Jewish people of Russian or Eastern European descent and is uncommon in people of Asian descent.

Acute lymphocytic leukemia (ALL) is a cancer of the lymph cells. It is characterized by large numbers of immature white blood cells that resemble lymphoblasts. These cells can be found in the blood, the bone marrow, the lymph nodes, the spleen, and other organs. This type of leukemia is responsible for 80 percent of the acute leukemias of childhood, with the peak incidence occurring between ages 3 and 7. ALL also occurs in adults, and comprises 20 percent of all adult leukemias.

In ALL, the blood cell loses its ability to mature and specialize (differentiate) its function. These malignant cells multiply rapidly and replace the normal cells. Bone marrow failure occurs

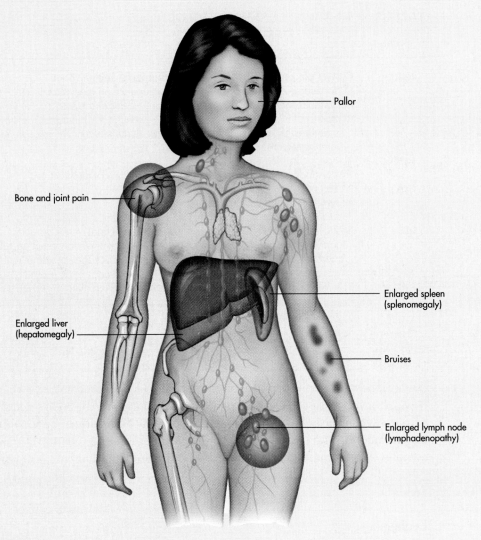

Pallor

Bone and joint pain

Enlarged spleen
(splenomegaly)

Enlarged liver
(hepatomegaly)

Bruises

Enlarged lymph node
(lymphadenopathy)

FIGURE 8–22

Signs and symptoms of leukemia.

as malignant cells replace normal bone marrow elements. The person becomes susceptible to bleeding and infection because the normal blood cells are reduced in number.

Most cases of ALL seem to have no apparent cause. However, radiation, some toxins such as benzene, and some chemotherapy agents are thought to contribute to this type of leukemia. Abnormalities in chromosomes may also play a role in the development of ALL.

✓PATHOLOGY CHECKPOINT

Following is a concise list of the pathology-related terms that you've seen in the chapter. Review this checklist to make sure that you are familiar with the meaning of each term before moving on to the next section.

Conditions and Symptoms

- ❏ acquired immunodeficiency syndrome (AIDS)
- ❏ allergy
- ❏ anaphylaxis
- ❏ anemia
- ❏ anisocytosis
- ❏ autoimmune disease
- ❏ creatinemia
- ❏ embolus
- ❏ erythrocytosis
- ❏ extravasation
- ❏ hematoma
- ❏ hemochromatosis
- ❏ hemophilia
- ❏ hemorrhage
- ❏ hypercalcemia
- ❏ hyperglycemia

- ❏ hyperlipemia
- ❏ hypoglycemia
- ❏ Kaposi's sarcoma
- ❏ leukemia
- ❏ leukocytopenia
- ❏ lymphadenitis
- ❏ lymphangitis
- ❏ lymphedema
- ❏ lymphoma
- ❏ mononucleosis
- ❏ opportunistic infection
- ❏ pancytopenia
- ❏ pneumocystis pneumonia
- ❏ polycythemia
- ❏ septicemia
- ❏ sideropenia
- ❏ splenomegaly
- ❏ thalassemia

- ❏ thrombosis
- ❏ thymoma
- ❏ tonsillectomy
- ❏ vasculitis

Diagnosis and Treatment

- ❏ anticoagulant
- ❏ autotransfusion
- ❏ hematocrit
- ❏ hemostasis
- ❏ leukapheresis
- ❏ lymphadenotomy
- ❏ lymphostasis
- ❏ plasmapheresis
- ❏ radioimmunoassay
- ❏ seroculture
- ❏ thrombectomy
- ❏ transfusion

DRUG HIGHLIGHTS

DRUG HIGHLIGHTS

Drugs that are generally used in blood and lymphatic diseases and disorders include anticoagulants, hemostatic agents, antianemic agents, epoetin alfa, and drugs used in treating megaloblastic anemias.

Anticoagulants

Used in inhibiting or preventing a blood clot formation. Hemorrhage can occur at almost any site in patients on anticoagulant therapy.

Examples: heparin sodium, Coumadin (warfarin sodium), and Lovenox (enoxaparin).

Hemostatic Agents

Used to control bleeding and may be administered systemically or topically.

Examples: Proplex (factor IX complement), Amicar (aminocaproic acid), vitamin K, and Surgicel (oxidized cellulose).

Antianemic Agents (*irons*)

Used to treat iron deficiency anemia. Oral iron preparations interfere with the absorption of oral tetracycline antibiotics. These products should not be taken within 2 hours of each other.

Examples: Femiron (ferrous fumarate), Fergon, Fertinic (ferrous gluconate), and Feosol (ferrous sulfate).

Epoetin Alfa (*EPO, Procrit*)

A genetically engineered hemopoietin that stimulates the production of red blood cells. It is a recombinant version of erythropoietin and is indicated for treating anemia in patients with chronic renal failure and HIV-infected patients taking zidovudine (AZT).

Agents

Used in treating megaloblastic anemias include *Folvite (folic acid) and vitamin B_{12} (cyanocobalamin).*

DIAGNOSTIC & LAB TESTS

DIAGNOSTIC & LAB TESTS

TEST	DESCRIPTION
antinuclear antibodies (ANA) (ăn″ tĭ-nū′ klē-ăr ăn′ tĭ-bŏd″ ēs)	A blood test to identify antigen–antibody reactions. ANA antibodies are present in a number of autoimmune diseases.
bleeding time (blēd′ ĭng tīm)	A puncture of the ear lobe or forearm to determine the time required for blood to stop flowing. Duke method (ear lobe) 1 to 3 minutes is the normal time, and with the Ivy (forearm), 1 to 9 minutes is the normal time for the flow of blood to cease. Times greater than these may indicate thrombocytopenia, aplastic anemia, leukemia, decreased platelet count, hemophilia, and potential hemorrhage. Anticoagulant drugs delay the bleeding time.

TEST	DESCRIPTION
blood typing (ABO group and Rh factor) (blod tīp′ ĭng)	A blood test to determine an individual's blood type and Rh factor. Blood types are A, B, AB, and O. Rh factor may be negative or positive.
bone marrow aspiration (bōn măr′ ō ăs-pĭ-rā′ shŭn)	Removal of bone marrow for examination; may be performed to determine aplastic anemia, leukemia, certain cancers, and polycythemia.
complete blood count (CBC) (kom-plēt′ blod kount)	This blood test includes a hematocrit, hemoglobin, red and white blood cell count, and differential. This test is usually a part of a complete physical examination and a good indicator of hematologic system functioning.
hematocrit (Hct) (hē-măt′ ō-krĭt)	A blood test performed on whole blood to determine the percentage of red blood cells in the total blood volume.
hemoglobin (Hb, Hgb) (hē″ mō-glō′ bĭn)	A blood test to determine the amount of iron-containing pigment of the red blood cells.
immunoglobulins (Ig) (ĭm″ u-nō-glob′ u-lĭns)	A serum blood test to determine the presence of IgA, IgD, IgE, IgG, and/or IgM. Lymphocytes and plasma cells produce immunoglobulins in response to antigen exposure. Increased and/or decreased values may indicate certain disease conditions.
partial thromboplastin time (PTT) (păr′ shāl thrŏm″ bō-plăs′ tĭn tīm)	A test performed on blood plasma to determine how long it takes for fibrin clots to form; used to regulate heparin dosage and to detect clotting disorders.
platelet count (plāt′ lĕt kount)	A test performed on whole blood to determine the number of thrombocytes present. Increased and/or decreased amounts may indicate certain disease conditions.
prothrombin time (PT) (prō-thrŏm′ bĭn tīm)	A test performed on blood plasma to determine the time needed for oxalated plasma to clot; used to regulate anticoagulant drug therapy and to detect clotting disorders.
red blood count (RBC) (red blod kount)	A test performed on whole blood to determine the number of erythrocytes present. Increased and/or decreased amounts may indicate certain disease conditions.
sedimentation rate (ESR) (sĕd″ -ĭmĕn-tā′ shŭn rāt)	A blood test to determine the rate at which red blood cells settle in a long, narrow tube. The distance the RBCs settle in 1 hour is the rate. Higher or lower rate may indicate certain disease conditions.
viral load (vī′ ral lōd)	A blood test that measures the amount of HIV in the blood. Results can range from 50 to over one million copies per milliliter (mL) of blood. Two tests that are used to measure viral load are bDNA and PCR.
white blood count (WBC) (wīt blod kount)	A blood test to determine the number of leukocytes present. Increased level indicates infection and/or inflammation and decreased level indicates aplastic anemia, pernicious anemia, and malaria.

ABBREVIATIONS

ABBREVIATION	MEANING	ABBREVIATION	MEANING
ABO	blood group	HIV	human immunodeficiency virus
AHF	antihemophilic factor		
AIDS	acquired immunodeficiency syndrome	lymphs	lymphocytes
		MCH	mean corpuscular hemoglobin
ALL	acute lymphocytic leukemia	MCHC	mean corpuscular hemoglobin concentration
BAC	blood alcohol concentration		
baso	basophil	MCV	mean corpuscular volume
BSI	body systems isolation	mono	monocyte
CBC	complete blood count	PCP	*Pneumocystis carinii* pneumonia
CLL	chronic lymphocytic leukemia		
CML	chronic myelogenous leukemia	PCV	packed cell volume
diff	differential count	PMN	polymorphonuclear neutrophil
EBV	Epstein–Barr virus	poly	polymorphonuclear
ELISA	enzyme-linked immunosorbent assay	PT	prothrombin time
		PTT	partial thromboplastin time
eos, eosin	eosinophil	RBC	red blood cell (count)
ESR	erythrocyte sedimentation rate	Rh	Rhesus (factor)
Hb, Hgb, HGB	hemoglobin	RIA	radioimmunoassay
		segs	segmented (mature RBCs)
Hct, HCT	hematocrit	SRS-A	slow-reacting substances of anaphylaxis
HDN	hemolytic disease of the newborn		
		WBC	white blood cell (count)

STUDY AND REVIEW

Anatomy and Physiology

Write your answers to the following questions. Do not refer to the text.

1. Name the three formed elements of blood.

   a. _____   b. _____

   c. _____

2. State the function of erythrocytes.

   _____

3. There are approximately _____ million erythrocytes per cubic millimeter of blood.

4. The life span of an erythrocyte is _____.

5. State the function of leukocytes. _____

   _____

6. There are approximately _____ thousand leukocytes per cubic millimeter of blood.

7. Name the five types of leukocytes.

   a. _____   b. _____

   c. _____   d. _____

   e. _____

8. State the function of thrombocytes. _____

   _____

9. There are approximately _____ thrombocytes per cubic millimeter of
   blood.

10. Name the four blood types.

    a. _____   b. _____

    c. _____   d. _____

11. State the three main functions of the lymphatic system.

    a. _____

    b. _____

    c. _____

12. Name the three accessory organs of the lymphatic system.

    a. _____

    b. _____

    c. _____

Word Parts

1. In the spaces provided, write the definition of these prefixes, roots, combining forms, and suffixes. Do not refer to the listings of medical words. Leave blank those words you cannot define.

2. After completing as many as you can, refer to the medical word listings to check your work. For each word missed or left blank, write the word and its definition several times on the margins of these pages or on a separate sheet of paper.

3. To maximize the learning process, it is to your advantage to do the following exercises as directed. To refer to the word building section before completing these exercises invalidates the learning process.

PREFIXES

Give the definitions of the following prefixes:

1. an- _____   2. anti- _____

3. auto- _____   4. ana- _____

5. extra- _____   6. hyper- _____

7. hypo- _____   8. mono- _____

9. pan- _____   10. poly- _____

11. pro- _____   12. trans- _____

ROOTS AND COMBINING FORMS

Give the definitions of the following roots and combining forms:

1. aden _____

2. aden/o _____

3. agglutinat _____

4. all _____

5. angi/o _____

6. anis/o _____

7. bas/o _____

8. calc _____

9. chromat _____

10. fus _____

11. coagul _____

12. creatin _____

13. cyt _____

14. cyth _____

15. cyt/o _____

16. eosin/o _____

17. erythr/o _____

18. globul _____

19. granul/o _____

20. hemat _____

21. hemat/o _____

22. hem/o _____

23. leuk _____

24. leuk/o _____

25. lip _____

26. log _____

27. lymph _____

28. lymph/o _____

29. macr/o _____

30. neutr/o _____

31. nucle _____

32. phag/o _____

33. plasma _____

34. reticul/o _____

35. septic _____

36. ser/o _____

37. sider/o _____

38. fibr _____

39. splen/o _____

40. thalass _____

41. thromb _____

42. thromb/o _____

43. thym _____

44. fibrin/o _____

45. tonsill _____

46. poiet _____

47. immun/o _____

48. ang _____

49. ser (a) _____

50. plast _____

51. vas (at) _____

52. vascul _____

SUFFIXES

Give the definitions of the following suffixes:

1. -able _____

2. -ant _____

3. -blast _____

4. -body _____

5. -edema _____

6. -crit _____

7. -culture _____

8. -cyte _____

9. -ectomy _____

10. -emia _____

11. -ergy _____

12. -gen _____

13. -phylaxis _____

14. -globin _____

15. -um _____

16. -ic _____

17. -in _____

18. -ion _____

19. -ist _____

20. -itis _____

21. -logy _____

22. -lysis _____

23. -megaly _____

24. -oma _____

25. -osis _____

26. -penia _____

27. -pheresis _____

28. -phil _____

29. -philia _____

30. -poiesis _____

31. -rrhage _____

32. -stasis _____

33. -tomy _____

Identifying Medical Terms

In the spaces provided, write the medical terms for the following meanings:

1. _____ Process of clumping together, as of blood cells that are incompatible

2. _____ Individual hypersensitivity to a substance that is usually harmless

3. _____ A protein substance produced in the body in response to an invading foreign substance

4. _____ An agent that works against the formation of blood clots

5. _____ An invading foreign substance that induces the formation of antibodies

6. _____ A base cell, leukocyte

7. _____ Capable of forming a clot

8. _____ Excess of creatine in the blood

9. _____ A cell that readily stains with the acid stain

10. _____ A granular leukocyte

11. _____ One who specializes in the study of the blood

12. _____ Blood protein

13. _____ Excessive amounts of sugar in the blood

14. _____ Excessive amounts of fat in the blood

15. _____ A white blood cell

16. _____ The control or stopping of the flow of lymph

17. _____ Condition of excessive amounts of mononuclear leukocytes in the blood

18. _____ A chemical substance that interacts with calcium salts to produce thrombin

19. _____ Surgical fixation of a movable spleen

20. _____ A clotting cell; a blood platelet

Spelling

In the spaces provided, write the correct spelling of these misspelled terms:

1. allregy _____

2. cretinemia _____

3. etravasation _____

4. erythcytosis _____

5. thrombplastin _____

6. hemacrit _____

7. hemorhage _____

8. lukemia _____

9. lymphadnotomy _____

10. anphylaxis _____

Matching

Select the appropriate lettered meaning for each word listed below.

_____ 1. autotransfusion

_____ 2. erythrocyte

_____ 3. erythropoietin

_____ 4. extravasation

_____ 5. hemorrhage

_____ 6. immunoglobulin

_____ 7. hemochromatosis

_____ 8. radioimmunoassay

_____ 9. reticulocyte

_____10. thrombectomy

a. A method of determining the concentration of protein-bound hormones in the blood plasma
b. A disease condition in which iron is not metabolized properly and accumulates in body tissues
c. A blood protein capable of acting as an antibody
d. A red blood cell
e. A hormone that stimulates the production of red blood cells
f. Excessive bleeding
g. The process whereby fluids and/or medications escape into surrounding tissue
h. The process of reinfusing a patient's own blood
i. Surgical excision of a blood clot
j. A red blood cell containing a network of granules
k. A white blood cell

Abbreviations

Place the correct word, phrase, or abbreviation in the space provided.

1. acquired immunodeficiency syndrome _____

2. body systems isolation _____

3. CML _____

4. hemoglobin _____

5. Hct _____

6. human immunodeficiency virus _____

7. PCP _____

8. PT _____

9. RBC _____

10. radioimmunoassay _____

Diagnostic and Laboratory Tests

Select the best answer to each multiple choice question. Circle the letter of your choice.

1. A blood test to identify antigen–antibody reactions.
   a. sedimentation rate
   b. hematocrit
   c. immunoglobulins
   d. antinuclear antibodies

2. This blood test includes a hematocrit, hemoglobin, red and white blood cell count, and differential.
   a. blood typing
   b. sedimentation rate
   c. CBC
   d. Hb, Hgb

3. A blood test performed on whole blood to determine the percentage of red blood cells in the total blood volume.
   a. RBC
   b. WBC
   c. Hct
   d. PTT

4. A blood test to determine the number of leukocytes present.
   a. RBC
   b. WBC
   c. Hct
   d. PTT

5. A puncture of the ear lobe or forearm to determine the time required for blood to stop flowing.
   a. bleeding time
   b. platelet count
   c. prothrombin time
   d. PTT

CASE STUDY

ACQUIRED IMMUNODEFICIENCY SYNDROME (AIDS)

Read the following case study and then answer the questions that follow.

A 52-year-old female was seen by a physician; the following is a synopsis of her visit. *Note: More than 10% of all AIDS cases in the United States have occurred in persons age 50 or older.*

Present History: The patient states that several months after the death of her husband she became sexually involved with a younger man. She states that they didn't use condoms, as they were not concerned about pregnancy, and now she has found out that he has AIDS. She is most anxious, and states that lately she has had "night sweats," weight loss for no apparent reason, constant fatigue, diarrhea, swollen lymph nodes, and unusual confusion.

Signs and Symptoms: Night sweats, weight loss, fatigue, diarrhea, swollen lymph nodes, and unusual confusion.

Diagnosis: Acquired immunodeficiency syndrome (AIDS). Diagnosis was determined by a complete medical and social history, a physical examination, CD_4 lymphocyte count, which was 180 cells/mm^3 (normal is 600 to 1200 cells/mm^3), and laboratory evidence of immune dysfunction, identification of HIV antibodies, and signs and symptoms.

Treatment: The regimen includes treating any associated condition with proper medical intervention, and starting the patient on a combination of antiretroviral therapy of three drugs: AZT—zidovudine; 3TC—lamiudine; and a protease inhibitor, Norvir—ritonavir. Drug therapy is carefully monitored for older adults, as they may have preexisting conditions, such as cardiac disease and/or renal insufficiency, that can make them less tolerant of drugs. Clinical evaluation and laboratory monitoring every 3 to 6 months and more frequently if needed. Provide for professional assistance as needed. Information on services available for the older adult with HIV infection and AIDS may be obtained by calling the CDC's AIDS Hotline at 1-800-342-AIDS.

CASE STUDY QUESTIONS

1. Signs and symptoms of AIDS include night sweats, weight loss, fatigue, _____, swollen lymph nodes, and confusion.

2. The diagnosis of AIDS was determined by a complete physical examination, laboratory evidence of _____ dysfunction, and a CD_4 lymphocyte count of 180 cells/mm^3.

3. _____ is an antiretroviral drug that is combined with two other drugs in the treatment of AIDS.

4. Why is drug therapy carefully monitored for older adults? _____

 MedMedia Wrap-Up
www.prenhall.com/rice

Additional interactive resources and activities for this chapter can be found on the Companion Website. For animation, videos, audio glossary, and review, access the accompanying CD-ROM in this book.

 Audio Glossary
Medical Terminology Exercises & Activities
Pathology Spotlights
Terminology Translator
Animations
Videos

 Objectives
Medical Terminology Exercises & Activities
Audio Glossary
Drug Updates
Medical Terminology in the News

ANSWER KEY

■ CHAPTER 1

WORD PARTS

Prefixes

1. without
2. away from
3. against
4. self
5. bad
6. a hundred
7. through
8. different
9. bad
10. small
11. one thousandth
12. many, much
13. new
14. beside
15. before
16. together
17. three
18. apart
19. upon
20. out
21. in, into

Roots and Combining Forms

1. stuck to
2. armpit
3. center
4. chemical
5. a shaping
6. formation, produce
7. a thousand
8. large
9. death
10. law
11. rule
12. tumor
13. organ
14. fever
15. heat, fire
16. ray
17. to examine
18. putrefaction
19. hot, heat
20. place
21. cough
22. infection
23. people
24. cause
25. to cut
26. bad kind
27. greatest
28. least
29. palm
30. guarding

Suffixes

1. related to
2. pertaining to
3. pertaining to
4. surgical puncture
5. a key
6. a course
7. shape
8. to flee
9. formation, produce
10. knowledge
11. a step
12. a weight
13. recording
14. condition
15. pertaining to
16. process
17. condition of
18. nature of, quality of
19. liter
20. study of
21. instrument to measure
22. condition of
23. pertaining to
24. disease
25. to carry
26. instrument
27. decay
28. treatment
29. pertaining to
30. condition

IDENTIFYING MEDICAL TERMS

1. adhesion
2. asepsis
3. axillary
4. chemotherapy
5. heterogeneous
6. malformation
7. microscope
8. multiform
9. neopathy
10. oncology

SPELLING

1. antiseptic
2. autonomy

3. centimeter
4. diaphoresis
5. milligram
6. necrosis
7. paracentesis
8. radiology

MATCHING

1. f   6. k
2. d   7. b
3. j   8. i
4. g   9. c
5. a   10. e

ABBREVIATIONS

1. abnormal
2. axillary
3. Bx
4. cardiovascular disease
5. diagnosis-related groups
6. ENT
7. FP
8. g
9. gynecology
10. pediatrics

■ CHAPTER 2

ANATOMY AND PHYSIOLOGY

1. body . . . cells . . . sustain
2. cell membrane
3. protoplasm . . . cytoplasm . . . karyoplasm
4. karyoplasm
5. cell reproduction. . . . control over activity within the cell's cytoplasm
6. a. protection
   b. absorption
   c. secretion
   d. excretion
7. connective
8. a. striated (voluntary)
   b. cardiac
   c. smooth (involuntary)
9. excitability . . . conductivity

10. A tissue serving a common purpose
11. A group of organs functioning together for a common purpose
12. a. integumentary
    b. skeletal
    c. muscular
    d. digestive
    e. cardiovascular
    f. blood and lymphatic
    g. respiratory
    h. urinary
    i. endocrine
    j. nervous
    k. reproductive
13. a. above, in an upward direction
    b. in front of, before
    c. toward the back
    d. toward the head
    e. nearest the middle
    f. to the side
    g. nearest the point of attachment
    h. away from the point of attachment
    i. the front side
    j. the back side
14. midsagittal plane
15. transverse or horizontal
16. coronal or frontal
17. a. thoracic
    b. abdominal
    c. pelvic
18. a. cranial
    b. spinal

WORD PARTS

Prefixes

1. both
2. up
3. two
4. color
5. down, away from
6. apart
7. outside

8. within
9. similar, same
10. middle
11. through
12. first
13. one

Roots and Combining Forms

1. fat
2. man
3. life
4. tail
5. cell
6. cell
7. to pour
8. formation, produce
9. tissue
10. water
11. cell's nucleus
12. side
13. disease
14. nature
15. to drink
16. body
17. place
18. a turning
19. body organs
20. toward the front
21. head
22. away from the point of origin
23. backward
24. to strain through
25. horizon
26. below
27. groin
28. within
29. side
30. toward the middle
31. organ
32. to show
33. behind, toward the back
34. near the point of origin
35. near the surface
36. upper
37. a composite whole
38. near the belly side

Suffixes

1. pertaining to
2. use, action
3. formation, produce
4. pertaining to
5. process
6. study of
7. form, shape
8. resemble
9. like
10. condition of
11. pertaining to
12. a thing formed, plasma
13. body
14. control, stopping
15. incision
16. a doer
17. pertaining to
18. type

IDENTIFYING MEDICAL TERMS

1. android
2. bilateral
3. cytology
4. ectomorph
5. karyogenesis
6. somatotrophic
7. unilateral

SPELLING

1. adipose
2. caudal
3. cytology
4. diffusion
5. histology
6. mesomorph
7. perfusion
8. proximal
9. somatotrophic
10. unilateral

MATCHING

1. c
2. d
3. e
4. f
5. a
6. i
7. g
8. h
9. j
10. b

ABBREVIATIONS

1. abd
2. anatomy and physiology
3. central nervous system
4. CV
5. GI
6. lateral
7. respiratory
8. endoplasmic reticulum
9. anteroposterior
10. posteroanterior

■ CHAPTER 3

ANATOMY AND PHYSIOLOGY

1. The skin
2. a. hair
   b. nails
   c. sebaceous glands
   d. sweat glands
3. a. protection
   b. regulation
   c. sensory reception
   d. secretion
4. epidermis . . . dermis
5. a. stratum corneum
   b. stratum lucidum
   c. stratum granulosum
   d. stratum germinativum
6. Keratin
7. Melanin
8. dermis
9. a. papillary layer
   b. reticular layer
10. lunula

WORD PARTS

Prefixes

1. without, lack of
2. self
3. out
4. down
5. out
6. excessive
7. under
8. within
9. around
10. below

Roots and Combining Forms

1. extremity
2. ray
3. gland
4. white
5. cancer
6. heat
7. juice
8. corium
9. skin
10. skin
11. skin
12. skin
13. skin
14. skin
15. fox mange
16. red
17. sweat
18. jaundice
19. tumor
20. horn
21. white
22. study of
23. black
24. black
25. fungus
26. nail
27. little cell
28. nail
29. thick
30. a louse
31. cord
32. wrinkle
33. hard
34. oil
35. old
36. hot, heat
37. to pull
38. hair
39. nail
40. yellow
41. dry
42. to lie

43. little bag
44. a covering
45. yellow
46. plate
47. millet (tiny)
48. itching
49. end, distant
50. vessel

Suffixes

1. pertaining to
2. pain
3. pertaining to
4. pertaining to
5. skin
6. pertaining to
7. sensation
8. pencil, grafting knife
9. condition
10. pertaining to
11. process
12. condition of
13. one who specializes
14. inflammation
15. study of
16. dilatation
17. resemble
18. tumor
19. condition of
20. pertaining to
21. surgical repair
22. flow, discharge
23. instrument to cut

IDENTIFYING MEDICAL TERMS

1. actinic dermatitis
2. cutaneous
3. dermatitis
4. dermatology
5. pruritus
6. hyperhidrosis
7. hypodermic
8. icteric
9. onychitis
10. pachyderma
11. thermanesthesia
12. xanthoderma

SPELLING

1. causalgia
2. dermomycosis
3. ecchymosis
4. excoriation
5. hyperhidrosis
6. melanoma
7. onychomycosis
8. rhytidoplasty
9. scleroderma
10. seborrhea

MATCHING

1. d   6. i
2. f   7. b
3. e   8. g
4. h   9. a
5. j   10. c

ABBREVIATIONS

1. FUO
2. TTS
3. hypodermic
4. I & D
5. SG
6. intradermal
7. T
8. UV
9. foreign body
10. psoralen-ultraviolet light

DIAGNOSTIC AND LABORATORY TESTS

1. c
2. d
3. a
4. b
5. a

■ CHAPTER 4

ANATOMY AND PHYSIOLOGY

1. 206
2. a. axial
   b. appendicular
3. a. flat . . . ribs, scapula, parts of the pelvic girdle, bones of the skull
   b. long . . . tibia, femur, humerus, radius

c. short . . . carpal, tarsal
d. irregular . . . vertebrae, ossicles of the ear
e. sesamoid . . . patella

*Optional answer to question 3:

f. sutural or wormian . . . between the flat bones of the skull

4. a. shape, support
   b. protection
   c. storage
   d. formation of blood cells
   e. attachment of skeletal muscles
   f. movement, through articulation
5. a. the ends of a developing bone
   b. the shaft of a long bone
   c. the membrane that forms the covering of bones, except at their articular surfaces
   d. the dense, hard layer of bone tissue
   e. a narrow space or cavity throughout the length of the diaphysis
   f. a tough connective tissue membrane lining the medullary canal and containing the bone marrow
   g. the reticular tissue that makes up most of the volume of bone
6. Numbers of the matching answers:
   a. 6
   b. 11
   c. 4
   d. 13
   e. 8
   f. 10
   g. 9
   h. 14
   i. 1
   j. 12

k. 2

l. 3

m. 7

n. 5

7. a. synarthrosis

b. amphiarthrosis

c. diarthrosis

8. Abduction

9. the process of moving a body part toward the midline

10. Circumduction

11. the process of bending a body part backward

12. Eversion

13. the process of straightening a flexed limb

14. Flexion

15. the process of turning inward

16. Pronation

17. the process of moving a body part forward

18. Retraction

19. the process of moving a body part around a central axis

20. Supination

WORD PARTS

Prefixes

1. without

2. apart

3. water

4. between

5. beyond

6. around

7. many, much

8. under, beneath

9. together

10. back

ROOTS AND COMBING FORMS

1. vinegar cup

2. gristle

3. extremity, point

4. extremity

5. stiffening, crooked

6. joint

7. joint

8. a pouch

9. heel bone

10. to place

11. cancer

12. wrist

13. wrist

14. cartilage

15. cartilage

16. little key

17. fastened

18. tail bone

19. tail bone

20. glue

21. to lead

22. to bind together

23. rib

24. rib

25. crescent

26. light

27. skull

28. skull

29. finger or toe

30. finger or toe

31. femur

32. carrying

33. fibula

34. ray

35. humerus

36. ilium

37. ilium

38. ischium

39. a hump

40. lamina (thin plate)

41. bending

42. loin

43. loin

44. lower jawbone

45. jawbone

46. jaw

47. marrow

48. marrow

49. discharge

50. elbow

51. bone

52. kneecap

53. to draw

54. foot

55. closely knit row

56. a passage

57. spine

58. radius

59. sacrum

60. flesh

61. shoulder blade

62. curvature

63. curvature

64. spine

65. vertebra

66. sternum

67. sternum

68. tendon

69. tibia

70. elbow

71. elbow

72. vertebra

73. vertebra

74. sword

Suffixes

1. pertaining to

2. pertaining to

3. pain

4. pertaining to

5. pertaining to

6. immature cell, germ cell

7. surgical puncture

8. related to

9. process

10. pain

11. excision

12. swelling

13. formation, produce

14. formation, produce

15. mark, record

16. to write

17. pertaining to

18. inflammation

19. nature of

20. instrument

21. softening

22. pertaining to

23. resemble

24. tumor

25. shoulder

26. condition of
27. lack of
28. growth
29. formation
30. surgical repair
31. formation
32. instrument to cut
33. incision

IDENTIFYING MEDICAL TERMS

1. acroarthritis
2. ankylosis
3. arthritis
4. calcaneal
5. chondral
6. coccygodynia
7. costal
8. craniectomy
9. dactylic
10. hydrarthrosis
11. intercostal
12. ischialgia
13. lumbar
14. myeloma
15. osteoarthritis
16. osteomyelitis or myelitis
17. osteopenia
18. pedal
19. xiphoid

SPELLING

1. acromion
2. arthroscope
3. bursitis
4. chrondroblast
5. connective
6. cranioplasty
7. dislocation
8. ischial
9. myelitis
10. osteochondritis
11. phosphorus
12. patellar
13. phalangeal
14. rachigraph
15. scoliosis
16. spondylitis

17. symphysis
18. tenonitis
19. ulnocarpal
20. vertebral

MATCHING

1. i
2. j
3. e
4. c
5. b
6. h
7. g
8. a
9. d
10. f

ABBREVIATIONS

1. CDH
2. DJD
3. long leg cast
4. osteoarthritis
5. PEMFs
6. rheumatoid arthritis
7. SPECT
8. thoracic vertebra, first
9. temporomandibular joint
10. Tx

DIAGNOSTIC AND LABORATORY TESTS

1. c
2. d
3. c
4. b
5. b

■ CHAPTER 5

ANATOMY AND PHYSIOLOGY

1. a. skeletal
   b. smooth
   c. cardiac
2. 42
3. a. nutrition
   b. oxygen
4. a. origin
   b. insertion
5. voluntary or striated
6. aponeurosis
7. a. body
   b. origin
   c. insertion

8. a. A muscle that counteracts the action of another muscle.
   b. A muscle that is primary in a given movement.
   c. A muscle that acts with another muscle to produce movement.
9. involuntary, visceral, or unstriated
10. a. digestive tract
    b. respiratory tract
    c. urinary tract
    d. eye
    e. skin
11. Cardiac
12. a. movement
    b. maintain posture
    c. produce heat

WORD PARTS

Prefixes

1. lack of
2. away from
3. toward
4. against
5. separation
6. two
7. slow
8. with
9. through
10. difficult
11. into
12. within
13. water
14. four
15. with, together
16. three

Roots and Combining Forms

1. agony
2. arm
3. clavicle
4. to cut through
5. neck
6. finger or toe
7. to lead
8. work

9. a band
10. skin
11. discharge
12. fiber
13. fiber
14. equal
15. a rind
16. lifter
17. an addition
18. breast
19. hot, heat
20. to measure
21. muscle
22. muscle
23. muscle
24. muscle
25. nerve
26. nerve
27. disease
28. to loosen
29. rod
30. to turn
31. a turning
32. flesh
33. hardening
34. to gain
35. convulsive
36. sternum
37. tendon
38. tone, tension
39. twisted
40. to draw
41. will
42. joint fluid
43. twisted

Suffixes

1. pain
2. pertaining to
3. pertaining to
4. weakness
5. immature cell, germ cell
6. head
7. binding
8. pain
9. chemical
10. treatment

11. to write, record
12. condition
13. pertaining to
14. process
15. agent
16. inflammation
17. condition
18. motion
19. motion
20. study of
21. process
22. softening
23. resemble
24. tumor
25. a doer
26. condition of
27. weakness
28. disease
29. a fence
30. surgical repair
31. stroke, paralysis
32. suture
33. pertaining to
34. tension, spasm
35. order
36. instrument to cut
37. incision
38. nourishment, development
39. condition of
40. condition of

IDENTIFYING MEDICAL TERMS

1. atonic
2. bradykinesia
3. dactylospasm
4. dystrophy
5. intramuscular
6. levator
7. myasthenia
8. myology
9. myoparesis
10. myoplasty
11. myosarcoma
12. myotomy
13. polyplegia
14. tenodesis

15. synergetic
16. triceps

SPELLING

1. fascia
2. myokinesis
3. dermatomyositis
4. rhabdomyoma
5. sarcolemma
6. sternocleidomastoid
7. dystrophin
8. torticollis

MATCHING

1. d		6. a	
2. i		7. h	
3. g		8. c	
4. e		9. b	
5. j		10. f	

ABBREVIATIONS

1. above elbow
2. aspartate aminotransferase
3. Ca
4. EMG
5. full range of motion
6. musculoskeletal
7. ROM
8. sh
9. total body weight
10. triceps jerk

DIAGNOSTIC AND LABORATORY TESTS

1. b	4. c
2. d	5. a
3. b	

■ CHAPTER 6

ANATOMY AND PHYSIOLOGY

1. a. mouth
   b. pharynx
   c. esophagus
   d. stomach
   e. small intestine
   f. large intestine
2. a. salivary glands
   b. liver

c. gallbladder

d. pancreas

3. a. digestion

b. absorption

c. elimination

4. A small mass of masticated food ready to be swallowed

5. A series of wave-like muscular contractions that are involuntary

6. Hydrochloric acid and gastric juices

7. duodenum

8. chyme

9. circulatory system

10. cecum, colon, rectum, and the anal canal

11. liver

12. Stores and concentrates bile

13. Produces digestive enzymes

14. a. It plays an important role in metabolism.

b. It manufactures bile.

c. It stores iron, vitamins B_{12}, A, D, E, and K

15. small intestine

16. parotid, sublingual, submandibular

17. a. insulin

b. glucagon

WORD PARTS

Prefixes

1. lack of

2. up

3. down

4. difficult

5. above

6. excessive, above

7. deficient, below

8. bad

9. through

10. around

11. after

12. through

13. below

Roots and Combining Forms

1. to suck in

2. gland

3. starch

4. orange-yellow

5. appendix

6. appendix

7. gall, bile

8. to cast, throw

9. cheek

10. abdomen, belly

11. lip

12. gall, bile

13. common bile duct

14. colon

15. colon

16. colon

17. colon

18. bladder

19. tooth

20. to press together

21. diverticula

22. duodenum

23. intestine

24. to remove dregs

25. esophagus

26. to carry

27. stomach

28. stomach

29. gums

30. tongue

31. sweet, sugar

32. blood

33. liver

34. liver

35. hernia

36. ileum

37. ileum

38. lip

39. flank, abdomen

40. to loosen

41. tongue

42. fat

43. study of

44. middle

45. pancreas

46. to digest

47. pharynx

48. meal

49. to vomit

50. rectum, anus

51. pylorus, gate keeper

52. rectum

53. saliva

54. sigmoid

55. spleen

56. mouth

57. poison

58. a breaking out

59. worm

60. breath

61. vein liable to bleed

62. nourishment

63. to chew

64. to disable; paralysis

65. hair

66. nest

67. to roll

68. tooth

Suffixes

1. pertaining to

2. pertaining to

3. pain

4. pertaining to

5. enzyme

6. hernia

7. resemble

8. condition of

9. excision

10. vomiting

11. shape

12. formation, produce

13. pertaining to

14. pertaining to

15. process

16. condition of

17. one who specializes

18. inflammation

19. nature of, quality of

20. study of

21. destruction, to separate

22. enlargement, large

23. tumor
24. appetite
25. condition of
26. flow
27. to digest
28. pertaining to
29. to eat
30. instrument
31. to view, examine
32. contraction
33. new opening
34. incision
35. pertaining to

IDENTIFYING MEDICAL TERMS

1. amylase
2. anabolism
3. anorexia
4. appendectomy
5. appendicitis
6. biliary
7. celiac
8. colorrhaphy
9. dysphagia
10. hepatitis
11. herniotomy
12. postprandial
13. proctalgia
14. splenomegaly
15. sigmoidoscope

SPELLING

1. biliary
2. colonoscopy
3. enteroclysis
4. gastroenterology
5. hepatotoxin
6. laxative
7. peristalsis
8. sialadenitis
9. vagotomy
10. vermiform

MATCHING

1. e	6. h
2. f	7. j
3. d	8. a
4. b	9. g
5. i	10. c

ABBREVIATIONS

1. ac
2. bowel movement
3. bowel sounds
4. cib
5. GB
6. HAV
7. nasogastric
8. nothing by mouth
9. pc
10. TPN

DIAGNOSTIC AND LABORATORY TESTS

1. a
2. c
3. d
4. c
5. c

■ CHAPTER 7

ANATOMY AND PHYSIOLOGY

1. a. heart
   b. arteries
   c. veins
   d. capillaries
2. a. endocardium
   b. myocardium
   c. pericardium
3. 300
4. atria . . . interatrial
5. ventricles . . . interventricular
6. a. superior and inferior vena cavae
   b. right atrium
   c. tricuspid valve
   d. right ventricle
   e. pulmonary semilunar valve
   f. left and right pulmonary arteries
   g. lungs
   h. left and right pulmonary veins
   i. left atrium
   j. bicuspid or mitral valve
   k. left ventricle
   l. aortic valve
   m. aorta
   n. capillaries
7. autonomic nervous system
8. sinoatrial node
9. Purkinje system
10. a. radial . . . on the radial side of the wrist
    b. brachial . . . in the antecubital space of the elbow
    c. carotid . . . in the neck
11. a. the pressure exerted by the blood on the walls of the vessels
    b. the difference between the systolic and diastolic readings
12. man's fist . . . 60 to 100
13. 100 and 140 . . . 60 and 90
14. transport blood from the right and left ventricles of the heart to all body parts
15. transport blood from peripheral tissues to the heart

WORD PARTS

Prefixes

1. lack of
2. two
3. slow
4. together
5. within
6. within
7. outside
8. excessive, above
9. deficient, below
10. around
11. difficult
12. half
13. fast
14. three

Roots and Combining Forms

1. vessel
2. to choke, quinsy
3. vessel
4. opening
5. aorta
6. artery

7. artery
8. artery
9. fatty substance, porridge
10. fatty substance, porridge
11. atrium
12. atrium
13. heart
14. heart
15. heart
16. dark blue
17. listen to
18. to widen
19. electricity
20. a throwing in
21. sweet, sugar
22. blood
23. to hold back
24. bile
25. study of
26. moon
27. thin
28. mitral valve
29. muscle
30. circular
31. sour, sharp, acid
32. vein
33. vein
34. sound
35. lung
36. rhythm
37. hardening
38. a curve
39. pulse
40. narrowing
41. chest
42. to draw, to bind
43. to limp
44. pressure
45. clot of blood
46. to expand
47. small vessel
48. vessel
49. echo
50. vein
51. body
52. ventricle

53. fibrils (small fibers)
54. blood
55. power
56. infarct (necrosis of an area)
57. fat
58. first
59. to shut up
60. oxygen
61. throbbing
62. a partition
63. contraction
64. end
65. clot of blood
66. solid (fat)

Suffixes
1. pertaining to
2. pertaining to
3. pertaining to
4. immature cell, germ cell
5. surgical puncture
6. small
7. point
8. measurement
9. dilatation
10. excision
11. blood condition
12. relating to
13. formation, produce
14. chemical
15. to write
16. recording
17. condition
18. pertaining to
19. having a particular quality
20. process
21. condition of
22. one who specializes
23. inflammation
24. nature of, quality of
25. study of
26. softening
27. enlargement, large
28. instrument to measure
29. tumor
30. one who
31. condition of
32. disease

33. surgical repair
34. to pierce
35. instrument
36. contraction, spasm
37. incision
38. tissue
39. pertaining to

IDENTIFYING MEDICAL TERMS
1. angioma
2. angioblast
3. angioplasty
4. angiostenosis
5. arteriotomy
6. arteritis
7. bicuspid
8. cardiologist
9. cardiomegaly
10. cardiopulmonary
11. constriction
12. embolism
13. phlebitis
14. tachycardia
15. vasodilator

SPELLING
1. anastomosis
2. atherosclerosis
3. atrioventricular
4. endocarditis
5. extracorporeal
6. ischemia
7. myocardial
8. oxygen
9. phlebitis
10. palpitation

MATCHING
1. d   6. c
2. c   7. a
3. f   8. i
4. g   9. j
5. b   10. h

ABBREVIATIONS
1. AMI
2. A-V, AV
3. blood pressure
4. coronary artery disease

5. CC
6. electrocardiogram
7. high-density lipoprotein
8. H & L
9. myocardial infarction
10. tissue plasminogen activator

DIAGNOSTIC AND LABORATORY TESTS

1. c
2. a
3. b
4. c
5. b

■ CHAPTER 8

ANATOMY AND PHYSIOLOGY

1. a. erythrocytes
   b. thrombocytes
   c. leukocytes
2. transport oxygen and carbon dioxide
3. 5
4. 80 to 120 days
5. body's main defense against the invasion of pathogens
6. 8000
7. a. neutrophils
   b. eosinophils
   c. basophils
   d. lymphocytes
   e. monocytes
8. play an important role in the clotting process
9. 200,000 to 500,000
10. a. A
    b. B
    c. AB
    d. O
11. a. It transports proteins and fluids
    b. It protects the body against pathogens
    c. It serves as a pathway for the absorption of fats
12. a. spleen
    b. tonsils
    c. thymus

WORD PARTS

Prefixes

1. lack of
2. against
3. self
4. up
5. beyond
6. excessive
7. deficient
8. one
9. all
10. many
11. before
12. across

Roots and Combining Forms

1. gland
2. gland
3. clumping
4. other
5. vessel
6. unequal
7. base
8. lime, calcium
9. color
10. to pour
11. clots, to clot
12. flesh, creatine
13. cell
14. cell
15. cell
16. rose-colored
17. red
18. globe
19. little grain, granular
20. blood
21. blood
22. blood
23. white
24. white
25. fat
26. study of
27. lymph
28. lymph
29. large
30. neither
31. kernel, nucleus
32. eat, engulf
33. a thing formed, plasma
34. net
35. putrefying
36. whey, serum
37. iron
38. fiber
39. spleen
40. sea
41. clot
42. clot
43. thymus
44. fiber
45. tonsil
46. formation
47. immunity
48. vessel
49. whey
50. a developing
51. vessel
52. small vessel

Suffixes

1. capable
2. forming
3. immature cell, germ cell
4. body
5. swelling
6. to separate
7. cultivation
8. cell
9. excision
10. blood condition
11. work
12. formation, produce
13. protection
14. protein
15. tissue
16. pertaining to
17. chemical
18. process
19. one who specializes
20. inflammation
21. study of
22. destruction
23. enlargement
24. tumor

25. condition of
26. lack of
27. removal
28. attraction
29. attraction
30. formation
31. bursting forth
32. control, stopping
33. incision

IDENTIFYING MEDICAL TERMS

1. agglutination
2. allergy
3. antibody
4. anticoagulant
5. antigen
6. basocyte
7. coagulable
8. creatinemia
9. eosinophil
10. granulocyte
11. hematologist
12. hemoglobin
13. hyperglycemia
14. hyperlipemia
15. leukocyte
16. lymphostasis
17. mononucleosis
18. prothrombin
19. splenopexy
20. thrombocyte

SPELLING

1. allergy
2. creatinemia
3. extravasation
4. erythrocytosis
5. thromboplastin
6. hematocrit
7. hemorrhage
8. leukemia
9. lymphadenotomy
10. anaphylaxis

MATCHING

1. h   4. g
2. d   5. f
3. e   6. c
7. b   9. j
8. a   10. i

ABBREVIATIONS

1. AIDS
2. BSI
3. chronic myelogenous leukemia
4. Hb, Hgb
5. hematocrit
6. HIV
7. *Pneumocystis carinii* pneumonia
8. prothrombin time
9. red blood cell (count)
10. RIA

DIAGNOSTIC AND LABORATORY TESTS

1. d
2. c
3. c
4. b
5. a

CASE STUDY ANSWERS

■ CHAPTER 3

1. pruritus
2. vesicle
3. contact dermatitis
4. antipruritic
5. corticosteroid
6. a. stay away from poison ivy
   b. when working outside, wear clothing that covers arms and legs
   c. after working in the yard, immediately take a bath or shower to remove any possible contamination of skin with poison ivy
7. erythroderma
8. edema

■ CHAPTER 4

1. humpback
2. one 5mg tablet orally, taken daily
3. Vitamin A
4. Vitamin C
5. Calcium

■ CHAPTER 5

1. waddling
2. electromyography
3. a. minimize deformities
   b. preserve mobility

■ CHAPTER 6

1. pyrosis
2. gastrointestinal
3. acidity
4. Mylanta
5. 300

■ CHAPTER 7

1. dyspnea
2. electrocardiogram
3. nitroglycerin
4. seek medical attention without delay

■ CHAPTER 8

1. diarrhea
2. immune
3. AZT and/or zidovudine
4. Pre-existing conditions can make them less tolerant of drugs.

GLOSSARY OF WORD PARTS

PREFIXES

a	no, not, without, lack of, apart	dif	apart, free from, separate	hyper	above, beyond, excessive		
ab	away from	dipl	double	hypo	below, under, deficient		
ad	toward, near	di (s)	two, apart	in	in, into, not		
ambi	both	dis	apart	infra	below		
an	no, not, without, lack of	dys	bad, difficult, painful	infer	below		
ana	up	ec	out, outside, outer	inter	between		
ant	against	ecto	out, outside, outer	intra	within		
ante	before	em	in	ir (in)	into		
anti	against	en	within	macro	large		
apo	separation	end	within, inner	mal	bad		
astro	star-shaped	endo	within, inner	mega	large, great		
auto	self	ep	upon, over, above	meso	middle		
bi	two, double	epi	upon, over, above	meta	beyond, over, between, change		
bin	twice	eso	inward				
brachy	short	eu	good, normal	micro	small		
brady	slow	ex	out, away from	milli	one-thousandth		
cac	bad	exo	out, away from	mon (o)	one		
cata	down	extra	outside, beyond	mono	one		
centi	a hundred	hemi	half	multi	many, much		
chromo	color	heter	different	neo	new		
circum	around	hetero	different	nulli	none		
con	with, together	homo	similar, same	olig	little, scanty		
contra	against	homeo	similar, same, likeness, constant	oligo	little, scanty		
de	down, away from			pan	all		
deca	ten	hydr	water	par	around, beside		
di (a)	through, between	hydro	water	para	beside, alongside, abnormal		
dia	through, between	hyp	below, deficient				

per	through	pyro	fire	sym	together
peri	around	quadri	four	syn	together, with
poly	many, much,	quint	five	tachy	fast
	excessive	re	back	tetra	four
post	after, behind	retro	backward	trans	across
pre	before	semi	half	tri	three
primi	first	sub	below, under,	ultra	beyond
pro	before		beneath	uni	one
proto	first	supra	above, beyond		
pseudo	false	super	above, beyond		

WORD ROOTS/COMBINING FORMS

abdomin	abdomen	andr	man	atri/o	atrium
abort	to miscarry	andr/o	man	aud/i	to hear
absorpt	to suck in	ang	vessel	audi/o	to hear
acanth	a thorn	ang/i	vessel	auditor	hearing
acetabul	vinegar cup	angin	to choke, quinsy	aur	ear
acid	acid	angi/o	vessel	aur/i	ear
acoust	hearing	anis/o	unequal	auscultat	listen to
acr	extremity, point	ankyl	stiffening, crooked	aut	self
acr/o	extremity, point	an/o	anus	axill	armpit
act	acting	anter/i	toward the front	bacter/i	bacteria
actin	ray	anthrac	coal	balan	glans penis
aden	gland	aort	aorta	bartholin	Bartholin's glands
aden/o	gland	aort/o	aorta	bas/o	base
adhes	stuck to	append	appendix	bil	bile, gall
adip	fat	arachn	spider	bil/i	bile, gall
agglutinat	clumping	arche	beginning	bi/o	life
agon	agony	arter	artery	blast/o	germ cell
agor/a	market place	arter/i	artery	blephar	eyelid
albin	white	arteri/o	artery	blephar/o	eyelid
albumin	protein	arthr	joint	bol	to cast, throw
alimentat	nourishment	arthr/o	joint	brach/i	arm
all	other	artific/i	not natural	bronch	bronchi
alveol	small, hollow air sac	aspirat	to draw in	bronch/i	bronchi
ambyl	dull	atel	imperfect	bronchiol	bronchiole
ambul	to walk	atel/o	imperfect	bronch/o	bronchi
amni/o	lamb	ather	fatty substance,	bucc	cheek
ampere	ampere		porridge	burs	a pouch
amputat	to cut though	ather/o	fatty substance,	calc	lime, calcium
amyl	starch		porridge	calc/i	calcium
anastom	opening	atri	atrium	calcan/e	heel bone

cancer	crab	circulat	circular	crur	leg
capn	smoke	cirrh	orange-yellow	cry/o	cold
capsul	a little box	cirrh/o	orange-yellow	crypt	hidden
carcin	cancer	cis	to cut	cubit	elbow, to lie
carcin/o	cancer	claudicat	to limp	culd/o	cul-de-sac
card	heart	clavicul	little key	curie	curie
card/i	heart	cleid/o	clavicle	cutane	skin
cardi/o	heart	coagul	to clot	cyan	dark blue
carp	wrist	coagulat	to clot	cycl	ciliary body
carp/o	wrist	coccyg/e	tailbone	cycl/o	ciliary body
cartil	gristle	coccyg/o	tail bone	cyst	bladder, sac
castr	to prune	cochle/o	land snail	cyst/o	bladder, sac
caud	tail	coit	a coming together	cyt	cell
caus	heat	col	colon	cyth	cell
cavit	cavity	coll/a	glue	cyt/o	cell
celi	abdomen, belly	collis	neck	dacry	tear
cellul	little cell	col/o	colon	dactyl	finger or toe
centr	center	colon	colon	dactyl/o	finger or toe
centr/i	center	colon/o	colon	defecat	to remove dregs
cephal	head	colp/o	vagina	dem	people
cept	receive	concuss	shaken violently	dendr/o	tree
cerebell	little brain	condyle	knuckle	dent	tooth
cerebell/o	little brain	con/i	dust	dent/i	tooth
cerebr/o	cerebrum	conjunctiv	to join together	derm	skin
cervic	cervix, neck	connect	to bind together	derm/a	skin
cheil	lip	constipat	to press together	dermat	skin
chem/o	chemical	continence	to hold	dermat/o	skin
chlor/o	green	cor	pupil	derm/o	skin
chol	gall, bile	coriat	corium	dextr/o	to the right
chole	gall, bile	corne	cornea	diast	to expand
chol/e	gall, bile	corpor	body	didym	testis
choledoch/o	common bile duct	corpor/e	body	digit	finger or toe
chondr	cartilage	cortic	cortex	dilat	to widen
chondr/o	cartilage	cortis	cortex	disk	a disk
chord	cord	cost	rib	dist	away from the point
chori/o	chorion	cost/o	rib		of origin
choroid	choroid	cox	hip	diverticul	diverticula
choroid/o	choroid	cran/i	skull	dors	backward
chromat	color	crani/o	skull	dors/i	backward
chrom/o	color	creat	flesh	duct	to lead
chym	juice	creatin	flesh, creatine	duoden	duodenum
cine	motion	crine	to secrete	dur	dura, hard
cinemat/o	motion	crin/o	to secrete	dur/o	dura, hard

dwarf	small	flex	to bend	halat	breathe
dynam	power	fluor/o	fluorescence	hallux	great (big) toe
ech/o	echo	foc	focus	hem	blood
ectop	displaced	follicul	little bag	hemat	blood
eg/o	I, self	format	a shaping	hemat/o	blood
ejaculat	to throw out	fungat	mushroom, fungus	hem/o	blood
electr/o	electricity	fus	to pour	hemorrh	vein liable to bleed
eme	to vomit	galact/o	milk	hepat	liver
embol	to cast, to throw	ganglion	knot	hepat/o	liver
emulsificat	disintergrate	gastr	stomach	herni/o	hernia
encephal	brain	gastr/o	stomach	hidr	sweat
encephal/o	brain	gen	formation, produce	hirsut	hairy
enchyma	to pour	gene	formation, produce	hist/o	tissue
enter	intestine	genet	formation, produce	hol/o	whole
enucleat	to remove the kernel of	genital	belonging to birth	horizont	horizon
		gen/o	kind	humer	humerus
eosin/o	rose-colored	ger	old age	hydr	water
episi/o	vulva, pudenda	gest	to carry	hymen	hymen
equ/i	equal	gester	to bear	hypn	sleep
erget	work	gigant	giant	hyster	womb, uterus
erg/o	work	gingiv	gums	hyster/o	womb, uterus
eructat	a breaking out	glandul	little acorn	icter	jaundice
erysi	red	gli	glue	ile	ileum
erythr/o	red	gli/o	glue	ile/o	ileum
esophag/e	esophagus	glob	globe	ili	ilium
esophag/o	esophagus	globin	globule	ili/o	ilium
esthesi/o	feeling	globul	globe	illus	foot
estr/o	mad desire	glomerul	glomerulus, little ball	immun/o	safe, immunity
eti/o	cause			infarct	infarct (necrosis of an area)
eunia	a bed	glomerul/o	glomerulus, little ball		
excret	sifted out			infect	infection
f(erat)	to bear	gloss/o	tongue	infer/i	below
fasc	a band (fascia)	gluc/o	sweet, sugar	inguin	groin
fasci/o	a band (fascia)	glyc	sweet, sugar	insul	insulin
femor	femur	glyc/o	glucose, sweet, sugar	insulin/o	insulin
fenestrat	window	glycos	sweet, sugar	integument	covering
fibr	fibrous tissue, fiber	gonad	seed	intern	within
fibrillat	fibrils (small fibers)	goni/o	angle	ionizat	ion (going)
fibrin/o	fiber	gon/o	genitals	ion/o	ion
fibr/o	fiber	granul/o	little grain, granular	iont/o	ion
fibul	fibula	gravida	pregnant	irid	iris
filtrat	to strain through	gryp	curve	irid/o	iris
fixat	fastened	gynec/o	female	isch	to hold back

ischi	ischium	log	study	micturit	to urinate
is/o	equal	log/o	word	miliar	millet (tiny)
jaund	yellow	lopec	fox mange	minim	least
kal	potassium	lord	bending	mi/o	less, smaller
kary/o	cell's nucleus	lucent	to shine	mit	thread
kel	tumor	lumb	loin	mitr	mitral valve
kerat	cornea	lumb/o	loin	mnes	memory
kerat/o	horn, cornea	lump	lump	mucos	mucus
keton	ketone	lun	moon	mucus	mucus
kil/o	a thousand	lymph	lymph, clear fluid	muscul	muscle
kinet	motion	lymph/o	lymph, clear fluid	muscul/o	muscle
kyph	a hump	malign	bad kind	muta	to change
labi	lip	mamm/o	breast	mutat	to change
labyrinth	maze	mandibul	lower jawbone	my	muscle
labyrinth/o	maze	man/o	thin	myc	fungus
lacrim	tear	mast	breast	myc/o	fungus
lamin	lamina, thin plate	masticat	to chew	mydriat	dilation, widen
lamp (s)	to shine	mast/o	breast	myel	bone marrow, spinal cord
lapar/o	flank, abdomen	maxill	jawbone		
laryng	larynx	maxilla	jaw	myel/o	marrow
laryng/e	larynx	maxim	greatest	my/o	muscle
laryng/o	larynx	meat	passage	my/os	muscle
later	side	meat/o	passage	myring	drum membrane
laxat	to loosen	med	middle	myring/o	drum membrane
lei/o	smooth	medi	toward the middle	myx	mucus
lemma	rind, sheath, husk	medull	marrow	narc/o	numbness
lent	lens	medull/o	marrow	nas/o	nose
lept	seizure	melan	black	nat	birth
letharg	drowsiness	melan/o	black	nat/o	birth
leuk	white	men	month	necr	death
leuk/o	white	mening	membrane (meninges)	necr/o	death
levat	lifter			nephr	kidney
libr/i	balance	mening/i	membrane	nephr/o	kidney
lingu	tongue	mening/o	membrane	neur	nerve
lip	fat	menise	crescent	neur/i	nerve
lipid	fat	men/o	month	neur/o	nerve
lip/o	fat	ment	mind	neutr/o	neither
lith	stone	mes	middle	nid	nest
lith/o	stone	mes/o	middle	noct	night
lob	lobe	mester	month	nom	law
lob/o	lobe	metr	to measure, womb, uterus	norm	rule
lobul	small lobe			nucl	nucleus
locat	to place	metr/i	womb, uterus	nucle	kernel, nucleus

nyctal	blind	para	to bear	physi/o	nature
nystagm	to nod	paralyt	to disable, paralysis	pil/o	hair
occlus	to shut up	partum	labor	pine	pine cone
ocul	eye	parturit	in labor	pineal	pineal body
odont	tooth	patell	kneecap, patella	pin/o	to drink
olecran	elbow	path	disease	pituitar	phlegm
onc/o	tumor	path/o	disease	plak	plate
onych	nail	pause	cessation	plasma	a thing formed,
onych/o	nail	pector	chest		plasma
o/o	ovum, egg	pectorat	breast	plast	a developing
oophor	ovary	ped	foot, child	pleur	pleura
ophthalm	eye	ped/i	foot, child	pleura	pleura
ophthalm/o	eye	pedicul	a louse	pleur/o	pleura
opt	eye	pelv/i	pelvis	plicat	to fold
opt/o	eye	pen	penis	pneum/o	lung, air
or	mouth	penile	penis	pneumon	lung
orch	testicle	pept	to digest	poiet	formation
orchid	testicle	perine	perineum	poli/o	gray
orchid/o	testicle	periton/e	peritoneum	pollex	thumb
organ	organ	phac	lens	por	a passage
orth	straight	phac/o	lens	porphyr	purple
orth/o	straight	phag	to eat, engulf	poster/i	behind, toward the
oscill	to swing	phag/o	to eat, engulf		back
oscill/o	to swing	phak	lentil, lens	prand/i	meal
oste	bone	phalang/e	closely knit row	presby	old
oste/o	bone	pharyng/o	pharynx	press	to press
ot	ear	pharyng	pharynx	proct	anus, rectum
ot/o	ear	phas	speech	proct/o	anus, rectum
ovar	ovary	phen/o	to show	prolif	fruitful
ovul	ovary	phe/o	dusky	prophylact	guarding
ovulat	ovary	phim	a muzzle	prostat	prostate
ox	oxygen	phleb	vein	prosth/e	an addition
ox/i	oxygen	phleb/o	vein	prot/e	first
oxy	sour, sharp, acid	phon	voice	proxim	near the point of
pachy	thick	phone	voice		origin
pancreat	pancreas	phon/o	sound	prurit	itching
paque	dark	phor	carrying	psych	mind
palat/o	palate	phos	light	psych/o	mind
palliat	cloaked	phot/o	light	pudend	external genitals
pallid/o	globus, pallidus	phragm	partition	pulm/o	lung
palm	palm	phragmat/o	partition	pulmon	lung
palpitat	throbbing	phras	speech	pulmonar	lung
papill	papilla	physic	nature	pupill	pupil

purpur	purple	scapul	shoulder blade	spondyl/o	vertebra
py	pus	scler	hardening	staped	stirrup
pyel	renal pelvis	scler/o	hardening, sclera	steat	fat
pyel/o	renal pelvis	scoli	curvature	sten	narrowing
pylor	pylorus, gate keeper	scoli/o	curvature	ster	solid
py/o	pus	scop	to examine	stern	sternum
pyret	fever	seb/o	oil	stern/o	sternum
pyr/o	heat, fire	secund	second	sterol	solid (fat)
rach	spine	semin	seed	steth	chest
rachi	spine	seminat	seed	steth/o	chest
radi	radius	senile	old	stigmat	point
rad/i	radiating out from a center	senil	old	stom	mouth
		sept	putrefaction	stomat	mouth
radiat	radiant	septic	putrefying	strabism	a squinting
radic/o	spinal nerve root	ser (a)	whey	strict	to draw, to bind
radicul	spinal nerve root	ser/o	whey, serum	superfic/i	near the surface
radi/o	ray	sert	to gain	super/i	upper
rect/o	rectum	sexu	sex	suppress	suppress
relaxat	to loosen	sial	saliva	surrog	substituted
remiss	remit	sial/o	salivary	sympath	sympathy
ren	kidney	sider/o	iron	synov	joint fluid
ren/o	kidney	sigmoid	sigmoid	syst	contraction
respirat	breathing	sigmoid/o	sigmoid	system	a composite whole
reticul/o	net	sin/o	a curve	systol	contraction
retin	retina	sinus	a hollow curve	tel	end, distant
retin/o	retina	situ	place	tele	distant
rhabd/o	rod	som	body	tempor	temples
rheumat	discharge	somat	body	tend/o	tendon
rheumat/o	discharge	somat/o	body	tendin	tendon
rhin/o	nose	somn	sleep	ten/o	tendon
rhonch	snore	son	sound	tenon	tendon
rhytid/o	wrinkle	son/o	sound	tenos	tendon
roent	roentgen	spadias	a rent, an opening	tens	tension
rotat	to turn	spastic	convulsive	tentori	tentorium, tent
rrhyth	rhythm	sperm	seed (sperm)	terat	monster
rrhythm	rhythm	spermi	seed (sperm)	testicul	testicle
rube/o	red	spermat	seed (sperm)	test/o	testicle
sacr	sacrum	spermat/o	seed (sperm)	thalass	sea
salping	tube, fallopian tube	sphygm/o	pulse	thel/i	nipple
salping/o	tube, fallopian tube	spin	spine, a thorn	therm	hot, heat
salpinx	tube, fallopian tube	spir/o	breath	therm/o	hot, heat
sarc	flesh	splen/o	spleen	thorac	chest
sarc/o	flesh	spondyl	vertebra	thorac/o	chest

thorax	chest	tubercul	a little swelling	venere	sexual intercourse
thromb	clot	tuss	cough	ven/i	vein
thromb/o	clot	tympan	ear drum	ven/o	vein
thym	thymus, mind, emotion	tympan/o	drum	ventilat	to air
		uln	ulna, elbow	ventr	near or on the belly
thyr	thyroid, shield	uln/o	ulna, elbow		side of the body
thyr/o	thyroid, shield	umbilic	navel	ventricul	ventricle
thyrox	thyroid, shield	ungu	nail	ventricul/o	little belly
tibi	tibia	ur	urine	vermi	worm
tinnit	a jingling	ure	urinate	vers	turning
toc	birth	urea	urea	vertebr	vertebra
tom/o	to cut	uret	urine	vertebr/o	vertebra
ton	tone, tension	ureter	ureter	vesic	bladder
ton/o	tone	ureter/o	ureter	vesicul	vesicle
tonsill	tonsil, almond	urethr	urethra	vir	virus (poison)
topic	place	urethr/o	urethra	viril	masculine
top/o	place	urin	urine	viscer	body organs
tors	twisted	urinat	urine	volt	volt
tort/i	twisted	urin/o	urine	volunt	will
tox	poison	ur/o	urine	volvul	to roll
toxic	poison	uter	uterus	vuls	to pull
trach/e	trachea	uter/o	uterus	watt	watt
trache/o	trachea	uve	uvea	xanth/o	yellow
tract	to draw	vagin	vagina	xen	foreign material
trephinat	a bore	vag/o	vagus, wandering	xer	dry
trich	hair	varic/o	twisted vein	xer/o	dry
trich/o	hair	vas	vessel	xiph	sword
trigon	trigone	vascul	small vessel	zo/o	animal
trism	grating	vas/o	vessel	zoon	life
trop	turning	vector	a carrier		
troph	a turning	ven	vein		

SUFFIXES

-able	capable	-ary	pertaining to	-cele	hernia, tumor,
-ac	pertaining to	-ase	enzyme		swelling
-ad	pertaining to	-asthenia	weakness	-centesis	surgical puncture
-age	related to	-ate	use, action	-ceps	head
-al	pertaining to	-ate (d)	use, action	-cide	to kill
-algesia	pain	-betes	to go	-clasia	a breaking
-algia	pain	-blast	immature cell, germ	-clave	a key
-ant	forming		cell	-cle	small
-ar	pertaining to	-body	body	-clysis	injection

-cope	strike	-ic	pertaining to	-opsy	to view
-crit	to separate	-ide	having a particular	-or	one who, a doer
-culture	cultivation		quality	-ory	like, resemble
-cusis	hearing	-in	chemical, pertaining	-orexia	appetite
-cuspid	point		to	-ose	like
-cyesis	pregnancy	-ine	pertaining to	-osis	condition
-cyst	bladder	-ing	quality of	-ous	pertaining to
-cyte	cell	-ion	process	-paresis	weakness
-derma	skin	-ism	condition	-pathy	disease
-dermis	skin	-ist	one who specializes,	-penia	lack of, deficiency
-desis	binding		agent	-pepsia	to digest
-dipsia	thirst	-itis	inflammation	-pexy	surgical fixation
-drome	a course	-ity	condition	-phagia	to eat
-dynia	pain	-ive	nature of, quality of	-phasia	to speak
-ectasia	dilatation	-kinesia	motion	-pheresis	removal
-ectasis	dilatation,	-kinesis	motion	-phil	attraction
	distention	-lalia	to talk	-philia	attraction
-ectasy	dilation	-lemma	a sheath, rind	-phobia	fear
-ectomy	surgical excision	-lepsy	seizure	-phoresis	to carry
-edema	swelling	-lexia	diction	-phragm	a fence
-emesis	vomiting	-liter	liter	-phraxis	to obstruct
-emia	blood condition	-lith	stone	-phylaxis	protection
-er	relating to, one who	-logy	study of	-physis	growth
-ergy	work	-lymph	clear fluid	-plakia	plate
-esthesia	feeling	-lysis	destruction, to	-plasia	formation, produce
-form	shape		separate	-plasm	a thing formed,
-fuge	to flee	-malacia	softening		plasma
-gen	formation, produce	-mania	madness	-plasty	surgical repair
-genes	produce	-megaly	enlargement, large	-plegia	stroke, paralysis
-genesis	formation, produce	-meter	instrument to	-pnea	breathing
-genic	formation, produce		measure	-poiesis	formation
-glia	glue	-metry	measurement	-praxia	action
-globin	protein	-mnesia	memory	-ptosis	prolapse, drooping
-gnosis	knowledge	-morph	form, shape	-ptysis	to spit, spitting
-grade	a step	-noia	mind	-puncture	to pierce
-graft	pencil, grafting knife	-oid	resemble	-rrhage	to burst forth, burst-
-gram	a weight, mark,	-ole	opening		ing forth
	record	-oma	tumor	-rrhagia	to burst forth, burst-
-graph	to write, record	-omion	shoulder		ing forth
-graphy	recording	-on	pertaining to	-rrhaphy	suture
-hexia	condition	-one	hormone	-rrhea	flow, discharge
-ia	condition	-opia	eye, vision	-rrhexis	rupture
-iasis	condition	-opsia	eye, vision	-scope	instrument

-scopy	to view, examine	-systole	contraction	-trophy	nourishment, development
-sepsis	decay	-taxia	order		
-sis	condition	-therapy	treatment	-type	type
-some	body	-thermy	heat	-um	tissue
-spasm	tension, spasm, contraction	-tic	pertaining to	-ure	process
		-tome	instrument to cut	-uria	urine
-stalsis	contraction	-tomy	incision	-us	pertaining to
-stasis	control, stopping	-tone	tension	-y	condition, pertaining to, process
-staxis	dripping, trickling	-tripsy	crushing		
-sthenia	strength	-troph (y)	nourishment, development		
-stomy	new opening				

ABBREVIATIONS AND SYMBOLS

A

a	ampere; anode; anterior; aqua; area; artery
AB	abortion; abnormal
Ab	antibody
ABC	aspiration biopsy cytology
ABGs	arterial blood gases
ABLB	alternate binaural loudness balance
ABO	blood group
ABR	auditory brainstem response
ac	before meals (ante cibum); acute
AC	air conduction; anticoagulant
Acc	accommodation
ACG	angiocardiography
Ach	acetylcholine
ACL	anterior cruciate ligament
ACR	American College of Rheumatology
ACS	American Cancer Society
ACTH	adrenocorticotropic hormone
AD	right ear (auris dexter); Alzheimer's Disease; advance directive
ADA	American Diabetes Association
ad lib	as desired; freely
adeno-CA	adenocarcinoma
ADH	antidiuretic hormone (vasopressin)
ADHD	attention-deficit hyperactivity disorder
ADP	adenosine diphosphate
AE	above the elbow
AF	atrial fibrillation
AFB	acid-fast bacillus (TB organism)
AFP	alpha-fetoprotein
A/G	albumin/globulin ratio
Ag	antigen
AGN	acute glomerulonephritis
AH	abdominal hysterectomy
AHF	antihemophilic factor VIII
AHG	antihemophillic globulin factor VIII

AI	artificial insemination; aortic insufficiency
AIDS	acquired immunodeficiency syndrome
AIH	artificial insemination homologous
AK	above knee
AKA	above-knee amputation
alk phos	alkaline phosphatase
ALD	aldolase
ALL	acute lymphocytic leukemia
ALS	amyotrophic lateral sclerosis
ALT	argon laser trabeculoplasty; alanine aminotransferase
AMA	American Medical Association
AMD	age-related macular degeneration
AMI	acute myocardial infarction
AML	acute myelogenous leukemia
ANS	autonomic nervous system
A&P	auscultation and percussion; anatomy and physiology
AP	anteroposterior
APTT	activated partial thromboplastin time
ARD	acute respiratory disease
ARDS	acute respiratory distress syndrome
ARF	acute renal failure
ARMD	age-related macular degeneration
AS	aortic stenosis; left ear (auris sinistra)
As, Ast, astigm	astigmatism
Ascus	atypical squamous cells of undetermined significance
ASD	atrial septal defect
ASH	asymmetrical septal hypertrophy
ASHD	arteriosclerotic heart disease
AST	aspartate aminotransferase
ATN	acute tubular necrosis
ATP	adenosine triphosphate
AU	both ears (auris unitas)

AV	atrioventricular; arteriovenous		cc	cubic centimeter
AVMs	arteriovenous malformations		CC	cardiac catheterization; chief complaint; clean catch
AVR	aortic valve replacement			
			CCU	coronary care unit
			CDC	Centers for Disease Control and Prevention
B				
Ba	barium		CDH	congenital dislocation of the hip
BAC	blood alcohol concentration		CEA	carcinoembryonic antigen
BaE	barium enema		CF	cystic fibrosis
baso	basophil		CGN	chronic glomerulonephritis
BBB	bundle branch block		CHD	coronary heart disease
BBT	basal body temperature		chem	chemotherapy
BC	bone conduction		CHF	congestive heart failure
BE	below elbow; barium enema		CHO	carbohydrate
BG, bG	blood glucose; blood sugar		chol	cholesterol
bid	twice a day		Ci	curie
BIN, bin	twice a night		Cib	food (cibus)
BK	below knee		CIN	cervical intraepithelial neoplasia
BKA	below-knee amputation		CIS	carcinoma in situ
BM	bowel movement		CK	creatine kinase
BMD	bone mineral density (test)		Cl	chlorine
BMR	basal metabolic rate		CLL	chronic lymphocytic leukemia
BNO	bladder neck obstruction		cm	centimeter
BP	blood pressure		CMG	cystometrogram
BPH	benign prostatic hyperplasia (hypertrophy)		CML	chronic myelogenous leukemia
			CMP	cardiomyopathy
BRP	bathroom privileges		CNS	central nervous system
BS	bowel sounds		c/o	complains of
BSE	breast self-examination		CO	cardiac output
BSI	body systems isolation		CO_2	carbon dioxide
BSP	bromsulphalein		COLD	chronic obstructive lung disease
BT	bleeding time		COPD	chronic obstructive pulmonary disease
BUN	blood urea nitrogen			
Bx	biopsy		CP	cerebral palsy
			CPD	cephalopelvic disproportion
			CPK	creatine phosphokinase
			CPM	continuous passive motion
C			CPR	cardiopulmonary resuscitation
c̄	with (cum)		CPS	cycles per second
C1, C2, etc.	first cervical vertebra; second cervical vertebra		CR	computerized radiography
			CRF	chronic renal failure; corticotropin-releasing factor
C&S	culture and sensitivity			
CA	cancer; carcinoembryonic antigen		CS, C-section	cesarean section
Ca	calcium		CSF	cerebrospinal fluid
CABG	coronary artery bypass graft		CT	computed tomography
CAD	coronary artery disease		CTS	carpal tunnel syndrome
CAM	complementary and alternative medicines		CUC	chronic ulcerative colitis
			CV	cardiovascular
cap	capsule		CVA	cerebrovascular accident (stroke)
CAPD	continuous ambulatory peritoneal dialysis		CVD	cardiovascular disease
			CVP	central venous pressure
cath	catheterization; catheter		CVS	chorionic villus sampling
CBC	complete blood count		CWP	childbirth without pain
CBS	chronic brain syndrome			

CXR	chest x-ray film; chest radiograph	ED	erectile dysfunction
cysto	cystoscopic examination	EDC	estimated date of confinement
		EEG	electroencephalogram; electroencephalograph

D

/d	per day	EENT	eye, ear, nose and throat
D	diopter (lens strength)	EGD	esophagogastroduodenoscopy
db, dB	decibel	ELISA	enzyme-linked immunosorbent assay
DBS	deep brain stimulation	EM	emmetropia
D&C	dilatation (dilatation) and curettage	EMG	electromyography
D&E	dilation and evacuation	ENG	electronystagmography
dc	discontinue	ENT	ear, nose and throat
DC	discharge	EOM	extraocular movement, extraocular muscles
DCIS	ductal carcinoma in situ	eos, eosin	eosinophil
DDS	Doctor of Dental Surgery; dorsal cord stimulation	ERCP	endoscopic retrograde cholangiopancreatography
decub	decubitus	ERT	estrogen replacement therapy; external radiation therapy
derm	dermatology		
DES	diethylstilbestrol	ERV	expiratory reserve volume
DHT	dihydrotestosterone	ESL, ESWL	extracorporeal shock-wave lithotripsy
DI	diabetes insipidus; diagnostic imaging	ESR, SR, sed rate	erythrocyte sedimentation rate; sedimentation rate
diff	differential count (white blood cells)		
dil	dilute; diluted	ESRD	end-stage renal disease
DJD	degenerative joint disease	EST	electroshock therapy
DM	diabetes mellitus	ESWL	extracorporeal shockwave lithotripsy
DNA	deoxyribonucleic acid		
DNR	do not resuscitate	ET	esotropia; endotracheal
DO	doctor of osteopathy	ETF	eustachian tube function
DOA	dead on arrival		
DOB	date of birth		
DRE	digital rectal examination		
DRGs	diagnostic related groups	**F**	
DSA	digital subtraction angiography	F	Fahrenheit
DTaP	diphtheria, tetanus and pertussis (vaccine)	FACP	Fellow, American College of Physicians
DTRs	deep tendon reflexes	FACS	Fellow, American College of Surgeons
DUB	dysfunctional uterine bleeding		
DVA	distance visual acuity	FBS	fasting blood sugar
DVT	deep vein thrombosis	FDA	Food and Drug Administration
Dx	diagnosis	FEF	forced expiratory flow
		FEKG	fetal electrocardiogram
		FEV	forced expiratory volume
		FH	family history
E		FHR	fetal heart rate
EBV	Epstein-Barr virus	FHS	fetal heart sound
ECC	extracorporeal circulation	FHT	fetal heart tone
ECCE	extracapsular cataract extraction	FMS	fibromyalgia syndrome
ECF	extracellular fluid; extended care facility	FROM	full range of motion
		FS	frozen section
ECG, EKG	electrocardiogram	FSH	follicle-stimulating hormone
ECHO	echocardiogram	FTA-ABS	fluorescent treponemal antibody absorption
E. coli	Escherichia coli		
ECSL	extracorporeal shockwave lithotriptor	FTND	fullterm normal delivery
ECT	electroconvulsive therapy		

FUO	fever of undetermined origin
FVC	forced vital capacity
Fx	fracture

G

g	gram
GB	gallbladder
GC	gonorrhea
GCSF	granulocyte colony-stimulating factor
GERD	gastroesophageal reflux disease
GGT	gamma-glutamyl transferase
GH	growth hormone
GI	gastrointestinal
GIFT	gamete intrafallopian transfer
GnRF	gonadotropin-releasing factor
GOT	glutamic oxaloacetic transaminase
Gpi	globus pallidus
GPT	glutamic pyruvic transaminase
gr	grain
grav I	pregnancy one
GTT	glucose tolerance test
gtt	drops (guttae)
GU	genitourinary
GYN	gynecology

H

h	hour
H	hypodermic; hydrogen
H&L	heart & lungs
HAA	hepatitis-associated antigen
HAV	hepatitis A virus
HBIG	hepatitis B immune globulin
HBOT	hyperbaric oxygen therapy
HBP	high blood pressure
HBV	hepatitis B virus
HCG	human chorionic gonadotropin
HCl	hydrochloric acid
HCO_3	bicarbonate
HCT, Hct	hematocrit
HD	hip disarticulation; hearing distance; Hodgkin's disease
HDL	high-density lipoprotein
HDN	hemolytic disease of the newborn
HDS	herniated disk syndrome
HEENT	head, eyes, ears, nose and throat
HF	heart failure
Hg	mercury
HGB, Hgb, Hb	hemoglobin
HIV	human immunodeficiency virus
HLA	human leukocyte antigen
HMD	hyaline membrane disease

HNP	herniated nucleus pulposus (herniated disk)
H_2O	water
Hpd	hematoporphyrin derivative
H. pylori	Heliocobacter pylori
HPV	human papillomavirus
HRT	hormone replacement therapy
hs	at bedtime
HSG	hysterosalpingography
HSV-2	herpes simplex virus-2
Ht	height
HT	hypermetropia (hyperopia)
HTLV	human T-cell leukemia-lymphoma virus
Hx	history
hypo	hypodermic

I

IAS	interatrial septum
IBS	irritable bowel syndrome
IC	interstitial cystitis
ICCE	intracapsular cataract cryoextraction
ICF	intracellular fluid
ICP	intracranial pressure
ICSH	interstitial cell-stimulating hormone
ICU	intensive care unit
ID	intradermal
I&D	incision and drainage
IDDM	insulin-dependent diabetes mellitus
Ig	immunoglobulin
IH	infectious hepatitis
IHSS	idiopathic hypertropic subaortic stenosis
IL-2	interleukin-2
IM	intramuscular
inj	injection
I&O	intake and output
IOL	intraocular lens
IOP	intraocular pressure
IPD	intermittent peritoneal dialysis
IPPB	intermittent positive-pressure breathing
IQ	intelligence quotient
IR	interventional radiologist
IRDS	infant respiratory distress syndrome
IRT	internal radiation therapy
IRV	inspiratory reserve volume
IS	intercostal space
ITP	idiopathic thrombocytopenia purpura
IU	international unit
IUD	intrauterine device

IUGR	intrauterine growth rate; intrauterine growth retardation	LMP	last menstrual period
IV	intravenous	LOM	limitation or loss of motion
IVC	inferior vena cava; intravenous cholangiography; intraventricular catheter	LP	lumbar puncture
		LPE	laser peripheral iridotomy
		LPF	low-power field
		LRQ	lower right quadrant
IVF	in vitro fertilization	L, lt	left
IVP	intravenous pyelogram	LTH	lactogenic hormone
IVS	interventricular septum	LUQ	left upper quadrant
IVU	intravenous urogram	LV	left ventricle
		lymphs	lymphocytes

J

J	joule		
JNC	Joint National Committee		

M

		M	molar; thousand; muscle
		m	male; meter; minim
		mA	milliampere

K

		mAs	milliampere second
K	potassium	MBC	maximal breathing capacity
KD	knee disarticulation	MCH	mean corpuscular hemoglobin
kg	kilogram	MCHC	mean corpuscular hemoglobin concentration
KS	Kaposi's sarcoma		
KUB	kidney, ureter and bladder	mCi	millicurie
kV	kilovolt	MCV	mean corpuscular volume
		MD	medical doctor; muscular dystrophy

L

		mEq	milliequivalent
L, l	liter	mets	metastases
L1, L2, etc.	first lumbar vertebra, second lumbar vertebra, etc.	MG	myasthenia gravis
		mg	milligram (0.001 gram)
LA	left atrium	MH	marital history
L&A	light and accommodation	MI	myocardial infarction; mitral insufficiency
lab	laboratory		
LAC	long arm cast	MIF	melanocyte-stimulating hormone release-inhibiting factor
LAK	lymphokine-activated killer (cells)		
LAT, lat	lateral	mix astig	mixed astigmatism
lb	pound	mL, ml	milliliter (0.001 liter)
LB	large bowel	mm	millimeter (0.001 meter; 0.039 inch)
LBBB	left bundle branch block		
LCIS	lobular carcinoma in situ	mMol	millimole
LD	lactate dehydrogenase	MMR	measles, mumps, and rubella (vaccine)
LDH	lactic dehydrogenase		
LDL	low-density lipoprotein	mol wt	molecular weight
LE	lupus erythematosus; lower extremity; left eye	mono	monocyte
		MR	mental retardation
LEDs	light-emitting diodes	MRI	magnetic resonance imaging
LES	lower esophageal sphincter	MS	mitral stenosis; multiple sclerosis; musculoskeletal
LH	luteinizing hormone		
LH-RH	luteinizing hormone-releasing hormone	MSH	melanocyte-stimulating hormone
		mV	millivolt
liq	liquid; fluid	MV	minute volume
LLC	long leg cast	MVP	mitral valve prolapse
		MVV	maximal voluntary ventilation
LLQ	left lower quadrant	MY	myopia

N

n	nerve
Na	sodium
NANBH	non-A, non-B hepatitis virus
NB	newborn
nCi	nanocurie
NCV	nerve conduction velocity
NIDDM	non-insulin-dependent diabetes mellitus
NG	nasogastric (tube)
NH_4	ammonia
NHLBI	National Heart, Lung and Blood Institute
NIH	National Institute of Health
NMR	nuclear magnetic resonance
NPH	nonprotein nitrogen
NPO, npo	nothing by mouth (nil per os)
NPT	nocturnal penile tumescence
NPUAP	National Pressure Ulcer Advisory Panel
NSAIDs	nonsteroidal anti-inflammatory drugs
N&V	nausea & vomiting
NVA	near visual acuity

O

O	pint
O_2	oxygen
OA	osteoarthritis
OB	obstetrics
OB-GYN	obstetrics and gynecology
OC	oral contraceptive
OCD	obsessive-compulsive disorder
OCPs	oral contraceptive pills
od	once a day
OD	right eye (oculus dexter); overdose
OHS	open heart surgery
OM	otitis media
O&P	ova and parasites
OR	operating room
ORTH, ortho	orthopedics; orthopaedics
os	mouth opening; bone
OS	left eye (oculus sinister)
OTC	over the counter
oto	otology
OU	both eyes (oculi unitas); each eye (oculus uterque)
OV	office visit
oz	ounce

P

P	pulse; phosphorus
PA	posteroanterior; pernicious anemia
PAC	premature arterial contraction
Pap	Papanicolaou (smear)
PAT	paroxysmal atrial tachycardia
Path	pathology
PBI	protein bound iodine
pc	after meals (post cibum)
PCL	posterior cruciate ligament
PCP	*Pneumocystis carinii* pneumonia
PCV	packed cell volume
PD	peritoneal dialysis
PDR	*Physicians' Desk Reference*
PE	physical examination; pulmonary embolism
PEEP	positive end-expiratory pressure
PEG	percutaneous endoscopic gastrostomy
PERRLA	pupils equal, regular, react to light and accommodation
PET	positron emission tomography
PE tube	polyethylene tube
PFT	pulmonary function test
pH	hydrogen ion concentration, degree of acidity
PH	past history
PID	pelvic inflammatory disease
PIF	prolactin release-inhibiting factor
PKU	phenylketonuria
PM, pm	afternoon, evening
PMH	past medical history
PMI	point of maximal impulse
PMN	polymorphonuclear neutrophil
PMP	previous menstrual period
PMR	physical medicine and rehabilitation
PMS	premenstrual syndrome
PND	paroxysmal nocturnal dyspnea; postnasal drip
PNS	peripheral nervous system
PO, po	orally, by mouth (per os)
poly	polymorphonuclear
PP	postprandial (after meals)
PPD	purified protein derivative (TB test)
PPI	proton pump inhibitors
pr	per rectum
PRF	prolactin-releasing factor
prn	as necessary, as required, when necessary
PSA	prostate-specific antigen
PT	physical therapy; prothrombin time
pt	patient; pint

PTC	percutaneous transhepatic cholangiography	
PTCA	percutaneous transluminal coronary angioplasty	
PTH	parathormone	
PTS	permanent threshold shift	
PTT	partial thromboplastin time	
PUD	peptic ulcer disease	
PUL	percutaneous ultrasonic lithotropsy	
PVC	premature ventricular contraction	
PVD	peripheral vascular disease	

Q

q	every
qam, qm	every morning
qd	every day (quaque die)
qh	every hour
q2h	every 2 hours
qid	four times a day
qns	quantity not sufficient
qpm, qn	every night
qs	quantity sufficient
qt	quart

R

R	respiration
R, rt	right
Ra	radium
RA	right atrium; rheumatoid arthritis
rad	radiation absorbed dose
RAI	radioactive iodine
RAIU	radioactive iodine uptake
RBC	red blood cell; red blood cell (count)
RD	respiratory disease
RDA	recommended dietary or daily allowance
RDS	respiratory distress syndrome
RE	right eye
REM	rapid eye movement
Rh	Rhesus (factor)
RIA	radioimmunoassay
RLQ	right lower quadrant
RNA	ribonucleic acid
R/O	rule out
ROM	range of motion; read only memory
RP	retrograde pyelogram
RPM	revolutions per minute
RQ	respiratory quotient

RT	radiation therapy
RUQ	right upper quadrant
RV	right ventricle
Rx	take thou; prescribe; treatment; therapy

S

$\bar{s}$	without
SA, S-A	sinoatrial (node)
SAC	short arm cast
SAD	seasonal affective disorder
SAH	subarachnoid hemorrhage
SALT	serum alanine aminotransferase
SARS	severe acute respiratory syndrome
SAST	serum aspartate aminotransferase
SBFT	small-bowel follow-through
SC, sc, subq	subcutaneous
SCD	sudden cardiac death
SD	shoulder disarticulation; standard deviation
seg, poly	polymorphonuclear neutrophil
segs	segmented (mature RBCs)
SG	skin graft
SGOT	serum glutamic oxaloacetic transaminase
SGPT	serum glutamic pyruvic transaminase
sh	shoulder
SH	serum hepatitis
SIDS	sudden infant death syndrome
SK	streptokinase
SLE	systemic lupus erythematosus
SMBG	self-monitoring of blood glucose
SOB	shortness of breath
SOM	serous otitis media
sono	sonogram, sonography
SOP	standard operating procedure
sp gr, SG	specific gravity
SPP	suprapubic prostatectomy
SR	sedimentation rate
ss	one half
St	stage (of disease)
ST	esotropia
staph	staphylococcus
stat	immediately
STDs	sexually transmitted diseases
STH	somatotropin hormone
strep	streptococcus
STS	serologic test for syphilis
STSG	split thickness skin graft
subcu, subq	subcutaneous

SVC	superior vena cava
SVD	spontaneous vaginal delivery
Sx	signs, symptoms
syr	syrup

T

T	temperature
T1, T2, etc.	thoracic vertebrae first, thoracic vertebrae second, etc.
T$_3$	triiodothyronine
T$_3$RU	triiodothyronine resin uptake
T$_4$	thyroxine
T&A	tonsillectomy and adenoidectomy
tab	tablet
TAH	total abdominal hysterectomy
TB	tuberculosis
TBW	total body weight
TENS	transcutaneous electrical nerve stimulation
TFS	thyroid function studies
THA	total hip arthroplasty
THR	total hip replacement
TIAs	transient ischemic attacks
tid	three times a day
TIMS	topical immunomodulators
TIPS	transjugular intrahepatic portosystemic shunt
TJ	triceps jerk
TKA	total knee arthroplasty
TKR	total knee replacement
TLC	tender loving care; total lung capacity
TMJ	temporomandibular joint
TNF	tumor necrosis factor
TNM	tumor, node, metastasis
TNS	transcutaneous nerve stimulation
top	topically
TPA	*Treponema pallidum* agglutination (test)
TPA, tPA	tissue plasminogen activator
TPN	total parenteral nutrition
TPR	temperature, pulse, respiration
tr, tinct	tincture
TSE	testicular self-exam
TSH	thyroid stimulating hormone
TSS	toxic shock syndrome
TTH	thyrotropic hormone
TTS	temporary threshold shift
TUIP	transurethral incision of the prostate
TUMP	transurethral microwave thermotherapy

TUNA	transurethral needle ablation
TUR, TURP	transurethral resection of the prostate
TV	tidal volume
Tx	traction; treatment; transplant

U

U	units
UA	urinalysis
UC	uterine contractions
UCHD	usual childhood diseases
UG	urogenital
UGI	upper gastrointestinal
U&L, U/L	upper and lower
ULQ	upper left quadrant
ung	ointment
URI	upper respiratory infection
URQ	upper right quadrant
US	ultrasound
USP	United States Pharmacopeia
UTI	urinary tract infection
UV	ultraviolet

V

v	vein
VA	visual acuity
VC	vital capacity
VCD	vacuum constriction device
VCG	vectorcardiogram
VCU, VCUG	voiding cystourethrogram
VD	venereal disease
VDRL	Venereal Disease Research Laboratory (syphilis test)
VF	visual field
VHD	ventricular heart disease
VLDL	very low density lipoprotein
vol	volume
vol %	volume percent
VMA	vanillylmandelic acid
VP	vasopressin
VSD	ventricular septal defect
VT	ventricular tachycardia

W

WBC	white blood cell; white blood (cell) count
WDWN	well developed, well nourished
WNL	within normal limits
wt	weight
w/v	weight by volume

X

x	multiplied by
XM	cross match for blood (type and cross match)
XP	xeroderma pigmentosum
XR	x-ray
XT	exotropia
XX	female sex chromosomes
XY	male sex chromosomes

Y

YAG	yttrium-aluminum-garnet (laser)
YOB	year of birth
yr	year

Z

z	atomic number

Charting Abbreviations and Symbols

āā	of each
ac	before meals (ante cibum)
AD	right ear (auris dextra)
ADL	activities of daily living
ad lib	as desired
adm	admission
AE	above elbow
AJ	ankle jerk
AK	above knee
alt dieb	every other day
alt hor	every other hour
alt noc	every other night
AM, am	before noon (ante meridiem); morning
AMA	against medical advice
AMB	ambulate; ambulatory
ant	anterior
AP	anteroposterior
A-P	anterior-posterior
approx	approximately
AQ, aq	water
ASAP	as soon as possible
AS or LE	left ear (auris sinistra)
AV	atrioventricular
BE	below elbow
bid	twice a day
bin	twice a night
BK	below knee
BM	bowel movement
BMR	basal metabolic rate
BRP	bathroom privileges

C	Centigrade, Celsius or calorie (kilocalorie)
caps	capsules
CBR	complete bed rest
CC	chief complaint; clean catch (urine)
CCU	cardiac (coronary) care unit
c/o	complains of
cont	continue
dc	discontinue
DC	discharge from hospital
DNA	does not apply
DNR	do not resuscitate
DNS	did not show
Dr	doctor
D/W	dextrose in water
Dx	diagnosis
EOM	extraocular movement
ER	emergency room
Ex	examination
F	Fahrenheit
FHS	fetal heart sounds
FHT	fetal heart tones
GB	gallbladder
GI	gastrointestinal
GU	genitourinary
h, hr	hour
hpf	high power field
hs	hour of sleep; bedtime (hora somni)
hypo	hypodermic injection
ICU	intensive care unit
IM	intramuscular
I&O	intake and output
IU	international unit
IV	intravenous
L	left
L&A	light and accommodation
LAT	lateral
L&W	living and well
LLQ	left lower quadrant
LMP	last menstrual period
LOA	left occipitoanterior
LPF	low power field (10x)
LUQ	left upper quadrant
MTD	right ear drum (membrana tympani dexter)
MTS	left ear drum (membrana tympani sinister)
neg	negative
NG	nasogastric
NPO	nothing by mouth
NS	normal saline
OD	right eye (oculus dexter)
OP	outpatient

OR	operating room	tabs	tablets
OS or OL	left eye (oculus sinister, oculus laevus)	TC&DB	turn, cough, deep breathe
		tid	three times a day
OU	each eye (oculus uterque)	tinct	tincture
P	pulse	TPN	total parenteral nutrition
PA	posteroanterior	trans	transverse
pc	after meals (post cibum)	ULQ	upper left quadrant
PI	present illness	ung	ointment
po	by mouth (per os)	URQ	upper right quadrant
PO	postoperative	VS	vital signs
PM, pm	afternoon or evening (post meridiem)	WBC	white blood cell; white blood (cell) count
prn	as necessary, as required, when necessary	WM, BM	white male, black male
		WF, BF	white female, black female
q	every (quaque)	×	times, power
qd	every day (quaque die)	−	negative
qh	every hour (quaque hora)	+	positive
q2h	every 2 hours	F	female
q4h	every 4 hours	M	male
qid	four times a day (quarter in die)	+/−	positive or negative
qm	every morning (quaque mane)	*	birth
qn	every night (quaque nocte)	†	death
R	right; respiration	%	percent
RBC	red blood cell; red blood (cell) count	#	number; pound
Rh	Rhesus blood factor (Rh + or Rh −)	&	and
RLQ	right lower quadrant	<	less than
R/O	rule out	=	equal
ROM	range of motion	>	greater than
RUQ	right upper quadrant	?	question
SC, sc, subq	subcutaneous	@	at
SOB	shortness of breath	^	increase
SOS	if necessary (si opus sit)	™	trade mark
stat	immediately	©	copyright
Sx	signs, symptoms	®	registered
T, temp	temperature	¶	paragraph

LABORATORY REFERENCE VALUES

ABBREVIATIONS USED IN REPORTING LABORATORY VALUES

cm^3	cubic centimeter
cu μ	cubic microns
dL	deciliter
fL	femtoliter
g	gram
g/dL	grams per deciliter
IU	International Unit
kg	kilogram
L	liter
mol (M)	mole
mEq	milliequivalent
mg	milligram
mg/dL	milligram per deciliter
mm	millimeter
mmol	millimole
mm^3	cubic millimeter
mm Hg	millimeter of mercury
ng	nanogram
ng/dL	nanogram per deciliter
ng/mL	nanogram per milliliter
pg	picogram
U	unit
U/L	units per liter
uIU/mL	units International Unit per milliliter
μg (mcg)	microgram

HEMATOLOGY TESTS

	Normal Ranges
Erythrocytes–Red blood cells (RBC)	
Females	$4.2–5.4$ million/mm^3
Males	$4.6–6.2$ million/mm^3
Children	$4.5–5.1$ million/mm^3

Hemoglobin (HGB, Hgb)	
Females	$12.0–14.0$ g/dL
Males	$14.0–16.0$ g/dL
Hematocrit (HCT)	$37.0–54$ %
Females	$37–47$ %
Males	$40–54$ %
Leukocytes–White blood cells (WBC)	$4500–11,000$/mm^3
Differential	
Neutrophils	$54–62$ %
Lymphocytes	$20–40$ %
Monocytes	$2–10$ %
Eosinophils	$1–2$ %
Basophils	$0–1$ %
Thrombocytes–Platelets	$200,000–400,000$/mm^3
Mean corpuscular volume (MCV)	$80–97$ fL
Mean corpuscular hemoglobin (MCH)	$27.0–31.2$ pg
Mean corpuscular hemoglobin concentration (MCHC)	$31.8–37.4$ g/dL

COAGULATION TESTS

Bleeding time	$2.75–8.0$ min
Coagulation time	$5–15$ min
Prothrombin time (PT)	$12–14$ sec

CHEMISTRIES

	Normal Ranges
Sodium (Na)	136–145 mEq/L
Potassium (K)	3.5–5.0 mEq/L
Calcium (Ca)	9.0–11.0 mg/dL
Chloride (Cl)	100–108 mmol/L
CO_2	21–32 mmol/L
Phosphate (PO_4)	3.0–4.5 mg/dL
Glucose (fasting)	70–115 mg/dL
Blood urea nitrogen (BUN)	8–20 mg/dL
Creatinine	0.9–1.5 mg/dL
Creatine phosphokinase (CPK)	
Females	30–135 U/L
Males	55–170 U/L
Anion gap	10–17 mEq/L
Alkaline phosphatase (ALP)	20–90U/L
Alanine aminotransferase (ALT, SGPT)	5–30 U/L
Albumin	3.5–5.5 g/dL
Globulin	1.4–4.8 g/dL
A/G ratio	0.7–2.0 g/dL
Aspartate aminotransferase (AST, SGOT)	10–30 U/L
Bilirubin	0.3–1.1 mg/dL
Cholesterol	<200 mg/dL
High density lipoprotein (HDL)	>60 mg/dL
Low density lipoprotein (LDL)	<100 mg/dL

Triglycerides	<150 mg/dL
Uric acid	
Females	1.5–7.0 mg/dL
Males	2.5–8.0 mg/dL
Lactate dehydrogenase (LDH)	100–190 U/L
Thyroxine (T_4)	4.4–9.9 µg/dL
Free T_4	0.8–1.8 ng/dL
Thyroid stimulating hormone (TSH)	0.5–6.0 uIU/mL
Prostate specific antigen (PSA) Male	0.0–4.0 ng/mL
Testosterone	241–827 ng/dL

URINALYSIS

	Normal Ranges
Color	Yellow to amber
Turbidity (Appearance)	Clear
Specific gravity	1.003–1.030
Reaction (pH)	5.0–7.0
Odor	Faintly aromatic
Protein	Negative
Glucose	Negative
Ketones	Negative
Bilirubin	Negative
Blood	Negative
Urobilinogen	0.1–1.0
Nitrite	Negative
Leukocytes	Negative

SINGLE PC LICENSE AGREEMENT AND LIMITED WARRANTY

READ THIS LICENSE CAREFULLY BEFORE OPENING THIS PACKAGE. BY OPENING THIS PACKAGE, YOU ARE AGREEING TO THE TERMS AND CONDITIONS OF THIS LICENSE. IF YOU DO NOT AGREE, DO NOT OPEN THE PACKAGE. PROMPTLY RETURN THE UNOPENED PACKAGE AND ALL ACCOMPANYING ITEMS TO THE PLACE YOU OBTAINED THEM. *THESE TERMS APPLY TO ALL LICENSED SOFTWARE ON THE DISK EXCEPT THAT THE TERMS FOR USE OF ANY SHAREWARE OR FREEWARE ON THE DISKETTES ARE AS SET FORTH IN THE ELECTRONIC LICENSE LOCATED ON THE DISK:*

1. GRANT OF LICENSE and OWNERSHIP: The enclosed computer programs and data ("Software") are licensed, not sold, to you by Pearson Education, Inc. ("We" or the "Company") and in consideration of your purchase or adoption of the accompanying Company textbooks and/or other materials, and your agreement to these terms. We reserve any rights not granted to you. You own only the disk(s) but we and/or our licensors own the Software itself. This license allows you to use and display your copy of the Software on a single computer (i.e., with a single CPU) at a single location for academic use only, so long as you comply with the terms of this Agreement. You may make one copy for back up, or transfer your copy to another CPU, provided that the Software is usable on only one computer

2. RESTRICTIONS: You may not transfer or distribute the Software or documentation to anyone else. Except for backup, you may not copy the documentation or the Software. You may not network the Software or otherwise use it on more than one computer or computer terminal at the same time. You may not reverse engineer, disassemble, decompile, modify, adapt, translate, or create derivative works based on the Software or the Documentation. You may be held legally responsible for any copying or copyright infringement which is caused by your failure to abide by the terms of these restrictions.

3. TERMINATION: This license is effective until terminated. This license will terminate automatically without notice from the Company if you fail to comply with any provisions or limitations of this license. Upon termination, you shall destroy the Documentation and all copies of the Software. All provisions of this Agreement as to limitation and disclaimer of warranties, limitation of liability, remedies or damages, and our ownership rights shall survive termination.

4. LIMITED WARRANTY AND DISCLAIMER OF WARRANTY: Company warrants that for a period of 60 days from the date you purchase this SOFTWARE (or purchase or adopt the accompanying textbook), the Software, when properly installed and used in accordance with the Documentation, will operate in substantial conformity with the description of the Software set forth in the Documentation, and that for a period of 30 days the disk(s) on which the Software is delivered shall be free from defects in materials and workmanship under normal use. The Company does not warrant that the Software will meet your requirements or that the operation of the Software will be uninterrupted or error-free. Your only remedy and the Company's only obligation under these limited warranties is, at the Company's

option, return of the disk for a refund of any amounts paid for it by you or replacement of the disk. THIS LIMITED WARRANTY IS THE ONLY WARRANTY PROVIDED BY THE COMPANY AND ITS LICENSORS, AND THE COMPANY AND ITS LICENSORS DISCLAIM ALL OTHER WARRANTIES, EXPRESS OR IMPLIED, INCLUDING WITHOUT LIMITATION, THE IMPLIED WARRANTIES OF MERCHANTABILITY AND FITNESS FOR A PARTICULAR PURPOSE. THE COMPANY DOES NOT WARRANT, GUARANTEE OR MAKE ANY REPRESENTATION REGARDING THE ACCURACY, RELIABILITY, CURRENTNESS, USE, OR RESULTS OF USE, OF THE SOFTWARE.

5. LIMITATION OF REMEDIES AND DAMAGES: IN NO EVENT, SHALL THE COMPANY OR ITS EMPLOYEES, AGENTS, LICENSORS, OR CONTRACTORS BE LIABLE FOR ANY INCIDENTAL, INDIRECT, SPECIAL, OR CONSEQUENTIAL DAMAGES ARISING OUT OF OR IN CONNECTION WITH THIS LICENSE OR THE SOFTWARE, INCLUDING FOR LOSS OF USE, LOSS OF DATA, LOSS OF INCOME OR PROFIT, OR OTHER LOSSES, SUSTAINED AS A RESULT OF INJURY TO ANY PERSON, OR LOSS OF OR DAMAGE TO PROPERTY, OR CLAIMS OF THIRD PARTIES, EVEN IF THE COMPANY OR AN AUTHORIZED REPRESENTATIVE OF THE COMPANY HAS BEEN ADVISED OF THE POSSIBILITY OF SUCH DAMAGES. IN NO EVENT SHALL THE LIABILITY OF THE COMPANY FOR DAMAGES WITH RESPECT TO THE SOFTWARE EXCEED THE AMOUNTS ACTUALLY PAID BY YOU, IF ANY, FOR THE SOFTWARE OR THE ACCOMPANYING TEXTBOOK. BECAUSE SOME JURISDICTIONS DO NOT ALLOW THE LIMITATION OF LIABILITY IN CERTAIN CIRCUMSTANCES, THE ABOVE LIMITATIONS MAY NOT ALWAYS APPLY TO YOU.

6. GENERAL: THIS AGREEMENT SHALL BE CONSTRUED IN ACCORDANCE WITH THE LAWS OF THE UNITED STATES OF AMERICA AND THE STATE OF NEW YORK, APPLICABLE TO CONTRACTS MADE IN NEW YORK, AND SHALL BENEFIT THE COMPANY, ITS AFFILIATES AND ASSIGNEES. HIS AGREEMENT IS THE COMPLETE AND EXCLUSIVE STATEMENT OF THE AGREEMENT BETWEEN YOU AND THE COMPANY AND SUPERSEDES ALL PROPOSALS OR PRIOR AGREEMENTS, ORAL, OR WRITTEN, AND ANY OTHER COMMUNICATIONS BETWEEN YOU AND THE COMPANY OR ANY REPRESENTATIVE OF THE COMPANY RELATING TO THE SUBJECT MATTER OF THIS AGREEMENT. If you are a U.S. Government user, this Software is licensed with "restricted rights" as set forth in subparagraphs (a)-(d) of the Commercial Computer-Restricted Rights clause at FAR 52.227-19 or in subparagraphs (c)(1)(ii) of the Rights in Technical Data and Computer Software clause at DFARS 252.227-7013, and similar clauses, as applicable.

Should you have any questions concerning this agreement or if you wish to contact the Company for any reason, please contact in writing: Prentice-Hall, New Media Department, One Lake Street, Upper Saddle River, NJ 07458.